Multicultural
Health

Second Edition

Lois A. Ritter, EdD, MS, MA, MS-HCA, PMP
Consultant, Health and Education

Donald H. Graham, JD, MA
Attorney and Consultant, Human Services

JONES & BARTLETT
LEARNING

World Headquarters
Jones & Bartlett Learning
5 Wall Street
Burlington, MA 01803
978-443-5000
info@jblearning.com
www.jblearning.com

Jones & Bartlett Learning books and products are available through most bookstores and online booksellers. To contact
Jones & Bartlett Learning directly, call 800-832-0034, fax 978-443-8000, or visit our website, www.jblearning.com.

Substantial discounts on bulk quantities of Jones & Bartlett Learning publications are available to corporations,
professional associations, and other qualified organizations. For details and specific discount information, contact
the special sales department at Jones & Bartlett Learning via the above contact information or send an email to
specialsales@jblearning.com.

Production Credits

Chief Executive Officer: Ty Field
Chief Product Officer: Eduardo Moura
VP, Executive Publisher: David D. Cella
Publisher: Cathy L. Esperti
Editorial Assistant: Sara J. Peterson
Associate Director of Production: Julie C. Bolduc
Production Manager: Tina Chen
Marketing Director: Andrea DeFronzo
Rights & Media Specialist: Jamey O'Quinn
Media Development Editor: Troy Liston
Cover Design: Theresa Manley
Text Design: Scott Moden

VP, Manufacturing and Inventory Control: Therese Connell
Composition: Cenveo® Publisher Services
Project Management: Cenveo Publisher Services
Cover Image: Backgrounds: © Click Bestsellers/Shutterstock,
© Ms.Moloko/Shutterstock; Portraits, clockwise from top left:
© Andresr/Shutterstock; © Nolte Lourens/Shutterstock; © wong
sze yuen/Shutterstock; © Monkey Business Images/Shutterstock;
© project1photography/Shutterstock; © project1photography/
Shutterstock; © Fotoluminate LLC/Shutterstock; © Stuart
Jenner/Shutterstock
Printing and Binding: LSC Communications
Cover Printing: LSC Communications

Library of Congress Cataloging-in-Publication Data
Names: Ritter, Lois A., author. | Graham, Donald H., author.
Title: Multicultural health / Lois A. Ritter, Donald H. Graham.
Description: Second edition. | Burlington, MA : Jones & Bartlett Learning, [2017] | Includes bibliographical
   references and index.
Identifiers: LCCN 2015048787 | ISBN 9781284021028 (pbk. : alk. paper)
Subjects: | MESH: Cultural Competency | Culturally Competent Care | Cross-Cultural Comparison | Ethnic Groups |
   United States
Classification: LCC RA418.5.T73 | NLM W 21 | DDC 362.1089—dc23 LC record
available at http://lccn.loc.gov/2015048787

6048

Printed in the United States of America
20 19 18   10 9 8 7 6 5 4

CONTENTS

UNIT II Specific Cultural Groups

UNIT III Looking Ahead

Dedication

To Gary and Samantha, for creating countless hours of laughter—lr

To Sarah—dg

Preface

Your mind is like a parachute . . . it functions only when open.
  ~ Author unknown

Health care professionals work in a diverse society that presents both opportunities and challenges, so being culturally competent is essential to their role. Although knowing about every culture is not possible, having an understanding of various cultures can improve effectiveness. *Multicultural Health* provides an introduction and overview to some of the major cultural variations related to health.

Throughout this text, those engaged in health care can acquire knowledge necessary to improve their effectiveness when working with diverse groups, regardless of the predominant culture of the community in which they live or work. The content of this book is useful when working in the field on both individual and community levels. It serves as a guide to the concepts and theories related to cultural issues in health and as a primer on health issues and practices specific to certain cultures and ethnic groups.

New to This Edition

- **NEW!** A Student Activity is added to each chapter to challenge student comprehension.
- **NEW!** Two new Feature Boxes appear in each chapter—**What Do You Think?** and **Did You Know?**—to engage readers and enhance critical thinking.
- **NEW! Chapter 3**, Worldview and Health Decisions, provides information

about the ways that worldview and communication affect health, the provision of health services, health care decisions, and communication.

- **Expanded!** Reiki has been added to **Chapter 4**, Complementary and Alternative Medicine. Chiropractic care, homeopathy, hypnosis, and hydrotherapy, although important treatment modalities, were removed to keep the chapter focused on culturally based CAM modalities.
- **Expanded!** In **Chapter 5**, Religion, Rituals, and Health, a section was added about the clinical implications of the relationships among religion, spirituality, and health.
- **Expanded!** In **Chapter 6**, Communication and Health Promotion in Diverse Societies, tips for communicating with people with limited English proficiency have been added.
- **Expanded! Chapters 7 through 12** have new sections on worldview, pregnancy, mental health, and death and dying as they relate to the cultural group discussed in each chapter.
- **Expanded! Chapter 12**, Nonethnic Cultures, has been expanded to include people with disabilities, immigrants and refugees, and the culture of commerce.
- **Expanded!** In **Chapter 13**, Closing the Gap: Strategies for Eliminating Health Disparities, information about the

Health and Humans Services Action Plan to reduce racial and ethnic health disparities and the National Stakeholder Strategy for Achieving Health Equality have been added.

- **Revised!** Laws and ethics material is now integrated throughout where appropriate.

- **Revised!** The model programs have been removed from **Chapters 7 through 12** and an activity has been added for learners to conduct research and identify a model program themselves.

About This Book

Multicultural Health is divided into three units.

UNIT I, The Foundations, includes Chapters 1 through 6 and focuses on the context of culture, cultural beliefs regarding health and illness, health disparities, models for cross-cultural health and communication, and approaches to culturally appropriate health promotion programs and evaluation.

- **Chapter 1**, Introduction to Multicultural Health, discusses the reasons for becoming knowledgeable about the cultural impact of health practices. It defines terminology and key concepts that set the foundation for the remainder of the text. The chapter addresses diversity in the United States and the racial makeup of the country, health disparities and their causes, and issues related to medical care in the context of culture.

- **Chapter 2**, Theories and Models Related to Multicultural Health, addresses theories regarding the occurrence of illness

and its treatment. Terms and theoretical models related to cultural competence are provided. Individual and organizational cultural competence assessments are included.

- **Chapter 3**, Worldview and Health Decisions, explores the concept of worldview on illness and treatment and cultural influences that affect health. Differences in worldview and how that affects perceptions about health, health behaviors, and interactions with health care providers are described. Verbal and nonverbal communication considerations are explained. The chapter closes with discussions about how worldview and communication influence specific areas of health, such as the use of birth control.

- **Chapter 4**, Complementary and Alternative Medicine, provides an introduction to complementary and alternative medicine and health practices. It explores the major non-Western medicine modalities of care, including Ayurvedic medicine, traditional Chinese medicine, herbal medicine, and holistic and naturopathic medicine. The history, theories, and beliefs regarding the source of illness and treatment modalities are described.

- **Chapter 5**, Religion, Rituals, and Health, explores the role of religion and spiritual beliefs in health and health behavior. The similarities and differences between religion and rituals are described. The chapter integrates examples of religious beliefs in the United States and their impact on health decisions and behaviors.

- **Chapter 6**, Communication and Health Promotion in Diverse Societies, includes information about culturally sensitive communication strategies used in public health. Considerations to making health care campaigns using various communication channels, such as social media, appropriate for diverse audiences are explained. A section on health literacy is included.

UNIT II, Specific Cultural Groups, includes Chapters 7 through 12 and addresses the history of specific cultural groups in the United States, beliefs regarding the causes of health and illness, healing traditions and practices, common health problems, and health promotion and program planning for the various cultural groups. These points are applied to specific cultural groups as follows:

- **Chapter 7**, Hispanic and Latino American Populations
- **Chapter 8**, American Indian and Alaskan Native Populations
- **Chapter 9**, African American Populations
- **Chapter 10**, Asian American Populations
- **Chapter 11**, European and Mediterranean American Populations
- **Chapter 12**, Nonethnic Cultures

UNIT III, Looking Ahead, outlines priority areas in health disparities and strategies to eliminate health disparities.

- **Chapter 13**, Closing the Gap: Strategies for Eliminating Health Disparities, explores the implications of the growth of diversity in the United States in relation to future disease prevention and treatment. It further addresses diversity in the health care workforce and its impact on care, as well as the need for ongoing education in cultural competence for health care practitioners.

Features and Benefits

Each chapter includes a **"Did You Know?"** and **"What Do You Think?"** section to stimulate critical thinking and classroom discussions. Also included are chapter review questions, related activities, and a case study. Key concepts are listed and their definitions are provided in the glossary.

We hope the information contained in *Multicultural Health* will introduce you to the rich and fascinating cultural landscape in the United States and the diverse health practices and beliefs of various cultural groups. This book is not intended to be an end point; rather, it is a starting point in the journey to becoming culturally competent in health care.

For the Instructor

Instructor resources, including Power-Point presentations, Instructor's Manual, and test bank questions, are available. Contact your sales representative or visit **go.jblearning.com/Ritter2e for access**.

Acknowledgments

We would like to express gratitude to the many dedicated people whose contributions made this book possible. We extend a special thanks to those who provided us with permission to reprint their work. We also are grateful to the Jones & Bartlett Learning team who assisted with the editing, design, and marketing of the book. We would like to particularly acknowledge Sara J. Peterson and Cathy Esperti at Jones & Bartlett Learning for their efforts. Cherilyn Aranzamendez and Jessica Ross, we appreciate your efforts to locate research on the topic of multicultural health. We are also indebted to the reviewers for their thoughtful and valuable suggestions:

First Edition

Patricia Coleman Burns, PhD, University of Michigan

Maureen J. Dunn, RN, Pennsylvania State University, Shenango Campus

Mary Hysell Lynd, PhD, Wright State University

Sharon B. McLaughlin, MS, ATC, CSCS, Mesa Community College

Melba I. Ovalle, MD, Nova Southeastern University

Second Edition

William C. Andress, DrPH, MCHES, La Sierra University

Debra L. Fetherman, PhD, CHES, ACSM-HFS, University of Scranton

Carmel D. Joseph, MPH, Nova Southeastern University

Kirsten Lupinski, PhD, Albany State University

Hendrika Maltby, PhD, RN, University of Vermont

Cindy K. Manjounes, MSHA, EdD, Lindenwood University–Belleville

Mary P. Martinasek, PhD, University of Tampa

To our family, friends, and colleagues, we want to express our gratitude because you provided continued encouragement, support, and recognition throughout the process.

About the Authors

Lois A. Ritter earned a doctorate in education and master's degrees in health science, health care administration, and cultural and social anthropology. She has taught at the university level for approximately 20 years and has led national and regional research studies on a broad range of health topics.

Donald H. Graham is an attorney and holds a master's degree in urban affairs. He has developed and managed client-centered and culturally appropriate health and human service programs for more than 30 years.

UNIT I

The Foundations

Courtesy of David Bartholomew

© Andresr/Shutterstock, Inc.   © Nolte Lourens/Shutterstock, Inc.   © Stuart Jenner/Shutterstock, Inc.

CHAPTER 1

Introduction to Multicultural Health

We have become not a melting pot but a beautiful mosaic.
   —Jimmy Carter

One day our descendants will think it incredible that we paid so much attention to things like the amount of melanin in our skin or the shape of our eyes or our gender instead of the unique identities of each of us as complex human beings.
   —Author unknown

Key Concepts

Multicultural health	Heritage consistency
Cultural competence	Health disparity
Culture	*Healthy People 2020*
Dominant culture	Hill-Burton Act
Race	Ethics
Racism	Morality
Discrimination	Autonomy
Ethnicity	Respect
Cultural ethnocentricity	Veracity
Cultural relativism	Fidelity
Cultural adaptation	Beneficence
Acculturation	Nonmaleficence
Minority	Justice
Assimilation	

Learning Objectives

After reading this chapter, you should be able to:

1. Explain why cultural considerations are important in health care.
2. Describe the processes of acculturation and assimilation.
3. Define race, culture, ethnicity, ethnocentricity, and cultural relativism.
4. Explain what cultural adaptation is and why it is important in health care.
5. Explain what health disparities are and their related causes.
6. List the five elements of the determinants of health and describe how they relate to health disparities.
7. Explain key legislation related to health and minority rights.

Why do we need to study multicultural health? Why is culture important if we all have the same basic biological makeup? Isn't health all about science? Shouldn't people from different cultural backgrounds just adapt to the way we provide health care in the United States if they are in this country?

For decades, the role that culture plays in health was virtually ignored, but the links have now become more apparent. As a result, the focus on the need to educate health care professionals about the important role that culture plays in health has escalated. Health is influenced by factors such as genetics, the environment, and socioeconomic status, as well as by other cultural and social forces. Culture affects people's perception of health and illness, how they pursue and adhere to treatment, their health behaviors, beliefs about why people become ill, how symptoms and concerns about the problem are expressed, what is considered to be a health problem, and ways to maintain and restore health. Recognizing cultural similarities and differences is an essential component for delivering effective health care services. To provide quality care, health care professionals need to provide services within a cultural context, which is the focus of multicultural health.

Multicultural health is the phrase used to reflect the need to provide health care services in a sensitive, knowledgeable, and nonjudgmental manner with respect for people's health beliefs and practices when they are different from our own. It entails challenging our own assumptions, asking the right questions, and working with the patient and the community in a manner that respects the patient's lifestyle and approach to maintaining health and treating illness. Multicultural health integrates different approaches to care and incorporates the culture and belief system of the health care recipient while providing care within the legal, ethical, and medically sound practices of the practitioner's medical system.

Knowing the health practices and cultures of all groups is not possible, but becoming familiar with various groups' general health beliefs and preferences can be very beneficial and improve the effectiveness of health care services. In this text, generalizations about cultural groups are provided, but it is important to realize that many subcultures exist within those cultures, and people vary in the degree to which they identify with the beliefs and practices of their culture of origin. Awareness of general differences can help health care professionals provide services within a cultural context, but it is important to distinguish between stereotyping (the mistaken assumption that everyone in a given culture is alike) and generalizations (awareness of cultural norms) (Juckett, 2005). Generalizations can serve as a starting point but do not preclude factoring in individual characteristics such as education, nationality, faith, and level of cultural adaptation. Stereotypes and assumptions can be problematic and can lead to errors and ineffective care. Remember, every person is unique, but understanding the generalizations can be beneficial because it moves people in the direction of becoming culturally competent.

Cultural competence refers to an individual's or an agency's ability to work effectively with people from diverse backgrounds. *Culture* refers to a group's integrated patterns of behavior, and *competency* is the capacity to function effectively. Cultural competence occurs on a continuum, and this text is geared toward helping you progress along the cultural competence continuum.

Specific terms related to multicultural health, such as *race* and *acculturation*, need to be clarified, and this chapter begins by defining some of these terms. Following that is a discussion of the demographic landscape of the U.S. population and how it is changing, types and degrees of cultural adaptation, and health disparities and their causes. The chapter concludes with an analysis of the legislation related to health care that is designed to protect minorities.

Key Concepts and Terms

Some of the terminology related to multicultural health can be confusing because the differences can be subtle. This section clarifies the meaning of terms such as *culture, race, ethnicity, ethnocentricity*, and *cultural relativism*.

Culture

There are countless definitions of culture. The short explanation is that **culture** is everything that makes us who we are. E. B. Tylor (1924/1871), who is considered to be the founder of cultural anthropology, provided the classical definition of culture. Tylor stated in 1871, "Culture, or civilization, taken in its broad, ethnographic sense, is that complex whole which includes knowledge, belief, art, morals, law, custom, and any other capabilities and habits acquired by man as a member of society" (p. 1). Tylor's definition is still widely cited today. A modern definition of culture is the "integrated patterns of human behavior that include the language, thoughts, communications, actions, customs, beliefs, values, and institutions of racial, ethnic, religious, or social groups" (Office of Minority Health, 2013).

Culture is learned, changes over time, and is passed on from generation to generation. It is a very complex system, and many subcultures exist within each culture. For example, universities, businesses, neighborhoods, age groups, homosexuals, athletic teams, and musicians are subcultures of the dominant American culture. **Dominant culture** refers to the primary or predominant culture of a region and does not indicate superiority. People simultaneously belong to numerous subcultures because we can be students, fathers or mothers, and bowling enthusiasts at the same time.

Race and Ethnicity

Race refers to a person's physical characteristics and genetic or biological makeup, but race is not a scientific construct. Race is a social construct that was developed to categorize people, and it was based on the notion that some "races" are superior to others. Many professionals in the fields of biology, sociology, and anthropology have determined that race is a social construct and not a biological one because not one characteristic, trait, or gene distinguishes all the members of one so-called race from all the members of another so-called race. "There is more genetic variation within races than between them, and racial categories do not capture biological distinctiveness" (Williams, Lavizzo-Mourey, & Warren, 1994).

Why is race important if it does not really exist? Race is important because society makes it important. Race shapes social, cultural, political, ideological, and legal functions in society. Race is an institutionalized concept that has had devastating consequences. Race has been the basis for deaths from wars and murders and suffering caused by discrimination, violence, torture, and hate crimes. The ideology of race has been the root of suffering and death for centuries even though it has little scientific merit.

The 2010 U.S. Census questions related to ethnicity and race can be found in **Figure 1.1** and **Figure 1.2**. **Box 1.1** explains how these terms were defined in the 2010 census. The U.S. government declared that Hispanics and Latinos are an ethnicity and not a race.

Is this person of Hispanic, Latino, or Spanish origin?

☐ **No**, not of Hispanic, Latino, or Spanish origin
☐ Yes, Mexican, Mexican Am., Chicano
☐ Yes, Puerto Rican
☐ Yes, Cuban
☐ Yes, another Hispanic, Latino, or Spanish origin—*Print origin, for example, Argentinean, Colombian, Dominican, Nicaraguan, Salvadoran, Spaniard, and so on.*

☐☐☐☐☐☐☐☐☐☐☐☐☐☐☐☐☐☐☐☐☐☐

FIGURE 1.1

U.S. Census origin question, 2010.

Source: Population Reference Bureau (2013).

What is this person's race? *Mark* ☒ *one or more boxes.*

☐ White
☐ Black, African Am., or Negro
☐ American Indian or Alaska Native—*Print name of enrolled or principal tribe.* ↴

☐☐☐☐☐☐☐☐☐☐☐☐☐☐☐☐☐☐☐☐☐

☐ Asian Indian ☐ Japanese ☐ Native Hawaiian
☐ Chinese ☐ Korean ☐ Guamanian or Chamorro
☐ Filipino ☐ Vietnamese ☐ Samoan
☐ Other Asian—*Print race, for example, Hmong, Laotian, Thai, Pakistani, Cambodian, and so on.* ↴ ☐ Other Pacific Islander—*Print race, for example, Fijian, Tongan, and so on.* ↴

☐☐☐☐☐☐☐☐☐☐☐☐☐☐☐☐☐☐☐☐☐

☐ Some other race—*Print race.* ↴

☐☐☐☐☐☐☐☐☐☐☐☐☐☐☐☐☐☐☐☐☐

FIGURE 1.2

U.S. Census race question, 2010.

Source: Population Reference Bureau (2013).

It is important to note that there is great variation within each of the racial and ethnic categories. For example, American Indians are grouped together even though there are variations between the tribes. It is essential to be aware of the differences that occur within these groups and not to stereotype people. Stereotyping people by their race and ethnicity is racism. **Racism** is the belief that some races are superior to others by nature. **Discrimination** occurs when people act on that belief and treat people differently as a result. Discrimination can occur because of beliefs related to factors such as race, sexual orientation, dialect, religion, or gender.

Ethnicity is the socially defined characteristic of a group of people who share common cultural factors such as race, history, national origin, religious belief, or language. So how is ethnicity different from race? Race is primarily based on physical characteristics, whereas ethnicity is based on social and cultural identities. For example, consider these terms in relation to a person born in Korea to Korean parents but adopted by a French family in France as an infant. Ethnically, the person may feel French: she or he eats French food, speaks French, celebrates French holidays, and learns French history and culture. This person knows nothing about Korean history and culture, but in the United States she or he would likely be treated racially as Asian. Let's consider another example. The physical characteristics of Caucasians (a race) are typically light skin and eyes, narrow noses, thin lips, and straight or wavy hair. A person whose appearance matches these characteristics is said to be a Caucasian. However, there are many ethnicities within the Caucasian race such as Dutch, Irish, Greek, German, French, and so on. What differentiates these Caucasian ethnic groups from one another is their country of origin, language, cultural heritage and traditions, beliefs, and rituals.

BOX 1.1   Definition of Race Categories Used in the 2010 Census

"White" refers to a person having origins in any of the original peoples of Europe, the Middle East, or North Africa. It includes people who indicated their race(s) as "White" or reported entries such as Irish, German, Italian, Lebanese, Arab, Moroccan, or Caucasian.

"Black or African American" refers to a person having origins in any of the black racial groups of Africa. It includes people who indicated their race(s) as "Black, African Am., or Negro" or reported entries such as African American, Kenyan, Nigerian, or Haitian.

"American Indian or Alaska Native" refers to a person having origins in any of the original peoples of North and South America (including Central America) and who maintains tribal affiliation or community attachment. This category includes people who indicated their race(s) as "American Indian or Alaska Native" or reported their enrolled or principal tribe, such as Navajo, Blackfeet, Inupiat, Yup'ik, or Central American Indian groups or South American Indian groups.

"Asian" refers to a person having origins in any of the original peoples of the Far East, Southeast Asia, or the Indian subcontinent, including, for example, Cambodia, China, India, Japan, Korea, Malaysia, Pakistan, the Philippine Islands, Thailand, and Vietnam. It includes people who indicated their race(s) as "Asian" or reported entries such as "Asian Indian," "Chinese," "Filipino," "Korean," "Japanese," "Vietnamese," and "Other Asian" or provided other detailed Asian responses.

"Native Hawaiian or Other Pacific Islander" refers to a person having origins in any of the original peoples of Hawaii, Guam, Samoa, or other Pacific Islands. It includes people who indicated their race(s) as "Pacific Islander" or reported entries such as "Native Hawaiian," "Guamanian or Chamorro," "Samoan," and "Other Pacific Islander" or provided other detailed Pacific Islander responses.

"Some Other Race" includes all other responses not included in the White, Black or African American, American Indian or Alaska Native, Asian, and Native Hawaiian or Other Pacific Islander race categories described above. Respondents reporting entries such as multiracial, mixed, interracial, or a Hispanic or Latino group (for example, Mexican, Puerto Rican, Cuban, or Spanish) in response to the race question are included in this category.

Source: Humes, Jones, & Ramirez (2011).

How is ethnicity different from culture? One can belong to a culture without having ancestral roots to that culture. For example, a person can belong to the hip-hop culture, but he or she is not born into the culture. With ethnicity, the culture is a part of the ethnic background, so culture is embedded within the ethnic group. Ethnic groups have shared beliefs, values, norms, and practices that are learned and shared. These patterned behaviors are passed down from one generation to another and are thus preserved.

Cultural Ethnocentricity and Cultural Relativism

Cultural ethnocentricity refers to a person's belief that his or her culture is superior to another one. This can cause problems in the health care field. If a professional believes that his or her way is the better way to prevent or treat a health problem, the health care worker may disrespect or ignore the patient's cultural beliefs and values. The health care professional may not take into consideration that the listener may have different views than the provider. This can lead to ineffective communication and treatment and leave the listener feeling unimportant, frustrated, disrespected, or confused about how to prevent or treat the health issue, and he or she might view the professional as uneducated, uncooperative, unapproachable, or closed-minded.

To be effective, one needs to see and appreciate the value of different cultures; this is referred to as **cultural relativism**. The phrase developed in the field of anthropology to refute the idea of cultural ethnocentricity. It posits that all cultures are of equal value and need to be studied from a neutral point of view. It rejects value judgments on cultures and holds the belief that no culture is superior to any other. Cultural relativism takes an objective view of cultures and incorporates the idea that a society's moral code defines whether something is right (or wrong) for members of that society.

What Do You Think?

Cultural imposition occurs when one cultural group, usually the majority group, forces their culture view on another culture or subculture. Can you provide examples of cultural imposition? Do you think it is ethical? Why or why not?

Diversity Within the United States

A great strength of the United States is the diversity of the people. Historically, waves of immigrants have come to the United States to live in the land of opportunity and pursue a better quality of life. Immigrants brought their traditions, languages, and cultures with them, creating a country that developed a very diverse landscape. Of course, some peoples, such as Native Americans, were already on the land, and others, such as African Americans, were forced to come to the United States. An unfortunate outcome was that despite its great advantages, this diversity contributed to racial and cultural clashes as well as to imbalances in equality and opportunities that continue today. These positive and adverse consequences of diversity must be considered in our health care approaches, particularly because the demographics are continuing to change and the inequalities persist. The delivery of health care to individuals, families, and communities must meet the needs of the wide variety of people who reside in and visit the United States.

The percentage of the U.S. population characterized as white is decreasing (see **Table 1.1**). This is an important consideration for health care providers because ethnic minorities experience poorer health status, which is usually due to economic disparities.

TABLE 1.1   Population Data Related to Origin and Race, 2010

Hispanic or Latino origin and race	2000 Number	2000 Percentage of total population	2010 Number	2010 Percentage of total population	Change, 2000 to 2010 Number	Change, 2000 to 2010 Percent
HISPANIC OR LATINO ORIGIN AND RACE						
Total population.	**281,421,906**	**100.0**	**308,745,538**	**100.0**	**27,323,632**	**9.7**
Hispanic or Latino	35,305,818	12.5	50,477,594	16.3	15,171,776	43.0
Not Hispanic or Latino	246,116,088	87.5	258,267,944	83.7	12,151,856	4.9
White alone	194,552,774	69.1	196,817,552	63.7	2,264,778	1.2
RACE						
Total population.	**281,421,906**	**100.0**	**308,745,538**	**100.0**	**27,323,632**	**9.7**
One Race	274,595,678	97.6	299,736,465	97.1	25,140,787	9.2
White	211,460,626	75.1	223,553,265	72.4	12,092,639	5.7
Black or African American	34,658,190	12.3	38,929,319	12.6	4,271,129	12.3
American Indian and Alaska Native	2,475,956	0.9	2,932,248	0.9	456,292	18.4
Asian	10,242,998	3.6	14,674,252	4.8	4,431,254	43.3
Native Hawaiian and Other Pacific Islander.	398,835	0.1	540,013	0.2	141,178	35.4
Some Other Race	15,359,073	5.5	19,107,368	6.2	3,748,295	24.4
Two or More Races[1]	6,826,228	2.4	9,009,073	2.9	2,182,845	32.0

[1] In Census 2000, an error in data processing resulted in an overstatement of the Two or More Races population by about 1 million people (about 15 percent) nationally, which almost entirely affected race combinations involving Some Other Race. Therefore, data users should assess observed changes in the Two or More Races population and race combinations involving Some Other Race between Census 2000 and the 2010 Census with caution. Changes in specific race combinations not involving Some Other Race, such as White and Black or Black or African American or White and Asian, generally should be more comparable.

Source: U.S. Census Bureau (2011, March). Sources: U.S. Census Bureau, Census 2000 Redistricting Data (Public Law 94-171) Summary File, Tables PL1 and PL2; and 2010 Census Redistricting Data (Public Law 94-171) Summary File, Tables P1 and P2.

Source: U.S. Census Bureau (2011).

Cultural Adaptation

With this changing landscape in the United States, professionals are encouraged to consider the degree of cultural adaptation that the person has experienced. **Cultural adaptation** refers to the degree to which a person or community has adapted to the dominant culture or retained their traditional practices. Generally, a first-generation individual will identify more with his or her culture of origin than a third-generation person. Therefore, when working with the first-generation person, the health care professional needs to be more sensitive to issues such as language barriers, distrust, lack of understanding of the American medical system, and the person's ties to his or her traditional beliefs.

Acculturation relates to the degree of adaptation that has taken place; a process in which members of one cultural group adopt the beliefs and behaviors of another group. Essentially, members of the **minority** cultural group take up many of the dominant culture's traits. Because of the great variety of peoples who have immigrated to the United States, the country is often said to be a melting pot. However, given the tendencies of cultural groups to locate together and maintain some familiar practices in a foreign land, the country also has been described as more like a salad bowl. Both of these analogies reflect the process of cultural interaction.

Except for the indigenous population, everyone in the United States is or is descended from immigrants and refugees. For instance, the Pilgrims of Plymouth Rock were refugees from religious persecution. Each group of people who traveled to America built on the strengths of their own culture while adapting to a new social and economic environment through acculturation. Acculturation can include adopting customs from one culture to another or direct change of customs as one culture dominates the other. Each of the cultures discussed in the text has adapted as new populations arrive, territory is acquired or conquered, or popular or useful practices and beliefs are invented and spread throughout the overall population. Some interactions between cultures generate discriminatory responses, individual stress, and family conflict, whereas others create an appreciation for variation as customs or practices are welcomed into other cultures. Whether melting or mixing, the interrelationship of cultures in the United States in constantly changing. The process continues as new people arrive in the country.

People can experience different levels of acculturation as illustrated in Berry and colleagues' acculturation framework (see **Figure 1.3**). The acculturation framework identifies four levels of integration:

1. An **assimilated** individual demonstrates high-dominant and low-ethnic society immersion. This entails moving away from one's ethnic society and immersing fully in the dominant society (Stephenson, 2000). As a result, the minority group disappears through the loss of particular identifying physical or sociocultural characteristics. This usually occurs when people immigrate to a new geographic region and in their desire to be part of the mainstream give up most of their culture traits of origin and take on a new cultural identity defined by the dominant culture. Many people do not fully assimilate, however, and tend to keep some of their original cultural beliefs.

2. An integrated person has high-dominant and high-ethnic immersion. Integration entails immersion in both ethnic and dominant societies (Stephenson, 2000). An example of an

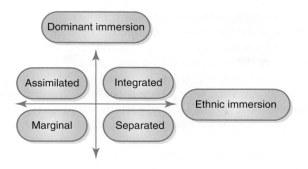

FIGURE 1.3

Acculturation framework.

integrated person is a Russian American who socializes with the dominant group but chooses to speak Russian at home and marries a person who is Russian.

3. Separated individuals have low-dominant and high-ethnic immersion. A separated individual withdraws from the dominant society and completely submerges into the ethnic society (Stephenson, 2000). An example is a person who lives in an ethnic community such as Little Italy or Chinatown.

4. A marginalized individual has low-dominant and low-ethnic immersion and does not identify with any particular culture or belief system.

Marginalized people tend to have the most psychological problems and the highest stress levels. These individuals often lack social support systems and are not accepted by the dominant society or their culture of origin. A person in the separated mode is accepted in his or her ethnic society but may not be accepted by the dominant culture, leaving the person feeling alienated. The integrated and assimilated modes are considered to be the most psychologically healthy adaptation styles, although some individuals benefit more from one than from the other. Western Europeans and individuals whose families have been in the United States for a number of generations (and are not discriminated against) are most likely to adopt an assimilated mode because they have many beliefs and attributes of the dominant society. Individuals who retain value structures from their country of origin and encounter discrimination benefit more from an integrated (bicultural) mode. To be bicultural one must be knowledgeable about both cultures and see the positive attributes of both of them.

The degree to which people identify with their culture of origin is sometimes referred to as **heritage consistency**. Some indicators that can help professionals assess the level of cultural adaptation are inquiring about how long the person has been in the country, how often the person returns to his or her culture of origin, what holidays the person celebrates, what language the person speaks at home, and how much knowledge the person has of his or her culture of origin.

Are people who have higher levels of cultural adaptation healthier? Despite increasing research on the relationships between acculturation and health, the answer to that question is not clear. Research on the influence of acculturation on health indicates con-tradictory results because the variables are complex. The answer also is dependent upon which health habits are incorporated into one's lifestyle and which are lost. For example, acculturation can have detrimental effects on one's dietary patterns if a person is from a culture where eating fruits and vegetables is common and the person incorporates the habit of eating at fast-food restaurants, which is common in the United States. On the other hand, if someone moves from a culture where smoking is common to a culture where it is frowned upon, the person may stop smoking and reduce his or her chances of serious illness.

Acculturation from traditional, nonindustrialized cultures to a modern westernized cul-ture generally has been associated with higher rates of disease. An example of this is the rate of cardiovascular disease among Japanese males in the United States. Increasing levels of acculturation also have been associated with higher rates of specific mental disorders and with substance abuse, suggesting that these disorders result from acculturation. Increasing levels of acculturation are correlated with advancing socioeconomic status, and higher socio-economic status is correlated with lower rates of disease and disorders. However, in some instances higher acculturation is correlated with higher rates of disease and disorders. What constitutes healthy acculturation, as contrasted with unhealthy acculturation, for which health outcomes, for whom, and under what conditions? Scientific answers to these questions may help empower diverse communities by promoting health and wellness in the presence of acculturation (González Castro, 2007).

Health Disparities

Health disparities "are differences in health outcomes and their determinants between seg-ments of the population, as defined by social, demographic, environmental, and geographic attributes" (Centers for Disease Control and Prevention, Division of Community Health, 2013, p. 4). Health disparities occur among groups who have persistently experienced historic trauma, social disadvantage, or discrimination. They are widespread in the United States as demonstrated by the fact that many minority groups in the United States have a higher inci-dence of chronic diseases, higher mortality, and poorer health outcomes when compared to Whites. Numerous other disparities exist such as the health of rural residents being poorer than urban residents and people with disabilities reporting poorer health when compared to those without disabilities.

Eliminating health disparities is an important goal for our nation and is one of the four overarching goals of *Healthy People 2020*. These four goals are:

1. "Attain high-quality, longer lives free of preventable disease, disability, injury, and pre-mature death.
2. Achieve health equity, eliminate disparities, and improve the health of all groups.
3. Create social and physical environments that promote good health for all.
4. Promote quality of life, healthy development, and healthy behaviors across all life stages" (U.S. Department of Health and Human Services [USHHS], 2014).

Some examples of health disparities follow, but numerous other statistics illuminate these differences as well.

- African Americans can expect to live 6 to 10 fewer years than whites and face higher rates of illness and mortality (Mead et al., 2008, p. 20).

- The prevalence of diabetes among American Indians and Alaska Natives is more than twice that for all adults in the United States (USHHS, 2009).

- Hispanic and Vietnamese women are twice as likely as white women to face cervical cancer (USHHS, 2009).

- African Americans experience rates of infant mortality that are 2.5 times higher than for whites (Mead et al., 2008, p. 20).

- Asian and Pacific Islanders make up less than 5% of the total population in the United States but account for more than 50% of Americans living with chronic hepatitis B (Centers for Disease Control and Prevention [CDC], 2014).

- A nationally representative study of adolescents in grades 7 to 12 found that lesbian, gay, and bisexual youth were more than twice as likely to have attempted suicide as their heterosexual peers (Russell & Joyner, 2001).

- Rural residents are more likely to be obese than urban residents, 27.4% versus 23.9% (Rural Health Research & Policies Centers, 2008).

- People with disabilities have the highest proportion of current smokers (29%), followed by American Indian/Alaska Natives (23%), blacks (22%), Hispanics (16%), and Asians (9%); (Drum, McClain, Horner-Johnson, & Taitano, 2011).

Did You Know?

… that April is National Minority Health month? The purpose is to raise awareness of health disparities. Public health agencies across the national engage in activities to raise awareness about the health disparities that exist around issues such as alcohol and drug use and infectious diseases.

Causes of Health Disparities

Health disparities exist due to both voluntary and involuntary factors. Voluntary factors related to health behaviors, such as smoking and diet, can be avoided. Factors such as genetics, living and working in unhealthy conditions, limited or no access to health care, and language barriers are often viewed as involuntary factors because they are not within that person's control.

Most experts agree that the causes of health disparities are multiple and complex; no single factor explains why disparities exist across such a wide range of health measures. Access to health care and the quality of health care are important factors, but they do not explain why some groups experience greater risks for poor health in the first place (Alliance for Health Reform, 2010).

Socioeconomic status (SES) is one of the most important predictors of health. Socioeconomic status is typically measured by educational attainment, income, wealth, occupation, or a combination of these factors. In general, the higher one's SES, the better one's health (Alliance for Health Reform, 2010). Socioeconomic status is thought to affect health in many ways, such as by increasing access to health-enhancing resources, access to health care, and living in healthier neighborhoods.

SES is related to health disparities, and racial and ethnic minorities are disproportionately found in lower socioeconomic levels. An important exception is the "Hispanic Epidemiologic Paradox." This refers to the fact that new Hispanic immigrants are found to have generally better health than U.S.-born individuals of the same SES (Alliance for Health Reform, 2010).

Another way to frame the causes of health disparities is via the factors affecting health that were identified in the 1974 Lalonde report, "A New Perspective on the Health of Canadians." This report probably was the first acknowledgment by a major industrialized country that health is determined by more than biological factors. The report led to the development of the "health field" concept, which identified four health fields that were interdependently responsible for individual health:

1. *Environment.* All matters related to health external to the human body and over which the individual has little or no control. Includes the physical and social environment.

2. *Human biology.* All aspects of health, physical and mental, developed within the human body as a result of organic makeup.

3. *Lifestyle.* The aggregation of personal decisions over which the individual has control. Self-imposed risks created by unhealthy lifestyle choices can be said to contribute to, or cause, illness or death.

4. *Health care organization.* The quantity, quality, arrangement, nature, and relationships of people and resources in the provision of health care.

These four domains were later refined to include five intersecting domains:

1. environmental exposures,
2. genetics,
3. behavior (lifestyle) choices,
4. social circumstances, and
5. medical care (Institute of Medicine [IOM], 2001).

All five domains are integrated and affected by one another. For example, people who have more education usually have higher incomes (social circumstances), are more likely to live in neighborhoods with fewer environmental health risks (environmental exposures), and have money to purchase healthier foods (lifestyle). Let's look at each of these domains in more detail.

Environmental Exposures

Environmental conditions are believed to play an important role in producing and maintaining health disparities. The environment influences our health in many ways, including through exposures to physical, chemical, and biological risk factors and through related changes in our behavior in response to those factors. In general, whites and minorities do not have the same exposure to environmental health threats because they live in different neighborhoods. Residential segregation still exists.

Residential segregation between white and black populations continues to be very high in U.S. metropolitan areas. Residential segregation of Hispanics/Latinos is not yet as high as that of African Americans, but it has been increasing over the past few decades; black segregation has modestly decreased (Iceland, Weinberg, & Steinmetz, 2002).

Growing evidence suggests that segregation is a key determinant of racial inequalities for a broad range of societal outcomes, including health disparities (Acevedo-Garcia, Osypuk, McArdle, & Williams, 2008). Segregation affects health outcomes in a multitude of ways. It limits the socioeconomic advancement of minorities through educational quality and employment, and lowers the returns of home ownership due to lower school quality, fewer job opportunities, and lower property values in disadvantaged neighborhoods. Segregation also leads to segregation in health care settings, which in turn is associated with disparities in the quality of treatment (Acevedo-Garcia et al., 2008).

Minorities tend to live in poorer areas (see **Figure 1.4**), and these disadvantaged neighborhoods are exposed to greater health hazards, including tobacco and alcohol advertisements,

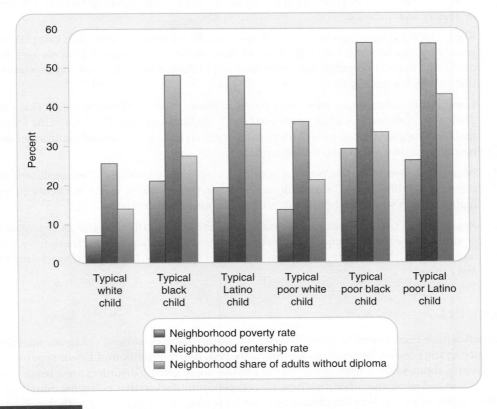

FIGURE 1.4

Racial and ethnic neighborhood disparities.

Source: Acevedo-Garcia et al. (2008).

toxic waste incinerators, and air pollution. Tiny particles of air pollution contain more hazardous ingredients in non-white and low-income communities than in affluent white ones (Katz, 2012). The greater the concentration of Hispanics, Asians, African Americans, or poor residents in an area, the more likely it is that potentially dangerous compounds such as vanadium, nitrates, and zinc are in the mix of fine particles they breathe. In a study conducted in 2012, the group with the highest exposure to the largest number of these ingredients was Latinos, while whites generally had the lowest exposure. Economic stress within a community may exacerbate tensions between social groups, magnify workplace stressors, induce maladaptive coping behaviors such as smoking and alcohol use, and translate into individual stress, all of which makes individuals more vulnerable to illness (e.g., depression, high blood pressure). Factors associated with living in poor neighborhoods—crime, noise, traffic, litter, crowding, and physical deterioration—also can cause stress.

Some health issues related to where one lives include the following (Cooper, 2014):

- Two to three times as many fast food outlets are located in segregated black neighborhoods than in white neighborhoods of comparable socioeconomic status, contributing to higher black consumption of fatty, salty meals and in turn widening racial disparities in obesity and diabetes.

- Black neighborhoods contain two to three times fewer supermarkets than comparable white neighborhoods, creating the kind of "food deserts" that make it difficult for residents who depend on public transportation to purchase the fresh fruits and vegetables that make for a healthy diet.

- Fewer African-Americans have ready access to places to work off excess weight that can gradually cause death. A study limited to New York, Maryland and North Carolina found that black neighborhoods were three times more likely to lack recreational facilities where residents could exercise and relieve stress.

- Because of "the deliberate placement of polluting factories and toxic waste dumps in minority neighborhoods," exposure to air pollutants and toxins is five to twenty times higher than in white neighborhoods with the same income levels.

- Regardless of their socioeconomic status, African-Americans who live in segregated communities receive unequal medical care because hospitals serving them have less technology, such as imaging equipment, and fewer specialists, like those in heart surgery and cancer.

Genetics

Genetics have been linked to many diseases, including diabetes, cancer, sickle-cell anemia, obesity, cystic fibrosis, hemophilia, Tay-Sachs disease, schizophrenia, and Down syndrome. Currently, about 4,000 genetic disorders are known. Some genetic disorders are a result of a single mutated gene, and other disorders are complex, multifactorial or polygenic mutations. (*Multifactorial* means that the disease or disorder is likely to be associated with the effects of multiple genes in combination with lifestyle and environmental factors.) Examples of multifactorial disorders are cancer, heart disease, and diabetes. Although numerous studies have linked genetics to health, social and cultural factors play a role as well. For example, smoking may trigger a genetic predisposition to lung cancer, but that gene may not have been expressed if the person did not smoke.

There are concerns about relating genetics and health disparities because race is not truly biologically determined, so the relationship between genetics and race is not clear cut. There are more genetic differences within races than among them, and racial categories do not capture biological distinctiveness. Another problem with linking genetics to race is that many people have a mixed gene pool due to interracial marriages and partnerships. Also, it is difficult at times to determine which diseases are related to genetics and which are related to other factors, such as lifestyle and the environment.

Sometimes disease is caused by a combination of factors. For example, African Americans have been shown to have higher rates of hypertension than whites, but is that difference due to genetics? African Americans tend to consume less potassium than whites and have stress related to discrimination, which could be the cause of their higher rates of hypertension. Health disparities also can be related to the level of exposure to environmental hazards, such as toxins and carcinogens, that some racial groups are exposed to more than others. Therefore, it is difficult to link health disparities to genetics alone because a variety of factors may be involved. Genetics does play a role in health however, and some clear links have been made, such as people with lighter skin tones being more prone to skin cancer.

Lifestyle

Behavior patterns are factors that the individual has more control over. Many of the diseases of the 21st century are caused by personally modifiable factors, such as smoking, poor diet, and physical inactivity. So how does lifestyle relate to ethnicity? Studies reveal that differences in health behaviors exist among racial and ethnic groups. For example, the national Youth Risk Behavior Survey (YRBS) monitors priority health risk behaviors that contribute to the leading causes of death, disability, and social problems among youth and adults in the United States. The national YRBS is conducted every 2 years during the spring semester and provides data representative of 9th through 12th grade students in public and private schools throughout the United States. Data shows racial and ethnic differences in behaviors such as alcohol consumption, use of sunscreen, physical activity levels, substance use, and being injured in a fight.

Social Circumstances

Social circumstances include factors such as SES, education level, stress, discrimination, marriage and partnerships, and family roles. SES is made up of a combination of variables including occupation, education, income, wealth, place of residence, and poverty. These variables do not have a direct effect on health, but they do have an indirect effect. For example, low SES does not cause disease, but poor nutrition, limited access to health care, and substandard housing certainly do, and these are just a few of the many indirect effects. Discrimination does not cause poor health directly either, but it can lead to depression and high blood pressure.

One variable of social circumstances, poverty, can be measured in many ways. One approach is to measure the number of people who are recipients of federal aid programs, such as food stamps, public housing, and Head Start. Another method is through labor statistics, but the most common way is through the federal government's measure of poverty based on income. The federal government's definition of poverty is based on a threshold defined by income, and it is updated annually. So how is poverty related to ethnicity?

Poverty is higher among certain racial and ethnic groups (see **Figure 1.5**) and is a contributing factor to health disparities because poverty affects many factors, including where people live and their access to health care. What may not be surprising is that low SES groups more often act in ways that harm their health than do high SES groups. It is perplexing that some of these unhealthy behaviors are adopted despite the monetary and health costs. For example, smoking cigarettes and alcohol consumption require that the person spend money on these items. Pampel, Krueger, and Denney (2010) noted some important facts

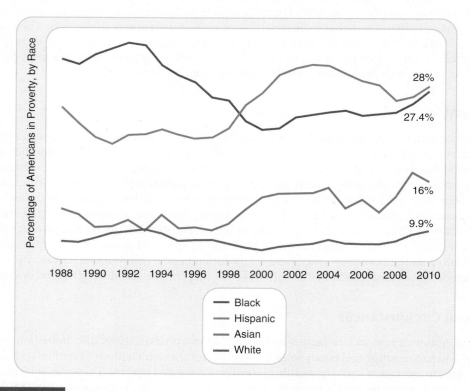

FIGURE 1.5

Poverty rates by race.

Source: Data from U.S. Census Bureau (2011).

related to socioeconomic factors in health behaviors. One example is access to health aids. Adopting many healthy behaviors does not require money, but having more money to pay for tobacco cessation aids, joining fitness clubs and weight loss programs, and buying more expensive fruits, vegetables, and lean meats can help people achieve better health.

Medical Care

The shortfalls for minorities in the health care system in the United States can be categorized into three general areas: (1) lack of access to care, (2) lower quality of care, and (3) limited providers with the same ethnic background.

Lack of Access to Medical Care

Research has shown that without access to timely and effective preventive care, people may be at risk for potentially avoidable conditions, such as asthma, diabetes, and immunizable conditions (National Center for Health Statistics, 2006). Access to health care is also important for prompt treatment and follow-up to illness and injury.

Access to health care is a problem for many Americans due to lack of health care insurance. According to the National Health Interview Survey (NHIS), in 2012, 45.5 million persons of all ages (14.7%) were uninsured at the time of interview (Cohen & Martinez, 2013). Access to health care is particularly problematic for minorities because they have higher rates of being uninsured than whites. Based on data from the 2012 NHIS, Hispanics were more likely than non-Hispanic whites, non-Hispanic blacks, and non-Hispanic Asians to be uninsured at the time of interview, to have been uninsured for at least part of the past 12 months, and to have been uninsured for more than a year. More than one quarter of Hispanics were uninsured at the time of interview, and one third had been uninsured for at least part of the past year (Cohen & Martinez, 2013).

The Patient Protection and Affordable Care Act (ACA), passed in 2010, was designed to increase the quality and affordability of health insurance, hence lowering the rate of uninsured. The ACA went into effect on January 1, 2014, but it is too soon to know whether it will achieve this goal.

Lower Quality of Care

Despite improvements, differences persist in health care quality among racial and ethnic minority groups. People in low-income families also experience poorer quality care. Disparities in quality of care are common. For example,

- Blacks and American Indians and Alaska Natives received worse care than whites for about 40% of measures.
- Asians received worse care than whites for about 20% of measures.
- Hispanics received worse care than non-Hispanic whites for about 60% of core measures.
- Poor people received worse care than high-income people for about 80% of core measures. (Agency for Healthcare Research and Quality, 2011a)

Disparities in access are also common, especially among Hispanics and poor people:

- Blacks had worse access to care than whites for one third of core measures.

- Asians and American Indians and Alaska Natives had worse access to care than whites for 1 of 5 core measures.

- Hispanics had worse access to care than non-Hispanic whites for 5 of 6 core measures.

- Poor people had worse access to care than high-income people for all 6 core measures. (Agency for Healthcare Research and Quality, 2011a.)

Examples of core measures include adults 40 and over with diabetes who received their exams, adults over age 50 who received a colonoscopy, and children ages 19 to 35 months who received their vaccines.

Limited Providers With the Same Ethnic Background

Ethnic minorities are poorly represented among physicians and other health care professionals. For almost all of the following list of health care occupations, Euro-Mediterraneans and Asians are overrepresented while blacks and Hispanics are underrepresented: physicians and surgeons, registered nurses, licensed practical and licensed vocational nurses, dentists, dental hygienists, dental assistants, pharmacists, occupational therapists, physical therapists, and speech-language pathologists (Agency for Healthcare Research and Quality, 2011b). Two exceptions were noted. Blacks are overrepresented among licensed practical and licensed vocational nurses, and Hispanics are overrepresented among dental assistants. Of the health care occupations tracked, these two require the least amount of education and have the lowest median annual wages (Agency for Healthcare Research and Quality, 2011b). More specifically, although African Americans, Hispanics, and Native Americans make up over a quarter of the nation's population, in 2007 African Americans accounted for only 3.5%, Hispanics 5%, and Native Americans/Native Alaskans 0.2% of physicians (American College of Physicians, 2010). Similar workforce disparities are found among some Asian subgroups, such as Samoans and Cambodians (American College of Physicians, 2010).

As a result, minority patients are frequently treated by professionals from a different racial or ethnic background. Many programs, funding agencies, and research studies suggest that more diversity is needed among health care professionals to improve quality of care and reduce health disparities. But is there evidence that racial concordance (patients being treated by people in the same ethnic group) accomplishes these goals?

A comprehensive review of research published between 1980 and 2008 was conducted by Meghani et al. (2009). Twenty-seven studies having at least one research question examining the effect of patient–provider race-concordance on minority patients' health outcomes and pertained to minorities in the United States were included in this review. Of the 27 studies, patient–provider race-concordance was associated with positive health outcomes for minorities in only 9 studies (33%); 8 studies (30%) found no association of race-concordance with the outcomes studied; and 10 studies (37%) presented mixed findings. The authors concluded that having a provider of same race did *not* improve "receipt of services" for minorities.

Legal Protections for Ethnic Minorities

Many laws have been passed to help reduce discrimination, including in the health care arena. The Civil Rights Act of 1964 was passed by Congress and signed into law by President Lyndon Baines Johnson. Title VI of the Civil Rights Act prohibits federally funded programs or activities from discriminating on the basis of race, color, or national origin. Federal agencies are responsible for enforcement of this law. In areas involving discrimination in health care, the Office for Civil Rights (OCR) of the Department of Health and Human Services (HHS), is responsible for enforcement. Title VI of the act is the operative section that informs nondiscrimination in health care. It has three key elements:

1. It established a national priority against discrimination in the use of federal funds.
2. It authorized federal agencies to establish standards of nondiscrimination.
3. It provided for enforcement by withholding funds or by any other means authorized by law.

Since the Civil Rights Act of 1964 was passed, numerous other statutes and regulations have been created to address discrimination against ethnic minorities in health care, including the **Hill-Burton Act**. The Hill-Burton Act has been amended a number of times since its inception. The amendment entitled "Community Service Assurance under Title IV of the U.S. Public Health Service Act" requires facilities to provide services to persons living within the service area without discrimination based on race, national origin, color, creed, or any other reason not related to the person's need for services. The subsequent HHS regulations set forth the requirements with which a Hill-Burton facility must comply (USHHS, Office for Civil Rights, 2006):

- A person residing in the Hill-Burton facility's service area has the right to medical treatment at the facility without regard to race, color, national origin, or creed.

- A Hill-Burton facility must post notices informing the public of its community service obligations in English and Spanish. If 10% or more of the households in the service area usually speak a language other than English or Spanish, the facility must translate the notice into that language and post it as well.

- A Hill-Burton facility may not deny emergency services to any person residing in the facility's service area on the grounds that the person is unable to pay for those services.

- A Hill-Burton facility may not adopt patient admission policies that have the effect of excluding persons on grounds of race, color, national origin, creed, or any other ground unrelated to the patient's need for the service or the availability of the needed service.

Title VI and HHS services regulations require recipients of federal financial assistance from HHS to take reasonable steps to provide meaningful access to limited English proficiency (LEP) persons. Federal financial assistance includes grants, training, use of equipment, donations of surplus property, and other assistance. Recipients of HHS assistance may include hospitals, nursing homes, home health agencies, managed care organizations, universities, and other entities with health or social service research programs. It also may include state Medicaid agencies; state, county, and local welfare agencies; programs for families, youth, and children; Head Start programs; public and private contractors, subcontractors, and vendors; and physicians and other providers who receive federal financial assistance from HHS (USHHS, Office for Civil Rights, n.d.).

Recipients are required to take reasonable steps to ensure meaningful access to their programs and activities by LEP persons. The obligation to provide meaningful access is fact dependent and starts with an individualized assessment that balances four factors: (1) the number or proportion of LEP persons eligible to be served or likely to be encountered by the program or grantee; (2) the frequency with which LEP individuals come into contact with the program; (3) the nature and importance of the program, activity, or service provided by the recipient to its beneficiaries; and (4) the resources available to the grantee/recipient and the costs of interpretation/translation services. There is no "one size fits all" solution for Title VI compliance with respect to LEP persons, and what constitutes "reasonable steps" for large providers may not be reasonable where small providers are concerned (USHHS, Office for Civil Rights, n.d.).

If, after completing the four-factor analysis, a recipient determines that it should provide language assistance services, a recipient may develop an implementation plan to address the identified needs of the LEP populations it serves. Recipients have considerable flexibility in developing this plan. The guidance provides five steps that may be helpful in designing such a plan: (1) identifying LEP individuals who need language assistance; (2) language assistance measures (such as how staff can obtain services or respond to LEP callers); (3) training staff; (4) providing notice to LEP persons (such as posting signs); and (5) monitoring and updating the LEP plan (USHHS, Office for Civil Rights, n.d.).

Culturally and Linguistically Appropriate Services (CLAS)

In compliance with Title VI and the LEP regulations, the HHS Office of Minority Health (OMH) has developed "National Standards for Culturally and Linguistically Appropriate Services in Health Care (CLAS)." In promulgating these standards, OMH provided its rationale for preparing the standards and recommendations for their use. The CLAS standards are intended to advance health equity, improve quality, and help eliminate health care disparities by providing a blueprint for individuals and health and health care organizations to implement culturally and linguistically appropriate services. Adoption of these standards is expected to help advance better health and health care in the United States. The CLAS standards are listed in **Table 1.2**.

It is worth noting that both federal and state governments have begun addressing the need for cultural competence through various standards and legislation. States are requiring cultural competence education in medical and nursing schools, and legislation in many states includes requiring cultural competence training for health care providers to receive licensure or relicensure. **Figure 1.6** highlights the states that are proposing to implement cultural competence training.

TABLE 1.2   National CLAS Standards

Principal Standard

1. Provide effective, equitable, understandable, and respectful quality care and services that are responsive to diverse cultural health beliefs and practices, preferred languages, health literacy, and other communication needs.

Governance, Leadership and Workforce

2. Advance and sustain organizational governance and leadership that promotes CLAS and health equity through policy, practices, and allocated resources.

3. Recruit, promote, and support a culturally and linguistically diverse governance, leadership, and workforce that are responsive to the population in the service area.

4. Educate and train governance, leadership, and workforce in culturally and linguistically appropriate policies and practices on an ongoing basis.

Communication and Language Assistance

5. Offer language assistance to individuals who have limited English proficiency and/or other communication needs, at no cost to them, to facilitate timely access to all health care and services.

6. Inform all individuals of the availability of language assistance services clearly and in their preferred language, verbally and in writing.

7. Ensure the competence of individuals providing language assistance, recognizing that the use of untrained individuals and/or minors as interpreters should be avoided.

8. Provide easy-to-understand print and multimedia materials and signage in the languages commonly used by the populations in the service area.

Engagement, Continuous Improvement, and Accountability

9. Establish culturally and linguistically appropriate goals, policies, and management accountability, and infuse them throughout the organization's planning and operations.

10. Conduct ongoing assessments of the organization's CLAS-related activities and integrate CLAS-related measures into measurement and continuous quality improvement activities.

11. Collect and maintain accurate and reliable demographic data to monitor and evaluate the impact of CLAS on health equity and outcomes and to inform service delivery.

12. Conduct regular assessments of community health assets and needs and use the results to plan and implement services that respond to the cultural and linguistic diversity of populations in the service area.

13. Partner with the community to design, implement, and evaluate policies, practices, and services to ensure cultural and linguistic appropriateness.

14. Create conflict and grievance resolution processes that are culturally and linguistically appropriate to identify, prevent, and resolve conflicts or complaints.

15. Communicate the organization's progress in implementing and sustaining CLAS to all stakeholders, constituents, and the general public.

Source: USHHS, Office of Minority Health (n.d.).

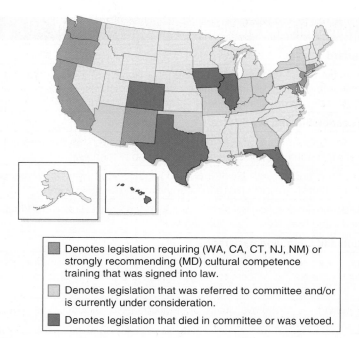

Denotes legislation requiring (WA, CA, CT, NJ, NM) or strongly recommending (MD) cultural competence training that was signed into law.

Denotes legislation that was referred to committee and/or is currently under consideration.

Denotes legislation that died in committee or was vetoed.

FIGURE 1.6

Map of states with cultural competence legislation.

Personal Health Decisions

Perhaps the area where law and cultural health issues intersect the most is in the area of personal health care decisions. How an individual approaches health care decisions is informed by his or her personal experiences as well as family, religious, and cultural influences. Different cultures approach how to undergo treatment, when to treat, and when to stop treatment differently. Even more important, who will make such decisions for a patient may differ from culture to culture.

Therefore, it is important to understand the legal construct that affects health care decisions. The laws of all the states reflect an individual's constitutional right to privacy and to make personal decisions free from outside influence. Consequently, the right to make health care decisions is personal to the patient involved, and no one else has the right to interfere. In cultures where family input is sought for such decisions, or a surrogate decision maker is used, this legal principle could create decision-making conflicts. A competent individual can appoint someone else to make decisions for him or her, thus removing the conflict.

The more problematic situation is when the patient is unable to make his or her wishes known because of the patient's medical condition. In that situation, it is important to have documents prepared in advance that name who will make decisions for the person and what decisions are to be made that are consistent with the person's cultural beliefs. Health care powers of attorney are documents that appoint who will make decisions for the person if he or she is unable to decide. A living will documents what decisions and desires a person has about his or her care and end-of-life decisions, and it can, and should, include instructions respecting the person's cultural beliefs. Many states have combined these two documents into one advance health care document that covers all the various decisions. Whatever format is utilized in a particular state, the importance of having these documents remains.

Ethical Considerations

Ethics point to standards or codes of behavior expected by the group to which the individual belongs. Ethics are different from morals in that **morality** refers to personal character and what the individual believes is right or wrong conduct. For example, a nurse's moral code may consider murder to be wrong, but the nurse has an ethical obligation to provide services for a murderer if the murderer is a patient in the medical facility.

The legal system is a set of rules and regulations that are binding on the members of a society and that set out what behavior is acceptable. They are subject to review and change as the society changes. The relationship between law and ethics significantly affects health care decisions and cultural influences. The ethical principles with the most impact on cultural issues in health care are autonomy, nonmaleficence, beneficence, and justice.

Autonomy is the ethical principle that embodies the right of self-determination. It is the right to choose what happens to one's self and decision making. It is embodied in the concept of informed consent in health care, which is the right to be informed about recommended treatment prior to consent. Autonomy requires that certain conditions exist, including understanding; an absence of controlling influences, which is traditionally understood as liberty; and agency, which is the ability to act intentionally (Beauchamp & Childress, 2001).

For this ethical principle to be achieved, the health care provider must respect and guard the patient's right to self-determination. This includes informing patients in a manner that considers both cultural and language barriers to understanding. The CLAS standards are an attempt to respect the ethical concept of autonomy. **Respect** takes into account individuals' rights to make determinations about their health and to live or die with the consequences. Respect for others does not allow cultural, gender, religious, or racial differences to interfere with that individual right. Respect is evident when the cultural heritage and practices of patients are considered in treatment even when the provider does not share that value.

In respect for autonomy, not only the right to choose is respected, but a right not to choose should be respected as well. Valuing a patient's right to defer decision making to another person, or not to be informed about the extent of his or her condition, is as essential to the principle of autonomy as ensuring that a patient who desires autonomy is fully informed about his or her treatment options.

Associated with respecting patient autonomy are two principles that should be followed by the caregiver: veracity and fidelity. **Veracity** involves being truthful and providing necessary information in an honest way. **Fidelity** entails keeping one's promises or commitments. It requires not promising what one cannot do or control. Both of these principles are necessary for patients to be truly informed about their care so they can make autonomous decisions.

Beneficence is the principle that requires doing good or removing harm. It is often intertwined with nonmaleficence, but it is a distinct ethical construct. Beneficence is at work when balancing the risk, benefit, harm, and effectiveness of treatment. When harm is found, positive actions are required to remove or limit it. This ethical principle was at work when segregated hospitals were outlawed by the Civil Rights Act.

Nonmaleficence is the principle that states that one should do no harm. Although simple in concept, it is often difficult in practice. In health care, actions can often cause harm, and very few treatment modalities are completely without risk of harm. Thus the practitioner must weigh the risks and benefits of any treatment.

However, it is the unknown harm that should be addressed in the cultural context. Practitioners should be aware that patients from cultures other than their own may perceive situations as harmful that are not readily apparent to them. For example, physical examination of a female by a male practitioner is considered to be unacceptable in some cultures and can lead to serious consequences for the female patient. Making arrangements for a female examiner would evidence the ethical concept of nonmaleficence.

Justice is the ethical principle that holds that people should be treated equally and fairly. Justice requires that people not be treated differently because of their culture or ethnic background. Justice is also at issue when the allocation and distribution of limited health resources are discussed. Ensuring that health resources are available to all without regard to race or ethnicity is the theory of distributive justice. It is this ethical principle that is breached when care is denied or withheld on racial or ethnic grounds.

The fair opportunity rule of justice states that no one should receive social benefits based on undeserved advantages or be denied benefits on the basis of disadvantages (Beauchamp & Childress, 2001). Although this may seem fairly straightforward, it becomes difficult to manage when applied to the variances of social inequalities. The rule states that discrimination is not ethically justifiable on the basis of social status or ethnicity.

Summary

One of the great attributes of the United States is its diverse landscape. Immigrants (voluntary and forced) who have come to the United States and natives of this country have experienced different levels of cultural adaptation to blend into the dominant society. Some have retained their strong cultural ties to create a society of rich and diverse cultures filled with various beliefs, traditions, languages, and societal norms. Understanding and respecting this diverse landscape is a goal for the nation, specifically for the health care industry. Health care providers need to be knowledgeable about and sensitive to cultural differences to provide effective care and education. Laws have been established to address inequalities.

This chapter provides an understanding of the foundations of multicultural health and the key terms and concepts associated with it, such as culture, race, assimilation, and cultural relativism. You should now have a general appreciation of how culture affects health, the breadth and depth of health disparities and their related causes, as well as the legal protections provided to people in the United States.

Review

1. What is the focus of multicultural health, and why is it important?

2. Is race a biological or a social construct? Why is race important?

3. What is the difference between ethnicity and culture? What is the difference between race and ethnicity?

4. Explain cultural ethnocentricity and cultural relativism.

5. Explain the differences between the concepts of acculturation, assimilation, and bicultural.

6. Does the level of acculturation have a positive or negative effect on health? Explain.

7. Explain what health disparities are and their causes.

8. Describe the key intentions of the Civil Rights Act and the Hill-Burton Act.

9. Explain the ethical principles related to health care decision making and how they influence health care services.

Activity

Conduct research to identify a legal case related to health and culture. Write a paper explaining the situation, the court's decision and the reason behind the decision, and your reaction to the outcome.

Case Study

The book titled *The Spirit Catches You and You Fall Down*, by Anne Fadiman, tells the story of Lia Lee, a Hmong child with epilepsy, who lived in Merced, California. When 3-month-old Lia Lee arrived at the county hospital emergency room in Merced, a chain of events was set in motion from which Lia, her parents, and her doctors would never recover. Lia's parents, Foua and Nao Kao, were part of a large Hmong community in Merced, refugees from the "Quiet War" in Laos. Her parents and doctors both wanted the best for Lia, but their ideas about the causes of her illness and its treatment were very different.

The Hmong see illness and healing as spiritual matters that are linked to virtually everything in the universe, but the U.S. medical community marks a division between body and soul and concerns itself almost exclusively with the former. Lia's doctors attributed her seizures to the misfiring of her cerebral neurons; her parents called her illness "qaug dab peg"—the spirit catches you and you fall down—and ascribed it to the wandering of her soul. The doctors prescribed anticonvulsants; her parents preferred animal sacrifices. *The Spirit Catches You and You Fall Down* moves from hospital corridors to healing ceremonies, and from the hill country of Laos to the living rooms of Merced, uncovering in its path the complex sources and implications of two dramatically clashing worldviews.

Lia's doctors prescribed a complex regimen of medication designed to control her seizures. However, her parents believed that the epilepsy was a result of Lia "losing her soul" and did not give her the medication as indicated because of the complexity of the drug therapy and the adverse side effects. Instead, they did everything logical in terms of their Hmong beliefs to help her. They took her to a clan leader and shaman, sacrificed animals, and bought expensive amulets to guide her soul's return. Lia's doctors believed that her parents were endangering her life by not giving her the medication, so they called child protective services, and Lia was placed in foster care. Lia was a victim of a misunderstanding between these two cultures that were both intent on saving her. The results were disastrous: a close family was separated, and Hmong community faith in Western doctors was shaken.

Lia was surrounded by people who wanted the best for her and her health. Unfortunately, the involved parties disagreed on the best treatment because they understood her epilepsy differently. The separate cultures of Lia's caretakers had different concepts of health and illness.

This example illustrates how culture and health influence each other and at times clash. To help ensure good care for diverse patients, health care providers must address cultural issues and respect the cultural values of each patient.

There are several issues to consider about this case:

- How can health care providers prepare for situations like Lia's?

- Should child protective services have been contacted?

- Were Lia's parents irresponsible?

- How did the parents' belief system affect Lia's health care?

- Were the parents' decisions morally and legally wrong?

References

Acevedo-Garcia, D., Osypuk, T. L., McArdle, N., & Williams, D. R. (2008, March). Toward a policy-relevant analysis of geographic and racial/ethnic disparities in child health. *Health Affairs, 27*(2), 321–333. Retrieved from http://content.healthaffairs.org/content/27/2/321.full

Agency for Healthcare Research and Quality. (2011a, March). *Disparities in healthcare quality among racial and ethnic minority groups: Selected findings from the 2010 national healthcare quality and disparities reports.* Retrieved from http://www.ahrq.gov/research/findings/nhqrdr/nhqrdr10/minority.html

Agency for Healthcare Research and Quality. (2011b). *National healthcare quality report, 2011.* Retrieved from http://www.ahrq.gov/research/findings/nhqrdr/nhqr11/nhqr11.pdf

Alliance for Health Reform. (2010). Disparities. *Covering health issues* (5th ed.). Retrieved from http://www.allhealth.org/sourcebook-content.asp?CHID=73

American College of Physicians. (2010). *Racial and ethnic disparities in health care, updated 2010.* Retrieved from http://www.acponline.org/advocacy/current_policy_papers/assets/racial_disparities.pdf

Beauchamp, T., & Childress, J. (2001). *Principles of biomedical ethics* (5th ed.). New York, NY: Oxford University Press.

Centers for Disease Control and Prevention. (2014, March). *Asian & Pacific Islanders.* Retrieved from http://www.cdc.gov/hepatitis/Populations/api.htm

Centers for Disease Control and Prevention, Division of Community Health. (2013). *A practitioner's guide for advancing health equity: Community strategies for preventing chronic disease.* Atlanta, GA: U.S. Department of Health and Human Services.

Cohen, R. A., & Martinez, M. E. (2013, June 20). *Health insurance coverage: Early release of estimates from the National Health Interview Survey, 2012.* Retrieved from http://www.cdc.gov/nchs/data/nhis/earlyrelease/insur201306.pdf

Cooper, K. J. (2014, September 21). *Residential segregation contributes to health disparities for people of color.* Retrieved from http://americaswire.org/drupal7/?q=content/residential-segregation-contributes-health-disparities-people-color

Drum, C., McClain, M. R., Horner-Johnson, W., & Taitano, G. (2011, August). *Health disparities chart book on disability, and racial and ethnic status in the United States.* Durham, NH: UNH Institute on Disability.

González Castro, F. (2007). Is acculturation really detrimental to health? *American Journal of Public Health, 97*(7), 1162. http://www.ncbi.nlm.nih.gov/pmc/articles/PMC1913069/

Humes, K. R., Jones, N. A., & Ramirez, R. R. (2011, March). Overview of race and Hispanic origin: 2010. Retrieved from http://www.census.gov/prod/cen2010/briefs/c2010br-02.pdf

Iceland, J., Weinberg, D. H., & Steinmetz, E. (2002). *Racial and ethnic residential segregation in the United States: 1980–2000* (US Census Bureau, Series CENSR-3). Washington, DC: U.S. Government Printing Office.

Institute of Medicine. (2001). *Health and behavior: The interplay of biological, behavioral, and societal influences.* Washington, DC: National Academies Press.

Juckett, G. (2005). Cross-cultural medicine. *American Family Physician, 72,* 2267–2274. Retrieved from http://www.aafp.org/afp/20051201/2267.html

Katz, C. (2012, November 1). Unequal exposures: People in poor, non-White neighborhoods breathe more hazardous particles. *Environmental Health News.* Retrieved from http://www.environmentalhealthnews.org/ehs/news/2012/unequal-exposures

Lalonde (1974). A new perspective on the health of Canadians. Retrieved from http://www.phac-aspc.gc.ca/ph-sp/pdf/perspect-eng.pdf

Mead, H., Cartwright-Smith, L., Jones, K., Ramos, C., Woods, K., & Siegel, B. (2008). *Racial and ethnic disparities in U.S. health care: A chart book.* New York, NY: The Commonwealth Fund. Retrieved from http://www.commonwealthfund.org/usr_doc/Mead_racialethnicdisparities_chartbook_1111.pdf

Meghani, S. H., Brooks, J. M., Gipson-Jones, T., Waite, R., Whitfield-Harris, L., & Deatrick, J. A. (2009). Patient–provider race-concordance: Does it matter in improving minority patients' health outcomes? *Ethnicity & Health, 14*(1), 107–130. doi: 10.1080/13557850802227031

National Center for Health Statistics. (2006). NCHS data on health insurance and access to care.

Office of Minority Health. (2013, May 9). *What is cultural competency?*

Pampel, Krueger, & Denney (2010). Socioeconomic Disparities in Health Behaviors. *Annual Review of Sociology, 36,* 349–370.

Population Reference Bureau. (2013). *The 2010 census questionnaire: Seven questions for everyone.* Retrieved from http://www.prb.org/Articles/2009/questionnaire.aspx

Rural Health Research & Policies Centers. (2008, June). *Health disparities: A rural–urban chartbook.*

Russell, S. T., & Joyner, K. (2001). Adolescent sexual orientation and suicide risk: Evidence from a national study. *American Journal of Public Health, 91,* 1276–1281.

Stephenson, M. (2000). Development and validation of the Stephenson Multigroup Acculturation Scale (SMAS). *Psychological Assessment, 12,* 77–88.

Tylor, E. B. (1924). *Primitive culture: Researches into the development of mythology, philosophy, religion, language, art, and custom* (7th ed.). New York, NY: Brentano. (Original work published 1871)

U.S. Census Bureau (2009, May 14). *Census Bureau estimates nearly half of children under 5 are minorities* (News release). Retrieved from www.census.gov/Press-Release/www/releases/archives/population/013733.html

U.S. Census Bureau. (2011, March). *Overview of race and Hispanic origin: 2010.* Retrieved from http://www.census.gov/prod/cen2010/briefs/c2010br-02.pdf

U.S. Department of Health and Human Services. (2009). *Health disparities: A case for closing the gap.* Retrieved from http://smhs.gwu.edu/rodhaminstitute/sites/rodhaminstitute/files/HCReform%20-%20Disparities%20Report.pdf

U.S. Department of Health and Human Services (2014, September). *About healthy people.* Retrieved from http://www.healthypeople.gov/2020/about/default.aspx

U.S. Department of Health and Human Services, Office for Civil Rights. (n.d.). *Guidance to federal financial assistance recipients regarding Title VI and the prohibition against national origin discrimination affecting limited English proficient persons—Summary.* Retrieved from http://www.hhs.gov/ocr/civilrights/resources/laws/summaryguidance.html

U.S. Department of Health and Human Services, Office for Civil Rights. (2006, June). *Your rights under Title VI of the Civil Rights Act of 1964.* Retrieved from http://www.hhs.gov/

U.S. Department of Health and Human Services, Office of Minority Health. (n.d.). *CLAS & the CLAS Standards.* Retrieved from https://www.thinkculturalhealth.hhs.gov/Content/clas.asp

Williams, D. R., Lavizzo-Mourey, R., & Warren, R. C. (1994). *The concept of race and health status in America.* Retrieved from http://www.pubmedcentral.nih.gov/picrender.fcgi?artid=1402239&blobtype=pdf

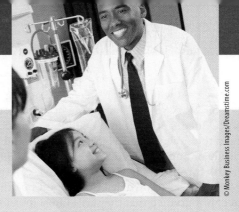

CHAPTER 2

Theories and Models Related to Multicultural Health

An understanding of the determinants of the different distribution of health problems among racial or ethnic groups is a prerequisite to the development and direction of effective programs and services to address them.
   —Williams, Lavizzo-Mourey, & Warren (1994)

Key Concepts

Personalistic belief system

Naturalistic theories of disease

Humoral system

Ayurvedic system

Vitalistic system

Biomedical (allopathic) medicine

Germ theory

Holistic medicine

Learning Objectives

After reading this chapter, you should be able to:

1. Explain three overarching theories of the causes of illness and provide examples of each.
2. Explain the differences between the biomedical and holistic systems of care.
3. Explain two models of cultural competence.

"Being cold will give you a cold," "cracking your knuckles will give you arthritis," and "feed a fever, starve a cold" are three of many commonly held beliefs by the dominant culture in the United States about how illness can occur and be cured. People from different cultures hold their own beliefs about the causes and cures of illness, and these beliefs influence their behavior and where and when they decide to seek care. Many others factors also affect our health care experience, such as how we communicate about health, whether we believe we have control over our own health, and how health care decisions are made. These factors can be so deeply ingrained that they are almost invisible. Because of this invisibility, health care professionals can overlook these key differences and forget that not all people who reside within the United States have the same beliefs about health and illness. Therefore, it is essential to bring these issues to light, which is the purpose of this chapter.

This chapter begins with a discussion of theories about how illness occurs and then presents models of care for when illness does occur. The chapter ends with a focus on cultural competence and ways to improve cultural competence.

Theories of Health and Illness

Theories about health and illness address the beliefs people hold about how to maintain health and the causes of illness. These ideas, beliefs, and attitudes are socially constructed and are deeply ingrained in people's cultural experience, and they can have a profound effect on medical care. Where people seek care and when are rooted in their cultural belief system (Carteret, 2011). Their beliefs influence prevention efforts, delay or prevent medical care, and complicate the care given (Carteret, 2011).

Ideas about health maintenance vary among cultures and include ideologies such as consuming a well-balanced diet, wearing amulets, rewards for good behavior, and prayer. Illness causation ideologies include breach of taboo, soul loss, exposure to germs, upset in the hot–cold balance of the body, or a weakening of the body's immune system. Treatment methods range from medications and surgeries to witchcraft and returning the soul to the ill person. In the Western world, the human body is thought of as a machine; when the machine breaks, illness occurs. Eastern philosophies generally view health as a state of balance between the physical and social environments as well as the supernatural environment (Carteret, 2011).

Theories of health and illness serve to create a context of meaning within which the patient can make sense of his or her bodily experience. They assist the patient in framing the illness in a meaningful and logical manner. A meaningful context for illness usually reflects core cultural values and helps the patient bring order to the chaotic world of serious illness and regain some sense of control in a frightening situation. Theories of illness shape how people receive and respond to prevention programs, treatment, and health education messages.

Theories of illness are often divided into three broad categories: personalistic, naturalistic, and biomedical (allopathic). In a personalistic system, illness is believed to be caused by the intentional intervention of an agent who may be a supernatural being (a deity or ancestral spirits) or a human being with special powers (a witch or sorcerer). The sick person's illness is considered to be a direct result of the harmful influence of these agents and is often linked to the ill person's behavior. In naturalistic causation, illness is explained in terms of a disturbed natural equilibrium. When the body is in balance with the natural environment, a state of health is achieved. When the balance no longer exists, then illness occurs. In the biomedical theory, illness is identified and cured using scientific evidence. The cause of illness is physiological in nature.

Many people's beliefs systems are a combination of these three theories. The theories are used by people to understand and respond to the illness. Through communication, patients and providers can work together and combine the theories to try to achieve a positive outcome for the patient.

Personalistic Theories

In the **personalistic belief system**, illness is believed to be caused by the person's misbehavior. The behavior could be related to violations of social or religious norms. As a result of moral or spiritual failings, the person may have punishment invoked in the form of illness by a supernatural being or a human with special powers. The supernatural being may be a dead ancestor or a deity (Carteret, 2011). A dead ancestor may retaliate for not carrying out proper rituals of respect for the dead ancestor. The deity may retaliate for breaching a religious taboo. Bad luck or karma also may cause illness.

Illness also can be caused by people who have the power to make others ill, such as witches, practitioners of voodoo, and sorcerers. These malevolent human beings manipulate secret rituals and charms to cause illness in their enemies.

Recovery from the illness involves healers using supernatural means to understand what is wrong with their patients and to return them to health. These supernatural means usually involves rituals or symbolisms used by healers, such as shaman, who are trained in the healing methods. Native Americans and people from Latin America and Asia often hold the personalistic belief system (Carteret, 2011). Preventing personalistic illness includes avoiding situations that can provoke jealousy or envy, wearing certain amulets, adhering to social norms and moral behaviors, adhering to food taboos and restrictions, and performing certain rituals. Several personalistic beliefs and practices are reviewed in later chapters.

Did You Know?

Osteopathic medicine is a form of medical care based on the philosophy that all body systems are interrelated and dependent upon one another for good health. In 1874, Dr. Andrew Taylor Still, who recognized the importance of treating illness within the context of the whole body, developed the philosophy of osteopathic medicine. In 1892, Dr. Still opened the first school of osteopathic medicine in Kirksville, Missouri. Physicians licensed as Doctors of Osteopathic Medicine (DOs) must pass a national or state medical board examination to obtain a license to practice medicine (American College of Osteopathic Medicine, 2014).

Osteopathic physicians utilize the same tools available through modern medicine including prescription medicine and surgery. In addition, DOs use osteopathic manipulative medicine (OMM) into their regimen of patient care when appropriate. "OMM is a set of manual medicine techniques that may be used to diagnose illness and injury, relieve pain, restore range of motion, and enhance the body's capacity to heal" (American College of Osteopathic Medicine, 2014).

Naturalistic Theories

Naturalistic theories of disease tend to view health as a state of harmony between the person and his or her environment; when this balance is upset, illness will result. The naturalistic explanation assumes that illness is due to impersonal, mechanistic causes in nature that potentially can be understood and cured by returning the patient to a balanced state. Humoral, Ayurvedic, and vitalistic are three of the widely practiced approaches to curing naturalitically caused illness or to explain what causes illness. Preventing naturalistic illness includes methods such as proper hygiene, a balanced diet, and meditation. These types of illness are treated by practitioners such as physicians, nurses, acupuncturists, and chiropractors. Methods include dietary changes, massage, medication, exercise, and physical adjustments.

Humoral

Humoral pathology was developed and became the basis of both ancient Greek and Roman medicine. It is part of the mainstream medical system in Latin America and Asia.

The **humoral system** is an ancient belief system based on the idea that our bodies have four important fluids, or humors: blood, phlegm, black bile, and yellow bile. These four fluids are related to seasons, internal organs, physical qualities (hot–cold; wet–dry), and human temperaments (see **Table 2.1**). Each humor is thought to have its own "complexion." For example, blood is hot and wet, and yellow bile is hot and dry. Different kinds of illnesses, medicines, foods, and most natural objects also have specific complexions.

Curing an illness involves discovering the complexion imbalance and rectifying it. A hot injury or illness must be treated with a cold remedy and vice versa (O'Neil, 2005). In the 19th century there was a radical transition from the humoral theory to the germ theory of disease, which involved new concepts, rules, and classifications, as well as the abandonment of old ones.

TABLE 2.1 Humor and Related Organ and Complexion

Humor (Fluid)	Associated Internal Organ	Associated Season	Associated Element	Normal Complexion	Temperament
Blood	Liver	Spring	Air	Hot and wet	Sanguine (cheerfully confident; optimistic)
Phlegm	Brain and lungs	Winter	Water	Cold and wet	Phlegmatic (calm, sluggish; apathetic)
Black bile	Spleen	Fall	Earth	Cold and dry	Melancholic (in low spirits; gloomy)
Yellow bile	Gallbladder	Summer	Fire	Hot and dry	Choleric (easily angered)

Ayurvedic

Ayurvedic is an ancient naturalistic approach to health that is used in India and other parts of the world. The term "ayurveda" is taken from the Sanskrit words *ayus,* meaning life or life span, and *veda,* meaning knowledge. In the **Ayurvedic system**, illness is caused by an energy imbalance. The belief system has a long history and embraces the ideology that disease is a result of an imbalance in vital energies, which distinguish living and nonliving matter. In ayurvedic medicine the vital force is called the *prana.*

Ayurveda suggests that three primary principles govern every human body. These principles, called *doshas*, are derived from the five elements: earth, air, water, fire, and space. Doshas regulate all actions of the body. Most people have a predominant dosha, and each dosha type has typical attributes or characteristics. The Ayurveda system of medicine uses a genetically determined concept, *prakriti,* to categorize the population into several subgroups based on phenotypic characters such as appearance, temperament, and habits. This system is useful in predicting an individual's susceptibility to a particular disease, prognosis for that illness and selection of therapy, and variations in platelet aggregation (Bhalerao, Deshpande, & Thatte, 2012).

When the doshas are balanced, we experience good health, vitality, ease, strength, flexibility, and emotional well-being. When the doshas fall out of balance, we experience energy loss, discomfort, pain, mental or emotional instability, and, ultimately, disease. Ayurvedic ways to restore balance include breathing exercises, rubbing the skin with herbalized oil, meditation, yoga, mantras, massage, and herbs. These modalities are energetic ways to balance the chakras.

The system links the body's *chakras,* or energy centers associated with organs of the body, with primal forces, such as *prana* (breath of life), *agni* (spirit of light or fire), and *soma* (manifestation of harmony). Each and every cell has a chakra, but like the doshas, one or more often can be found to be more dominant than some of the others. When the life force withdraws, the physical body dies; if the life force becomes blocked or compromised, illness or disease is the likely result. Two ways in which the life force enters the body are through breath and through the chakra system.

Breath sustains all life, and when we breathe we take in life-force energy and move the energy to the entire body via the respiratory and circulatory system. The chakra system is another way in which that energy force enters the body. *Chakra* means "wheels of life," and these invisible "wheels" pull in this vital life force. Our physical bodies contain seven major chakras between the base of the spine and the top of the head as well as many minor chakras (see **Figure 2.1**). Each chakra is associated with a major gland or organ and plays an important role in our emotional well-being. As we become older or ill, these chakras may slow down or become blocked, reducing the amount of life force taken into the body, which compromises health and vitality. Our life force also may become depleted due to prolonged stress, poor health habits, or unexpressed emotions (Gilberti, 2004).

Vitalistic

In China a system similar to Ayurveda was developed. The **vitalistic system** can be defined as the concept that bodily functions are due to a vital principle or "life force" that is distinct from physical forces explainable by the laws of chemistry and physics and is not detectable by scientific instrumentation. The system is built on the belief that an imbalance in vital energies causes disease.

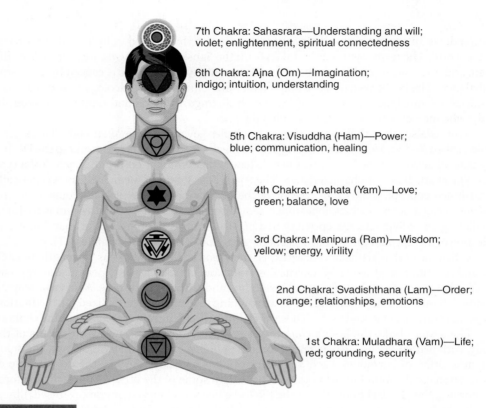

7th Chakra: Sahasrara—Understanding and will; violet; enlightenment, spiritual connectedness

6th Chakra: Ajna (Om)—Imagination; indigo; intuition, understanding

5th Chakra: Visuddha (Ham)—Power; blue; communication, healing

4th Chakra: Anahata (Yam)—Love; green; balance, love

3rd Chakra: Manipura (Ram)—Wisdom; yellow; energy, virility

2nd Chakra: Svadishthana (Lam)—Order; orange; relationships, emotions

1st Chakra: Muladhara (Vam)—Life; red; grounding, security

FIGURE 2.1

Chakra system.

The imbalance is related to the polar opposites *yin* (female, dark, cold) and *yang* (male, light, hot) in which one combines the interaction of body fluids and energy channels, or meridians. This vitalistic belief system is widespread in China, South Asia, and Southeast Asia. In the Chinese system, the vital force is called the *chi*; in the ayurvedic system it is the prana. When vital forces within the body flow in a harmonious pattern, a positive state of health is maintained. Illness results when this smooth flow of energy is disrupted, and therapeutic measures are aimed at restoring a normal flow of energy in the body. In China the ancient art of acupuncture is based on this understanding of the body. Acupuncture needles help restore a proper flow of energy within the body.

Biomedical Theory

Biomedical medicine (also known as **allopathic medicine**) is based on the mechanical view, or machine view, of the body; when the machine breaks illness occurs. Spirituality is generally kept separate from health and healing matters. Spirituality is usually viewed as a nonscientific approach to health and healing. Mental health problems are generally viewed as disorders of the mind, and physicians tend to treat these disorders by affecting brain physiology with pharmaceuticals or with counseling or behavior modification.

Allopathic medicine is the type of medicine most familiar to westerners today. Allopathy is a biologically based approach to healing. For instance, if a patient has high blood pressure, an allopathic physician might give him or her a drug that lowers blood pressure. A core assumption of the value system of allopathic medicine is that diagnosis and treatment should be based on scientific data. The system is built on a molecular understanding of the mechanisms underlying disease, and this lays the foundation for all medical application, diagnosis, and treatment (Carteret, 2011).

Allopathic medicine quickly rose to dominance in the West, in part due to successful scientific progress in developing specific drugs that treat disease. The discovery of antibiotics also triggered rapid growth of the pharmaceutical industry. Pharmacy evolved as an enabling discipline to allopathic medicine, helping it to achieve and maintain its dominance through many successful treatments and cures.

The germ theory of disease is a core component of contemporary allopathic medicine. **Germ theory** proposes that microorganisms are the cause of many diseases. Although highly controversial when first introduced, it is now a cornerstone of modern medicine and has led to innovations and concepts such as antibiotics and hygienic practices.

Typical causes of illness, according to the allopathic belief, are (O'Neil, 2005):

- Organic breakdown or deterioration (e.g., tooth decay, heart failure, senility)
- Obstruction (e.g., kidney stones, arterial blockage due to plaque buildup)
- Injury (e.g., broken bones, bullet wounds)
- Imbalance (e.g., too much or too little of specific hormones and salts in the blood)
- Malnutrition (e.g., too much or too little food, not enough proteins, vitamins, or minerals)
- Parasites (e.g., bacteria, viruses, amoebas, worms)

What Do You Think?

What are your personal beliefs about how health is maintained and illness occurs? Do you hold any beliefs such as that a glass of milk will help you fall asleep? Where does that belief come from? Is it valid? How do your beliefs affect your behavior?

Pathways to Care

The theory of illness with which a person identifies has an impact on where he or she seeks care. Within the United States there are two general systems of care to choose from: the allopathic (biomedical) approach and the holistic approach. The allopathic approach is often viewed as being scientific and focuses more on the physical components of illness than on the

TABLE 2.2   Two Health Paradigms

Allopathic	Holistic
Focuses on measurements: symptoms	Focuses on experience: causes and patterns
Disease as entity: pain avoiding	Disease as process: pain reading
General classified diagnosis	Specific individual needs
Health as commodity	Health as process
Technical tools	Integrated therapies
Remedial, combative, reactive	Preventive, corrective, proactive
Crisis oriented: occasional intervention	Lifestyle oriented: sustained maintenance
Radical, defensive	Natural, ecological
Medicine as counteragent	Medicine as coagent
Side effects: chemicals, surgery, radiation, replacement	Low risk: conservative, organic, purification, manipulation, correction
Emphasis on cure	Emphasis on healing
Speed, comfort, convenience	Restoration, regeneration, transformation
Practitioner as authority: pacifying	Practitioner as educator: activating
Patient as passive recipient	Patient as source of healing
Mechanical, analytical, biophysical	Systemic, multidimensional, body–mind–spirit
Best for infectious diseases, trauma, structural damage, organ failure, acute conditions	Best for degeneration, chronic stress and lifestyle disorders, toxemia, glandular conditions, weakness, systemic imbalances, immunity

Source: © Lonny J. Brown is the author of *Enlightenment in Our Time* (www.BookLocker.com/LonnyBrown), *Meditation—Beginners' Questions & Answers* (www.SelfHelpGuides.com), and *Self-Actuated Healing* (www .amazon.com). www.LonnyBrown.com

social aspects. Holistic medicine is viewed by some as being unscientific, and it is based on a psychosocial model of health care. A comparison of these two approaches can be found in **Table 2.2**. People select one health care delivery system over the other for a variety of reasons, and this decision-making process includes considerations such as culture, access to care, health beliefs, and affordability, but many people use both systems.

Allopathic Medicine

In the Western world, the theoretical construct about the cause of illness is biomedicine. In biomedicine, the body is viewed as a machine, and a core assumption of biomedicine is that scientific data should be the basis of diagnosis and treatment. The approach is built on the ideology that illness occurs when the human biological system goes out of balance and that microorganisms are the cause of many diseases.

Care in the biomedical system is provided by a variety of types of professionals with diverse expertise and levels of training. Allopathic physicians include doctors of medicine (MDs) and doctors of osteopathic medicine (DOs). Numerous allied health professionals, such as nurses, respiratory therapists, physical therapists, physician assistants, health educators, and radiologists, also practice allopathic medicine.

Holistic Medicine

The holistic approach (also called alternative medicine or complementary medicine) has a long history and has been rapidly gaining popularity worldwide. **Holistic medicine** is an approach to maintaining and resuming health that takes the body, mind, and spiritual being into consideration. Holistic medicine uses a variety of therapies, such as massage, prayer, herbal remedies, and reiki. More detail about these therapies is provided in Chapter 4.

Holistic providers have vast differences in their levels of training. These differences include length of training, certification and licensing requirements, and required experience. For example, people who study ayurvedic medicine in India often have four or more years of training, and in the United States it is often much less. Because of this broad range of training and educational requirements, it is essential to inquire about education and experience when seeking a provider. Providers include professionals such as homeopaths, naturopaths, acupuncturists, and hypnotherapists.

Cultural Competence

Cultural competence occurs when an individual or organization has the ability to function effectively within the cultural context of beliefs, behaviors, and needs of the patients or community it serves. Campinha-Bacote (2009) defined cultural competence as "the process in which the healthcare professional continually strives to achieve the ability and availability to effectively work within the cultural context of a client." Cultural competence requires a set of skills and knowledge that all health care professionals and organizations should strive to acquire. The ability to be culturally competent is on a continuum, with cultural destructiveness on one end of the continuum and cultural proficiency at the other end, as illustrated in **Figure 2.2**.

Being culturally competent does not mean that people need to know everything about every culture because that is not possible. What it does mean is that people are respectful and sensitive to cultural differences and can work with clients' cultural beliefs and practices.

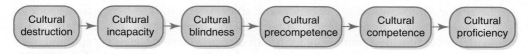

FIGURE 2.2

Cultural competence continuum.

Source: Adapted from University of Michigan Health System, Program for Multicultural Health.

To be culturally competent, one needs to understand his or her own worldviews and those of the person or community in which he or she serves while avoiding stereotyping, judgment, and misapplication of scientific knowledge. Becoming culturally competent is a process that health care professionals should continue to strive to achieve. Models have been developed to assist individuals and organizations in achieving this goal.

Cultural Competence Models

Models are tools that assist with understanding the causes of behaviors, predicting behaviors, and evaluating interventions. Cultural competence models help the learner understand the different components of cultural competence, guide their interactions with people of different cultural groups, and help them identify areas in which they may need to increase their education.

The Process of Cultural Competence in the Delivery of Health Care Services

Josepha Campinha-Bacote (2009) developed a model of cultural competence that is based on five constructs:

1. *Cultural awareness.* The process of conducting a self-examination of one's own biases toward other cultures and the in-depth exploration of one's cultural and professional background.
2. *Cultural knowledge.* The process in which the health care professional seeks and obtains a sound information base regarding the worldviews of different cultural and ethnic groups as well as biological variations, diseases and health conditions, and variations in drug metabolism found among ethnic groups (biocultural ecology).
3. *Cultural skill.* The ability to conduct a cultural assessment to collect relevant cultural data regarding the client's presenting problem as well as accurately conducting a culturally based physical assessment.
4. *Cultural encounter.* The process that encourages the health care professional to directly engage in face-to-face cultural interactions and other types of encounters with clients from culturally diverse backgrounds to modify existing beliefs about a cultural group and to prevent possible stereotyping.
5. *Cultural desire.* The motivation of the health care professional to "want to" rather than to "have to" engage in the process of becoming culturally aware, culturally knowledgeable, culturally skillful, and to seek cultural encounters.

The Purnell Model for Cultural Competence

The Purnell model for cultural competence started as an organizing framework in 1991 when Dr. Larry Purnell discovered the need for both students and staff to have a framework for learning about their cultures and the cultures of their patients and families. The purposes of the model are to provide a framework for health care providers to learn concepts and characteristics of culture and to define circumstances that affect a person's cultural worldview in the context of historic perspectives (Purnell, 2005).

The model (illustrated in **Figure 2.3**) is a circle in which an outlying rim represents global society, a second rim represents community, a third rim represents family, and an inner rim

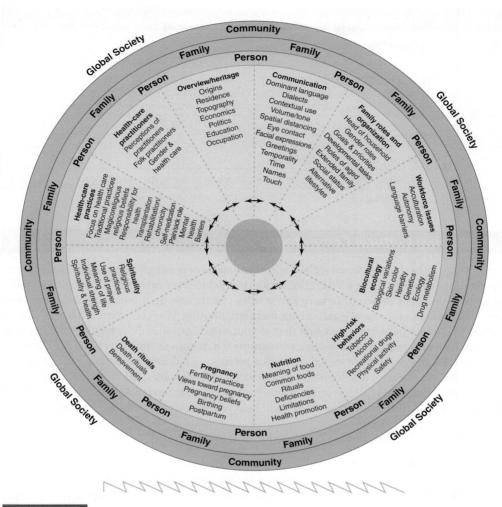

FIGURE 2.3

The Purnell model for cultural competence.

Source: Reprinted with permission from Dr. Larry Purnell, University of Delaware.

represents the person. **Table 2.3** lists the four rings with their related definitions. The interior of the circle is divided into 12 pie-shaped wedges that depict cultural domains and their concepts. The dark center of the circle represents unknown phenomena. Along the bottom of the model is a jagged line that represents the nonlinear concept of cultural consciousness. The 12 cultural domains (constructs) provide the organizing framework of the model. Health care providers can use this same process to understand their own cultural beliefs, attitudes, values, practices, and behaviors.

TABLE 2.3   The Rings of the Purnell Model for Cultural Competence

Ring	Definition
Global society	World communications and politics; conflicts and warfare; natural disasters and famines; international exchanges in business, commerce, and information technology; advances in the health sciences; space exploration; and the increased ability for people to travel around the world and to interact with diverse societies
Community	A group of people who have a common interest or identity and live in a specified locality
Family	Two or more people who are emotionally involved with each other and who may or may not be blood relatives
Person	A biopsychosociocultural human being who is constantly adapting

Source: Reprinted with permission from Dr. Larry Purnell, University of Delaware.

Promoting Cultural Competence

Promoting cultural competence within organizations is increasingly becoming a higher priority in the health care industry. The rationale for this includes the existence of health disparities, existing differences in access to care and quality of care among minorities, concerns about providing quality of care and legal actions, and credentialing. Ways to promote and assess your own level of cultural competence and that of your organization are the focus of this section.

Implementing cultural competence programs is a nonlinear, multilevel, complex process. The paths to progression are varied. Areas for promoting cultural competence are related to policies, human resource development, and services. Two tools are used to assess cultural competence: one at an individual level and the other at an organizational level. These types of assessments are a good place to start, and they will help you identify areas in need of improvement.

Individual Assessment of Cultural Competence

As a member of the organization, the knowledge you have of yourself and others is important and is reflected in the ways you communicate and interact. The individual assessment instrument in **Table 2.4** was developed to assist you in reflecting on and examining your journey toward cultural competence.

The following statements are about you and your cultural beliefs and values as they relate to the organization. Please check the *one* answer that *best describes* your response to each of the statements.

Organizational Assessment of Cultural Competence

Table 2.5 offers a means of assessing an organization's cultural competence. Some suggestions for achieving a culturally competent organization include the following:

- Maximize diversity among the workforce.
- Involve community representatives in the organization's planning and quality improvement meetings.

TABLE 2.4   Individual Cultural Assessment

Individual Assessment	Almost Always	Often	Sometimes	Almost Never
1. I reflect on and examine my own cultural background, biases, and prejudices related to race, culture, and sexual orientation that may influence my behaviors.				
2. I continue to learn about the cultures of the consumers and families who are served in the program, in particular attitudes toward disability; cultural beliefs and values; and health, spiritual, and religious practices.				
3. I recognize and accept that the consumer and family members make the ultimate decisions even though they may be different compared to my personal and professional values and beliefs.				
4. I intervene, in an appropriate manner, when I observe other staff members engaging in behaviors that appear culturally insensitive or reflect prejudice.				
5. I attempt to learn and use key words and colloquialisms of the languages used by the consumers and families who are served.				
6. I utilize interpreters for the assessment of consumers and their families whose spoken language is one for which I am not fluent.				
7. I have developed skills to utilize an interpreter effectively.				
8. I utilize methods of communication, including written, verbal, pictures, and diagrams, that will be most helpful to the consumers, families, and other program participants.				
9. I write reports, or any form of written communication, in a style and at a level that consumers, families, and other program participants will understand.				
10. I am flexible, adaptive, and will initiate changes that will better serve consumers, families, and other program participants from diverse cultures.				
11. I am mindful of cultural factors that may influence the behaviors of consumers, families, and other program participants.				

Source: Reprinted with permission from the Committee of the Association of University Centers on Disabilities (AUCD) Multicultural Council.

TABLE 2.5   Organizational Cultural Assessment

Please check the *one* answer that *best describes* your response to each of the statements.

A. Organization	Yes	No	Don't Know
1. Cultural competence is included in the mission statement, policies, and procedures.			
2. A committee/task force/program area addresses issues of cultural competence.			
3. Partnerships with representatives of ethnic communities actively incorporate their knowledge and experience in organizational planning.			
4. The organization supports involvement with and/or utilization of the resources of regional and/or national forums that promote cultural competence.			

B. Administration	Almost Always	Often	Sometimes	Almost Never	Don't Know
1. Personnel recruitment, hiring, and retention practices reflect the goal to achieve ethnic diversity and cultural competence.					
2. Resources are in place to support initial and ongoing training for personnel to develop cultural competence.					
3. Position descriptions and personnel performance measures include skills related to cultural competence.					
4. Participants for all advisory committees and councils are recruited and supported to ensure the diverse cultural representation of the organization's geographic area.					
5. Personnel are respected and supported for their desire to honor and participate in cultural celebrations.					
6. Fiscal resources are available to support translation and interpretation services.					

C. Clinical Services	Almost Always	Often	Sometimes	Almost Never	Don't Know
Important: If your organization does not provide these services, please check here and proceed to the next section. _____					
1. Clinical services are routinely and systematically reviewed for methods, strategies, and ways of serving consumers and their families in culturally competent ways.					
2. Cultural bias of assessment tools is considered when interpreting results and making recommendations.					
3. Translation and interpretation assistance is available and utilized when needed.					
4. Forms of communication (reports, appointment notices, telephone message greetings, etc.) are culturally and linguistically appropriate for the populations that are served.					
5. Pictures, posters, printed materials, and toys reflect the culture and ethnic backgrounds of the consumers and families who are served.					
6. When food is discussed or used in assessment or treatment, the cultural and ethnic background of the consumer and family is considered.					

(*Continues*)

TABLE 2.5   Organizational Cultural Assessment (*Continued*)

D. Research and Program Evaluation	Almost Always	Often	Sometimes	Almost Never	Don't Know
Important: If your organization is not involved in these activities, please check here and proceed to the next section. ___					
1. Input on research priorities is sought from consumers and/or their families who represent diverse cultures.					
2. Research projects include subjects of diverse cultures that are representative of the targeted research population.					
3. The researchers include members of the racial/ethnic groups to be studied and/or individuals who have acquired knowledge and skills to work with subjects from those specific groups.					
4. Consumers and families who represent diverse cultures provide input regarding the design, methods, and outcome measures of research and program evaluation projects.					
E. Technical Assistance/Consultation	**Almost Always**	**Often**	**Sometimes**	**Almost Never**	**Don't Know**
Important: If your organization is not involved in these activities, please check here and proceed to the next section. ___					
1. Technical assistance/consultation activities are routinely and systematically reviewed for methods, strategies, and ways of serving communities in culturally competent ways.					
2. When assessing the need for technical assistance/consultation in communities, input from members who reflect the diverse cultural makeup of these communities is sought and utilized.					
3. Efforts are made to involve consultants who have knowledge of and experience with the cultural group who requested the technical assistance/consultation.					
4. Evaluation from the recipients of technical assistance/consultation activities includes components of cultural competence.					

F. Education/Training	Almost Always	Often	Sometimes	Almost Never	Don't Know
Important: If your organization is not involved in these activities, please check here and proceed to the next section. _____					
1. Trainees/students are actively recruited from diverse cultures.					
2. Trainees/students from diverse cultures are mentored.					
3. Representatives of the diverse cultures are actively sought to participate in the planning and presentation of training activities.					
4. The training curriculum and activities incorporate content for the development of cultural competence.					
5. The training curriculum, materials, and activities are systemically evaluated to determine if they achieve cultural competence.					

G. Community/Continuing Education	Almost Always	Often	Sometimes	Almost Never	Don't Know
Important: If your organization is not involved in these activities, please check here. _____					
1. Participants are actively recruited from diverse cultures.					
2. Representatives of diverse cultures are actively sought to participate in the planning and presentation of these activities.					
3. The content and activities are culturally and linguistically appropriate.					
4. Participant evaluation of community/continuing education activities includes components of cultural competence.					

Source: Reprinted with permission from the Committee of the Association of University Centers on Disabilities (AUCD) Multicultural Council.

- Establish a cultural competence board to help guide the implementation of culturally sensitive prevention and treatment efforts.
- Provide ongoing training to staff members.
- Develop health materials for the target population written at the appropriate literacy level, in a variety of languages, and with culturally appropriate images—this includes materials such as educational brochures, consent forms, signage, postprocedural directions, and advance directives.
- Make onsite interpretation services available when possible, and be sure that all appropriate staff members are educated about how to use telephone interpretation services.
- Assess customer satisfaction and clinical outcomes regularly.
- Consider the health disparities that exist in your community when planning outreach efforts.

When an individual, organization, or system has implemented change to progress toward cultural competence, the change process should be measured. This is important because it can indicate the progress that has been made and identify areas that are in need of improvement. The measurement process itself can be a catalyst for change.

Summary

We have all heard an abundance of stories about how illness can occur and how it can be cured. Some of these belief systems are ancient and are believed to be true, regardless of whether or not controversial evidence exists. These beliefs influence who we ask for medical advice and when. This is part of our worldview, which is our perception of how the world works. Health care professionals need to take these issues into consideration, and that is a step toward the progression of cultural competence.

Several concepts that one needs to consider when working with people from different cultures have been identified in this chapter. These concepts include different beliefs about how illness occurs, which affects how, where, and when people seek medical care. Health care professionals should assess the person's worldview and tailor their approach and communication to successfully prevent and treat illness. Because of these differences, health care professionals need to become culturally competent. The concept of cultural competence and what that means has been discussed, and two tools to assess the level of cultural competence among individuals and organizations are included to assist with assessing cultural competence at both the individual and organizational levels.

Review

1. Explain three overarching theories about the causes of illness.

2. Explain the two overarching systems of care in the United States and their differences.

3. Explain the components of the process of cultural competence in the delivery of health care services model.

4. Explain the components of the Purnell model for cultural competence.

5. List ways to improve cultural competence within an organization.

Activity

Write a research paper on three types of holistic healers (e.g., shamans, medicine men, accupuncturists). Include information about their training, approaches to healing, and evidence-based patient outcomes.

Case Study

Public health workers are offering free measles vaccinations to children. The worker is speaking with the parents of a child and explaining why the vaccination is important. The parents express concerns that the vaccine will interfere with God's plan, and they refuse to have the child vaccinated.

Consider these related questions:

- What are the parents' beliefs about how health is maintained?

- How do the theories of health and illness discussed in this chapter apply to this case study?

- Using the Purnell model for cultural competence, what approach, if any, should the public health workers take to help protect the child by assisting the parents with understanding the need for the vaccination?

References

American College of Osteopathic Medicine. (2014). *The history of osteopathic medicine*. Retrieved from http://www.aacom.org /about/osteomed/Pages/History.aspx)

Bhalerao, S., Deshpande, T., & Thatte, U. (2012). Prakriti (Ayurvedic concept of constitution) and variations in platelet aggregation. *BMC Complementary & Alternative Medicine*, *12*, 248.

Campinha-Bacote, J. (2009). *The process of cultural competence in the delivery of healthcare services*. Retrieved from http:// www.transculturalcare.net/Cultural _Competence_Model.htm

Carteret, M. (2011). *Culturally-based beliefs about illness causation*. Retrieved from http://www .dimensionsofculture.com/2011/02/culturally -based-beliefs-about-illness-causation/

Gilberti, T. C. (2004). Reiki: The re-emergence of an ancient healing art in modern times. *Home Health Care Management Practice*, *16*(6), 480–486.

O'Neil, D. (2005). *Explanations of illness*. Retrieved from http://anthro.palomar.edu/medical/med_1.htm

Purnell, L. (2005, Summer). The Purnell model for cultural competence. *Journal of Multicultural Nursing & Health*, *11*:(2), 7–15.

Williams, D. R., Lavizzo-Mourey, R., & Warren, R. C. (1994). The concept of race and health status in America. *Public Health Reports*, January–February, *109*(1), 26–41.

CHAPTER 3

Worldview and Health Decisions

After all, when you come right down to it, how many people speak the same language even when they speak the same language?
　—Russell Hoban

Key Concepts

Worldview
Temporal relationships
Proxemics
Individualism
Collectivism
Fate versus free will
Euthanasia

Karma
Ahimsa
Advance directive
Living will
Durable power of attorney
Biomedical worldview
Mind–body integration

Learning Objectives

After reading this chapter, you should be able to:

1. Explain what worldview means and how it is related to culture.
2. Describe at least three components of worldview that affect health.
3. Explain how worldview influences beginning- and end-of-life medical decisions.
4. Describe how worldview is related to how health is perceived and how problems are expressed.

A person's worldview is closely linked to his or her cultural and religious background, and it has profound implications for health care. Worldview influences lifestyle, and it is imperative that health care professionals understand its impact on health care decisions, involve patients in decisions and actions, and accommodate patients' beliefs to provide congruent care.

This chapter begins with a discussion of worldview, particularly in terms of time, personal space, individual autonomy, free will, and fate, and explains how these major components relate to health care. Then we move into more specific ways that worldview affects medical decisions and how people perceive and respond to illness.

Worldview

A **worldview** is a set of cultural assumptions and beliefs that express how people see, interpret, and explain their experience (Tilbert, 2010). It helps us make sense of our lives. Worldview includes our relationships with nature, our social relationships, our ethical reasoning, and cosmology (study of the universe and humanity's place) (Purnell, 2013). It even affects our view of aesthetics. For example, most of us know that sun exposure contributes to skin cancer, but some cultures view tans as healthy whereas others see very white skin as beautiful (e.g., the Japanese culture), which is why skin lightening is done.

Culture fits within the larger structure of worldviews. Worldviews are the beliefs and assumptions by which an individual can make sense of experiences, and these are what culture is built upon. Cultural groups have varied views of the world, and when they clash, people may find the behavior of others offensive or confusing. Some of the prominent variances in worldviews include health beliefs, orientation toward time, use of space, social and family organization, and communication.

Because worldviews contain and shape cultures (shared starting points and values), working effectively across cultures requires some understanding of the soil from which cultures grow—the seedbed called worldviews.

> Worldviews can be resources for understanding and analyzing conflicts when fundamental differences divide groups of people. By looking at the stories, rituals, myths, and metaphors used by a group, we can learn efficiently and deeply about group members' identities (who they see themselves to be) and meanings (what matters to them and how they make meaning). When we do this with each side to a conflict, places of connection and divergence may become clearer, leading to a better understanding of the conflict in context. (LeBaron, 2003)

Worldview encourages a broader understanding of and elaborates on the implicit content of culture. For example, a health care professional may know that a patient or a family holds many unfamiliar beliefs, but by understanding worldviews the health care professional can appreciate the mind-set that those beliefs create (Tilbert, 2010).

A person's worldview is closely linked with his or her cultural and religious background and has profound health care implications. For example, people with chronic diseases who believe in fatalism (predetermined fate) may not adhere to treatment because they believe that medical intervention cannot affect their outcomes. Worldview is an equally important concept for educating health professionals about their own beliefs and assumptions that may influence the care they deliver. Health care providers play a mediating role in whether or not populations experience health disparities. A weakness of the medical profession is that not all of its members appreciate and accept that it has a professional culture (and subcultures) that consists of its own beliefs and assumptions just as do the cultures of the patients (Tilbert, 2010). Some of the major components of worldview that affect health care professionals are discussed in the following sections.

Temporal Relationships

Temporal relationships refers to people's worldview in terms of time. These perceptions of time vary among cultures. In the West, time tends to be seen as quantitative elements of past, present, and future and is measured in units that reflect the march of progress. It is logical, sequential, and present focused, moving with incremental certainty toward a future. In the East, time feels like it has unlimited continuity, and it does not have a defined boundary. Birth and death are not such absolute ends because the universe continues, and humans, though changing form, continue as part of it.

Some cultures are present oriented, and others focus on the past or future. Time perspective affects our health behaviors and expectations of health care behavior. In general, people in the West understand that healthy behaviors in the present will affect our health in the future, and future-oriented people are willing to make sacrifices now for future benefits. Present-focused people are not willing to make sacrifices for the future and engage in behaviors to satisfy their immediate desire regardless of the long-term consequences. Future-oriented individuals place value on getting screenings and preventive measures for future payoffs. Present-oriented cultures, including American Indians and African Americans, may see living in the moment as the priority and are less willing to forgo immediate pleasures for future benefits. Cultures that are past oriented tend to value elders and honor traditions. For example, the Asian culture is generally past oriented, and they value and perform traditional healing practices, such as acupuncture and herbal remedies.

Another component of time related to health care is expectations related to punctuality. Some cultures are very punctual, and people in these groups (for example, people with a Polish culture) will arrive for appointments on time. Others are less rigid and will arrive around the time of the appointment. Some clinics who serve cultures who have less rigidity around time have stopped making appointments and changed to seeing patients on a first-come, first-served basis.

Space (Proxemics)

Another variable across cultures is perception of space, or **proxemics**, which includes interpersonal distance and boundaries. North Americans tend to prefer a large amount of space, and Europeans tend to stand more closely together when talking and are accustomed to smaller personal spaces (LeBaron, 2003).

Violating these boundaries can lead to conflict, stress, anxiety, miscommunication, or discomfort. If someone is accustomed to standing or sitting very close when he or she is talking with another, that person may see the other's attempt to create more space as evidence of coldness, condescension, or a lack of interest. Those who are accustomed to more personal space may view attempts to get closer as pushy, disrespectful, or aggressive (LeBaron, 2003).

Also related to space is the degree of comfort we feel when furniture or other objects are moved. A German executive working in the United States became so upset with visitors to his office moving the guest chair to suit themselves that he had it bolted to the floor (LeBaron, 2003). Contrast this with United States and Canadian mediators and conflict-resolution trainers, whose first step in preparing for a meeting is frequently a complete rearrangement of the furniture (LeBaron, 2003).

Social Organization and Family Relationships

Social organization refers to patterns of social interactions. Examples include how people interact and communicate, the kinship system, marriage residency patterns, division of labor, who has access to specific goods and knowledge, social hierarchy, religion, and economic systems. Four components of social organization that have an immense impact in health care are explored here: individualism versus collectivism, fate versus free will, communication, and family relationships.

Individualism Versus Collectivism

Individualism and collectivism are contrasting perspectives and values (see **Table 3.1**). In **individualism** each person is seen as a social unit, and each person has primary responsibility for him- or herself. In the United States the overarching culture values of individualism, autonomy, and independence are rewarded and respected. Other individualistic cultures

TABLE 3.1   Individualism Versus Collectivism

Individualism	Collectivism
Focus on self rather than group	Focus on group rather than self
Guilt	Shame
Self-respect	Saving face
Behavior primarily regulated by likes and dislikes	Behavior primarily regulated by group norms
Conflict more acceptable	Conflict avoidance; emphasis on harmony and hierarchy
Person is basic unit of analysis and reality	Group is basic unit of analysis and reality
Focus on being unique	Focus on fitting in
Direct	Indirect
Achievement is a product of personal qualities	Achievement is a product of society
Priority given to promotion of own goals	Priority given to promotion of goals of others

include Germany, Canada, and Sweden (Purnell, 2013). If someone is successful, it is primarily because of these personal qualities.

In **collectivism**, people are socialized to view themselves as part of a larger group, such as a family, a community, or a tribe. The group is the social unit, and dependence and connections within the group are valued. An individual's identity is determined by his or her relationship and position within the group. People make decisions based on what is good for the group rather than on what is good for themselves. Saving face is valued as is showing respect for others. The needs and goals of the individual are subordinate to those of the larger group and should be sacrificed when the collective good so requires. Collectivists believe that achievement is a product of society. Examples of collectivist cultures include the Amish, Chinese, Mexicans, and Vietnamese (Purnell, 2013).

Why are these two opposing views important in health care? People from individualistic cultures make their health care decisions independently whereas individuals in collectivist cultures involve their families in the decision-making process. Health care professionals need to be aware of these differences in worldview. In collectivist cultures, illness is considered to be a family event rather than an individual occurrence. Knowledge transmission, personal responsibility, shame and guilt, help-seeking behaviors, competitiveness, and communication are affected by this aspect of worldview (Purnell, 2013). In individualistic cultures, direct questioning, sharing personal issues, and asking personal questions are typical. In a collectivist culture, disagreeing or saying "no" to a health care professional is considered rude; therefore, when a health care professional asks if the patient understands, the patient may answer "yes" even though understanding has really not occurred. In addition, disabilities, mental health issues, and other health problems that are stigmatized may be kept hidden to save face, and treatment may be delayed and care provided in the home (Purnell, 2013).

In the United States, legal documents such as advance directives and durable powers of attorney are strategies to prolong autonomy in situations in which patients can no longer represent themselves (Searight & Gafford, 2005). Other cultures de-emphasize autonomy, perceiving it as isolating rather than empowering. Their belief is that communities and families, not individuals alone, are affected by life-threatening illnesses and that they should be involved in making medical decisions (Searight & Gafford, 2005).

Fate Versus Free Will

"Fate and free will" refer to the degree to which people believe they are the masters of their own lives (**free will**) or believe they are subject to events outside their control (**fate**). Basically, fate and free will refer to the beliefs people hold about their ability to change and maneuver the course of their lives and relationships. This concept also is called *locus of control*. People who believe that they have control over their health have an internal locus of control (free will belief), and people who believe that it is outside of their control (fate belief) have an external locus of control. In some ethnic groups, factors outside medical intervention, such as a divine plan and personal coping skills, may be more important for health and survival than medical intervention and health behaviors.

Health care professionals need to consider this aspect of social organization. For example, when health outreach workers in India attempted to provide children with free polio vaccinations, they found that many parents refused the immunization because they believed Allah would take care of their children's health. Providing preventive care and treatment can be challenging when people believe that fate will determine their health and that their health behaviors will not change what the master plan is for them.

Communication

Communication is an interactive process that involves sending and receiving information, emotions, thoughts, and ideas through verbal and nonverbal means. It is the basis of human interaction. Effective communication enables health care professionals to accurately exchange information, establish relationships, and understand the person's needs and concerns. Effective communication is important in all facets of life, but in health care it can be the deciding factor between life and death.

Intercultural communication is sensitive to exchanging information across cultural boundaries in a way that preserves mutual respect and minimizes miscommunication and conflict. If communication is hindered, patients who utilize traditional remedies may be reluctant to inform their biomedical providers about them, leading to potentially dangerous interactions between medications prescribed by the two types of providers.

In addition to better health outcomes, effective communication can lead to higher patient satisfaction, continued care, and better adherence to treatment recommendations while reducing conflict and errors, lost opportunities for encouraging health behavior changes, misinterpretations of treatment plans, damaged relationships (including a loss of trust) between provider and patient or community member, and legal actions. All of these reasons illustrate why culturally competent communication is a vital component of health care.

Verbal Communication

As indicated in the quotation of Hoban at the beginning of this chapter, even people who speak the same language do not necessarily communicate even when using the same words. For example, in some age groups the word "fox" means attractive, but someone from a different generation may think of the animal. People in the United States whose first language is English have a difficult time communicating, so imagine how difficult it must be to communicate with people when English is not their first language. The limitations of language to convey experience—even between people who speak the same language—are extremely obvious when we cannot explain something as important as the intensity of pain we feel or the unrelenting worry and frustration pain sometimes causes. To further complicate communications, not all cultures describe health problems in the same way, and words from their language may not be easily translated to English and vice versa. For example, words used to describe pain typically include "sharp," "throbbing," "stabbing," or "aching." But in many tribal cultures, stories or symbols are essential in relating one's worldview, so very different words are used to describe pain. Clinicians might be baffled by patients explaining their pain using natural symbols like lightning, trees with deep spreading roots, spider webs, or the tones of drums and flutes (Carteret, 2011a).

In addition to the risks of everyday language breeding possibilities for miscommunication, health care has a language of its own with specialized terminology that can increase the chances of communication mishaps. Health care providers should avoid jargon and select words that people will understand without making them feel like you are talking down to them. Ask the receiver to summarize what you said to check for understanding, and look for nonverbal cues that indicate when miscommunication has occurred. A few cultural communication differences are described in the following paragraphs.

In some cultures, asking questions of health care providers is not an acceptable behavior. Patients from these cultures may be less likely to ask even clarifying questions and, subsequently, may not understand their condition or be able to follow their treatment plan, potentially resulting in a lower quality of care or even medical error.

In some cultures doctors do not want to inform the patient about his or her health problem. This nondisclosure may be because of the belief that the discussion about illness may eliminate or reduce the patient's hope or induce depression or anxiety. Others believe that discussing the illness may make the person worse or that it is disrespectful. This issue also is a concern with regard to consent forms. The patient may believe that discussing the possible death or side effects of a medical procedure or medication may make it self-fulfilling and actually happen.

Some cultures dictate that doctors protect patients from the emotional and physical harm caused by directly addressing death and end-of-life care. Many Asian and American Indian cultures value beneficence (physician's obligation to promote patient welfare) by encouraging the patient's hope, even in the face of terminal illness (Searight & Gafford, 2005). Emotional reaction to news of serious illness may be considered to be directly harmful to health. It is thought that a patient who is already in pain should not have to struggle with depression or stress as well. This negative emotional impact on health appears to be one of the primary reasons Chinese patients are less likely to sign do not resuscitate (DNR) orders (Searight & Gafford, 2005). This concern, together with Asian values of admiration for the elderly, may be especially pronounced in senior patients who, because of their frailty, are perceived to be more vulnerable to being upset by bad news. In addition, the special status of the elderly in Asian cultures includes a value that they should not be burdened unnecessarily when they are ill.

Direct disclosure of bad health news may eliminate patient hope. Bosnian respondents indicated that they expected physicians to maintain patients' optimism by not revealing terminal diagnoses (Searight & Gafford, 2005). Filipino patients may not want to discuss end-of-life care because these exchanges demonstrate a lack of respect for the belief that individual fate is determined by God (Searight & Gafford, 2005). American Indian, Filipino, and Bosnian cultures emphasize that words should be carefully chosen because when they are spoken they may become a reality (Searight & Gafford, 2005). Carrese and Rhodes (1995) noted that Navajo informants place a particularly high value on thinking and speaking in a "positive way." About one half of their Navajo informants would not even discuss advance directives or anticipated therapeutic support status with patients because these discussions were considered to be potentially injurious.

Nonverbal Communication

Communication is more than just words, and much information is conveyed nonverbally. Our system of nonverbal communication includes gestures, posture, silence, spatial relations, emotional expression, touch, and physical appearance (LeBaron, 2003). Our sense of what nonverbal behavior is appropriate is derived from our culture. Differences in nonverbal communication may lead to misunderstandings, misinterpretations about the person's character, damaged relationships, conflict, or escalate an existing conflict. For example, people in some cultures attach great superstition to particular numbers, and smiling does not suggest feeling good in all cultures. In some Asian cultures, people tend to smile when they are embarrassed or angry (Carteret, 2011b).

Differences in nonverbal communication can be seen in the following ways:

- Voice tone and volume
- Pace of speech
- Tolerance of silence
- Physical distance between speakers
- Posture
- Eye contact
- Gestures
- Direct versus indirect approaches
- Ways of greeting people
- Amount and location of touch

Nonverbal communication can be received in three general ways: (1) the nonverbal message may exist in both cultures but not have the same meaning, (2) the nonverbal message exists in the sender's culture but not in the receiver's culture, or (3) the nonverbal message exists in both cultures and has the same meaning. Here are some examples of nonverbal communications that have different meanings in various parts of the world:

- In Asian cultures smiling is used to show pleasure, and it also is used to cover emotional pain or embarrassment. When a patient is asked if he or she understands the treatment plan, if the person does not understand he or she may smile to cover embarrassment.

- The "ring" or "okay" gesture has different meaning in different countries. In the United States and other English-speaking countries, the ring or okay gesture means "everything is okay." In Japan it can mean money; in some Mediterranean countries it is used to infer that a man is homosexual; in Indonesia it means zero.

- In the United States, getting someone to come toward you by motioning with your index finger is common or acceptable; however, in the Philippines, Korea, and parts of Latin America, as well as other countries, the same gesture is considered to be rude.

- In some cultures, direct eye contact is an indication of honestly, listening, and respect. People from some other cultures consider direct eye contact to be rude and feel as though they are being disrespected or challenged; therefore, they may avoid direct eye contact.

- Touch has variations of meanings among cultures as well. For some, casual touching is seen as a sexual overture and should be avoided. People of the same sex (especially men) or opposite sex do not generally touch one another. In other cultures, especially among collectivist ones, same genders can touch without having a sexual connotation. Health care providers should ask permission before touching someone (Purnell, 2013).

Family Relationships

Family relationships include issues such as who makes the decisions in the home, family goals and priorities, child-rearing practices, family and community social status, marriage decisions, divorce acceptance, the roles of the elderly and extended family, and acceptance of alternative lifestyles. These factors influence related issues such as health behaviors and decisions, living situations, and age to marry. Family structure is an important consideration because the quality of social support from family, a practice highly driven by culture, has been shown to have significant consequences for health.

What Do You Think?

Reflect on your own worldview and how it differ from others. What are the philosophical reasons for how your worldview differs from others? How do these beliefs affect relationships and possibly lead to conflict? Consider the following questions:

- How comfortable are you with being touched?
- What is your perspective of time?
- What does it mean to you when people are late?
- How do you make health care decisions?
- How do you view illness?

Worldview and Medical Decisions

Medical decisions such as abortion, the use of birth control, permission to allow blood transfusion, utilization of chemotherapy, advance directives, and euthanasia are difficult and life altering. In this section the focus is on two areas of medical decisions: beginning-of-life and end-of-life decisions.

Beginning-of-Life Decisions

The beginning-of-life decisions include choices related to pregnancy, abortion, birth control use, fertility practices, birthing, and the postpartum period. Some of these decisions have deep ties to religious beliefs.

Birth Control

Decisions surrounding the use of birth control center around the view about the purpose of sexual intercourse. Is it for procreation or other reasons? The use of birth control is prohibited by some religions for reasons such as that men are not permitted to waste "their seed" or that it is a violation of the design built into the human race by God. Other religions permit the use of hormonal birth control methods such as pills, patches, injections, and implants, but they do not allow the use of birth control methods that block or destroy sperm, such as condoms and vasectomies. Condom use may be permitted to protect one from sexually transmitted infections, and birth control may be allowed when a woman needs a rest between pregnancies, when pregnancy poses a risk to the mother or baby, or when the man cannot financially support another child.

Abortion

A central issue surrounding abortion is related to the core question about when life begins. Does it begin when the egg is fertilized, when the soul enters the fetus, when consciousness occurs, when the embryo becomes embedded in the uterine wall, when the fetus moves, or when the birth occurs? The answer to this question depends on who you ask, and the answer one gives will shape his or her views on the morality of abortion. Some religions prohibit abortion because it is viewed as murder, because it brings bad karma, or because it is an act of violence regardless of when or why the abortion takes place.

Many religions approve of abortion under certain circumstances, such as when

- the health of the mother is at risk if the pregnancy is continued,
- the child may be born with a disability that will cause suffering, or
- in cases of rape or incest.

End-of-Life Decisions

In "The Parable of the Mustard Seed," the Buddha teaches a lesson that is valid for all cultures: human beings receive no exemption from mortality. Deep in the throes of grief after the death of her son, a woman seeks wisdom from the Buddha, who says that he does indeed have an answer to her queries. Before giving it, however, he insists that she must first collect a mustard seed from every house that has not been touched by death. She canvasses her entire community but fails to collect a single seed. Returning to the Buddha, she understands that, like all other living beings, we are destined to die.

Death is inevitable, but how people respond to death has cultural ties. In some cultures it is appropriate to cry, sob, and wail loudly, whereas mourning in other cultures requires controlling grief and being stoic in public. Variations in burial practices also are culturally determined.

Although death is inevitable, modern life-extending technologies have changed the process. Organ transplantation, respirators, antibiotics, surgical procedures, and feeding tubes enable life to be prolonged. Other technologies, such as lethal injections, may hasten death. Using these technologies is a complex choice. In some situations, prolonging life in these ways may be contradictory to another fundamental human value—going against God's will. Human beings struggle with not overstepping these boundaries or playing God with life and death. Individual wishes may be subsumed by the will of other family members or the dictates of their religion.

Decisions surrounding continuing treatment, discontinuing treatment, or hastening death are difficult and agonizing. As individuals and their families face these controversial questions and as many states consider revising their laws about end-of-life choices, religious traditions and values can offer guidance and insight, if not solutions, for some.

In the remainder of this section the more controversial and general decisions are addressed, but there are many other end-of-life decisions to consider, such as burial versus cremation, timing of the burial, length of the mourning process, appropriate dress and behavior before and during the service and after the burial, and permission to conduct an autopsy.

Organ Transplants

Organ transplantation is the removal of tissues of the human body from a person who has recently died or from a living donor for the purpose of transplanting or grafting them into other persons. Cultural and religious views regarding organ transplantation are changing. Some religions that previously prohibited organ donation are now altering their views and seeing it as an act of compassion, but others continue to prohibit organ donation. Religions that prohibit organ transplants do so because of their beliefs regarding life after death and resurrection. Some religions will consent to an organ donation if they are certain that it is for the health and welfare of the transplant recipient, but if the outcome is questionable, then the donation is not encouraged.

Euthanasia

Euthanasia is a Greek term that means "good death." Also called mercy killing, it is the act or practice of ending the life of an individual who is suffering from a terminal illness or an incurable condition by lethal injection or the suspension of extraordinary medical treatment. The person who is suffering from the painful and incurable disease or incapacitating physical disorder is painlessly put to death. Because there is no specific provision for it in most legal systems, it is usually regarded as a crime: suicide (if performed by the patient) or murder (if performed by another person, which includes physician-assisted suicide).

Murder and suicide are against the belief systems of most religions, so in those systems it would be considered morally wrong. In some religions, such as Hinduism, suicide is acceptable if it is done by fasting because it is nonviolent. Other reasons for religious opposition are the concern for patients who may be in vulnerable positions because of their illness or their lack of social and economic resources. There is fear that patients who cannot afford expensive treatment, for example, will be pressured to accept euthanasia. There also is great concern about the moral nature of the doctor's professional self.

Karma and rebirth are other considerations for not supporting euthanasia. Karma is the total effect of a person's actions and conduct during the successive phases of the person's existence, which is regarded as determining the person's destiny. Karma extends beyond one's present life to all past and future lives as well. In Hinduism and Buddhism, human beings are believed to be captured in endless cycles of rebirth and reincarnation. In both traditions, all living creatures (humans, animals, and plants) represent manifestations of the laws of karmic rebirth. To honor these laws, one must show great respect for the preservation of life and the noninjury of conscious beings. Acts that are destructive of life are morally condemned by the principle of **ahimsa**, which is the conceptual equivalent of the Western principle of the sanctity of life. Religions may permit physicians to hasten death in the very few jurisdictions that allow it through legal injection but not by withholding care.

On the other side of the issue, most religions also consider acts of compassion and concern about the dignity of the dying person to be part of humanity. Concern for the welfare of others as one is dying is seen as a sign of spiritual enlightenment. A person can decide to forgo treatment to avoid imposing a heavy burden of caregiving on family or friends. He or she may also stop treatment to relieve loved ones of the emotional or economic distress of prolonged dying.

These two different perspectives lead to the dilemma of whether euthanasia is an act of compassion or murder. Different cultures and religions answer the question differently, and debate exists within religions. This personal and difficult decision obviously needs to be made on an individual basis, but health care professionals should be aware of the conflicting perspectives and the rationale behind them.

Advance Directives and End-of-Life Care

Advance directives are legal documents that enable a person to convey his or her decisions about end-of-life care ahead of time. Advance directives include the living will and durable power of attorney, and they provide a way for patients to communicate their wishes to their family, friends, and health care professionals and to avoid confusion later in the event that the person becomes unable to communicate.

A **living will** is a set of instructions that documents a person's wishes about medical care intended to sustain life. People can accept or refuse medical care, and many types of life-sustaining care should be taken into consideration when drafting a living will:

- The use of life-sustaining equipment, such as dialysis and breathing machines
- Resuscitation if breathing or heart beat stops
- Artificial hydration and nutrition (tube feeding)
- Withholding food and fluids
- Organ or tissue donation
- Comfort care

A **durable power of attorney** for health care is a document that names your health care representative who can speak for you when you cannot. This is someone you trust to make health care decisions if you are unable to do so. Survey data suggest that about 26% of the U.S. population has an advance directive, with significantly lower rates among nonwhite races (Rao, Anderson, Lin, & Laux, 2014). For example, one study revealed significant differences among racial and ethnic groups in the rate of completion of advance directives, with about twice as many whites as African Americans completing advance directives (Morhaim & Pollack, 2013). This difference is likely attributable to several factors, including cultural differences in family-centered decision making, distrust of the health care system, and poor communication between health care professionals and patients. Collectivist groups, such as Hispanics, may be reluctant to formally appoint a specific family member to be in charge because of concerns about isolating this person or offending other relatives. Instead, a consensual decision-making approach seems to be more acceptable in this population. Among Asian Americans, aggressive treatment for elderly family members is likely to be frowned upon because family members should have love and respect for their parents and ancestors and because of their high respect for the elderly.

Did You Know?

The ability to take medical histories and diagnose current symptoms may be adversely affected by the patient's comfort with modesty. Cultural values surrounding modesty are more than one's comfort level with covering the intimate body parts. By definition, modesty is about respect. A provider who takes cultural modesty into consideration shows respect and caring in the highest degree. Modesty in many cultures often means showing good manners via verbal communication, dress, or behavior.

"In societies that place a high value on modesty, it is important for both sexes, but particularly emphasized for women. A woman's sexual purity and chastity honors her entire family. American women may view this as more discriminatory than protective. It is important not to assume that women in high-modesty cultures are forced to accept the restrictions placed on them by men. In fact, for many women in these cultures modesty is an attribute to be admired and attained. Women often impose modesty on themselves and other women as a way of keeping boundaries of privacy and respect" (Carteret, 2011b).

Worldview and Response to Illness

Worldview has an impact on how people perceive and respond to illness. The dominant values and standards regarding pain and illness affect the behaviors of the individual. When people with a **biomedical worldview** of the mind and body being separate was shared by providers and most patients, this shared belief often contributed to substantial patient stress and alienation. In contrast, in a study conducted in Puerto Rico, providers and patients often shared a view of **mind–body integration** in illness and valued treatments that addressed chronic pain as a biopsychosocial experience. In this setting, shared views and values contributed to more supportive patient–provider relationships, and patients thus experienced less treatment-related stress (Bates, Rankin-Hill, & Sanchez-Ayendez, 1997).

The level of stigma plays a role in how people respond to illness as well. Mental health issues, tuberculosis, HIV, and other illnesses create a sense of embarrassment and shame in some cultures. As a result, people may not seek care or delay seeking care. If the person is diagnosed with a stigmatized illness, it can affect how the family responds. For example, the person may be "hidden" from the public, the family may be embarrassed by the ill family member and distance themselves from the patient, or the patient may be shunned. In some cultures chronic illness and disability are viewed as forms of punishment, and the patient is viewed as being evil.

How people express and communicate about the illness has cultural roots. Most people experience pain sensations similarly, yet studies show there are important differences in the way people express their pain and expect others to respond to their discomfort. Stoic and emotive are two categories in which patients' culturally based responses to pain are often divided. Stoic patients are less expressive of their pain, tend to "grin and bear it," and socially withdraw. Emotive patients are more likely to verbalize their expressions of pain, prefer to have people around, and expect others to react to their pain to validate their discomfort. A broad generalization is that expressive patients often come from Hispanic, Middle Eastern, and Mediterranean backgrounds, and stoic patients often come from Northern European and Asian backgrounds. There are also culturally based attitudes about using pain medication. For example, a Filipino or an East Indian patient might not take pain medications due to being fearful of harmful effects, including addiction (Carteret, 2011a).

The family structure and child-rearing practices also influence the expression and communication of illness and pain. Stoicism in European American culture has a long history. For many generations, children, especially boys, would be reprimanded for crying like babies but applauded for keeping a stiff upper lip. In general, people made as little fuss as possible over injuries and illness. Children socialized in this manner will grow up to be "easy patients" who behave in ways consistent with the values of the Western medical system. In other cultures a child's crying immediately elicits the greatest sympathy, concern, and aid. In such cultures, children's health is fretted over constantly—even a sneeze can be seen as illness. This predisposes children to become more anxious about their health in general, and as adults, they may need greater reassurance from caregivers even when their symptoms are minor. In general, when people are ill, they revert to childhood behavior. If complaining brought them attention as children, they will likely complain out of habit as adults—even if the desired results are not provided by their caregivers (Carteret, 2011a).

Patients from Asian cultures are often stoic in the face of pain because self-restraint is a strong cultural value. Complaining is viewed as having poor social skills. In traditional Asian cultures, preserving harmony in interactions with others is very important, so an individual should never draw personal attention, especially in negative ways. Though an individual may feel sadness or pain, it is not customary to make this obvious. This translates to communications with doctors and nurses, who have high status in Asian cultures. People of high status should not be bothered with complaints and should not be questioned (Carteret, 2011a).

Summary

Worldview is our perception of how the world works. It includes issues such as moral and ethical reasoning, social relationships, and communication. Health care professionals need to take a person's worldview into consideration because it affects behaviors, perceptions, communication, and decisions. Some decisions are made daily, such as whether to take a medication or not, but major health decisions, such as beginning- and end-of-life decisions, are also subject to patients' worldview.

Review

1. What does worldview mean? Provide examples of why it is important to consider worldview in health care.

2. Provide examples of differences in verbal and nonverbal communication methods among different cultures.

3. Explain some beginning- and end-of-life decisions related to worldview and culture.

Activity

Select a culture of your choice. Write a paper explaining some key components of their worldview and explain how these views relate to health.

Case Study

A physician receives the pathology report from a recent endoscopy of her patient, a 78-year-old Japanese man. The report reveals adenocarcinoma of the stomach. The physician intends to disclose the diagnosis to the patient. However, as the provider approaches the patient's room, the patient's daughter stops her. The daughter demands to know the diagnosis and states that, if indeed it is cancer, her father should not be told. The daughter insists that she and her mother will decide what is best for her father. She argues that in her father's culture, family members make the decisions for the patient.

Consider these related questions:

- Is it the physician's duty to disclose the truth to her patient?

- How can the physician–patient relationship be preserved while taking into consideration the wishes of family members?

- What role should culture play in how a case is handled?

Source: Rosen, et al. (2004).

References

Bates, M. S., Rankin-Hill, L., & Sanchez-Ayendez, M. (1997). The effects of the cultural context of health care on treatment of and response to chronic pain and illness. *Social Science & Medicine, 45*(9), 1433–1447.

Carrese, J. A., & Rhodes, L. A. (1995). Western bioethics on the Navajo reservation. Benefit or harm? *Journal of the American Medical Association, 274*, 826–829.

Carteret, M. (2011a). *Cultural aspects of pain management*. Retrieved from http://www.dimensionsofculture.com/2010/11/cultural-aspects-of-pain-management/

Carteret, M. (2011b). *Modesty in health care: A cross-cultural perspective*. Retrieved from http://www.dimensionsofculture.com/2010/11/modesty-in-health-care-a-cross-cultural-perspective/

LeBaron, M. (2003, August). *Cultural and worldview frames.* Retrieved from http://www.beyondintractability.org/essay/cultural-frames

Morhaim, D. K., & Pollack, K. M. (2013). Rate of Americans who have completed advance directives. *American Journal of Public Health, 103*(6), e8–e10.

Purnell, L. D. (2013). *Transcultural health care.* Philadelphia, PA: F. A. Davis Company.

Rao, J. K., Anderson, L. A., Lin, F-C., & Laux, J. P. (2014). Completion of advanced directives among U.S. consumers. *American Journal of Prevention Medicine, 46*(1), 65–70. Retrieved from http://www.ajpmonline.org/article/S0749-3797(13)00521-7/pdf

Rosen, J., Spatz, E. S., Gaaserud, A. M. J., Abramovitch, H., Weinreb, B., Wenger, N. S., & Margolis, C. Z. (2004). A new approach to developing cross cultural communication skills. Medical Teacher, *26*(2), 126–132.

Searight, H. R., & Gafford, J. (2005). Cultural diversity at the end of life: Issues and guidelines for family physicians. *American Family Physician, 71*(3), 515–622. Retrieved from http://www.aafp.org/afp/20050201/515.html

Tilbert, J. C. (2010). The role of worldviews in health disparities education. *Journal of General Internal Medicine, 25*(Suppl. 2), 178–181. Retrieved from http://www.ncbi.nlm.nih.gov/pmc/articles/PMC2847101/

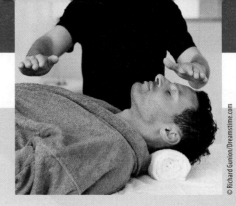

CHAPTER 4

Complementary and Alternative Medicine

Everyone has a doctor in him or her; we just have to help it in its work.
The natural healing force within each one of us is the greatest force in getting well.
Our food should be our medicine.
Our medicine should be our food.
    —Hippocrates

Key Concepts

Complementary medicine	Acupuncture
Alternative medicine	Qigong
Doshas	Tai chi
Prakriti	Naturopathy
Yoga	Hydrotherapy
Qi	Reiki
Five elements	Meditation
Yin and yang	Mindfulness meditation
Meridians	Transcendental meditation

Learning Objectives

After reading this chapter, you should be able to:

1. Identify the difference between complementary and alternative medicine (CAM) practices.
2. Understand the various types of CAM practices.
3. Discuss the potential benefits and risks of CAM practices.
4. Appreciate the cultural influences on CAM practices.

It is not entirely clear when humans began to develop modalities to deal with pain, injury, and disease. However, we know that these practices have been in existence for ages. The various practices to treat disease and injury have been passed down through the centuries from person to person and family member to family member. The practices have been influenced by observation and experimentation, as well as religious, social, and cultural practices. Over time, the various forms of these practices have taken on the unique characteristics of the people and cultures that utilize them.

These practices have been termed "folk medicine" by the mainstream science-based medical professions. With the advent of the scientific approach to medicine, it might be assumed that the various traditional folk medicine practices would die out. However, that has not been the case. As new cultures immigrated to the United States, so did their traditional healing practices. Increased interest in these traditional practices has spurred research into their efficacy and recharacterized them as complementary and alternative medical practices.

Complementary medicine refers to using a non-mainstream approach *together with* conventional medicine. **Alternative medicine** refers to using a non-mainstream approach *in place of* conventional medicine. Complementary and alternative medicine (CAM) is a broad range of modalities outside the traditional Western medicine approach to care (see **Box 4.1**). Folk medicine, or the use of traditional remedies, is considered to be a form of complementary and alternative medicine. Folk remedies include, but are not limited to long-existing practices, such as Chinese medicine, acupuncture, and naturopathy, to name a few. The history and utilization of CAM, along with culturally based CAM modalities and related laws, are the focus of this chapter.

BOX 4.1   CAM Systems of Health Care

I. Alternative health care systems

Ayurvedic medicine

Chiropractic

Homeopathic medicine

American Indian medicine (e.g., sweat lodge, medicine wheel)

Naturopathic medicine

Traditional Chinese medicine (e.g., acupuncture, Chinese herbal medicine)

II. Mind–body interventions

Meditation

Hypnosis

Guided imagery

Dance therapy

Music therapy

Art therapy

Prayer and mental healing

III. Biological-based therapies

Herbal therapies

Special diets (e.g., macrobiotics, extremely low fat or high carbohydrate diets)

Orthomolecular medicine (e.g., megavitamin therapy)

Individual biological therapies (e.g., shark cartilage, bee pollen)

IV. Therapeutic massage, body work, and somatic movement therapies

Massage

Feldenkrais

Alexander method

V. Energy therapies

Qigong

Reiki

Therapeutic touch

VI. Bioelectromagnetics

Magnet therapy

Source: White House Commission on Complementary and Alternative Medicine Policy (2002).

History of Complementary and Alternative Medicine

CAM predates the history of the United States. Prior to the latter part of the 19th century, medical care was provided by lay healers, naturopaths, homeopaths, midwives, and botanical healers as well as formally trained doctors. Nineteenth-century advances in science, such as germ theory, antisepsis, and anesthesia, spurred the trend to scientific medical education. Nonconventional treatments were marginalized in the first half of the 20th century after Abraham Flexner's 1910 report on the need for standardization in medical education. Interest in whole foods and dietary supplements in the 1950s began a resurgence of interest in alternative medical practices. The traditional health practices of immigrant cultures exposed Americans to alternatives, and the counterculture movements of the 1960s renewed the interest in natural healing practices. In the 1970s, the holistic health approach began incorporating Eastern medical traditions with conventional Western medical practices (White House Commission, 2002).

This resurgent public interest in modalities, characterized as folk medicine, has encouraged medical practitioners to investigate their efficacy and impact on conventional medical practices. It has been noted that many folk medicine traditions have common features. Hufford (1988, 1997) noted that folk traditions tend to view the cause of disease as an imbalance or lack of harmony; they are based on personal responsibility and connections between health and the person's environment; they tend to be complex practices that involve a holistic approach to disease; and they often include an energy that provides harmony and balance. Being aware of cultural differences in beliefs regarding disease and treatment is imperative to a modern medical practitioner because patients who engage in CAM practices may also seek help from Western medicine.

Use of Complementary and Alternative Medicine

The 2007 National Health Interview Survey (NHIS) gathered data from 23,393 interviews with U.S. adults and 9,417 interviews for U.S. children aged 0 to 17. The 2007 CAM section included questions on 36 types of CAM therapies commonly used in the United States: 10 types of provider-based therapies, such as acupuncture and chiropractic, and 26 other therapies that do not require a provider, such as herbal supplements and meditation. In 2007, approximately 38% of U.S. adults and approximately 12% of children used some form of CAM (Barnes, Bloom, & Nahin, 2008). In that same year, U.S. adults spent $33.9 billion out-of-pocket on visits to CAM practitioners and purchases of CAM products, classes, and materials (Nahin, Barnes, Stussman, & Bloom, 2009). **Figure 4.1** through **Figure 4.5** provide additional information on CAM usage.

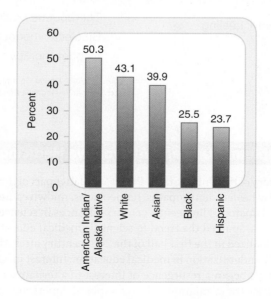

FIGURE 4.1

CAM use by race/ethnicity among adults, 2007.

Source: Barnes, Bloom, & Nahin (2008).

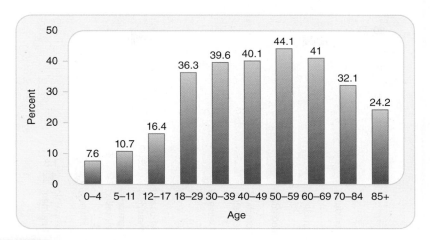

FIGURE 4.2

CAM use by age, 2007.

Source: Barnes, Bloom, & Nahin (2008).

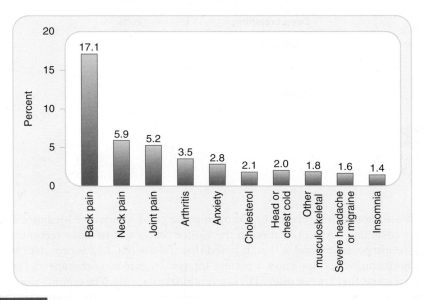

FIGURE 4.3

Diseases/conditions for which CAM is most frequently used among adults, 2007.

Source: Barnes, Bloom, & Nahin (2008).

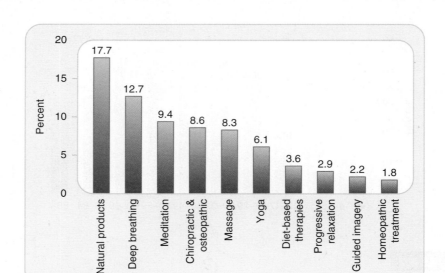

FIGURE 4.4

Ten most common CAM therapies among adults, 2007.

Source: Barnes, Bloom, & Nahin (2008).

The White House Commission on Complementary and Alternative Medicine Policy was convened to evaluate CAM utilization in the United States and to make recommendations regarding future governmental action. It noted that the use of CAM is prevalent in the U.S. patient population, which indicates a patient interest in exploring therapeutic options for chronic conditions that are not offered by conventional medicine. The commission produced 25 recommendations for further action by the government and private enterprises that focus on the coordination of research, education and training of health practitioners, CAM information and development and dissemination, access and delivery, coverage and reimbursement, and coordination of federal efforts.

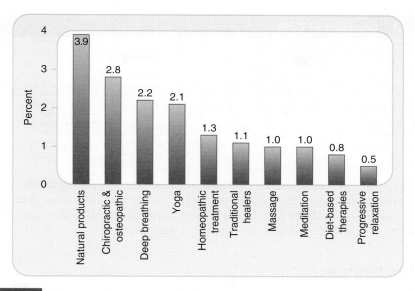

FIGURE 4.5

Ten most common therapies among children, 2007.

Source: Barnes, Bloom, & Nahin (2008).

Reviewing the White House commission's recommendations, the National Center for Complementary and Alternative Medicine ([NCCAM] 2011) released its third strategic plan, which specifically addressed racial and ethnic health disparities in the utilization of CAM practices. The plan presents a series of goals and objectives to guide NCCAM in determining priorities for future research in complementary and alternative medicine. The five strategic objectives are as follows:

Strategic Objective 1. Advance research on mind and body interventions, practices, and disciplines

Strategic Objective 2. Advance research on CAM natural products

Strategic Objective 3. Increase understanding of "real-world" patterns and outcomes of CAM use and its integration into health care and health promotion

Strategic Objective 4. Improve the capacity of the field to carry out rigorous research

Strategic Objective 5. Develop and disseminate objective, evidence-based information on CAM interventions

Complementary and Alternative Health Care Modalities

The White House Commission on Complementary and Alternative Medicine Policy noted that the major CAM systems have common characteristics that include focusing on individual treatment, a holistic approach to care, promotion of self-care and self-healing, and

TABLE 4.1   Domains of CAM

Biologically based practices. Uses substances found in nature, like herbs or vitamins, in doses that are not used in mainstream medicine
Energy medicine. Uses energy fields that are believed to surround and penetrate the body
Manipulative and body-based practices. Uses manipulation and movement of body parts
Mind–body medicine. Uses techniques to enhance the mind's ability to affect the body

Source: White House Commission on Complementary and Alternative Medicine Policy (2002).

addressing spiritual influences on health. The commission then created a classification model for CAM systems that listed the various practices by their major domains (**Table 4.1**) and policy recommendations (**Table 4.2**). The major modalities of complementary and alternative medicine that are culturally related are included in this chapter.

Ayurvedic Medicine

Ayurveda, a Sanskrit word meaning science of life, was originally described in the ancient Hindu texts called Vedas. This ancient practice is based on the theory that the five great elements—ether, air, fire, water, and earth—are the basis for all living systems. The five elements are in constant interaction and are constantly changing. The elements combine in pairs to form **doshas**, the three vital energies that regulate everything in nature (see **Table 4.3**).

At the time of conception, the doshas combine in a unique way for each individual. This combination is known as **prakriti**. A person's physiology, personality, intellect, and weaknesses are governed by two dominant doshas. If the doshas become imbalanced, the flow of *prana* (life energy) and *agni* (digestion) become upset. It is these imbalances that result in illness.

TABLE 4.2   White House Commission on Complementary and Alternative Medicine Policy Recommendations and Actions

Coordination of Research
Recommendation 1: Federal agencies should receive increased funding for clinical, basic, and health services research on CAM.
Recommendation 2: Congress and the Administration should consider enacting legislative and administrative incentives to stimulate private sector investment in CAM research on products that may not be patentable.
Recommendation 3: Federal, private, and nonprofit sectors should support research on CAM modalities and approaches that are designed to improve self-care and behaviors that promote health.
Recommendation 4: Federal, private, and nonprofit sectors should support new and innovative CAM research on core questions posed by frontier areas of scientific study associated with CAM that might expand our understanding of health and disease.

TABLE 4.2   White House Commission on Complementary and Alternative Medicine Policy Recommendations and Actions (*Continued*)

Coordination of Research
Recommendation 5: Investigators engaged in research of CAM should ensure that human subjects participating in clinical studies receive the same protections as are required in conventional medical research and to which they are entitled.
Recommendation 6: The Commission recommends that state professional regulatory bodies include language in their guidelines stating that licensed, certified, or otherwise authorized practitioners who are engaged in research on CAM will not be sanctioned solely because they are engaged in such research if they:
1. Are engaged in well-designed research that is approved by appropriately constituted Institutional Review Boards.
2. Are following the requirements for the protection of human subjects.
3. Are meeting their professional and ethical responsibilities. All CAM and conventional practitioners, whether or not they are engaged in research, must meet whatever State practice requirements or standards govern their authorization to practice.
Recommendation 7: Increased efforts should be made to strengthen the emerging dialogue among CAM and conventional medical practitioners, researchers, and accredited research institutions; federal and state research, health care, and regulatory agencies; the private and nonprofit sectors; and the general public.
Recommendation 8: Public and private resources should be increased to strengthen the infrastructure for CAM research and research training at conventional medical and CAM institutions and to expand the cadre of basic, clinical, and health services researchers who are knowledgeable about CAM and have received rigorous research training.
Recommendation 9: Public and private resources should be used to support, conduct, and update systematic reviews of the peer-reviewed research literature on the safety, efficacy, and cost–benefit of CAM practices and products.
Education and Training of Health Care Practitioners
Recommendation 10: The education and training of CAM and conventional practitioners should be designed to ensure public safety, improve health, and increase availability of qualified and knowledgeable CAM and conventional practitioners and enhance the collaboration among them.
Recommendation 11: The federal government should make available accurate, useful, and easily accessible information on CAM practices and products, including information on safety and effectiveness.
Recommendation 12: The quality and accuracy of CAM information on the Internet should be improved by establishing a voluntary standards board, a public education campaign, and actions to protect consumers' privacy.
Recommendation 13: Information on the training and education of providers of CAM services should be made easily available to the public.

(*Continues*)

TABLE 4.2   White House Commission on Complementary and Alternative Medicine Policy Recommendations and Actions (*Continued*)

Education and Training of Health Care Practitioners
Recommendation 14: CAM products that are available to U.S. consumers should be safe and meet appropriate standards of quality and consistency.
Recommendation 15: Provision of the Federal Food, Drug and Cosmetic Act, as modified by the Dietary Supplement Health and Education Act of 1994, should be fully implemented, funded, enforced, and evaluated.
Recommendation 16: Activities to ensure that advertising of dietary supplements and other CAM practices and products is truthful and not misleading should be increased.
Recommendation 17: The collection and dissemination of information about adverse events stemming from the use of dietary supplements should be improved.
Access and Delivery
Recommendation 18: The Department of Health and Human Services should evaluate current barriers to consumer access to safe and effective CAM practices and to qualified practitioners and should develop strategies for removing those barriers to increase access and to ensure accountability.
Recommendation 19: The federal government should offer assistance to states and professional organizations in (1) developing and evaluating guidelines for practitioner accountability and competence in CAM delivery, including regulation of practice, and (2) periodically reviewing and assessing the effects of regulations on consumer protection.
Recommendation 20: States should evaluate and review their regulation of CAM practitioners and ensure their accountability to the public. States should, as appropriate, implement provisions for licensure, registration, and exemption that are consistent with the practitioners' education, training, and scope of practice.
Recommendation 21: Nationally recognized accrediting bodies should evaluate how health care organizations under their oversight are using CAM practices and should develop strategies for the safe and appropriate use of qualified CAM practitioners and safe and effective products in these organizations.
Recommendation 22: The federal government should facilitate and support the evaluation and implementation of safe and effective CAM practices to help meet the health care needs of special and vulnerable populations.
Recommendation 23: Evidence should be developed and disseminated regarding safety, benefits, and cost-effectiveness of CAM interventions, as well as the optimum models for complementary and integrated care.
Recommendation 24: Insurers and managed care organizations should offer purchasers the option of health benefit plans that incorporate coverage of safe and effective CAM interventions provided by qualified practitioners.
Recommendation 25: Purchasers, including federal agencies and employers, should evaluate the possibility of covering benefits or adding health benefit plans that incorporate sage and effective CAM interventions.

Source: White House Commission on Complementary and Alternative Medicine Policy (2002).

TABLE 4.3   The Doshas
Vata. Composed of air and ether
Pita. Composed of fire and water
Kapha. Composed of water and earth

Ayurvedic practitioners seek to balance the doshas through methods such as herbal remedies, yoga, meditation, and massage. For example, *Panchakarma* is a purification process used to remove impurities and restore balance to the doshas. Panchakarma is a set of therapeutic procedures that is intended to improve health and expand the life span. The specific treatments vary and may include using a special diet, emetics, herbal enemas, massage, herbs, and nose cleaning.

Yoga

Yoga is an ancient system of exercises and breathing techniques designed to encourage physical and spiritual well-being. It incorporates a number of guidelines for well-being, including good nutrition and hygiene. The physical practice of yoga consists of going through *asanas* (physical postures) to improve the physical body and calm the nerves. *Pranayamas* are breathing techniques and meditations designed to improve spiritual well-being.

Some yoga practitioners teach that centers of energy, known as *chakras*, are connected to the nerves and spinal cord. It is believed that certain asanas and meditations can positively influence the chakras, improving physical and mental health. The exercise and relaxation techniques utilized in yoga are practiced by many people every day.

Traditional Chinese Medicine

Traditional Chinese medicine (TCM) is the term used for a group of ancient healing practices that date back some 2,000 years to 200 BCE. The concepts utilized have been adapted by the Koreans, Japanese, and Vietnamese into their own versions of treatment. The system includes, among other treatments, herbalism, acupuncture, *qigong*, and *tai chi*.

TCM is based on diagnosis from the pattern of symptoms rather than on endeavoring to identify a specific illness. It is believed that the cause of disease must be cured, not just its symptoms. TCM considers a person's body, mind, spirit, and emotions as part of one complete whole rather than individual parts that are to be treated separately. TCM is based on a number of interrelated theories: the theory of Qi, the theory of the five elements, the theory of yin and yang, and the meridian theory.

The Theory of Qi

Qi, pronounced "chee," is the vital life force that animates all things. Qi flows through the 12 meridians that run through the body. Physical, emotional, and mental harmony rely on the flow of qi. Qi has two parts, energy or power, and conscious intelligence. These parts are found in organ systems and allow them to perform their physical and energetic functions. Qi also can be described by how it functions. Qi creates all movement, protects the body, provides for harmonious transformation, such as water being turned into urine, keeps the organs and body parts in proper position, and warms the body. This theory holds that qi:

- Is spiritual in origin
- Makes up and moves through all living things
- Is available in infinite quantities, is positive in nature, and is important to all aspects of health
- Is present both inside the body and on its surface
- Flows throughout the body in specific channels
- Has its flow disturbed by negative thoughts or feelings

Qi deficiency can result in problems, such as what Western medicine calls chronic fatigue syndrome or a fever. Qi stagnation, where the energy cannot flow correctly, can result in what Western medicine calls pain.

The Five Elements Theory

The **five elements** are based on the perception of the relationships between all things. These patterns are grouped and named for the five elements: (1) wood, (2) fire, (3) earth, (4) metal, and (5) water. This theory states that the five organ systems are each tied to a particular element and to a broader group of phenomena that are associated with their elements, including the seasons, colors, emotions, and foods (see **Table 4.4**). This theory illustrates the interrelatedness of all things.

The Yin and Yang Theory

The **yin and yang** theory holds that everything is made up of two polar energies. Neither can exist without the other, and they never separate. It is the principle of interconnectedness and

TABLE 4.4 The Characteristics of the Five Elements

	Fire	Earth	Metal	Water	Wood
Season	Summer	Indian summer	Autumn	Winter	Spring
Taste	Bitter	Sweet	Pungent	Salty	Sour
Emotion	Joy	Worry	Grief	Fear	Anger
Body	Heart	Spleen	Lungs	Kidneys	Liver
	Small intestine	Stomach	Large intestine	Bladder	Gallbladder
	Tongue	Mouth	Nose	Hair	Tendons
	Blood vessels	Muscles	Skin	Bones	Eye
Energy/control	Melts metal	Dries water	Cuts wood	Douses fire	Breaks earth
	Water douses it	Wood breaks it	Fire melts it	Earth dries it	Metal cuts it

interdependence. Yin and yang describe how things function in relation to one another and the important principle of harmony where things blend together into a whole.

Yin is female and is associated with the moon and night, late afternoon, cold, rest, responsiveness, passivity, darkness, interiority, downwardness, inwardness, and decrease. Yang is male and is associated with the sun and daytime, early morning, heat, stimulation, movement, activity, excitement, vigor, light, exteriority, upwardness, outwardness, and increase (see **Figure 4.6**).

The Meridian Theory

Meridians are channels through which qi, blood, and information flow to all parts of the body (**Figure 4.7**). There are 12 meridians in the body; 6 are yin and 6 are yang. Although each meridian is attributed to, and named for, an organ or body function, the network of meridians connects the meridians to one another and all parts of the body, and they connect the body to the universe. When qi flows easily, the body is balanced and healthy. The meridians work to regulate the energy functions of the body and keep it balanced and in harmony.

TCM encompasses many different treatment modalities. Some of the treatment options utilized include acupuncture, herbal therapies, and qigong.

Acupuncture

Acupuncture is one of the most researched and accepted complementary practices in the United States today. It is experiencing greater acceptance by traditional medical practitioners, and research of its efficacy in treating various conditions has been undertaken, although it has proven to be a difficult subject to study.

Acupuncture involves stimulating specific points along the meridians to achieve a therapeutic purpose. The usual practice involves inserting a needle into one of the acupoints along a meridian associated with that organ or function. Besides puncturing the skin, practitioners also use other methods, including pressure, heat, friction, or electrical stimulation of the needle.

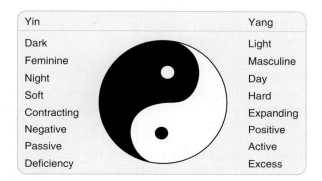

Yin	Yang
Dark	Light
Feminine	Masculine
Night	Day
Soft	Hard
Contracting	Expanding
Negative	Positive
Passive	Active
Deficiency	Excess

FIGURE 4.6

The symbol of yin and yang is a circle with two equal and opposite halves.

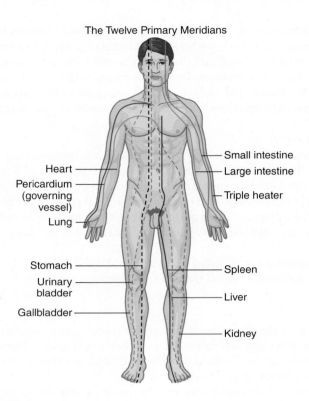

The Twelve Primary Meridians

Small intestine
Large intestine
Heart
Triple heater
Pericardium (governing vessel)
Lung
Stomach
Spleen
Urinary bladder
Liver
Gallbladder
Kidney

FIGURE 4.7

Meridians.

The TCM theory is that acupuncture works by bringing healing energy, qi, to the affected part of the body through the meridians. The stimulation of the appropriate meridian can assist in bringing the affected organ into balance.

Chinese Herbal Therapies

Another significant aspect of traditional Chinese medicine is the use of herbal remedies. Although it is not as prevalent in the United States as acupuncture, the use of herbal remedies is widespread in China and other Asian countries as well as among immigrants from Asian countries. Like acupuncture, herbal remedies are used to bring balance back to the body. Herbs are classified according to the five elements and their yin and yang properties to determine how they will be used. Herbs are combined according to their properties to treat a particular disharmony. They are usually administered as teas, pills, powders, or creams. Safety and efficacy issues related to herbal remedies are discussed in the "Herbal Remedies" section of this chapter.

Qigong

The term **qigong** translates to "energy work." It is a part of TCM that involves movement, breathing, and meditation, and it is intended to improve the flow of qi throughout the body. Qigong is an ancient technique that is practiced by millions of people every day. It involves a number of basic postures that are involved in daily practice, and a master can tailor the techniques to address specific problems.

The ancient noncombative martial art, **tai chi**, is a form of qigong. The purpose of tai chi is to improve the flow of qi through the body to encourage balance and harmony.

© Tyler Olson/Dreamstime

Naturopathy

Naturopathy, also known as naturopathic medicine, is a holistic system of medicine based on the healing power of nature. Naturopathy originated in Germany during the late 19th century. The system is built on the ancient belief in the healing power of nature and that natural organisms have the ability to heal themselves and maintain health. Such systems include **hydrotherapy** (water therapy), which was popular in Germany, and nature cure, developed in Austria, based on the use of food, air, light, water, and herbs to treat illness (University of Maryland, 2011). In 1902 naturopathy was introduced to the United States by Benjamin Lust, a German immigrant. Mr. Lust founded the American School of Naturopathy. The school emphasized the use of natural cures, proper bowel habits, and good hygiene as the tools for health. This was the first time that principles of a healthy diet, such as increasing fiber intake and reducing saturated fats, became popular (University of Maryland, 2011).

Naturopathic doctors (NDs) or naturopathic medical doctors (NMDs) work to identify the cause of disease through an understanding of the body, mind, and spirit of the person. Naturopathic doctors use a variety of therapies and techniques including nutrition, behavior change, herbal medicine, homeopathy, and acupuncture. Naturopathy has two major focus areas: (1) supporting the body's own healing abilities, and (2) empowering people to make lifestyle changes necessary to achieve the best possible health. Naturopathic doctors emphasize prevention and patient education; they treat both acute and chronic conditions (University of Maryland, 2011).

Naturopaths believe that the body strives to maintain a state of equilibrium, known as homeostasis, and unhealthy environments, diets, physical or emotional stress, and lack of sleep or fresh air can disrupt that balance (see **Table 4.5**). When homeostasis is upset, naturopaths utilize any number of treatments to return the body to balance. All treatments are designed to enhance the body's ability to heal itself. Modalities include diet, yoga, manipulation, massage, hydrotherapy, and natural herbs. Naturopathic practitioners take a holistic approach to treatment and focus on the cause of a disruption of homeostasis rather than treating only symptoms.

Herbal Remedies

Plants used for medicinal purposes are classified as medicinal herbs. Herbs have been used to treat diseases for centuries. Many conventional medications were originally developed from herbs. Naturopaths as well as other types of practitioners use herbs to restore homeostasis through treating the cause of diseases.

Herbal preparations use either whole plants or parts of plants. Many herbalists believe in synergy, the idea that whole plants are more effective than their individual parts. Herbal remedies are prepared in pill or liquid form for ingestion or as tinctures, creams, or ointments for external use.

In the United States, herbal products are sold as dietary supplements. They are not regulated by the U.S. Food and Drug Administration (FDA) as foods. This means that they do not have to meet the same standards as drugs and over-the-counter medications for proof of safety, effectiveness, and what the FDA calls Good Manufacturing Practices (see **Table 4.6**).

When considering using herbal remedies, it is important to consult a professional who is informed about the use of these remedies. Because a product is labeled "natural" does not mean it is safe or does not have harmful effects. Further, the product may not be recommended for

TABLE 4.5   The Six Key Principles of Naturopathy
1. Promote the healing power of nature.
2. Do no harm.
3. Treat the whole person.
4. Treat the cause.
5. Prevention is the best cure.
6. The physician is a teacher.

Source: National Center for Complementary and Alternative Medicine (2007).

TABLE 4.6   About Dietary Supplements

Dietary supplements were defined in a law passed by Congress in 1994. A dietary supplement is a product that contains vitamins, minerals, herbs or other botanicals, amino acids, enzymes, and/or other ingredients intended to supplement the diet. The U.S. Food and Drug Administration has special labeling requirements for dietary supplements and treats them as foods, not drugs. Dietary supplements must meet all of the following conditions:

- It is a product (other than tobacco) intended to supplement the diet, which contains one or more of the following: vitamins, minerals, herbs or other botanicals, amino acids, or any combination of these ingredients.
- It is intended to be taken in tablet, capsule, powder, softgel, gelcap, or liquid form.
- It is not represented for use as a conventional food or as a sole item of a meal or diet.
- It is labeled as being a dietary supplement.

Source: National Center for Complementary and Alternative Medicine (2009).

a person's specific situation, such as pregnancy. It should be remembered that these remedies can act in the same way as many prescription or over-the-counter drugs and can cause side effects or interfere with the actions of other medications. As with any medication, herbal remedies are not without hazards, and their use must be properly monitored.

Did You Know?

Ephedra is a plant native to Central Asia and Mongolia. Ephedrine, the main ingredient in ephedra, is a compound that can powerfully stimulate the nervous system and heart. Ephedra has been used for more than 5,000 years in China and India to treat conditions such as colds, fever, flu, headaches, asthma, wheezing, and nasal congestion. More recently, ephedra was used as an ingredient in dietary supplements for weight loss, increased energy, and enhanced athletic performance.

In 2004, the FDA banned the U.S. sale of dietary supplements containing ephedra. The FDA found that these supplements had an unreasonable risk of injury or illness. This includes the risk of anxiety, cardiovascular complications, headache, seizures, and death (National Center for Complementary and Alternative Medicine, 2013a).

Reiki

Reiki, pronounced "ray-kee," is a complementary health approach in which practitioners place their hands lightly on or just above a person, with the goal of facilitating the person's own healing response (see **Figure 4.8**). More high-quality research in this field is needed to determine its effectiveness. Despite the lack of evidence, more than 1.2 million adults—0.5% of the U.S. general adult population—used an energy healing therapy, such as Reiki, in 2006, according to the 2007 National Health Interview Survey. Reiki appears to be generally safe, and no serious

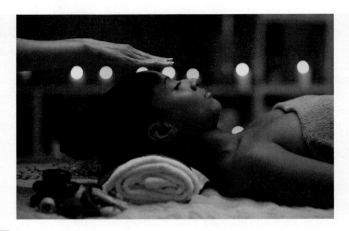

FIGURE 4.8

Reiki being performed by a practitioner.

© Dragon Images/Shutterstock

side effects have been reported. There are many different forms of Reiki, and no special background is needed to receive training (National Center for Complementary and Alternative Medicine, 2013b). Training programs and certification are available from Reiki organizations; however, these organizations are not regulated by any government agency.

The basis for modern-day Reiki practice may have started in Tibet more than 2,500 years ago. Reiki was rediscovered in the early 1900s by a Japanese man named Mikao Usui. During a lengthy period of travel and research, Usui found ancient texts that described Reiki and its power to heal by using the energy that flows through all living things. From his studies and meditations, he developed what came to be known as the Usui system of Reiki. Other systems of Reiki have been developed as well. The word *Reiki* comes from Japanese terms that translate as "universal life energy" (American Cancer Society, 2012).

Reiki is not used to diagnose or treat specific illnesses. Reiki is used to promote relaxation, decrease stress and anxiety, and increase a person's general sense of well-being. Therapy is delivered through the Reiki practitioner's hands, with the goal of raising the amount of universal life energy in and around the client. "Reiki practitioners intend to strengthen the flow of energy, which they say will decrease pain, ease muscle tension, speed healing, improve sleep, and generally enhance the body's ability to heal itself" (American Cancer Society, 2012).

A Reiki session is usually about an hour. The practitioner places his or her hands in 12 to 15 positions on or above parts of the patient's clothed body. Each hand position is sustained for 2 to 5 minutes. The hands are intended to be a conduit for universal life energy, balancing energy within and around the body. Some practitioners believe that the best results occur when patients have three Reiki sessions within a relatively short time, take a break, and then repeat the process. There are three levels of Reiki practice. A Reiki I practitioner can offer hands-on sessions; a Reiki II practitioner can offer hands-on or distant Reiki; and a Reiki master can offer hands-on Reiki, distant Reiki, and Reiki instruction (American Cancer Society, 2012).

What Do You Think?

Many of the CAM modalities do not have scientific evidence that they work yet they are frequently used. Should a hospital offer these services if there is no scientific merit for their use? Is a hospital that does not offer CAM culturally insensitive? Does a hospital that does offer CAM give users the impression that the hospital believes in these practices and encourages their use?

Meditation

Meditation refers to a group of mental techniques intended to provide relaxation and mental harmony, quiet one's mind, and increase awareness. It has been a practice in many cultures for thousands of years. Meditative practices are found in Christian, Jewish, Buddhist, Hindu, and Islamic religious traditions. Although meditation found its origins in religious practices, it is currently utilized for nonreligious purposes, such as improved emotional and physical health. Meditation is utilized to decrease stress and anxiety, decrease pain, improve mood, and positively affect heart disease and the symptoms of physical illness. Scientific research indicates that meditation decreases oxygen consumption, decreases heart and respiratory rates, and influences brain wave and hormone activity (Freeman, 2004).

Various techniques are used by different groups and religions. All techniques have some common factors, namely, use of a quiet location, assuming a comfortable position, focusing one's attention by concentrating on one's breath or a mantra (word or sound), and having an open attitude by not allowing distractions to disrupt focus. There are two common types of meditation practices: mindfulness meditation and transcendental meditation.

Mindfulness meditation originated in the Buddhist traditions. It is the concept of increasing awareness and acceptance of the present. During meditation one observes thoughts and images in a nonjudgmental manner with the goal of learning to experience thoughts and feelings with greater balance and acceptance. This technique has been used to treat posttraumatic stress disorder, drug abuse, chronic pain, and to increase cognitive function in the elderly.

Transcendental meditation found its origins in the Indian Vedic tradition. This practice is designed to allow the practitioner to experience ever-finer levels of thought until the source of thought is experienced. A mantra (a sound uttered repeatedly) is used to focus the mind, and the choice of mantra is vital to success. Transcendental meditation enables the mind to reach a quiet state and strives to create a state of relaxed alertness. Transcendental meditation has been found to stimulate what is termed the "relaxation response," which is responsible for decreased blood pressure, muscular relaxation, decreased heart and respiratory rate, and a decrease in lactate levels, which are associated with anxiety. Research shows that a number of relaxation meditation techniques include four parts: a mental focus, passive attitude, decreased muscle tone, and a quiet environment (Freeman, 2004). One relaxation technique is described in **Table 4.7**.

Studies have shown that transcendental meditation has a positive effect on blood pressure, cardiovascular disease, and overall health. Mindfulness meditation is useful in the treatment of chronic pain and certain psychological disorders. The only situation in which meditation is

TABLE 4.7   Relaxation Technique

1. Find a quiet place to sit.
2. Sit in a comfortable position with your feet on the floor, hands relaxed, and eyes closed.
3. Take three slow, deep breaths.
4. Begin to relax your muscles starting with your toes and progressing upward to your feet and ankles, then lower legs, then upper legs, and so on, until you reach your face and head. Sometimes it is helpful to contract the muscles and then allow them to relax.
5. Breathe through your nose, concentrating on the breath going in and out. As you exhale, say a word in your mind like "calm" or "relax."
6. Continue to concentrate on your breathing for 10 to 20 minutes. At the end of the time, sit quietly for a few minutes and gradually begin to arouse.

There is no failure in meditation. The benefit comes from maintaining a positive attitude and allowing relaxation to happen and ignoring distracting thoughts by gently pushing them from your mind when they appear.

considered to be unsafe is for people with serious mental disorders such as psychosis and schizophrenia. Otherwise, meditation has been determined to be a safe practice for almost everyone.

Laws Affecting Cultural Practices and Health

Many cultures have traditions and practices that involve health and healing. The members of the cultural group are familiar with the healing practices and find them normative. However, those practices often conflict with state and federal laws intended to protect the welfare of the community.

Unlicensed Practices

Every state licenses those who engage in the provision of health care services. Physicians, nurses, pharmacists, dentists, and so on must meet certain state-mandated requirements for education and testing before receiving a license to practice their profession. Again, the state's concern is protecting its citizens from unsafe practitioners. Those who attempt to practice the healing arts without obtaining the requisite license and complying with the licensing laws are prosecuted for the unlicensed practice of the particular profession. Penalties for unlawful practice can be stiff and include both prison time and monetary penalties.

Practitioners of various cultural healing traditions must be aware of and cautious regarding these types of laws. An example of a common area where these laws come in conflict with cultural practices is midwifery. Many cultures have customs regarding childbirth. Those who assist the mother in the delivery must be aware of the state's laws regarding that practice. For many years the practice of midwifery was banned by the great majority of states on the premise propounded by the medical associations that modern medical care during childbirth was safer for the mother and infant. Although those ideas have changed, and many states now sanction the practice of midwifery, the midwife must comply with licensing laws or risk sanctions for the unlawful practice of medicine or nursing. Therefore, traditional practitioners must be informed about both the legal requirements and the liabilities that exist in their practice.

Another area of cultural practice that attracts scrutiny is the use of herbs and other natural products in the treatment of illness or disease. We are all familiar with herbal dietary supplements that are available in practically every store in the country. In ethnic areas of many cities in the United States, shops offer various products common to ethnic or cultural tradition. On the surface it appears that no difference exists between those herb shops and the over-the-counter dietary supplements at the local drug store. However, herbal treatments are often treated differently from dietary supplements.

Ethnic healers and herbalists risk running afoul of licensing laws in the manner in which they apply their healing practices. If the healer is merely making available various herbs or natural products to the public, then they are no different from over-the-counter preparations at the local drug store. However, when the healer begins to evaluate and diagnose symptoms and prescribe treatment, healers are considered to be invading the domain of medical practitioners and become subject to sanctions for unlicensed practice.

For example, Lee Wah was a healer in the ancient Chinese traditions. A patient came to Lee's herb shop, described her ailment to him, and he prescribed certain herbs for the problem. He then chose the herbs and prepared them for her use. Lee was convicted of the unlicensed practice of medicine and was imprisoned (*People v. Lee Wah*, 1886).

Mexican Americans are very familiar with *curanderas*, traditional Mexican healers. Curanderas have treated illness in rural areas of Mexico for hundreds of years. It is not unexpected, then, that they should continue those practices in Mexican communities in the United States. However, the licensing laws apply to their practices as well. When a curandera visited an ill person in his home and prescribed a mixture of rhubarb, soda, glycerin, and spirits of peppermint for the patient's ailment, he was found to be in violation of the licensing laws (*People v. Machado*, 1929).

Many states now have licensing or registration requirements for herbal practitioners, and anyone engaging in those activities should consult local and state regulations to determine the rules with which they must comply.

Ethnic Remedies

The remedies utilized by traditional healers are often prepared by the healer or herbalist or are brought to the United States from the native country. These remedies are subject to government oversight and regulation to ensure safety. The FDA is responsible for ensuring the safety of all foods, drugs, and medical devices marketed and distributed in the United States. How the FDA views a particular remedy, and therefore the amount of regulation applicable to it, depends on how that remedy is classified.

Pharmaceutical products are subject to stringent regulation and testing both before and after approval by the FDA for placement on the market. These drugs are researched for mass production and distribution. No traditional ethnic remedy has ever been taken through the rigorous process for FDA approval.

Because traditional folk remedies contain ingredients such as vitamins, minerals, herbs, or other botanicals and substances such as enzymes and glandular and organ tissues, they are more likely to be viewed as dietary supplements and subject to less stringent regulation. The Dietary Supplement Health and Education Act of 1994 (DSHEA) established the FDA's current authority to regulate dietary supplements. A dietary supplement is a product taken by mouth that contains a "dietary ingredient" intended to supplement the diet. Those ingredients often are the very things that were previously noted as the components of ethnic remedies.

According to the DSHEA, a producer is responsible for determining that the dietary supplements it manufactures or distributes are safe and that any representations or claims made about them are substantiated by adequate evidence to show that they are not false or misleading. Dietary supplements do not need approval from the FDA before they are marketed (Center for Food Safety and Applied Nutrition, 2001). After a dietary supplement is on the market, the FDA has the responsibility of monitoring its safety and, if found to be unsafe, to take action to remove it from the market. Further, a product may not be sold as a dietary supplement and promoted as a treatment, prevention, or cure for a specific disease or condition. Such an action would be considered the distribution of an illegal drug (Center for Food Safety and Applied Nutrition, 2001). Although most ethnic healers would not consider their practices to include marketing a dietary supplement, nonetheless a traditional healer who provides any type of remedy is technically subject to these regulations and could be held responsible for their violation.

On a more local level, the state and county health departments are responsible for ensuring the health of the local community. It is not unusual for local health departments to investigate traditional healing practitioners for the unauthorized practice of medicine or the provision of remedies as treatments rather than as dietary supplements. For example, health investigators in Houston, Texas, investigated the lead poisoning of siblings where the children had been given a traditional Mexican remedy for stomach ailments that was found to be 90% lead (Rhor, 2008). Serious consequences for the health and welfare of an unwary population such as this demand government involvement to protect the general welfare.

Summary

This chapter includes descriptions of complementary and alternative health care modalities that are associated with a number of cultures. Many are ancient practices that continue to exist despite the emergence of modern Western medicine. Although research on the efficacy of many of these practices is scarce, the prevalence of use indicates a need for further investigation of the risks and benefits of these practices. People using this modalities and preparing ethnic remedies need to be aware of the laws in the United States to avoid violating them.

Review

1. Describe the advantages and disadvantages of three of the CAM modalities discussed in this chapter.

2. Discuss how meditation could be used in Western health care practice.

3. Describe the relationship between ethnic cultures and CAM in the United States.

4. Describe how the laws in the United States affect CAM practitioners.

Activity

Select a CAM method that interests you. Conduct research on the topic and interview a practitioner in the field. Write a paper explaining what you learned from the research and the interview. Include a list of the questions that you asked the practitioner and his or her responses in the appendix of the paper.

Case Study

Some cultural practices used to treat illness produce marks on the body that can mimic abuse. Coining and cupping are two such examples. Coining is a form of dermabrasion commonly used in Southeast Asian cultures to rid the body of "bad winds" by bringing bad blood to the surface (Harris, 2010). The process of coining involves applying ointment to the skin and using a coin or spoon to firmly rub the skin until purple-colored spots and patches appear on the skin. The result is a distinct, symmetrical pattern of bruises typically on the back, shoulders, chest, temples, and forehead that resolve without residual effects (see **Figure 4.9**). Cupping is another cultural practice used to treat illness. Cupping has been practiced by Russian, Asian, and Mexican cultures (Harris, 2010). A heated cup is applied to the skin, which creates suction on the skin, causing bruises that have been mistaken for abuse (see **Figure 4.10**). Both of these practices leaves burns or bruises on the child's skin, but they are cultural norms.

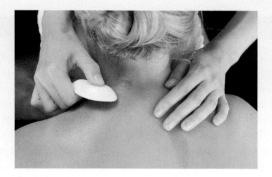

FIGURE 4.9

Coining.

© Tyler Olson/Shutterstock

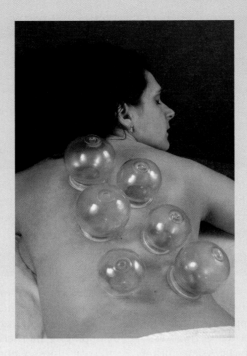

FIGURE 4.10

Cupping.

© Alfred Wekelo/Shutterstock

Consider these related questions:

- Are coining and cupping child abuse? Why or why not?

- When do cultural practices cross over to being abuse?

References

American Cancer Society. (2012, March 8). *Reiki*. Retrieved from http://www.cancer.org/treatment/treatmentsandsideeffects/complementaryandalternativemedicine/manualhealingandphysicaltouch/reiki

Barnes, P. M., Bloom, B., & Nahin, R. (2008, December 10). *Complementary and alternative medicine use among adults and children: United States, 2007.* (CDC National Health Statistics Report #12.) Washington, DC: U.S. Department of Health and Human Services.

Center for Food Safety and Applied Nutrition. (2001, January 3). *About the Center for Food Safety and Applied Nutrition*. Retrieved from http://www.fda.gov/AboutFDA/CentersOffices/OfficeofFoods/CFSAN/default.htm

Freeman, L. (2004). *Complementary and alternative medicine: A research-based approach* (2nd ed.). St. Louis, MO: Mosby.

Harris, T. S. (2010). Bruises in children: Normal or child abuse? *Journal of Pediatric Health Care, 24*(4), 216–221.

Hufford, D. J. (1988). Contemporary folk medicine. In N. Gevitz (Ed.), *Other healers: Unorthodox medicine in the United States*. Baltimore, MD: Johns Hopkins University Press.

Hufford, D. J. (1997). Folk medicine and health culture in contemporary society. *Primary Care, 24*, 723–741.

Nahin, R. L., Barnes, P. M., Stussman, B. J., & Bloom, B. (2009). *Costs of complementary and alternative medicine (CAM) and frequency of visits to CAM practitioners: United States, 2007*. (National Health Statistics Reports, No. 18.) Hyattsville, MD: National Center for Health Statistics.

National Center for Complementary and Alternative Medicine. (2007). *Backgrounder: An introduction to naturopathy*. Retrieved from http://www.nccam.nih.gov/health/naturopathy

National Center for Complementary and Alternative Medicine. (2009). *Using dietary supplements wisely*. Retrieved from http://nccam.nih.gov/health/supplements/wiseuse.htm

National Center for Complementary and Alternative Medicine. (2011). *Exploring the science of complementary and alternative medicine: NCCAM third strategic plan: 2011–2015*. Retrieved from http://nccam.nih.gov/about/plans/2011

National Center for Complementary and Alternative Medicine. (2013a, June), *Ephedra*. Retrieved from http://nccam.nih.gov/health/ephedra

National Center for Complementary and Alternative Medicine. (2013b, April). *Reiki: An introduction*. Retrieved from http://nccam.nih.gov/health/reiki/introduction.htm

People v. Lee Wah, 71 C. 80 (1886).

People v. Machado, 99 CA 702 (1929).

Rhor, M. (2008, January 23). Folk medicines pose poison risk. *San Francisco Chronicle*, p. A8.

University of Maryland. (2011). *Naturopathy*. Retrieved from http://umm.edu/health/medical/altmed/treatment/naturopathy

White House Commission on Complementary and Alternative Medicine Policy. (2002). *Chapter 10: Recommendations and actions*. Retrieved from http://www.whccamp.hhs.gov/fr10.html

© Janetto/Dreamstime.com

CHAPTER 5

Religion, Rituals, and Health

Nothing is so conducive to good health as the regularity of life without haste and without worry which the rational practice of religion brings in its train.
　—*James J. Walsh*

To prevent disease or to cure it, the power of truth, of divine Spirit, must break down the dream of the material senses.
　—*Mary Baker Eddy*

KEY CONCEPTS

Spirituality
Religion
Rituals

Shrines
Animal sacrifice

LEARNING OBJECTIVES

After reading this chapter, you should be able to:

1. Describe the role religion plays in people's lives.
2. Explain how religion influences health behaviors and the rationale behind these choices.
3. Describe ways that religion can have positive and negative effects on physical and mental health.
4. Describe religious differences in birthing and death rituals.
5. Explain the difference between spirituality and religion.

Have you ever prayed for a loved one or yourself when ill? If so, you fall within the majority of Americans. In 2007, almost 50% of adults said they had prayed about their health during the previous 12 months, up from 43% in 2002 and 14% in 1999 (Wachholtz & Sambamoorthi, 2011). Thirty-six percent of Americans surveyed reported that they had experienced or witnessed a divine healing of an illness or injury (Pew Forum on Religion & Public Life, 2008).

Spirituality, religion, and health have been related in all population groups since the beginning of recorded history (Koenig, 2012). In earlier times, physicians were often clergy, and for hundreds of years religious organizations were responsible for licensing physicians (Koenig, 2012). Belief in the ability of the supernatural to heal surfaced in shamanism thousands of years ago. Recorded history describing spiritual healing includes Egyptian belief in the healing power of a particular holy site and Greek and Roman temples built to the healing gods. These types of practices are still known today. Shamanic traditions continue today in Africa, Central and South America, and among some American Indian tribes, and Christians continue to make pilgrimages to holy sites that are believed to heal, such as the Sanctuary of Our Lady of Lourdes in France.

© Andrij Vatsyk/Shutterstock

Spirituality is often described as a belief in a higher power, something beyond the human experience. For many people, spirituality is a means of living with, confronting, or otherwise addressing universally mysterious events and occurrences. These events include birth, death, health, personal challenges, and tragedies. Scientific research has determined that spiritual practices positively influence health and increase longevity. However, there is disagreement as to the mechanism of these benefits.

Closely related but distinctive is **religion**, which is the acceptance of the specific beliefs and practices of an organized religion. Religion is generally an organized approach to practicing a form of spiritual belief in and respect for a supernatural power or powers, which is regarded as a creator or a governing framework of the universe and is supported by personal or institutionalized systems grounded in belief and worship.

Although many people find spirituality in the form of religious practice, religion and spirituality are conceptually different. A person may be spiritual without being religious, or may be both. Research has shown that both spirituality and religious beliefs have positive effects on health.

Those who practice Eastern religions seek to refine the life force within themselves, and they attempt to find meaning and purpose in life through these efforts. Practitioners of Western Christianity may focus more on faith and belief in external guidance and salvation from a supreme being, a god, or gods.

Although much human conduct is related to spiritualism that goes beyond practicing formal religious teachings, these two concepts flow universally throughout all cultures. However, most of the research has focused on health and religion, as opposed to health and spirituality, primarily because religion is associated with behaviors that can be quantified (e.g., how often one prays or attends a place of worship), it can be categorized by type of religion, and there is more agreement about its meaning. Religion has a significant role in the United States and in the health. It has an impact on social lives and health behaviors and, hence, on physical and mental well-being.

Religion and rituals overlap, but not all rituals are related to religion. Rituals such as baptism and the burning of ghost money when a person dies (a tradition in China) are related to religious practices, but other rituals are not tied to religion, such as drinking tea at 3 o'clock in the afternoon every day. The chapter begins with a discussion of religion and then moves into rituals, but the separation is not definitive. We discuss how religion in America influences health. Then we focus on rituals related to health. Because these topics have such a vast scope, only a few religious practices within the United States are discussed.

Religion in the United States

Spirtualism was part of the indigenous populations when the Europeans first arrived in what would become the United States. The conquering Spanish brought their Catholic priests not only for their own guidance but also to impose Christian beliefs on the natives. To a large extent the United States was established by people of strong religious beliefs, including Protestants from Europe seeking a place to practice their beliefs free from religious conflict with other European religions including Catholicism. In part because of the successful establishment of religious colonies, the United States has become "The Land of the Free," drawing immigrants from all over the world. The result is that almost every religion is represented and practiced somewhere in the United States.

In the 2011 Gallup poll, about 91% of the U.S. population reported a belief in God or a universal spirit (Newport, 2011). In 2008, 65% of Americans had reported that religion is an important part of their daily lives (Newport, 2009).

Religion and race/ethnicity are linked, but it is important not to assume a person's religion is based on his or her ethnicity (see **Table 5.1**). It also is not safe to assume that a person strictly adheres to the practices of a religion. Adherence to religious practices exists on a continuum, with some strictly adhering to all of the guidelines and others having looser ties.

TABLE 5.1   Religious Groups in the United States by Denomination, 2015

U.S. Religious Traditions	White (non-Hispanic) %	Black (non-Hispanic) %	Asian (non-Hispanic) %	Other/ Mixed (non-Hispanic) %	Hispanic %	Sample Size
National Total:	71	11	3	3	12	35,101
Evangelical Churches	81	6	2	4	7	9,380
Mainline Churches	91	2	1	3	3	7,383
Historically Black Churches	2	92	0	1	4	1,990
Catholics	65	2	2	2	29	7,987
Mormons	86	3	1	3	7	571
Orthodox	87	6	2	3	1	358
Jehovah's Witnesses	48	22	0	5	24	212
Other Christians	77	11	0	8	4	126
Jews	95	1	0	2	3	671
Muslims	37	24	20	15	4	1,030
Buddhists	53	4	32	5	6	405
Hindus	5	1	88	4	2	255
Other Faiths	80	2	1	13	5	436
Unaffiliated	73	8	4	4	11	4,955

Data from Muslims from "Muslim Americans: Middle Class and Mostly Mainstream," Pew Research Center, 2007. For more information, please see the detailed tables in the Full Reports section.
Source: Pew Research Center (2015). Comparisons. Retrieved from http://religions.pewforum.org/comparisons#

Religion and Health Behaviors

Lifestyle represents the single most prominent influence on our health today. As a result, the United States is seeing the need for more emphasis on prevention and behavior modification. People with religious ties of any kind have been shown to engage in healthier behavioral patterns, and these positive lifestyle choices lead to improved health and longer lives. Why do people with stronger religious ties have better health? The answer includes several possible factors, such as proscribed behaviors, closer social relationships, and improved coping mechanisms.

Health behaviors encouraged or proscribed by particular religions are one possible explanation for how religion can positively affect health. Some religions prohibit tobacco, alcohol, caffeine, certain sexual practices, and premarital sex, and some encourage vegetarianism. Social relationships are another potential explanatory factor for the connection between religion and improved health indicators. Social ties can provide both support and a sense of connectedness. Many churches and temples offer workshops, health fairs, and craft fairs, which provide social interactions. Social relationships also are tied to coping mechanisms because they provide support in multiple forms during times of stress. For example, financial support may be provided to people who have incurred a tragedy, such as a disability, loss of job, or a house fire. Religious organizations also conduct fundraisers for families who have experienced a death or personal tragedy in the family. Churches and temples assist elders by providing transportation or taking food to the homebound. Friendships and a sense of purpose also are methods of support.

Dietary Practices

Dietary practices have a long history of being incorporated into religions around the world. Some religions prohibit followers from consuming certain foods and drinks all of the time or on certain holy days; require or encourage specific dietary and food preparation practices and/or fasting (going without food and/or drink for a specified time); or prohibit eating certain foods at the same meal, such as dairy and meat products. Other religions require certain methods of food preparation and have special rules about the use of pans, plates, utensils, and how the food is to be cooked. Foods and drinks also may be a part of religious celebrations or rituals.

The restriction of certain foods and beverages may have a positive impact on the health of those engaged in such practices. For example, restricting consumption of animal products, such as beef and pork or all animal products, may reduce the risk of health problems. Many religions, such as Hinduism and Buddhism, practice or promote vegetarianism, and these diets have been shown to have several health effects, such as the reduction of heart disease, cancer, obesity, and stroke. Some religions help prevent obesity through beliefs that gluttony is a sin, only take what you need, and the need for self-discipline. **Table 5.2** presents a list of religions, their related dietary practices and restrictions, and the rationale behind them.

Religions may incorporate some element of fasting in their practices. In many religions, the general purpose for fasting is to become closer to God, show respect for the body (temple) that is a gift from God, understand and appreciate the suffering that the poor experience,

TABLE 5.2   Religions and Their Related Food and Substance Practices and Restrictions and Related Rationales

Type of Religion	Practice or Restriction	Rationale
Buddhism	• Vegetarian diet is desirable. • All foods in moderation.	• Natural foods of the earth are considered to be the most pure. • Encourage nonviolence (some Buddhists believe that the cause of human aggression is violence against animals).
Eastern Orthodox Christianity	• Restrictions on meat and fish. • Fasting selectively. • The ritual of the transubstantiation (changing) of bread and wine into the body and blood of Jesus Christ is believed to occur at communion.	• Observance of Holy Days includes fasting and restrictions to increase spiritual progress.
Hinduism	• Beef is forbidden. • Vegetarian diet is advocated. • Alcohol is avoided. • Numerous fasting days—may depend on the person's caste (or social standing) and the occasion.	• Cows are sacred and cannot be eaten, but the products of the "sacred" cow are pure and desirable. • Fasting promotes spiritual growth.
Islam	• Pork and certain birds are forbidden. • Alcohol is prohibited. • Coffee, tea, and stimulants are avoided. • Fasting from all food and drink during specific periods.	• Eating is for good health. • Failure to eat correctly minimizes spiritual awareness. • Fasting has a cleansing effect on evil elements.
Judaism	• Consumption of certain foods, including dairy products and fish, is subject to restrictions; for example, pork and shellfish are prohibited, and so is consuming meat and dairy at the same meal. • Leavened food is restricted. • Foods must be prepared in the right way to be kosher; for example, animals that provide meat must be slaughtered correctly. • Fasting is practiced.	• Land animals that do not have cloven hooves and that do not chew their cud are forbidden as unclean (e.g., hare, pig, camel). • The kosher process is based on the Torah. • The Passover commemorates the birth of the Jewish nation, and the food eaten helps tell the story of the exodus; for example, bitter herbs recall the suffering of the Israelites under Egyptian rule.

TABLE 5.2   Religions and Their Related Food and Substance Practices and Restrictions and Related Rationales (*Continued*)

Type of Religion	Practice or Restriction	Rationale
Mormonism	• Caffeinated and alcoholic beverages are forbidden. • All foods should be consumed in moderation. • Fasting is practiced.	• Caffeine is addictive and leads to poor physical and emotional health. • Fasting is the discipline of self-control and honoring God.
Protestantism	• Few restrictions of food or fasting observations. • Moderation in eating, drinking, and exercise is promoted.	• God made all animal and natural products for humans' enjoyment. • Gluttony and drunkenness are sins to be controlled.
Rastafarianism	• Meat and fish are restricted. • Vegetarian diets only, with salts, preservatives, and condiments prohibited. • Herbal drinks are permitted; alcohol, coffee, and soft drinks are prohibited. • Marijuana used extensively for religious and medicinal purposes.	• Pigs and shellfish are unclean; they are viewed as scavengers. • Foods grown with chemicals are unnatural and prohibited. • Biblical texts support the use of herbs (marijuana and other herbs).
Roman Catholicism	• Meat is restricted on certain days. • Fasting is practiced. • The ritual of the transubstantiation (changing) of bread and wine into the body and blood of Jesus Christ is believed to occur at communion. • Fast for at least 1 hour prior to communion.	• Restrictions are consistent with specified days of the church year.
Seventh-day Adventist	• Encourages adherence to kosher laws. • Pork is prohibited, and meat and fish are avoided unless animals chew the cud and have split hooves; fish must have scales and fins. • Recommends vegetarian diet. • Alcohol, tobacco, and illegal drugs are prohibited. • Avoid caffeinated beverages.	• Diet is related to honoring and glorifying God. • Body is to be treated as the temple of the Holy Ghost.

Source: Adapted from Advameg Inc. (2008).

acquire the discipline required to resist temptation, atone for sinful acts, and/or cleanse evil from within the body (Advameg Inc., 2008). Fasting may be recommended for specific times of the day; for a specified number of hours; on designated days of the week, month, or year; or on holy days.

During times of fasting, most but not all religions permit the consumption of water. Water restriction can lead to a risk of dehydration. Some fasters may not take their medication during the fast, which may put their health at risk. Prolonged fasting and/or restrictions from water and/or medications may pose health risks for some followers. Because of these health risks, certain groups are often excused from fasting. These groups include people with chronic diseases, frail elderly, pregnant and lactating women, people who engage in strenuous labor, young children, and people suffering from malnutrition.

Did You Know?

Most Hindus prefer to die at home. If that cannot occur, then certain rituals are to be performed at the hospital. Examples include assisting the patient with facing east and lighting a lamp near the patient's head. Often family and friends will be present, singing hymns or chanting mantras from sacred scriptures.

Holy ash or sandalwood paste is applied on the forehead after the patient dies. Members of the family may want the body to face south as that symbolizes facing the god of death. A few drops of holy water are trickled into the mouth, and the incense near the head of the deceased remains burning.

Use of Stimulants and Depressants

In addition to foods, some religions prohibit or restrict the use of stimulants. A stimulant is a product (including medications), food, or drink that stimulates the nervous system and alters the recipient's physiology. Stimulants include substances that contain caffeine, including some teas, coffee, chocolate, and energy drinks. Caffeine is prohibited or restricted by many religions because of its addictive properties. A depressant slows down the nervous system. Alcohol is an example. Many religions also restrict spices and certain condiments, such as pepper, pickles, or foods with preservatives because they are believed to be harmful by nature and favor the natural taste and effect of foods (Advameg Inc., 2008).

Some religions prohibit the use of stimulants and depressants, but others use them during ceremonies. For example, Roman Catholics, Eastern Orthodox Christians, and certain Protestant denominations use wine as a sacramental product to represent the blood of Christ in communion services (Advameg Inc., 2008). Rastafarians introduced marijuana into their religious rites because they consider it to be the "weed of wisdom," and they believe it contains healing ingredients (Advameg Inc., 2008). American Indians use tobacco and the hallucinogenic peyote as part of their spiritual ceremonies.

Cigarette Smoking

The influence of religion and spirituality is most evident in its "effects" on cigarette smoking. At least 137 studies have examined relationship between religion and spirituality and smoking, and of those, 123 (90%) reported statistically significant inverse relationships (including three at a trend level), and no studies found either a significant or even a trend association in the other direction. Of the 83 methodologically most rigorous studies, 75 (90%) reported inverse relationships with religion and spirituality involvement. Not surprisingly, the physical health consequences of not smoking are enormous. Decreased cigarette smoking will mean a reduction in chronic lung disease, lung cancer, all cancers (30% being related to smoking), coronary artery disease, hypertension, stroke, and other cardiovascular diseases (Koenig, 2012).

Exercise

Level of exercise and physical activity also appears linked to religion and spirituality. Koenig (2012) located 37 studies that examined this relationship. Of those, 25 (68%) reported significant positive relationships between religion and spiritual involvement and greater exercise or physical activity, whereas 6 (16%) found significant inverse relationships. Of 21 studies with the highest quality ratings, 16 (76%) reported positive associations and 2 (10%) found negative associations (Koenig, 2012).

Religion and Health Outcomes

As a result of religion's effects on health behaviors, it is not surprising that religion has been shown to have positive effects on both physical and mental health. Over the last several decades, a notable body of empirical evidence has emerged that examines the relationship between religion or religious practices and a host of outcomes. Most of the outcomes have been positive, but it is important to note that religion does not always have favorable effects on health.

Religion has sometimes been used to justify hatred, aggression, and prejudice (Lee & Newberg, 2005). Religion can be judgmental, alienating, and exclusive. Religious conflict is perhaps the greatest controllable threat to health and well-being in the modern era. Though raised as a Christian, during World War II, Adolph Hitler intentionally murdered 6 million Jews. Jews and Muslims repeatedly attack one another, keeping the Middle East in a constant state of tension over the last 50 years. Islamic extremists have declared war on Christian believers and used explosives on subways in Spain, crashed jetliners into high rises in New York, and used modern media to display multiple and serial beheadings while ostensibly practicing their religion. Threats of nuclear proliferation and potential use of "dirty" nuclear weapons have been driven by religious conflict.

Religion also may have a negative impact on health through the failure to conform to community norms. Open criticism by other congregation members or clergy can increase stress in social relationships. Feelings of religious guilt and the failure to meet religious expectations or cope with religious fears can contribute to illness. In some cases, parents' reliance on religion instead of traditional medical care has led to children's deaths. Also, people may not participate in healthy behaviors because they believe that their health is in God's hands, so their behaviors will not change God's plan. This is referred to as a fatalistic attitude.

In terms of positive effects, an abundance of research supports religion's constructive effect on health outcomes. Koenig (2012) found that religion and spirituality were related to lower levels of depression and anxiety and an improved ability to cope with adversity. Studies of health behavior have found that higher levels of religious involvement are inversely related to alcohol and drug use, smoking, sexual activity, depressive symptoms, and suicide risk (Koenig, 2012; Williams & Sternthal, 2007). These studies also found that spirituality and religion are positively related to immune system function. A review of 35 studies of the relationship between religion and health-related physiological processes found that both Judeo–Christian and Eastern religious practices were associated with reduced blood pressure and improved immune function; moreover, Zen, yoga, and meditation practices correlated with lower levels of stress hormones and cholesterol and better overall health outcomes in clinical patient populations (Williams & Sternthal, 2007).

In an important publication, Duke University researcher Harold Koenig and colleagues Michael McCullough and David Larson (2000) systematically reviewed much of the research on religion and health. This lengthy and detailed review of hundreds of studies focuses on scholarship from refereed journals. In sum, the review demonstrates that the majority of published research is consistent with the notion that religious practices or religious involvement are associated with beneficial outcomes in mental and physical health (Johnson, Tompkins, & Webb, 2008). These outcome categories include hypertension, mortality, depression, alcohol use or abuse, drug use or abuse, and suicide. Reviews of additional social science research also confirm that religious commitment and involvement in religious practices are significantly linked to reductions not only in delinquency among youth and adolescent populations but also in criminality among adult populations. Part of the following information is a summary of the findings from an extensive literature review conducted by Johnson, Tompkins, and Webb (2008). This information is reprinted with permission from the Baylor Institute for Studies of Religion.

Hypertension

As of 2012, nearly 1 in 3 adults (about 67 million) had high blood pressure, also known as hypertension (Centers for Disease Control and Prevention, 2012b). Though there is strong evidence that pharmacologic treatment can lower blood pressure, there remains concern about the adverse side effects of such treatments. For this reason, social epidemiologists are interested in the effects of socioenvironmental determinants of blood pressure. Among the factors shown to correlate with hypertension is religion. Epidemiological studies have found that individuals who report higher levels of religious activities tend to have lower blood pressure. Johnson, Tompkins, and Webb's (2008) review of the research indicates that 76% of the studies found that religious activities or involvement tend to be linked with reduced levels of hypertension (see **Table 5.3**).

TABLE 5.3   Results of Religion and Health Outcomes Studies

	Hypertension (%)	Mortality (%)	Depression (%)	Suicide (%)	Sexual Behavior (%)	Alcohol Use (%)	Drug Use (%)	Delinquency (%)
Beneficial outcomes	76	76	67	87	97	88	91	76
NA/mixed outcomes	20	21	27	14	3	10	8	17
Harmful outcomes	4	3	7	0	0	3	2	2

The data represent the percentage of published studies that were reviewed.
Source: Johnson, Tompkins, & Webb (2008). Reprinted with permission from The Baylor Institute for Studies of Religion.

Koenig (2012) found that at least 63 studies have examined the relationship between religion and spirituality and blood pressure, of which 36 (57%) reported significantly lower blood pressure in those who are more religious or spiritual and 7 (11%) reported significantly higher blood pressure.

Mortality

A substantial body of research reveals an association between intensity of participation in religious activities and greater longevity. Studies reviewed for the report done by Johnson, Tompkins, and Webb (2008) examined the association between degree of religious involvement and survival (see Table 5.3). Involvement in a religious community is consistently related to lower mortality and longer life spans. Johnson, Tompkins, and Webb's (2008) review of this literature revealed that 75% of these published studies conclude that higher levels of religious involvement have a sizable and consistent relationship with greater longevity (see **Figure 5.1**). This association was found to be independent of the effect of variables such as age, sex, race, education, and health. In a separate analysis, McCullough and colleagues conducted a meta-analytic review that incorporated data from more than 125,000 people and similarly concluded that religious involvement had a significant and substantial association with increased length of life (as cited in Johnson et al., 2008). In fact, longitudinal research in a variety of different cohorts also has documented that frequent religious attendance is associated with a significant reduction in the risk of dying during study follow-up periods ranging from 5 to 28 years.

Cancer

At least 29 studies have examined relationships between religion/spirituality and either the onset or the outcome of cancer (including cancer mortality). Of those, 16 (55%) found that those who are more religious or spiritual had a lower risk of developing cancer or a

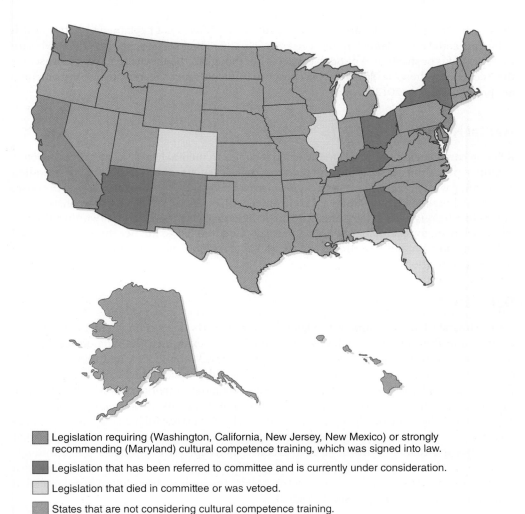

Legislation requiring (Washington, California, New Jersey, New Mexico) or strongly recommending (Maryland) cultural competence training, which was signed into law.

Legislation that has been referred to committee and is currently under consideration.

Legislation that died in committee or was vetoed.

States that are not considering cultural competence training.

FIGURE 5.1

Research examining the relationship between religion and health outcomes (total of 498 studies reviewed).

Source: Johnson, Tompkins, & Webb (2008). Reprinted with permission from The Baylor Institute for Studies of Religion.

better prognosis, although 2 (7%) studies reported a significantly worse prognosis. Of the 20 methodologically most rigorous studies, 12 (60%) found an association between religion or spirituality and lower risk or better outcomes, and none reported worse risk or outcomes. The results from some of these studies can be partially explained by better health behaviors (less cigarette smoking, alcohol abuse, etc.), but not all. Effects not explained by better health behaviors could be explained by lower stress levels and higher social support in those who are more religious or spiritual. Although cancer is not thought to be as sensitive as cardiovascular disorders to psychosocial stressors, psychosocial influences on cancer incidence and outcome are present (Koenig, 2012).

Mental Health

Religion can be helpful or problematic when it comes to mental health. Generally, religion is helpful in providing explanations and practices that can support individuals in understanding and dealing with distress. However, religion also can be a contributor to distress and the onset of mental illness when individuals are confronted with distress that seems to demonstrate the failure of religious beliefs (Pargament, 2013). Religion has been used to justify unhealthy and lethal behavior, for example, when a woman says God told her to kill her three children. Bad judgment and mental illness are no excuse to blame religion, but unhealthy acts do occur in the name of religion.

Depression

Approximately 1 in 10 adults in the United States reports depression (Centers for Disease Control and Prevention, 2012a). Over 100 studies that examined the religion–depression relationship were reviewed by Johnson, Tompkins, and Webb (2008), and they found that religious involvement tends to be associated with less depression in 68% of the articles (see Figure 5.1). People who are frequently involved in religious activities and who highly value their religious faith are at reduced risk for depression. Religious involvement seems to play an important role in helping people cope with the effects of stressful life circumstances. Prospective cohort studies and quasi-experimental and experimental research all suggest that religious or spiritual activities may lead to a reduction in depressive symptoms. These findings have been replicated across a number of large, well-designed studies and are consistent with much of the cross-sectional and prospective cohort research that has found less depression among more religious people (see Table 5.3).

Suicide

Suicide was the 10th leading cause of death for all ages in 2010 (Centers for Disease Control and Prevention, National Center for Injury Prevention and Control, 2010). A substantial body of literature documents that religious involvement (e.g., measured by frequency of religious attendance, frequency of prayer, and degree of religious salience) is associated with less suicide, suicidal behavior, and suicidal ideation, as well as less tolerant attitudes toward suicide across a variety of samples from many nations. This consistent inverse association is found in studies using both group and individual-level data. In total, 87% of the studies reviewed on suicide found these beneficial outcomes (see Figure 5.1). However, with increasing use of suicide bombers as agents of religious practice, such as the U.S. World

Trade Center attacks and individuals boarding U.S. – bound airplanes with explosive material in shoes, this area may need further review. Constructive peaceful religious practice has apparently proven to mediate isolated suicide behavior. But what is the prognosis for religion that encourages suicide?

Promiscuous Sexual Behaviors

Out-of-wedlock pregnancy is associated with poverty, higher infant mortality rates, increased risk of contracting sexually transmitted diseases, and other issues. Studies in the Johnson, Tompkins, and Webb (2008) review generally show that those who are religious are less likely to engage in premarital sex or extramarital affairs or to have multiple sexual partners (see Table 5.3). In fact, approximately 97% of the studies that were reviewed reported significant correlations between increased religious involvement and lower likelihood of promiscuous sexual behaviors (see Figure 5.1). None of the studies found that increased religious participation or commitment was linked to increases in promiscuous behavior.

Drug and Alcohol Use

In 2011, an estimated 22.5 million Americans aged 12 or older—or 8.7% of the population—had used an illicit drug or abused a psychotherapeutic medication (such as a pain reliever, stimulant, or tranquilizer) in the past month (National Institute on Drug Abuse, 2014). Both chronic alcohol consumption and abuse of drugs are associated with increased risks of morbidity and mortality. Johnson, Tompkins, and Webb (2008) reviewed over 150 studies that examined the relationship between religiosity and drug use ($n = 54$) or alcohol use ($n = 97$) and abuse. The vast majority of these studies demonstrate that participation in religious activities is associated with less of a tendency to use or abuse drugs (87%) or alcohol (94%). These findings are consistent regardless of the population under study (children, adolescents, or adults) or whether the research was conducted prospectively or retrospectively (see Table 5.3). The greater a person's religious involvement, the less likely he or she will be to initiate alcohol or drug use or have problems with these substances if they are used (see Table 5.3). Only four of the studies that were reviewed reported a positive correlation between religious involvement and increased alcohol or drug use. Interestingly, these four tended to be some of the weaker studies with regard to methodological design and statistical analyses.

Delinquency

There is growing evidence that religious commitment and involvement helps protect youth from delinquent behavior and deviant activities. Recent evidence suggests that such effects persist even if there is not a strong prevailing social control against delinquent behavior in the surrounding community. There is mounting evidence that religious involvement may lower the risks of a broad range of delinquent behaviors, including both minor and serious forms of criminal behavior. There is also evidence that religious involvement has a cumulative effect throughout adolescence and thus may significantly lessen the risk of later adult criminality. There is growing evidence that religion can be used as a tool to help prevent high-risk urban youths from engaging in delinquent behavior. Religious involvement may help adolescents learn prosocial behavior that emphasizes concern for other people's welfare. Such prosocial skills may give adolescents a greater sense of empathy toward others, which makes them less likely to commit acts that harm others. Similarly, when individuals become involved in deviant behavior, it is possible that participation in specific kinds of religious activities can help steer them back to a course of less deviant behavior and, more important, away from potential career criminal paths.

Research on adult samples is less common but tends to represent the same general pattern—that religion reduces criminal activity by adults. An important study by T. David Evans and colleagues found that religion, indicated by religious activities, reduced the likelihood of adult criminality as measured by a broad range of criminal acts (as cited in Johnson et al., 2008). The relationship persisted even after secular controls were added to the model. Further, the finding did not depend on social or religious contexts. A small but growing body of literature focuses on the links between religion and family violence. Several recent studies found that regular religious attendance is inversely related to abuse among both men and women. As can be seen in Figure 5.1, 78% of these studies report reductions in delinquency and criminal acts to be associated with higher levels of religious activity and involvements.

In sum, Johnson, Tompkins, and Webb's (2008) review of the research on religious practices and health outcomes indicates that, in general, higher levels of religious involvement are associated with reduced hypertension, longer survival, less depression, lower level of drug and alcohol use and abuse, a reduction in promiscuous sexual behaviors, reduced likelihood of suicide, lower rates of delinquency among youth, and reduced criminal activity among adults. As can be seen in Figure 5.1, this substantial body of empirical evidence demonstrates a very clear picture: People who are most involved in religious activities tend to fare better with respect to important and yet diverse outcome factors. Thus, aided by appropriate documentation, religiosity is now beginning to be acknowledged as a key protective factor, reducing the deleterious effects of a number of harmful outcomes.

Religion and Well-Being

Well-being has been referred to as the positive side of mental health. Symptoms for well-being include happiness, joy, satisfaction, fulfillment, pleasure, contentment, and other indicators of a life that is full and complete (Johnson et al., 2008). Many studies have examined the relationship between religion and the promotion of beneficial outcomes (see **Table 5.4**). Many of these studies tend to be cross-sectional in design, but a significant number are important prospective cohort studies. As reported in **Figure 5.2**, Johnson, Tompkins, and Webb (2008) found that the vast majority of these studies, some 81% of the 99 studies reviewed, reported some positive association between religious involvement and greater happiness, life satisfaction, morale, positive affect, or some other measure of well-being.

TABLE 5.4   Results of Religion and Well-Being Outcomes Studies

	Well-Being (%)	Hope (%)	Self Esteem (%)	Educational Attainment (%)
Beneficial outcomes	81	81	68	87
NA/mixed outcomes	16	16	30	10
Harmful outcomes	4	0	5	5

The data represent the percentage of published studies that were reviewed.
Source: Johnson, Tompkins, & Webb (2008). Reprinted with permission from The Baylor Institute for Studies of Religion.

Koenig (2012) found that out of the 256 studies he reviewed, 79% of them found only a positive relationship between religion and spirituality and well-being and three studies showed a significant inverse relationship. The vast number of studies on religion and well-being have included younger and older populations as well as African Americans and Caucasians from various denominational affiliations. Only one study found a negative correlation between religiosity and well-being, and this study was conducted in a small, nonrandom sample of college students.

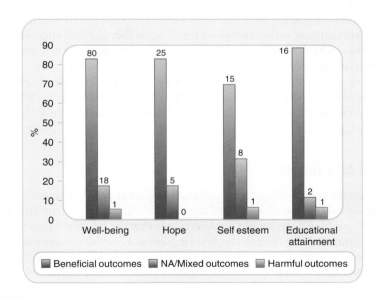

FIGURE 5.2

Research examining the relationship between religion and well-being outcomes (total of 171 studies reviewed).

Source: Johnson, Tompkins, & Webb (2008). Reprinted with permission from The Baylor Institute for Studies of Religion.

Hope, Purpose, and Meaning in Life

Many religious traditions and beliefs have long promoted positive thinking and an optimistic outlook on life. Not surprisingly, researchers have examined the role religion may or may not play in instilling hope and meaning or a sense of purpose in life for adherents. Researchers have found, on the whole, a positive relationship between measures of religiosity and hope in varied clinical and nonclinical settings. In total, 25 of the 30 studies reviewed (83%) document that increases in religious involvement or commitment are associated with having hope or a sense of purpose or meaning in life (see Figure 5.2). Similarly, studies show that increasing religiousness also is associated with optimism as well as larger support networks, more social contacts, and greater satisfaction with support. In fact, 19 out of the 23 studies reviewed by Johnson, Tompkins, and Webb (2008) conclude that increases in religious involvement and commitment are associated with increased social support.

Koenig (2012) reviewed 40 studies on the relationship between hope and religion and spirituality. Seventy-three percent (*n* = 29) reported significant positive relationships with hope; none of these reported the inverse. Koenig (2012) identified six studies with the highest quality, and of those six, half found a positive relationship.

Self-Esteem

Most people would agree that contemporary American culture places too much significance on physical appearance and the idea that one's esteem is bolstered by his or her looks. Conversely, a common theme of various religious teachings is that physical appearance, for example, should not be the basis of self-esteem. Religion provides a basis for self-esteem that is not dependent upon individual accomplishments, relationships with others (e.g., who you know), or talent. In other words, a person's self-esteem is rooted in the individual's religious faith as well as the faith community as a whole. Of the studies Johnson, Tompkins, and Webb (2008) reviewed, 65% conclude that religious commitment and activities are related to increases in self-esteem (see Figure 5.2).

Educational Attainment

The literature on the role of religious practices or religiosity on educational attainment represents a relatively recent development in the research literature. In the last decade or so, a number of researchers have sought to determine whether religion hampers or enhances educational attainment. Even though the development of a body of evidence is just beginning to emerge, some 84% of the studies reviewed concluded that religiosity or religious activities are positively correlated with improved educational attainment (see Figure 5.2). Educational attainment is relevant to health because those with a higher education tend to have higher socioeconomic status, and hence, better health status.

To summarize, a review of the research on religious practices and various measures of well-being reveals that, in general, higher levels of religious involvement are associated with increased levels of well-being, hope, purpose, meaning in life, and educational attainment.

As can be seen in Figure 5.2, this substantial body of evidence shows quite clearly that those who are most involved in religious activities tend to be better off, which is one of the critical indicators of well-being. Just as the studies reviewed earlier (see Table 5.3 and Figure 5.1) document that religious commitment is a protective factor that buffers individuals from various harmful outcomes (e.g., hypertension, depression, suicide, and delinquency), there is mounting empirical evidence to suggest that religious commitment is also a source for promoting or enhancing beneficial outcomes (e.g., well-being, purpose, or meaning in life). This review of a large number of diverse studies leaves one with the observation that, in general, the effect of religion on physical and mental health outcomes is remarkably positive. These findings have led some religious health care practitioners to conclude that further collaboration between religious organizations and health services may be desirable (see **Box 5.1**).

BOX 5.1 Clinical Implications of the Relationship Between Religion, Spirituality, and Health

There are many practical reasons for addressing spiritual issues in clinical practice. Here are eight important reasons for doing so, and there are others as well.

First, many patients are religious or spiritual and have spiritual needs related to medical or psychiatric illness. Studies of medical and psychiatric patients and those with terminal illnesses report that the vast majority have such needs, and most of those needs currently go unmet. Unmet spiritual needs, especially if they involve spiritual struggles, can adversely affect health and may increase mortality independent of mental, physical, or social health.

Second, religion and spirituality influence the patient's ability to cope with illness. In some areas of the country, 90% of hospitalized patients use religion to enable them to cope with their illnesses and over 40% indicate it is their primary coping behavior. Poor coping has adverse effects on medical outcomes, both in terms of lengthening hospital stay and increasing mortality.

Third, religious and spiritual beliefs affect patients' medical decisions, may conflict with medical treatments, and can influence compliance with those treatments. Studies have shown that religious and spiritual beliefs influence medical decisions among those with serious medical illness, and especially among those with advanced cancer or HIV/AIDs.

Fourth, physicians' own religious or spiritual beliefs often influence medical decisions they make and affect the type of care they offer to patients, including decisions about use of pain medications, abortion, vaccinations, and contraception. Physician views about such matters and how they influence the physician's decisions, however, are usually not discussed with a patient.

Fifth, as noted earlier, religion and spirituality are associated with both mental and physical health and likely affect medical outcomes. If so, then health professionals need to know about such influences, just as they need to know if a person smokes cigarettes or uses alcohol or drugs. Those who provide health care to the patient need to be aware of all of the factors that influence health and health care.

Sixth, religion and spirituality influence the kind of support and care that patients receive once they return home. A supportive faith community may ensure that patients receive medical follow-up (by providing rides to doctors' offices) and comply with their medications. It is important to know whether this is the case or whether the patient will return to an apartment to live alone with little social interaction or support.

Seventh, research shows that failure to address patients' spiritual needs increases health care costs, especially toward the end of life. This is a time when patients and families may demand medical care (often very expensive medical care) even when continued treatment is futile. For example, patients or families may be praying for a miracle. "Giving up" by withdrawing life support or agreeing to hospice care may be viewed as a lack of faith or lack of belief in the healing power of God. If health professionals do not take a spiritual history so that patients and their families feel comfortable discussing such issues openly, these situations may go on indefinitely and consume huge amounts of medical resources.

Finally, standards set by the Joint Commission and Medicare require that providers of health care show respect for patients' cultural and personal values, beliefs, and preferences (including religious or spiritual beliefs). If health professionals are unaware of those beliefs, they cannot show respect for them and adjust care accordingly.

Source: Koenig (2012).

What Do You Think?

Health care professionals should take a patient's religion and spirituality into consideration, but to what extent should a health care professional's beliefs be taken into consideration? If a pharmacist has religious beliefs against abortion, should he or she be required to fill prescriptions for the emergency contraceptive? If a pharmacist works in Oregon, where doctors are, by law, permitted to write life-ending prescriptions for dying patients, should a pharmacist who believes that such a practice is murder be required to fill that prescription? Should a faith-based hospital be able to prohibit providing an abortion? Would your answer be different if it was the only hospital in a large rural region so women wanting an abortion would have to travel for 5 hours to reach a clinic? Should the rural hospital be able to prohibit providing an abortion if the life of the mother is threatened?

Rituals

A **ritual** is a set of actions that usually is structured and has a symbolic value or meaning. The performance of rituals is usually tied to religion or traditions, and their forms, purposes, and functions vary. These include compliance with religious obligations or ideals, satisfaction of spiritual or emotional needs of the practitioners, to ward off evil, to ensure the favor of a divine being, to maintain or restore health, as a demonstration of respect or submission, stating one's affiliation, obtaining social acceptance, or for the pleasure of the ritual itself. A ritual may be performed on certain occasions, at regular intervals, or at the discretion of individuals or communities. It may be performed by an individual, a small group, or the community, and it may occur in arbitrary places or specified locations. The ritual may be performed in private or public, or in front of specific people. The participants may be restricted to certain community members, with limitations related to age, gender, or type of activity (hunting and birthing rituals).

Rituals are related to numerous activities and events, such as birth, death, puberty, marriages, sporting events, club meetings, holidays, graduations, and presidential inaugurations. Handshaking, saying hello and good-bye, and taking your shoes off before entering a home are also rituals. These actions and their symbolism are neither arbitrarily chosen by the performers nor dictated by logic or necessity, but they either are prescribed and imposed upon the performers by some external source or are inherited unconsciously from social traditions. Many have practical roots. Shaking hands originated as a gesture to assure each person that neither was carrying a weapon, and taking off shoes before entering a home helps keep it clean.

The biomedical system contains numerous rituals, including its own language filled with scientific terminology, jargon, and abbreviations (e.g., MRI, CAT scan). There are formal rules of behavior and communication, such as how physicians should be addressed and where the patient should sit. There are rituals such as hand washing, how to perform a physical examination, how to make a hospital bed, and how to document information in medical records. The values and expectations include being on time for your appointment and adhering to the treatment regimen. People who are unaccustomed to this culture and these rituals can experience difficulty with them, and this includes maneuvering through the complex health insurance system, which is laden with unfamiliar rituals and rules. This can be particularly challenging if English is the patient's second language and if the patient did not come from a place with a similar system, such as socialized medicine.

In addition to rituals within health care systems numerous rituals are related to health. These rituals are discussed here to help prompt people who are working in health care to ask about, be sensitive to, and not be surprised about these key differences.

Objects as Rituals

People wear various items to maintain their health. These may include amulets that may be worn on a necklace or strung around the neck, wrist, or waist. For example, people from Puerto Rico may place a bracelet on the wrist of a baby to ward off the evil eye. In addition to being worn, amulets may be placed in the home. For example, items such as written documents, statues, crosses, or horseshoes may be hung on the home to protect the family's health as well as other factors. It is important to ask about removing these objects first because removal may cause great stress and concern for the person.

Shrines

For centuries people have described certain places as being holy or magic, as having a concentrated power, or having the presence of spirit. Ancient legends, historic records, and contemporary reports tell of extraordinary, even miraculous, happenings at these places. Different sacred sites have the power to heal the body, enlighten the mind, increase creativity, develop psychic abilities, and awaken the soul to a knowing of its true purpose in life. **Shrines** are located at some of these sacred sites. A shrine was originally a container, usually made of precious materials, but it has come to mean a holy or sacred place. Shrines may be enclosures within temples, home altars, and sacred burial places. Secular meanings have developed by association, and some of the associations are related to health and healing. People visit numerous shrines that represent health to maintain or restore health. Some examples of these shrines are Our Lady of La Leche, Our Lady of San Juan, and St. Peregrine. These shrines can be associated with healing for a specific disease or condition or with healing in general.

Animal Sacrifice

Animal sacrifice is not only practiced for food consumption but also is believed to be needed for one to build and maintain a personal relationship with the spirit. It is also believed that it brings worshippers closer to their Creator or spirit and makes them aware of the spirit in them. Sacrifices are performed for events such as birth, marriage, and death. They are also used for healing. Animals are killed in a way similar to a kosher slaughter. Animals are cooked and eaten following most rituals, except for some healing and death rituals in which the animal is not eaten because it is believed that the sickness is passed into the dead animal.

Birthing Rituals

The birth of an infant is a life-altering event that is surrounded by many traditional and ancient rituals. These rituals are often related to protecting the health of the child, which includes protecting him or her from evil spirits. The rituals are related to events prior to, during, and after the birth. Because the rituals are so numerous, we have listed the general variations, but the list is not exhaustive.

Prior to birth:

- Food restrictions
- Wearing of amulets
- The fulfilling of food cravings
- Exposure to cold air
- Avoidance of loud noises or viewing certain types of people (i.e., deformed people)

During labor:

- How the placenta is discarded
- Silent birth (some cultures require that no words or sounds are spoken by the woman and/or family members)
- People present during labor
- Utilization of a midwife
- Place of delivery
- Medications used

After birth:

- Breastfeeding
- Amulets (placed on the baby, crib, or in the newborn's room)
- Female and male circumcision
- Baptism
- Animal sacrifice
- Cutting of child's lock of hair
- Bathing of baby
- Food restrictions
- When the naming of the baby occurs
- Rubbing the baby with oils or herbs
- Acceptance of postpartum depression
- Woman's and child's confinement period

Death Rituals

Responses to death vary widely across cultures. Although some cultures may perform the same or similar rituals, they may have different meaning among the cultures. The rituals, in part, are related to beliefs about the meaning of life and life after death. Is death the end of existence or a transition to another life? Rituals play a role in behaviors, such as how people discuss death, respond to death, handle the deceased's body, the behaviors that occur at the funeral, and the mourning process.

Some general variations include:

- The method of disposing of the body
- Open versus closed casket
- The length of the mourning process and appropriate behavior

- Dress, including colors, at the funeral ceremony and afterward
- Food restrictions or traditions
- Appropriate emotional responses
- The role of the family
- Use of prayer
- What is buried with the body
- Rituals engaged in before, during, and after the ceremony (e.g., burning of ghost money or candles, use of flowers)
- Animal sacrifice

Summary

Religion plays a major role in the lives of Americans. It shapes our health behaviors and has been shown to have an overall positive effect on health behaviors. Religion also guides people when making difficult and sometimes life-altering decisions. With technological advances, medical decisions can be complicated. Some people find the answers within their religion, but many people within religious sectors have differences in opinions. It is important for health care professionals not to assume someone's religion based upon their ethnicity and not to assume that everyone strictly adheres to the religious practices.

In this chapter we have described how important religion is in the lives of Americans as well as the reasons religion can influence health behaviors and decisions. In addition, some reasons people who are religious may have positive health habits and outcomes as well as the potential negative effects of religion were discussed. The chapter ended with a discussion about rituals that are related to health. Many of those rituals are tied to religious beliefs, and health care professionals should make an effort to adhere to these rituals.

Review

1. Provide examples of how religion shapes health behaviors and the rationale behind them.
2. Explain some of the positive and negatives effects religion can have on health outcomes.
3. Provide examples of medical decisions that are made based on religion and the rationale behind them.
4. Explain issues that health care professionals should take into consideration related to beginning- and end-of-life transitions.

Activity

Select a religion that you are interested in learning more about. Write a three-page paper about the practices and beliefs of that religion that are related to health.

Case Study

This case focuses on a Hasidic Judaism patient with cystic fibrosis and her family. Hasidic Judaism, sometimes referred to as Hasidic, refers to members of a Jewish religious movement founded in the 18th century in eastern Europe that maintains that God's presence is in all of one's surroundings and that one should serve God in one's every deed and word. As you read through this study, pay particular attention to the multiple cultural and religious factors that influence this child's medical management.

Judy Cohen is 6 years old. Much of her life in the Hasidic Jewish community revolves around the neighborhood synagogue, her extended family, and their Hasidic Jewish community. She lives with her parents and four siblings in a house packed closely against her grandparents' house next door. The Cohen house is awash in the smells of Mrs. Cohen's cooking, the sounds of Yiddish prayer and conversation, and the laughter of children. The Cohens speak English fluently, but they prefer to speak their native language. They speak English only when necessary.

Judy's mother stays home to care for Judy and her four siblings, ages 3, 7, 9, and 10 years. Judy's father, Mr. Cohen, works for a family business. When the father is not working, he is usually praying, socializing, and consulting with the rabbi at the synagogue.

When she was 12 months old, Judy was diagnosed with cystic fibrosis (CF), which is an inherited chronic disease that affects the lungs and digestive system. At the time, the medical team that specialized in CF recommended that her siblings have sweat tests, which is the test used for diagnosing cystic fibrosis. Judy's parents declined because they believed that their children's health was in God's hands. Judy's condition was stable then, and she and her mother attended regularly scheduled appointments with the CF team. Judy's father, although he was concerned, did not usually come to Judy's appointments.

When Judy was 18 months old, she went to the clinic with an increased cough and weight loss. The team recommended that she be hospitalized. Judy's parents initially declined but agreed a week later after her cough had worsened.

At age 4 years, Judy again went into the hospital for pneumonia. Mr. and Mrs. Cohen reluctantly agreed to the hospital admission. When Judy appeared to be responding to the intravenous antibiotics, her parents convinced the medical team to allow Judy to complete her regimen of antibiotics at home. When she was home, the family did have their daughter complete the course of antibiotics that was recommended, but they refused visiting nurse services because they did not want the neighbors to know about Judy's illness.

When Mrs. Cohen became pregnant with her fifth child, the medical team strongly suggested that she go for genetic counseling and possibly testing. After discussing the issue with their rabbi, Mr. and Mrs. Cohen decided not to have genetic testing. Again, they believed that "whatever will be, will be" and that the unborn child's health was in God's hands.

Today, Judy went to the clinic for a routine follow-up appointment. This is her first visit since beginning school. Her respiratory status is good, but she is having more frequent stools. After being questioned, Mr. and Mrs. Cohen admit that they do not want the school to give Judy the required enzymes, which are recommended so that she can digest her food. They have not told anyone at the school that Judy has CF.

There are several issues to consider about this case:

- What are the various ways in which religious beliefs can affect the understanding of illness?

- How did the Cohens' Hasidic belief system affect Judy's treatment?

- What are some of the main tenets of Hasidic Judaism?

- Do you believe that the Cohens should have been required to have genetic testing done?

- Do you think the Cohens mishandled Judy's illness?

Source: Cross Cultural Health Care (2003).

References

Advameg Inc. (2008). *Religion and dietary practices.* Retrieved from http://www.faqs.org /nutrition/Pre-Sma/Religion-and-Dietary -Practices.html

Centers for Disease Control and Prevention. (2012a, April 20). *An estimated 1 in 10 U.S. adults report depression.* Retrieved from http://www.cdc.gov/features/dsdepression/

Centers for Disease Control and Prevention. (2012b, September). *Getting blood pressure under control.* Retrieved from http://www .cdc.gov/vitalsigns/Hypertension/index.html

Centers for Disease Control and Prevention, National Center for Injury Prevention and Control. (2010). *Web-based Injury Statistics Query and Reporting System (WISQARS)* [online]. Retrieved from www.cdc.gov /injury/wisqars/index.html

Cross Cultural Health Care (2003). Cross cultural health care-case studies. Retrieved from http:// support.mchtraining.net/national_ccce/

Johnson, B. R., Tompkins, R. B., & Webb, D. (2008). *Assessing the effectiveness of faith-based organizations: A review of the literature.* Waco, TX: Baylor University.

Koenig, H. G. (2012). Religion, spirituality, and health: The research and clinical implications. *Psychiatry.* Retrieved from http://www.hindawi.com/journals/isrn /2012/278730/

Koenig, H. G., McCullough, M. E., & Larson, D. B. (2000). *Handbook of religion and health.* New York: Oxford University Press.

Lee, B. Y., & Newberg, A. B. (2005). Religion and health: A review and critical analysis. *Zygon,* *40,* 443–468.

National Institute on Drug Abuse. (2014, January). *DrugFacts: Nationwide trends.* Retrieved from http://www.drugabuse.gov /publications/drugfacts/nationwide-trends

Newport, F. (2009, January 28). *State of the states: Importance of religion.* Retrieved from http:// www.gallup.com/poll/114022/State-States-Importance-Religion.aspx

Newport, F. (2011, June 3). *More than 9 in 10 Americans continue to believe in God.* Retrieved from http://www.gallup.com /poll/147887/americans-continue-believe-god.aspx

Pargament, K. I. (2013, March 22). *What role do religion and spirituality play in mental health?* Retrieved from http://www.apa.org /news/press/releases/2013/03/religion-spirituality.aspx

Pew Forum on Religion & Public Life. (2008, February). *2008 U.S. Religious Landscape Survey*. Retrieved from http://religions.pewforum.org/pdf/report-religious-landscape-study-full.pdf

Pew Research Center. (2015). *Comparisons*. Retrieved from http://religions.pewforum.org/comparisons#

Wachholtz, A., & Sambamoorthi, U. (2011). National trends in prayer use as a coping mechanism for health: Changes from 2002 to 2007. *Psychology of Religion and Spirituality*, 3(2), 67–77. Retrieved from http://www.apa.org/pubs/journals/releases/rel-3-2-67.pdf

Williams, D. R., & Sternthal, M. J. (2007). Spirituality, religion and health: Evidence and research directions. *The Medical Journal of Australia*. Retrieved from http://www.mja.com.au/public/issues/186_10_210507/wil11060_fm.html

CHAPTER 6

Communication and Health Promotion in Diverse Societies

People who are Promotores(as) have a gift for service and a noble and kind heart. We think about things and take care of people. We identify with the people and the needs of the community.
  —Mirian Perez, Promotora

There is a push, sometimes—"what's the recipe" or "what are the ten things you have to do in every multicultural community." My experience says that there is a contextualization that needs to happen.
  —Zoe Cardoza Clayson

Key Concepts

Fotonovela   Multicultural evaluation
Digital divide   Reciprocity
Promotores

Learning Objectives

After reading this chapter, you should be able to:

1. Explain at least three ways to deliver health information.
2. Identify at least four issues to consider when developing printed materials.
3. Describe the Health Belief and PRECEDE–PROCEED models and how they can be utilized when working with diverse populations.
4. Describe at least three differences between traditional evaluation and multicultural evaluation.

In this chapter the focus is on communication in a one-to-one situation, as in patient-provider, or a one-to-many situation, as in a public health program. The chapter begins with a discussion about health communication, then addresses the delivery of the health message. It ends with a focus on models that can be used for developing a health promotion program and multicultural evaluation. Communication is the basis of any health promotion effort, but in this chapter special attention is paid to considerations that need to be taken into account when working with diverse populations.

Health Communication

Consider the following case study. An elderly Irish woman was hospitalized and scheduled to have surgery at the end of the week. A few days before the surgery, she suddenly started complaining of pain to her family but said nothing to her physician. Her physician was also unaware of evidence that the Irish, as a group, tend to minimize expressions of pain. Confronted by the family, the physician expressed little concern because in the physician's country, women having serious pain are much more vocal than this patient was being. The physician ignored their requests that the surgery be done sooner, deeming it unnecessary. By the time the patient went to surgery, her condition had worsened, and she died during the operation. Her daughter-in-law, a nurse, felt that had the surgeon operated when the patient first complained, she might have lived. In this case, the surgeon made the mistake of stereotyping the patient—she was a woman, and in the physician's experience, women complained loudly when in pain. Therefore, the physician failed to even reexamine the patient (in itself, bad medical judgment). If the physician had been aware of the generalization about Irish people in pain, the patient's complaints may have been taken more seriously, which may have led to an earlier operation. (Galanti, 2000, p. 335)

Health communication encompasses the study and use of communication strategies to inform and influence individual and community decisions that enhance health. It can occur on a one-to-one basis or one-to-many (which is the focus of public health discussed specifically later in the chapter). It links the domains of communication and health and is increasingly recognized as a necessary element of efforts to improve personal and public health. Health communication can contribute to all aspects of disease prevention and health promotion and is relevant in a number of contexts, including (1) health professional–patient relations, (2) individuals' exposure to, search for, and use and understanding of health information, (3) individuals' adherence to clinical recommendations and regimens, (4) the construction of public health messages and campaigns, (5) the dissemination of individual and population health risk information (i.e., risk communication), (6) images of health in the mass media and the culture at large, and (7) the education of consumers about how to gain access to the public health and health care systems.

Effective health communication can help raise awareness of health risks and solutions, provide the motivation and skills needed to reduce these risks, help individuals find support from other people in similar situations, and affect or reinforce attitudes.

Health communication also can increase demand for appropriate health services and decrease demand for inappropriate health services. It can make information available to assist in making complex choices, such as selecting health plans, care providers, and treatments. For the community, health communication can be used to advocate for policies and programs, promote positive changes in the socioeconomic and physical environments, improve the delivery of public health and health care services, and encourage social norms that benefit health and quality of life.

The practice of health communication has contributed to health promotion and disease prevention in several areas. One is the improvement of interpersonal and group interactions in clinical situations (e.g., provider–patient, provider–provider, and among members of a health care team) through training health professionals and patients in effective communication skills. Collaborative relationships are enhanced when all parties are capable of good communication.

Another area is the dissemination of health messages through public education campaigns that seek to change the social climate to encourage healthy behaviors, create awareness, change attitudes, and motivate individuals to adopt recommended behaviors. Campaigns traditionally have relied on mass communication (such as public service announcements on billboards, radio, and television) and educational messages in printed materials (such as pamphlets) to deliver health messages. With advances in technology, newer methods of message delivery now exist, such a text messaging. Many campaigns have used social marketing techniques. Social marketing is the systematic application of marketing used to achieve specific behavioral goals for a social good. **Table 6.1** provides a list of attributes of effective health communication.

Increasingly, health improvement activities are taking advantage of digital technologies, such as social media sites, health games, mobile applications, and the Internet, that can target audiences, tailor messages, and engage people in interactive, ongoing exchanges about health. As a result, a growing area is health communication to support community-centered prevention. Community-centered prevention shifts attention from the individual to group-level change and emphasizes the empowerment of individuals and communities to effect change on multiple levels.

On a community level, the promotion of regular physical activity, healthy weight, good nutrition, and responsible sexual behavior requires a range of information, education, and advocacy efforts, as does the reduction of tobacco use, substance abuse, injuries, and violence. Public information campaigns are used to promote increased fruit and vegetable consumption (such as the Fruits & Veggies—More Matters campaign), higher rates of preventive screening (such as mammograms and colonoscopies), higher rates of clinical preventive services (such as immunizations), and greater rates of adoption of risk-reducing behaviors (such as the Back to Sleep and Buckle Up America! campaigns). On a one-to-one or among small groups, effective counseling and patient education for behavior change require health care providers and patients to have good communication skills.

Health communication alone, however, cannot change systemic problems related to health, such as poverty, environmental degradation, or lack of access to health care. However, comprehensive health communication programs should include a systematic exploration of all the factors that contribute to health and the strategies that could be used to influence these

TABLE 6.1   Attributes of Effective Health Communication
Accuracy: The content is valid and without errors of fact, interpretation, or judgment.
Availability: The content (whether targeted message or other information) is delivered or placed where the audience can access it. Placement varies according to audience, message complexity, and purpose, ranging from interpersonal and social networks to billboards and mass transit signs to prime-time TV or radio, to public kiosks (print or electronic), to the Internet.
Balance: Where appropriate, the content presents the benefits and risks of potential actions or recognizes different and valid perspectives on the issue.
Consistency: The content remains internally consistent over time and also is consistent with information from other sources (the latter is a problem when other widely available content is not accurate or reliable).
Cultural competence: The design, implementation, and evaluation process accounts for special issues for select population groups (for example, ethnic, racial, and linguistic) and also educational levels and disability.
Evidence base: Relevant scientific evidence that has undergone comprehensive review and rigorous analysis to formulate practice guidelines, performance measures, review criteria, and technology assessments for telehealth applications.
Reach: The content gets to or is available to the largest possible number of people in the target population.
Reliability: The source of the content is credible, and the content itself is kept up to date.
Repetition: The delivery of/access to the content is continued or repeated over time, both to reinforce the impact with a given audience and to reach new generations.
Timeliness: The content is provided or available when the audience is most receptive to, or in need of, the specific information.
Understandability: The reading or language level and format (including multimedia) are appropriate for the specific audience.

Source: U.S. Department of Health and Human Services (2001).

factors. Well-designed health communication activities help individuals better understand their own and their communities' needs so that they can take appropriate actions to maximize health.

The environment for communicating about health has changed significantly. These changes include dramatic increases in the number of communication channels and the number of health issues vying for public attention, as well as consumer demands for more and better quality health information and the increased sophistication of marketing and sales techniques, such as direct-to-consumer advertising of prescription drugs and sales of medical devices and medications over the Internet.

The expansion of communication channels and health issues on the public agenda increases competition for people's time and attention; at the same time, people have more opportunities to select information based on their personal interests and preferences. The trend toward commercialization of the Internet suggests that the marketing models of other mass media will be applied to emerging media, which has important consequences for the ability of noncommercial and public-health-oriented communications to stand out in a cluttered information environment.

Communication occurs in a variety of contexts (e.g., school, home, and work); through a variety of channels (e.g., interpersonal, small group, organizational, community, text messages, and mass media) with a variety of messages; and for a variety of reasons. In such an environment, people do not pay attention to all communications they receive but selectively attend to and purposefully seek out information. One of the main challenges in the design of effective health communication programs is to identify the optimal contexts, channels, content, and reasons that will motivate people to pay attention to and use health information.

A one-dimensional approach to health promotion, such as reliance on mass media campaigns or other single-component communication activities, has been shown to be insufficient to achieve program goals. Successful health promotion efforts increasingly rely on multidimensional interventions to reach diverse audiences about complex health concerns, and communication is integrated from the beginning with other components, such as community-based programs, policy changes, and improvements in services and the health delivery system. Research shows that health communication best supports health promotion when multiple communication channels are used to reach specific audience segments with information that is appropriate and relevant to them. An important factor in the design of multidimensional programs is to allot sufficient time for planning, implementation, and evaluation and sufficient money to support the many elements of the program. Public–private partnerships and collaborations can leverage resources to strengthen the impact of multidimensional efforts. Collaboration can have the added benefit of reducing message clutter and targeting health concerns that cannot be fully addressed by public resources or market incentives alone.

Research indicates that effective health promotion and communication initiatives adopt an audience-centered perspective, which means that promotion and communication activities reflect audiences' preferred formats, channels, and contexts. These considerations are particularly relevant for racial and ethnic populations, who may have different languages and sources of information. In these cases, public education campaigns must be conceptualized and developed by individuals with specific knowledge of the cultural characteristics, media habits, and language preferences of intended audiences. While designing materials for your target audience, you also do not want to portray an issue as only relevant to that group. For example, providing a public message about HIV prevention in which all of the photos show one ethnic or racial group could be offensive to that group as HIV affects everyone.

Direct translation of health information or health promotion materials should be avoided. Credible channels of communication need to be identified for each major group. Television and radio stations that serve specific racial and ethnic populations can be effective means to deliver health messages when care is taken to account for the language, culture, and socioeconomic situations of intended audiences.

An audience-centered perspective also reflects the realities of people's everyday lives and their current practices, attitudes, beliefs, and lifestyles. Some specific audience characteristics that are relevant include gender, age, education and income levels, ethnicity, sexual orientation, cultural beliefs and values, primary language(s), and physical and mental functioning. Additional considerations include their experience with the health care system, attitudes toward different types of health problems, and willingness to use certain types of health services. Particular attention should be paid to the needs of underserved audience members.

Targeting specific segments of a population and tailoring messages for individual use are two methods to make health promotion activities relevant to audiences. Examples include the targeted use of mass media messages for adolescent girls at increased risk of smoking, tailoring computer-generated nutritional information to help individuals reduce their fat intake and increase fruit and vegetable consumption, and a text campaign in Spanish to provide pregnant women with health information.

Interventions that account for the cultural practices and needs of specific populations have shown some success. For example, a breastfeeding promotion program for Navajo women that was based on investigations of their cultural beliefs about infant feeding practices showed increased rates of breastfeeding. Similarly, an intervention that used the **fotonovela**, a popular form of Latino mass media, to reach young people and their parents sought to improve parent–youth communication in Hispanic families and to influence the adolescents' attitudes about alcohol.

Advances in medical and consumer health informatics are changing the delivery of health information and services and are likely to have a growing impact on individual and community health. The convergence of media (computers, cell phones, television, radio, video, print, and audio) and the emergence of the Internet and social media create a nearly ubiquitous networked communication infrastructure. This infrastructure facilitates access to an increasing array of health information and health-related support services and extends the reach of health communication efforts. Delivery channels, such as text messaging, email, and electronic health records, expand the choices available for health professionals to reach patients and consumers and for patients and consumers to interact with health professionals and with one another (e.g., in online support groups).

Compared to traditional mass media, interactive media may have several advantages for health communication efforts. These advantages include (1) improved access to personalized health information, (2) access to health information, support, and services on demand, (3) enhanced ability to distribute materials widely and update content or functions rapidly, (4) just-in-time expert decision support, and (5) more choices for consumers. The health impact of interactivity, customization, and enhanced multimedia is just beginning to be explored, and already interactive health communication technologies are being used to exchange information, facilitate informed decision making, promote healthy behaviors, enhance peer and emotional support, promote self-care, manage demand for health services, and support clinical care.

Widespread availability and use of interactive health communication create at least two serious challenges. One is related to the risks associated with consumers' use of poor quality health information to make decisions. Concerns are growing about the Internet and social media making available large amounts of information that may be misleading, inaccurate, or inappropriate, which may put consumers at unnecessary risk. Although many health professionals agree that the technology is a boon for consumers because they have easier access to much more information than before, professionals also are concerned that the poor quality of a lot of information will undermine informed decision making. These concerns are driving the development of a quality standards agenda to help health professionals and consumers find reliable health information. An expert panel convened by the U.S. Department of Health and Human Services describes high-quality health information as accurate, current, valid, appropriate, intelligible, and free of bias.

The other challenge is related to the protection of privacy and confidentiality of personal health information, which are major issues for consumers, and these concerns are magnified when information is collected, stored, and made available online. As the availability and variety of interactive health applications grow, consumer confidence about developers' ability or intent to ensure privacy will be challenged. Protected health information is collected during both clinical and nonclinical encounters in disparate settings, such as schools, mobile clinics, public places, and homes, and is, at times, available for administrative, financial, clinical, and research purposes. Although public health and health services research may require anonymous personal health information, policies and procedures to protect privacy will need to ensure a balance between confidentiality and appropriate access to protected health information.

The trend of rapidly expanding opportunities in health communication intersects with recent demands for more rigorous evaluation of all aspects of the health care and public health delivery systems and for evidence-based practices. Numerous studies of provider–patient communication support the connection among the quality of the provider–patient interaction, patient behavior, and health outcomes. As the knowledge base about provider–patient interactions increases, the need for practice guidelines to promote better provider–patient communication becomes apparent. Additional evidence also is needed to understand the process people use in seeking health information and the role of health information in their decision making. Health communication campaigns could benefit as well from more rigorous formative research and evaluation of outcomes. Expected outcomes should be an important consideration and central element of campaign design. Because health communication increasingly involves electronic media, new evaluation approaches are emerging. Given the critical role communication plays in all aspects of public health and health care, health communication and outcomes research should become more tightly linked across all health communication domains.

Health-conscious consumers increasingly are proactive in seeking out health information. Individuals want information about prevention and wellness as much as about medical problems. Public health and the medical community share an interest in promoting—and sustaining—informed decisions for better health. Surveys suggest that people want to get health information from a professional and that counseling by health professionals can be effective both in reducing lifestyle risks and in supporting self-management of chronic diseases such as diabetes. However, diminished time in clinical visits and some clinicians' discomfort with open communication work against optimum information exchange. In addition, many people want information to be available when and where they need it most. Health information should be easily accessible, of good quality, and relevant for the needs of the individual. The increasing use of the Internet as a source for health information requires greater awareness of the importance of the quality of information.

People with the greatest health burdens often have the least access to information, communication technologies, health care, and supporting social services. Even the most carefully designed health communication programs will have limited impact if underserved communities lack access to crucial health professionals, services, and communication channels that are part of a health improvement project. Research indicates that even after targeted health communication interventions, low-education and low-income groups remain less knowledgeable and less likely to change behavior than higher education and income groups, which creates a knowledge gap and leaves some people chronically uninformed. With communication technologies, the disparity in access to electronic information resources is commonly referred to as the **digital divide**, which becomes more critical as the amount and variety of health resources available over the Internet increase and as people need more sophisticated skills to use electronic resources.

Even with access to information and services, disparities may still exist because many people lack health literacy, which is increasingly vital to help people navigate a complex health care system and better manage their own health. Differences in the ability to read and understand materials related to personal health and knowing how to navigate the health system contribute to health disparities. People with low health literacy are more likely to report poor health, have an incomplete understanding of their health problems and treatment, and be at greater risk of hospitalization. People with chronic conditions, such as asthma, hypertension, and diabetes, and with low reading skills have been found to have less knowledge of their conditions than people with higher reading skills.

To complicate the issue is the fact that health care has a language of its own. There is certainly no shortage of acronyms and new and complex medical terms. In addition, how words are used can be a cause of communication errors. For example, to say that someone has tested positive for cancer may be interpreted as good news to someone whose first language is English. After all, positive means good, right?

According to *Healthy People 2020* (U.S. Department of Health and Human Services, 2010), an individual is considered to be "health literate" when he or she possesses the skills to understand information and services and use them to make appropriate decisions about health. Areas commonly associated with health literacy include:

Patient–physician communication
Drug labeling medical instructions and medical compliance
Health information publications and other resources
Informed consent
Responding to medical and insurance forms
Giving patient history
Public health training
Assessments for allied professional programs, such as social work and speech-language pathology

It is alarming that these skills and strategies are absent in more than half of the U.S. population. This fact is more disturbing when one considers that these are the very skills and strategies that often lead to longer life, improved quality of life, reduction of both chronic disease and health disparities, and cost savings. Health literacy is estimated to cost $106 billion to $238 billion annually (National Network of Libraries of Medicine, 2014).

According to the Agency for Healthcare Research and Quality (AHRQ), low health literacy is linked to higher risk of death and more emergency room visits and hospitalizations. Health literacy may not be related to years of education or general reading ability. A person who functions adequately at home or work may have marginal or inadequate literacy in a health care environment (National Network of Libraries of Medicine, 2014).

The National Assessment of Adult Literacy (NAAL) measures the health literacy of adults living in the United States. Health literacy was reported using four performance levels: Below Basic, Basic, Intermediate, and Proficient. According to the NAAL, approximately 36% of adults in the United States have limited health literacy: 22% have Basic and 14% have Below Basic health literacy. An additional 5% of the population is not literate in English. Only 12% of the population has a proficient health literacy level (National Network of Libraries of Medicine, 2014).

Here are some tips for working with people with low literacy:

- Speak Slowly and Clearly: Not Loudly.

- Repeat if Necessary: Make it clear at the outset that you are happy to repeat anything you say in conversation.

- Avoid Acronyms, Idioms, and Abbreviations: The medical culture has a language of its own that includes many acronyms such as ED, HMO, and NPO. Take the time to say words the long way and avoid terms that will create confusion for non-native speakers. It is best when setting appointments to say "eight o'clock in the morning" instead of "8 a.m." Common expressions and idioms also can block communication. If you say "I'll run that past the doctor," a patient with limited English proficiency may literally picture you running to the doctor, which sounds urgent when you intended a casual tone.

- Write It Down and Demonstrate While Speaking: Providing simple notes about the key points of an office visit and expectations for patient follow-up can be very useful to patients and families with limited English proficiency. Written material with more detailed information about medications and treatments also can be very helpful. Checking for understanding via open ended questions, gesturing while speaking, and demonstrating actions is recommended. Instead of explaining how a topical medication is applied, the health professional can demonstrate how it is done (Carteret, 2012).

For health communication to contribute to the improvement of personal and community health stakeholders, health professionals, researchers, public officials, and the lay public must collaborate on a range of activities. These activities include (1) initiatives to build a robust health information system that provides equitable access; (2) development of high-quality, audience-appropriate information and support services for specific health problems and health-related decisions for all segments of the population, especially for underserved segments; (3) training health professionals in the science of communication and the use of communication technologies; (4) evaluation of interventions; and (5) promotion of a critical understanding and practice of effective health communication.

Closing the gap in health literacy is an issue of fundamental fairness and equity and is essential to reduce health disparities. Public and private efforts need to occur in two areas:

the development of appropriate written materials and improvement in skills of those persons with limited literacy. Effective, culturally and linguistically appropriate, plain language health communications can be created. Professional publications and federal documents provide the criteria to integrate and apply the principles of organization, writing style, layout, and design for effective communication. These criteria should be widely distributed and used. Many organizations, such as public and medical libraries, voluntary, professional, and community groups, and schools, could offer health literacy programs that target skill improvement for low-literacy and limited English proficient individuals. If appropriate materials exist and people receive the training to use them, measurable improvements in health literacy for the least literate can occur.

With the rapidly growing volume of health information, advertising, products, and services available on web and social media sites, serious concerns arise regarding the accuracy, appropriateness, and potential health impact of these sites. People are using the Internet to look up information, purchase medications, consult remotely with providers, and maintain their personal health records. The potential for harm from inaccurate information, inferior quality goods, and inappropriate services is significant. Many initiatives are under way to identify appropriate and feasible approaches to evaluate online health sites. Professional associations are issuing guidelines and recommendations. Federal agencies, such as the Federal Trade Commission, are actively monitoring and sanctioning owners of websites that are false or misleading, and developers and purchasers of online health resources are being urged to adopt standards for quality assurance.

To allow users to evaluate the quality and appropriateness of Internet health resources, health-related sites should publicly disclose the following essential information: (1) the identity of the developers and sponsors of the site (and how to contact them) and information about any potential conflicts of interest or biases; (2) the explicit purpose of the site, including any commercial purposes and advertising; (3) the original sources of the content on the site; (4) how the privacy and confidentiality of any personal information collected from users is protected; (5) how the site is evaluated; and (6) how the content is updated. An additional mark of quality relates to the site's accessibility by all users. Content should be presented in a way that it can be used by people with disabilities and low-end technology.

Culture affects how people perceive and respond to health messages and materials, and it is related to how health behaviors and materials convey culture. Although it is important to acknowledge and understand the cultures within an intended audience, developing separate messages and materials for each cultural group is not necessary or even advisable. For example, when print materials for a state program for low-income people depicted people of only one race, some intended audience members felt singled out and said the materials suggested that only members of their racial group were poor. Careful audience research can help your program identify messages and images that resonate across groups or identify situations in which different messages or images are likely to work best.

That being said, it does not mean that culture should be ignored. According to a Center for Substance Abuse Prevention *Technical Assistance Bulletin*, culturally sensitive communications:

1. Acknowledge culture as a predominant force in shaping behaviors, values, and institutions.

2. Understand and reflect the diversity within cultures. In designing messages that are culturally appropriate, the following dimensions are important:
   - *Primary cultural factors* linked to race, ethnicity, language, nationality, and religion
   - *Secondary cultural factors* linked to age, gender, sexual orientation, educational level, occupation, income level, and acculturation to mainstream society

3. Reflect and respect the attitudes and values of the intended audience; some examples of attitudes and values that are interrelated to culture include:
   - Whether the individual or the community is of primary importance
   - Accepted roles of men, women, and children
   - Preferred family structure (nuclear or extended)
   - Relative importance of folk wisdom, life experience, and value of common sense compared to formal-education-specific situations and advanced degrees
   - Ways that wealth is measured (material goods, personal relationships)
   - Relative value put on different age groups (youth versus elders)
   - Whether people are more comfortable with traditions or open to new ways
   - Favorite and forbidden foods
   - Body language, particularly whether touching or proximity is permitted in specific situations
   - Manner of dress and adornment

4. Refer to cultural groups using terms that members of the group prefer (e.g., many people resent the term "minority" or "nonwhite." Preferred terms are often based on nationality, such as Japanese or Lakota).

5. Substituting culturally specific images, spokespeople, language, or other executional detail is not sufficient unless the messages have been tested and found to resonate with the intended audience.

6. Use the language of the intended audience, carefully developed and tested with the involvement of the audience.

You may have a message that you want to target to a particular cultural group in which you need to take specific cultural factors into consideration. For example, if you have developed a suicide prevention hotline for Asian Americans that provides services in a variety of Asian languages, you would not want the hotline number to contain a number that means death in any of the Asian cultures. Colors also have a wide variety of meanings in different cultures, so do your research. Also, some cultures do not respond well to health messages that try to induce change through fear, so be cautious of the images that you use. Of course, be sure to deliver your message at the appropriate language(s) and literacy levels.

Delivering Your Health Message

There are many ways to deliver your health message. Some methods have been shown to work better with specific cultures. For example, promotores(as) programs often are successful with the Hispanic population, and ethnic newspapers work well with older Asian

Americans. It is important to look for model programs (also known as promising practices) when designing your implementation strategy. Two interventions you may not be familiar with that have been shown to be popular among certain ethnic groups are presented in the following sections.

Promotores

Promotores and promotoras are community members who promote health in their own communities. They provide leadership, peer education, and resources to support community empowerment (Migrant Health Promotion, 2005). As members of minority and underserved populations, they are in a unique position to build on strengths and to address unmet health needs in their communities. Promotores(as) integrate information about health and the health care system into the community's culture, language, and value system, thus reducing many of the barriers to health services. They provide peer education, support, and links to services. They also help make health care systems more responsive. With the appropriate resources, training, and support, promotores(as) improve the health of their communities by linking their neighbors to health care and social services, by educating their peers about disease and injury prevention, by working to make available services more accessible, and by mobilizing their communities to create positive change.

Organizations may refer to promotores(as) as "promotores(as) de salud," which literally means "health promoters." In English, most promotores(as) call themselves community health workers, but there are many additional labels, including:

- Camp health aides
- Colonia health workers
- Lay health advisers
- Outreach workers
- Community health representatives
- Indigenous or village health workers

Promotores(as) conduct outreach in clients' homes and at community centers, clinics, hospitals, schools, work sites, shelters, and farmworker labor camps. Many promotores(as) programs focus on serving the needs of specific ethnic or racial groups, and others focus on vulnerable segments of the population or prominent health problems. Promotores(as) engage in a broad range of activities, but they share a number of common roles by providing (Migrant Health Promotion, 2005):

- A link between communities and health and human service agencies
- Informal counseling and support
- Culturally competent health education
- Advocacy

- Capacity building on individual and community levels
- First aid and emergency assistance

Promotores(as) effectively address many barriers to better health for underserved populations. Some of their accomplishments include (Migrant Health Promotion, 2005):

- Improving access to services
- Helping people understand the health and social service system
- Enhancing client and health provider communication
- Increasing appropriate rates of service utilization
- Decreasing costs for organizations and government programs
- Improving adherence to health recommendations
- Reducing the need for emergency and specialty services
- Improving overall community health status

Promotores(as) accomplish these and other outcomes by providing education and advocacy and building capacity in their communities (Migrant Health Promotion, 2005).

Fotonovelas

Fotonovelas are imaged-based interventions that are popular among Mexicans and Latin Americans. Fotonovelas are illustrated with photos, and these comic books with complex perspectives and dark imagery have had a long history and a far-reaching impact within the Latino and Chicano communities in the United States as well as Mexico and Latin America, where they continue to thrive in the popular culture (Independent Television Service, 2008).

In the United States, the fotonovela/historieta has a distinct manifestation in the Chicano/Latino community, providing a unique idiom through which the community addresses social concerns using a highly innovative visual language (Independent Television Service, 2008). Because of its popularity and flexibility, the fotonovela has been used in increasingly fresh ways by visual artists and writers to address important social issues within the Chicano/Latino community (Independent Television Service, 2008). Activists and religious groups also have turned to the form as an organizational tool for outreach and education, and to induce someone to convert to their own religious faith or political party. Fotonovelas are becoming more commonly used in public health as a way of delivering health information in a more creative manner. A representative from the Rural Women's Health Project ([RWHP] n.d.) stated:

> RWHP fotonovelas reflect the struggles of communities in a positive light, incorporating role models who balance socio-cultural obstacles and disease prevention. The visual aspects of the novela are enticing and the style allows the reader to explore the health topics, increase self-identification and risk, and strengthen cultural identity.

According to RWHP, the organization utilizes community actors and messages specific to the target community, and the fotonovelas successfully present health messages, document the work of communities, and unify them to both improve individual and community well-being. "The minimal text, popular language, and visuals of the fotonovelas allow them to be easily read by any community. These elements make fotonovelas an excellent educational tool for outreach workers, youth, and discussion groups" (RWHP, n.d.).

Source: Reprinted with permission from Rural Women's Health Project.

Printed Materials

Printed materials can be created in numerous forms, including newsletters, booklets, pamphlets, flyers, and newspapers. They can be placed on billboards, bathroom walls, and buses, or they can be inserted in envelopes with paychecks. Regardless of where they are, be sure your message is appropriate for your target audience.

Some issues to consider are literacy levels and language. You can check the literacy level by using the Fry Readability Graph (see **Figure 6.1**) or the Flesch-Kincaid Grade Level score, which is built into Microsoft Word.

Source: Reprinted with permission from Rural Women's Health Project (n.d.).

Fry Readability Graph

Directions for use of the Fry Readability Graph:

- Randomly select three 100-word passages from a book or an article.
- Plot the average number of syllables and the average number of sentences per 100 words on the graph to determine the grade level of the material.
- Choose more passages per book if great variability is observed and conclude that the book has uneven readability.
- Few books will fall into the solid black area, but when they do, grade level scores are invalid.

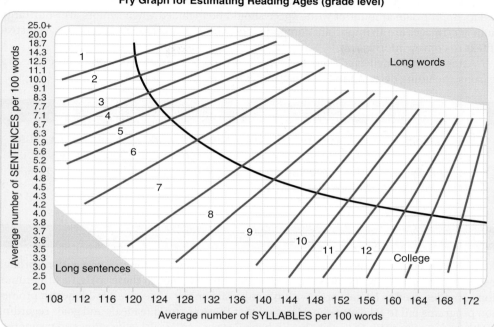

Fry Graph for Estimating Reading Ages (grade level)

FIGURE 6.1

Fry Readability Graph.

Source: Discovery Education (1995).

Additional Directions for Working Readability Graph:

• Randomly select three sample passages and count exactly 100 words beginning with the beginning of a sentence. Do not count numbers. Do count proper nouns.

• Count the number of sentences in the 100 words, estimating length of the fraction of the last sentence to the nearest 1/10th.

• Count the total number of syllables in the 100-word passage. If you do not have a hand counter available, an easy way is to simply place a mark above each syllable in the word, then, when you get to the end of the passage, count the number of marks and add 100.

• Enter graph with average sentence length and number of syllables; plot dot where the two lines intersect. Area where dot is plotted will give you the approximate grade level.

• If a great deal of variability is found, putting more sample counts into the average is desirable (Discovery Education, 1995).

You also will want to consider visual readability. For example, fonts should be made larger and an appropriate amount of white space should be included when seniors are your target audience. Images are an important component of printed materials. They can be used instead of text to convey information.

After you have delivered your message, you need to evaluate your program for several reasons, including determining its effectiveness.

What Do You Think?

What are some communication methods that would work well with your culture? What images or phrases do you suggest? What communication channels would work well? Why would you recommend these? What methods, images, phrases, or channels would not work well and why?

Public Health Programs

Public health efforts focus on health promotion and disease and injury prevention through research, community intervention, and education. To accomplish these goals, health promotion activities need to be delivered within a cultural context. One-size-fits-all health promotion programs fail to take into consideration that there are unique ideals and goals regarding health and various ways to initiate health behavior change. Health education and promotion programs for diverse populations are challenging, but to be successful, the cultural dimensions of the target audience must be considered.

Interventions for promoting health and disease prevention in any population require systematic planning. This organized effort requires an understanding of the culture of the target audience because culture is a strong force in the determinants of health and behavior change. Although the overall steps to program development are the same, distinct factors need to be taken into consideration when your audience is diverse. Planning models can be useful in this process.

Planning Models

Models and theories are planning tools that assist with understanding the causes of behaviors, predicting behaviors, and evaluating programs. Models are the starting place on which to build, and they can serve different purposes, which is why so many models exist. Promoting health in a multicultural setting requires using models that take the cultural context into consideration. Two planning models are briefly described here: the Health Belief Model and the PRECEDE–PROCEED model. An in-depth discussion of program planning models is outside the scope of this chapter.

Health Belief Model

The Health Belief Model (HBM) is a psychological model that attempts to explain and predict health behaviors by focusing on the attitudes and beliefs of individuals. The HBM was

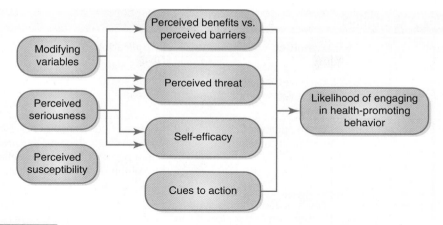

FIGURE 6.2

Health Belief Model.

developed in the 1950s as part of an effort by social psychologists in the U.S. Public Health Service to explain the lack of public participation in health screening and prevention programs (e.g., a free and conveniently located tuberculosis screening project). Their focus was on increasing the use of preventive services, such as chest x-rays for tuberculosis screening and immunizations.

The developers assumed that people feared diseases and that health actions were motivated in relation to the degree of fear (perceived threat). If the potential benefits outweighed practical and psychological obstacles to taking action (net benefits), they expected that action would occur. The HBM was one of the first models that adapted theory from the behavioral sciences to health problems, and it remains one of the most widely recognized conceptual frameworks of health behavior. The HBM has been adapted to explore a variety of long- and short-term health behaviors, including sexual risk behaviors and the transmission of HIV. The key variables of the HBM are given in **Figure 6.2**.

It is important to note that a wide variety of demographic (i.e., age, gender, ethnicity, race), social and psychological (i.e., personality, social status, group pressure), and structural variables (i.e., prior experience with the disease, knowledge about the health condition) also may influence people's perceptions and have an impact on their health behaviors. Ways that these constructs can be applied are described in **Table 6.2**.

The HBM can be applied to multicultural health in several ways. For example, if a person has a fatalistic perception of how disease develops, the program planner should work with that ideology because that person's idea about perceived susceptibility would be very different from that of a person with a Western perspective.

PRECEDE–PROCEED Framework

The PRECEDE–PROCEED framework, illustrated in **Figure 6.3**, is an approach to planning that examines the factors that contribute to behavior change. PRECEDE is an acronym for

TABLE 6.2   Applications of the Health Belief Model

Concept	Definition	Application
Perceived threat	Consists of two parts: perceived susceptibility and perceived severity of a health condition.	Explain how anyone can contract the disease and how easily it is spread.
Perceived susceptibility	One's opinion of chances of getting a condition.	Define population(s) at risk and the degree of risk. Personalize risk based on a person's features or behavior. Heighten perceived susceptibility if it is too low.
Perceived severity	One's opinion of how serious a condition and the condition that follows are as a result of the disease.	Explain the consequences of the risk and the condition.
Perceived benefits	One's opinion of the benefits of the action to reduce risk or seriousness of impact.	Clarify the positive effects to be expected from the behavior change.
Perceived barriers	One's opinion of the tangible and psychological costs of the advised action.	Identify and reduce barriers through reassurance, incentives, education, and assistance.
Cues to action	Strategies to activate change.	Provide how-to information, promote awareness, initiate media campaigns, write a newspaper or magazine article, provide reminders such as a postcard from a dentist or physician, obtain a friend's or family member's recommendation.
Self-efficacy	Confidence in one's ability to take action.	Provide training, guidance in performing action, and role modeling.

Source: Adapted from The Communication Initiative Network (2003).

Predisposing, **R**einforcing, and **E**nabling **C**onstructs in **E**ducational/ **E**cological **D**iagnosis and **E**valuation, and PROCEED is an acronym for **P**olicy, **R**egulatory, and **O**rganizational **C**onstructs in **E**ducational and **E**nvironmental **D**evelopment (McKenzie, Neiger, & Thackeray, 2009).

The factors that contribute to behavior change are described as follows:

- *Predisposing factors.* The individual's knowledge, attitudes, behavior, beliefs, and values before the intervention that affect their willingness to change

- *Enabling factors.* Factors in the environment or community of an individual that facilitate change

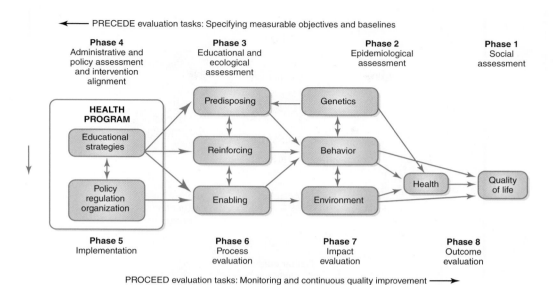

←—— PRECEDE evaluation tasks: Specifying measurable objectives and baselines

Phase 4	Phase 3	Phase 2	Phase 1
Administrative and policy assessment and intervention alignment	Educational and ecological assessment	Epidemiological assessment	Social assessment

Phase 5	Phase 6	Phase 7	Phase 8
Implementation	Process evaluation	Impact evaluation	Outcome evaluation

PROCEED evaluation tasks: Monitoring and continuous quality improvement ——→

FIGURE 6.3

PRECEDE–PROCEED Model.

Source: Reprinted with permission from The Community Toolbox (2007).

- *Reinforcing factors.* The positive or negative effects of adopting the behavior that influence continuing the behavior

The PRECEDE part of the model entails the planning steps that should occur prior to the intervention, and the PROCEED component includes the phases that should occur during and after the intervention.

Evaluating Your Multicultural Health Program

Effective program evaluation is a systematic way to improve and account for public health actions by involving procedures that are useful, feasible, ethical, and accurate. The Centers for Disease Control and Prevention ([CDC] 1999) developed a framework to guide public health professionals in using program evaluations. It is a practical, nonprescriptive tool designed to summarize and organize the essential elements of effective program evaluation (see **Figure 6.4**).

The framework is composed of six steps that must be taken in any evaluation. They are starting points for tailoring an evaluation to a particular public health effort at a particular time. Because the steps are all interdependent, they might be encountered in a nonlinear

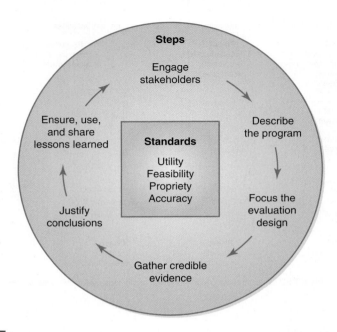

FIGURE 6.4

Recommended framework for program evaluation.

Source: Centers for Disease Control and Prevention (1999).

sequence; however, an order exists for fulfilling each—earlier steps provide the foundation for subsequent progress (see **Figure 6.4**).

Evaluation is a large subject and will not be covered in detail here because there are many other resources on the topic. For general information on public health evaluation, we suggest that you review the CDC (1999) document. There are numerous other sources as well.

The focus here is on illuminating the differences between traditional evaluation and **multicultural evaluation** and presenting strategies for making your program evaluation sensitive to diverse populations. The information in this section includes excerpts from *Commissioning Multicultural Evaluation: A Foundation Resource Guide* (Inouye, Yu, & Adefuin, 2005). Other resources include *Voices from the Field: Health and Evaluation Leaders on Multicultural Evaluation* (The California Endowment, 2003), which offers different perspectives on multicultural evaluation and how to advance this approach in the health field, and *Multicultural Health Evaluation: An Annotated Bibliography* (Adefuin & Endo, 2003), which highlights key literature on the theory and practice of multicultural evaluation.

Evaluation has come to serve a vital function for foundations, policy makers, and programs as they rely on evaluation as a tool for management, strategic planning, and accountability. In recent years, however, critical questions have been raised about how existing evaluation is still largely rooted in a Eurocentric worldview. Researchers are beginning to question the extent to which existing evaluation frameworks and measures present valid findings across multiple dimensions of diversity, such as race, ethnicity, economic status, gender, sexual orientation, age, religion, disability, or immigration status.

Multicultural evaluation integrates cultural considerations into its theory, measures, analysis, and practice. It requires a conceptual framework that incorporates different world-views and value systems, engages in data collection strategies that take into account potential cultural and linguistic barriers, includes a reexamination of established evaluation measures for cultural appropriateness, and incorporates creative strategies for ensuring culturally competent analysis and creative dissemination of findings to diverse audiences. Multicultural evaluation, like traditional evaluation, prioritizes impartial inquiry designed to provide information to decision makers and other parties interested in a particular program, policy, or intervention. In addition, multicultural evaluation aims to:

• Demystify issues of cultural difference so that relevant, culturally based knowledge can be brought to bear in problem solving and strategic planning

• Distinguish the effects of race and ethnicity, immigrant status, age, socioeconomic factors, gender, sexual orientation, and so forth

• Build diverse community members' and target populations' capacities for self-assessing community needs, cultural resources, and solutions

Principles stand as a professional cornerstone to create standards of excellence, but a widely adopted set of principles for multicultural evaluation has not yet been formalized. However, philanthropic leaders, scholars, evaluators, practitioners, and others are beginning to unite around a common set of principles for multicultural evaluation. A synthesis of some of the key principles includes:

Inclusion in design and implementation

• Multicultural evaluation is not imposed on diverse communities; communities understand and support the rationale for the research and agree with the methods used to answer key evaluation questions.

• Diverse beneficiary stakeholders are actively involved in all phases of the evaluation, including problem definition, development of research questions, methods chosen, data collection, analysis, and reporting.

• To the extent possible, multicultural evaluation empowers diverse communities to do self-evaluation through intentional capacity building in evaluation.

Acknowledgment/infusion of multiple worldviews

• Evaluators in multicultural evaluations have a genuine respect for communities that are being studied and seek deep understanding of different cultural contexts, practices, and paradigms of thinking.

• Expert knowledge does not exclusively reside with the evaluator; the community being studied is assumed to know best their issues, strengths, and challenges.

- The diversity of the communities being studied is represented in multicultural evaluation staffing and expertise whenever possible.

Cultural and systems analysis

- Multicultural evaluations take into account how historical and current social systems, institutions, and societal norms contribute to power and outcome disparities across different racial and ethnic communities.
- Multicultural evaluations incorporate and trace impacts of factors related to racial, cultural, gender, religious, economic, and other differences.
- Multicultural evaluation questions take a multilevel approach to understanding root causes and impact at the individual, interpersonal, institutional, cultural, system, and policy levels, rather than focusing the analysis solely on individual behavior.

Appropriate measures of success

- Measures of success in multicultural evaluations are discussed and/or collaboratively developed with those being evaluated.
- Data collection instruments and outcome measures are tested for multicultural validity across populations that may be non-English speaking, less literate, or from a different culture.
- Multicultural evaluation data collection methods and instruments accommodate different cultural contexts and consider alternative or nontraditional ways of collecting data.

Relevance to diverse communities

- Multicultural evaluations inform community decision making and program design.
- Findings from multicultural evaluations are co-owned with diverse communities and shared in culturally appropriate ways.

These principles align closely with the five guiding principles adopted by the American Evaluation Association as quality standards of practice for the profession: (1) systematic inquiry, (2) competence, (3) integrity/honesty, (4) respect for people, and (5) responsibilities for general and public welfare. The guiding principles for multicultural evaluation, however, imply a higher threshold that takes into account these generally accepted standards of quality evaluation while overlaying explicit consideration of differences related to diversity in race and ethnicity, age, gender, sexual orientation, socioeconomic status, religion, disability, and/or immigrant status.

Multicultural evaluation is built from core elements of sound evaluation practices, such as data-based inquiry, valid and reliable measures, and impartial assessment. Multicultural evaluation also reflects characteristics of quality evaluations based on guidelines set forth by the American Evaluation Association, such as strongly respecting stakeholders' self-worth, considering perspectives of a full range of stakeholders, and (where feasible) providing benefit to those who contribute data. When the principles of multicultural evaluation are applied to all aspects of evaluation—from the evaluator; to design and planning; to data collection, analysis, reporting, and application of findings—the result is a significant shift in how evaluation is implemented. The characteristics of a multicultural evaluation are shown in **Table 6.3**.

Traditional evaluation is based on a long history in which formally trained evaluators implement needs or impact assessments based on established measures of what is good practice. Multicultural evaluation is characterized by **reciprocity**. Evaluators integrate their own expertise throughout the evaluation, but the evaluator does not presume to understand the cultural context of diverse communities that are being studied. As a result, multicultural evaluation is characterized by a fundamental shift in how the evaluation is conceptualized and designed, how communities are engaged in data collection and analysis, and how the findings from the evaluation are ultimately communicated and used.

TABLE 6.3   Characteristics of a Multicultural Evaluation

	Traditional Evaluation	→	Multicultural Evaluation
Evaluator			
Where knowledge resides	Formally trained evaluators are the experts	→	Grantees, community members, and formally trained evaluators each have expertise. Each knows best their issues and strengths.
Evaluator role	Leader, judge, expert	→	Facilitator, translator, convener.
Design and planning	Evaluator presents design to commissioning entity for approval	→	Prioritizes developing rapport and trust with stakeholders to engage them in an inclusive planning process that infuses multiple worldviews.
Data collection	Conducted by evaluation professional	→	Conducted by all players. Facilitated by the evaluator; stakeholders are often trained in some collection methods and then implement them.
Data analysis	Results and their meaning are analyzed by evaluation professionals	→	Results and their meaning are derived with a focus on culture and system analysis.
Reporting	Written report, usually accompanied by brief presentation to commissioning entity	→	Jointly disseminated and presented in nontraditional formats. Results have relevance and utility to diverse communities.
Application of findings	Findings used as monitoring, judging device	→	Findings used to build capacity of community and community organizations.

Source: Inouye, Yu, and Adefuin (2005).

Closely related to understanding the principles and characteristics of multicultural evaluation is defining the characteristics of evaluators that make them culturally competent. Attributes of multicultural evaluators' competence do not lend themselves to a checklist or a formula. Rather, the multicultural knowledge, attitudes, and skill sets that evaluators bring to their work can best be viewed as evolving human skills that are developed over time. Some of the most often described characteristics are:

- *Experience in diverse communities.* Although an evaluator may not necessarily be from the same cultural background as the people in the communities he or she is evaluating, cultural competence involves a broader world perspective, often gained from experience living or working with different cultural groups.

- *Openness to learning about cultural complexities.* Culturally competent evaluators exhibit humility about what they think they already know and are open to in-depth understanding of the nuances and complexities of inter- and intracultural influences and variations.

- *Flexibility in evaluation design and practice.* Rather than coming in with prescriptive evaluation strategies, culturally competent evaluators realize limitations to established approaches and are willing to adapt to honor different cultural contexts.

- *Rapport and trust with diverse communities.* Culturally competent evaluators prioritize relationship building with diverse communities rather than viewing them solely as data sources. Relationships are viewed as mutually beneficial.

- *Acknowledgment of power differentials.* Culturally competent evaluators acknowledge the various power differentials possible in an evaluation, including those between the evaluator and those being evaluated, or between the commissioning entity (often a foundation) and those being evaluated.

- *Self-reflection for recognizing cultural biases.* Culturally competent evaluators take the time to become mindful of potential biases and prejudices and how they might be incorporated into their research.

- *Translation and mediation across diverse groups.* Culturally competent evaluators are skilled in translating jargon-laden evaluation findings to those who may not be trained in evaluation or have high levels of education, literacy, or English-language fluency. Likewise, evaluators also must be adept in communicating cultural paradigms and community voice back to funders.

- *Comprehension of historic and institutional oppression.* An understanding of oppression is critical for designing evaluations that integrate how historic and current social systems, institutions, and societal norms contribute to disparities among different communities.

The power imbalances that are inherent within both funder–grantee relationships and evaluator–community relationships require specific and explicit attention throughout the evaluation process. Understanding and implementing multicultural evaluation approaches is an ongoing process. A meaningful shift toward multicultural evaluation will be determined greatly by the individual and collective beliefs, experiences, and will of the people within the organization. Therefore, as with many personal or institutional journeys toward change, the path toward multicultural evaluation can be considered a progression along a continuum.

Table 6.4 maps the implementation of multicultural evaluation principles (outlined earlier) along a stepwise continuum. This continuum is adapted from the stages of cultural

TABLE 6.4   Continuum of Multicultural Evaluation

Principle	Cultural Incompetence	Cultural Blindness	Cultural Sensitivity	Cultural Proficiency
Inclusive design and implementation.	Evaluation designed to be accountable to the board; community largely unaware evaluation is happening and is uninvolved in any aspect of the evaluation.	Communities may be involved in evaluation, but no consideration for representation of multiple and diverse community voices.	Recognizing different cultural contexts, evaluation gathers input from diverse communities, typically through one-time requests for feedback. Community members may feel that their input is tokenized.	Diverse communities are involved in meaningful ways from start to finish. Evaluation is accountable to *multiple* stakeholders, including grantees and community beneficiaries.
Acknowledgment and infusion of multiple worldviews.	Funder assumptions and beliefs drive the evaluation; different perspectives and worldviews not acknowledged.	Mainstream values, beliefs, and perspectives drive evaluation; these are presumed to apply to diverse communities being studied.	Culturally competent evaluation strategies in place (e.g., translation of survey instruments; evaluators that reflect the diversity of community being studied; co-interpretation of findings). Evaluator still holds primary expertise.	Culturally competent evaluation strategies in place; evaluator approaches study with an intentional sense of humility; and expert knowledge is equally shared by evaluator and community being studied.

(Continues)

TABLE 6.4   Continuum of Multicultural Evaluation *(Continued)*

Principle	Cultural Incompetence	Cultural Blindness	Cultural Sensitivity	Cultural Proficiency
Cultural and systems analysis.	Cultural and systemic power differences are not realized.	Cultural and systemic power differences are ignored.	Cultural and systemic power differences are acknowledged, but not analyzed.	In-depth analysis of cultural and systemic power influences on a community is incorporated into findings.
Appropriate measures of success.	Evaluation does not consider the diversity of data sources or the relevance of methodology or measures.	Diversity may be acknowledged, but grantees and/or community success still judged using traditional methods and measures (often for the sake of "technical rigor").	Although traditional evaluation measures may still be used, additional strategies are in place to strengthen multicultural validity of findings (e.g., multimethod data collection, diversity considerations incorporated in analysis).	Validity of frameworks, tools, measures tested across *multiple* cultural groups, languages, and contexts; they are accordingly modified and/or new measures developed.
Relevance and utility to diverse community.	Funder and/or evaluator priorities drive evaluation; results kept from communities because there is no recognition of their value to community or because it is assumed that they won't understand.	Results might be shared back but with no consideration of how they might be interpreted or used. Results are not useful because they are not rooted in multicultural analysis.	Results consider cultural context and are shared with community, but community may not feel ownership of results and dissemination because of their limited role in the evaluation.	Because of joint development, results are culturally relevant and used constructively for program improvement for diverse communities. There is consideration of how to share findings in culturally appropriate ways.

Source: Inouye, Yu, and Adefuin (2005).

competency that were developed for the service delivery field. It assumes that the implementation of evaluation principles unfolds in four stages:

- *Cultural incompetence.* Diverse cultures are not acknowledged in evaluation.
- *Cultural blindness.* Awareness of diversity may exist but is not presumed to be a critical factor within evaluation design or implementation.
- *Cultural sensitivity.* Acknowledgment of cultural differences exists, and steps are taken to incorporate cultural considerations within existing evaluation models.
- *Cultural proficiency.* The way that evaluations are designed and implemented are fundamentally shifted to honor and capitalize upon the diverse cultural contexts in which target populations exist.

A true shift to a multicultural paradigm takes time. The extent to which some or all of the multicultural evaluation steps are incorporated into evaluation practice will determine whether researchers and foundations are harbingers of the shifts that can revolutionize the evaluation world.

Summary

Communication is central to health and must take cultural, literacy, and language barriers into consideration. When developing and delivering a health promotion program, there are additional considerations when the audience is a cultural group other than your own or composed of a diverse group. It is important that planners are sensitive and considerate of these differences to avoid wasting resources and possibly offending people.

In this chapter models for program planning and ways to deliver and evaluate your program were provided. The delivery method includes considering the content of your message as well as how it is disseminated. Some methods of delivery, such as promotores(as), work better with some cultural and ethnic groups than others. After the program is complete, evaluation is essential. You will want to be sure that your message is received as you intended and see what impact it has had on your target audience. We outlined some differences between traditional and multicultural evaluation, which should be considered.

Review

1. What is health communication?
2. What are some issues to consider when using written communication?
3. What is health literacy and why is it important?
4. How can you check the reading level of a document?
5. What are promotores (as) and fotonovelas?
6. What are the concepts of the Health Belief Model and the PRECEDE–PROCEED Model?
7. How are traditional and multicultural evaluations different?

Activity

Locate six to eight written health communication documents that are targeted to the same population. In a paper, describe the similarities and differences in the outreach documents and discuss why you expect that they would be successful or unsuccessful. Support your statements by referring to published literature. For example, if you state that the images include staple foods in that culture, cite literature indicating that the foods in the written materials are staple foods in that culture.

Case Study

In a city in Northern California, the Director in the Department of Public Health, Alice, noticed that the county has a very high rate of hepatitis B among the Asian American population. Hepatitis B is a disease caused by the hepatitis B virus. The most common ways that most people get hepatitis B are sexual contact with a person infected with hepatitis B, exposure to needles, medical or dental procedures where instruments are contaminated with hepatitis B virus, or when a mother passes hepatitis B to an infant at birth. The virus can live outside of the body for up to seven days. The disease can be prevented by a vaccine, and blood tests are used to determine if someone is infected. Alice knows that most Asians become infected while in the womb and not by sexual contact or exposure to needles from drug use. She is concerned that a major public information campaign must be designed to engage the Asian population but not imply to the general community that Asians have a major drug abuse problem. She has organized a meeting with her staff to discuss how to address the disparity.

Consider these related questions:

1. What information should Alice ask her staff to collect about the Asian American population in the county?
2. How should Alice and her team decide what communication campaign is best to use?
3. How should the materials be developed and tested?

References

Adefuin, J., & Edo, T. (2003). *Multicultural health evaluation: An annotated bibliography*. Woodland Hills, CA: The California Endowment.

California Endowment, The. (2003). *Voices from the field: Health and evaluation leaders on multicultural evaluation.* Woodland Hills, CA: Author.

Carteret, M. (2012). *8 tips for communicating with limited English proficiency patients.* Retrieved from http://www.dimensionsofculture.com/2010/10/8-tips-for-communicating-with-limited-english-proficiency-patients/

Centers for Disease Control and Prevention. (1999, September 17). Framework for public health and evaluation. *Morbidity and Mortality Weekly Report, 48.*

Communication Initiative Network, The. (2003). *Health belief model.*

Community Toolbox, The. (2007). *PRECEDE–PROCEED.* Retrieved from http://ctb.ku.edu/tools/sub_section_main_1008.htm

Discovery Education. (1995). *Kathy Schrock's guide for educators. Fry's readability graph.* Retrieved from http://school.discovery.com/schrockguide/fry/fry.html

Galanti, G. (2000, May). Culture and medicine. An introduction to cultural differences. *Caring for Patients from Different Cultures, 172,* 335–336. Retrieved from http://gagalanti.com/articles/Intro.pdf

Independent Television Service. (2008). *What is a foto-novela?* Retrieved from http://www.pbs.org/independentlens/fotonovelas2/what.html

Inouye, T. E., Yu, H. C., & Adefuin, J. (2005). *Commissioning multicultural evaluation: A foundation resource guide.* Retrieved from https://www.leadershiplearning.org/system.files/multicult_eval_rpt.pdf

Kung, E. Y. L., Chan, A. C., Chong, Y. S., Pham, T., & Hsu-Hage, B. H. H. (1997). Promoting breast screen in Melbourne Chinese women using ethnic-specific health promotion strategies. *Internet Journal of Health Promotion.* Retrieved from http://rhpeo.net/ijhp-articles/1997/3/index.htm

McKenzie, J. F., Neiger, B. L., & Thackeray, R. (2009). *Planning, implementing, & evaluating health promotion programs: A primer.* San Francisco, CA: Pearson/Benjamin Cummings.

Migrant Health Promotion. (2005). *Who are promotores(as)?* Retrieved from http://www.migranthealth.org/our_programs/who_are_promotora.php

National Network of Libraries of Medicine. (2014). *Health literacy.* Retrieved from http://nnlm.gov/outreach/consumer/hlthlit.html#A4

Rural Women's Health Project. (n.d.). *What is a fotonovela?* Retrieved from http://www.rwhp.org/catalog_info/whatis.html

U.S. Department of Health and Human Services. (2020). *Healthy people 2020: Understanding and improving health.* Washington, DC: US Government Printing Office.

U.S. Department of Health and Human Services. (2001). *Making health communications programs work* (NIH Publication No. 04-5145). Bethesda, MD: Author.

UNIT II

Specific Cultural Groups

© Diana Lundin/Dreamstime.com

© wong sze yuen/Shutterstock, Inc.

© Fotoluminate LLC/Shutterstock, Inc.

© Monkey Business Images/Shutterstock, Inc.

© Larry Dale Gordon/Getty Images

CHAPTER 7

Hispanic and Latino American Populations

Preservation of one's own culture does not require contempt or disrespect for other cultures.
—Cesar Chavez

Key Concepts

Familismo

Respeto

Hispanic paradox

Susto

Mal de ojo

Evil eye

Empacho

Curandero(a)

Santeria

Orishas

Espiritismo

Learning Objectives

After reading this chapter, you should be able to:

1. Provide an overview of the social and economic circumstances of Hispanics in the United States.
2. Provide an overview of Hispanic beliefs about the causes of illness.
3. Describe at least three culture-bound illnesses among Hispanics.
4. Describe Hispanics' health risk behaviors and common illnesses.
5. List at least six tips for working with Hispanic populations.

formally (e.g., Mrs. Martinez), but also personally (e.g., How are your children?). The length of the social interaction is often viewed to be less important than the quality (Rhode Island Department of Health, n.d.).

Hispanics tend to avoid conflict and criticism and prefer smooth social relations based on politeness and respect (Rhode Island Department of Health, n.d.). Overt disagreement is not considered appropriate behavior. Many Hispanics are characterized by warm, friendly, and affectionate relationships. Personal space is close and frequently shared with family members or close friends. Many Hispanics, particularly if they were not raised in the United States, may avoid direct eye contact with authority figures or in awkward situations. Many will nod affirmatively but not necessarily mean agreement. Silence may mean failure to understand and embarrassment about asking or disagreeing.

The family is considered a reliable source of health information. The family also is influential in health-seeking behaviors. They generally have a fatalistic worldview and an external locus of control, and this influences their help-seeking behaviors as well. There also is a belief that poor health is the fault of the individual and hence illness is a punishment from God. Expressing negative feelings is impolite, and people from this cultural group may not complain when health problems occur. Consistent with the importance of respect, modesty and privacy are important; therefore, health issues that are stigmatized should be discussed through an interpreter and not family members. Legally, family members should not be used as interpreters, but when one is used as interpreter, if the issue is personal, try to use a family member of the same gender. Sexuality issues are difficult to discuss. Often the word for sex (*sexo*) is not even used; *tener relaciones* (to have relations) is used instead (Rhode Island Department of Health, n.d.).

It is believed that the close family structure is a contributing factor to what is called the **Hispanic paradox**. In 1986, Kyriakos Markides coined the expression "Hispanic epidemiological paradox" to refer to what appears to be surprisingly good health outcomes for Hispanics for mortality relative to non-Hispanic whites and other minorities (Markides & Coreil, 1986). For example, mortality among Hispanic males has been reported as being 26% lower in 2012 than non-Hispanic white males, and mortality among Hispanic females is 39% lower for non-Hispanic white females (National Center for Health Statistics [NCHS], 2014). In 2013, a review of 58 studies conducted between 1990 and 2010 and involving 4,615,747 participants showed that Hispanic populations had a 17.5% lower risk of mortality compared with other racial groups (Ruis, Steffen, & Smith, 2013). Several efforts to explain this as errors in reporting, self-selection of healthy people entering the United States, or that Hispanics who are ill return to their prior country have not been sustained. It has likewise been suggested and conceded by Kyriako Markides that the support and "love" associated with strong family ties may contribute to the apparent positive outcomes (Yasmin, 2014).

General Philosophy About Disease Prevention and Health Maintenance

Hispanics generallly view health as being and looking clean, being able to rest and sleep well, feeling good and happy, and having the ability to perform in one's expected role as mother, father, worker, and so forth. In Puerto Rico, the phrase *llenitos y limpios* (clean and not too thin) is used (Rhode Island Department of Health, n.d.). A person's well-being depends upon a balance of emotional, physical, and social factors, and when they are not in balance, illness occurs. Some attribute physical illness to *los nervios*, believing that illness results from having experienced a strong emotional state. Thus they try to prevent illness by avoiding intense rage, sadness, and other emotions (Rhode Island Department of Health, n.d.). Depression is not talked about openly.

Did You Know?

Even though you might think low income is always associated with health risks, the rate for low-birth-weight infants born to first-generation and less acculturated Mexican immigrant women is the same as that of non-Hispanic whites, and half that of African Americans with similar risks. It appears that sociocultural rather than genetic variables are the primary factors associated with this phenomenon. Higher levels of acculturation to North American values and lifestyle in Mexican American childbearing women have been correlated with poor perinatal outcomes, including low birth weight (Callister & Birkhead, 2002).

Worldview

Hispanics tend to value closeness, so touching and embracing are common. Sustained eye contact with an older person is considered rude; direct eye contact with superiors is viewed as being disrespectful. This may not be relevant to second and third generation Hispanics. Using formal names and greeting with a handshake are signs of respect, and health care providers should address and greet Hispanics in this way. Inquiring about family before discussing the health issues is a way of gaining trust. Health care providers should engage in "small talk" before addressing the patient's health concerns (Purnell, 2013). Hispanics are reluctant to speak about some topics with health care providers, such as sexuality, but otherwise they are open to discussing their physical problems with providers. This group uses both complementary and alternative medicine (CAM) and allopathic medical care. It is important for health care providers to inquire about the CAM used.

Hispanics tend to be present oriented, so disease prevention may not be a priority. They may arrive late for appointments due to their relaxed sense of time. The social structure is a collectivistic one that values interdependence and cooperation. In the family, traditional gender roles are followed, with women making decisions related to the health of the family. Families are close and decisions are made jointly. This closeness is why Hispanics tend to refrain from putting family members in long-term care, caring instead for them at home.

Catholicism is the predominant religion among Hispanics, and the spirit is important in terms of health. Most people in this culture enjoy discussing spirituality, especially in times of illness. This may make some health care practitioners uncomfortable. Families may occasionally pray as a group, and rosaries may be present. Hispanics have a fatalistic worldview and believe that their health is in God's hands. Illness may be viewed as a punishment from God.

Many Hispanics view pain as a test of faith, and this view may affect a health care provider's pain management interventions. Pain also is sometimes viewed as a result of immoral behavior, yet Hispanics do tend to express pain and discomfort with others. They are very verbal and will moan and cry in response to pain (Purnell, 2013).

Blood transfusions are acceptable to Hispanics, but organ donations are infrequent, especially with regard to donating organs while the person is still living. Some frown upon organ transplants. In 2012, more than half of the organs recovered from Hispanic American patients were from deceased donors, and only 13% of organ donations were from people of Hispanic origin (Office of Minority Health, 2013b). Compared to whites, fewer Hispanics know about and have formally signed an advanced directive (Searight & Gafford, 2005).

Pregnancy, Birth, and Child Rearing

Family, marriage, and child rearing are highly valued in Hispanic culture. Although Hispanics have more conservative attitudes toward sexuality than whites or blacks, they are more likely to enter sexual relationships at a young age (Ford, 1993). In 2010, Hispanic females aged 15 to 19 had a birthrate higher than any other racial or ethnic group and approximately twice that of non-Hispanic whites. However, this rate has declined continually since 1991, as have rates for teenagers among all other race/ethnic groups (Office of Minority Health, 2014a).

Birth control, no matter how practiced, is against Catholic doctrine but is utilized by many. Creams, foams, and diaphragms are not commonly used for birth control for two major reasons: (1) they are not approved by Catholic doctrine, and (2) the belief that women are not supposed to touch their genitals. Birth control pills are not used because they are artificial, and condoms are usually not used because women may find it offensive because condoms are associated with prostitutes. Condom use can imply that the woman is dirty, and men believe that condoms should only be used for disease control (Purnell, 2013). As would be expected from the general nature of the family traditions, elder female family members such as mothers and older sisters provide support and advice to pregnant women and young mothers. In addition, the father will often attend prenatal medical appointments in support of the pregnancy (Kemp, 2005).

At the prenatal state, avoiding foods that are considered "hot" (spicy or physically hot) by their culture is thought to be beneficial because eating hot foods can cause the baby to be born with spots and susceptible to rashes. Eating foods with iron, avoiding greasy foods, eating soup and dairy products, keeping active, and seeking advice from older family members is customary. Not wearing tight clothing and wearing a rosary or talisman to ward off malformation are also traditions. It is believed that pregnant women should not walk in the moonlight because it might cause a birth deformity. Other ways to prevent birth deformities include wearing a metal key, safety pin, or some other metal object on the abdomen (Purnell, 2013).

During labor and delivery, Medication is thought to be detrimental to the baby as is screaming during labor. Makeup is not worn during labor and delivery. Some Hispanic traditions hold that the mother and child should be in the *Quarentena* for about 40 days after the birth, remaining home with limited visitors to enable the mother–child bond to develop and to avoid exposure to infections. Tradition also suggests that fresh air is healthiest for the baby and that perfumes and scented cleaning agents should not be used in the home with the baby. Hispanic culture is traditionally very modest. Male nurses may not be well accepted, and nurses and doctors are expected to be competent and knowledgeable on all topics. Their advice and directions will almost always be followed strictly (Paulank & Purnell, 2005).

Child rearing is consistent with the concepts of formality, distinctly defined parental roles, and extended family. The child is raised by a family not only to reach adulthood but also to be part of a family throughout life. Child-rearing goals for social, educational, and financial development are important not only for the child but also so that the child becomes a sustaining member of the extended family.

Older children often have significant responsibility for younger siblings or relatives and generally are actively engaged in the care of older family members as well (Kempe, 2005). Grandparent involvement in child rearing not only helps the parent but also helps engender a deep sense of family loyalty in the child and a sense of responsibility for providing extended social support to other family members, including the elderly. A well-raised child is generally expected to be calm, obedient, and respectful toward adults and to be courteous to others. Nevertheless, Hispanic adolescents report similar levels of conflict and cohesion with their parents as do teenagers of other groups (Dixon, Gaber, & Brooks-Gunn, 2008).

Nutrition and Exercise

Many Hispanics retain core elements of the traditional Hispanic diet, including grains, beans, and fresh fruits and vegetables. The typical diet is high in fiber with beans and grains (rice) as staple foods, and they generally rely on beans as a source of protein rather than meat. Leafy green vegetables and dairy are not a usual part of the diet (Rhode Island Department of Health, n.d.). Generally, Hispanics eat a good deal of tropical fruits, fruit juices, and starchy root vegetables (e.g., potatoes, cassava, and plantains). The food pyramid for the traditional Latino diet is shown in **Figure 7.1**.

Family life has traditionally occupied a central place in Hispanic culture and contributed to dietary behaviors supporting home preparation of meals and families eating together. Ironically, the lifestyle of Hispanic Americans is undergoing a transition as they begin to adopt the values and behaviors of the United States. Acculturation typically results in a more sedentary lifestyle and a change in dietary patterns even as economic status increases. National survey data show that Spanish-speaking households have more healthful diets than those who have English as a primary language. These healthier eating behaviors include lower consumption of fat, saturated fat, and cholesterol. Additional analysis of these survey data reveals that these dietary differences do not appear to be the result of greater nutritional knowledge or greater awareness of food–disease relationships (Aldrich & Variyam, 2000).

Mental Health

Acculturation into the U.S. society also may have a negative impact on mental health for Hispanics. U.S.-born and long-term residents have significantly greater rates of mental disorders and substance abuse than recent Hispanic immigrants (Vega et al., 1998). Findings from the 2013 Monitoring the Future study reveal that 12th grade Hispanics had the highest rates for

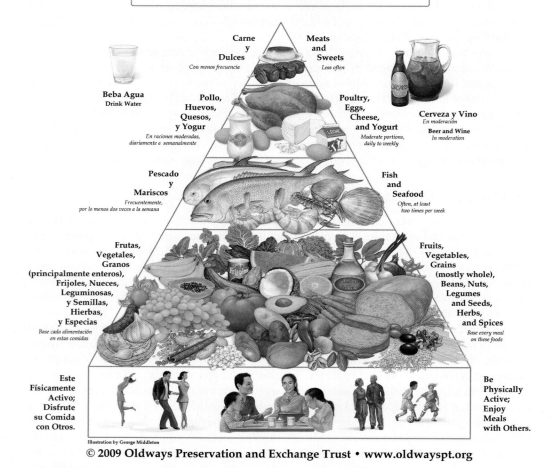

La Pirámide de La Dieta Latinoamericana

Una Propuesta Contemporánea a una Sana y Tradicional Dieta Latina

Latin American Diet Pyramid

A Contemporary Approach to the Healthy and Traditional Latino Diet

Carne
y
Dulces
Con menos frecuencia

Meats
and
Sweets
Less often

Beba Agua
Drink Water

Pollo,
Huevos,
Quesos,
y Yogur
*En raciones moderadas,
diariamente a semanalmente*

Poultry,
Eggs,
Cheese,
and Yogurt
*Moderate portions,
daily to weekly*

Cerveza y Vino
En moderación
Beer and Wine
In moderation

Pescado
y
Mariscos
*Frecuentemente,
por lo menos dos veces a la semana*

Fish
and
Seafood
*Often, at least
two times per week*

Frutas,
Vegetales,
Granos
(principalmente enteros),
Frijoles, Nueces,
Leguminosas,
y Semillas,
Hierbas,
y Especias
*Base cada alimentación
en estas comidas*

Fruits,
Vegetables,
Grains
(mostly whole),
Beans, Nuts,
Legumes
and Seeds,
Herbs,
and Spices
*Base every meal
on these foods*

Este
Físicamente
Activo;
Disfrute
su Comida
con Otros.

Be
Physically
Active;
Enjoy
Meals
with Others.

Illustration by George Middleton

© 2009 Oldways Preservation and Exchange Trust • www.oldwayspt.org

FIGURE 7.1

Food pyramid for traditional Latino diet.

use of a number of substances including marijuana, inhalants, ecstasy, cocaine, crack, salvia, Vicodin, methamphetamine, crystal methamphetamine, over-the-counter cough/cold medicines, and tobacco using a hookah. Hispanic students generally have lower rates than white students of misusing any of the prescription drugs (Johnston, O'Malley, Miech, Bachman, & Schulenberg, 2014).

Research on suicide found that foreign-born Mexican Americans are at significantly lower risk of suicide and depression than those born in the United States. In spite of the higher-than-average report of suicidal behavior among Hispanic youth, their suicide rate is lower than for non-Hispanic white and Native American adolescents, but higher than for non-Hispanic black youth (Zayas & Pilat, 2008).

Thousands in this population often go without professional mental health treatment. This is partly due to a sense of stigma associated with mental illness. Latino study participants receiving treatment for depression believed this condition carries a negative label. When asked about complications adhering to a prescribed antidepressant medication regimen, 73% of participants made comments related to stigma (Interian, Martinez, Guamaccia, Vega, & Escobar, 2007).

Death and Dying

Women tend to care for the seriously ill and dying. Men may stay close but usually do not provide hands-on care. Death rites are derived from Catholic Church customs and generally include confession and last rites. Based on both family respect and religious custom, funerals usually involve burial and often include a wake or social gathering where food is served and the life of the deceased is remembered positively and without grim mourning (Lobar, Youngblut, & Brooten, 2006).

Latino patients have lower rates of advance directive care than non-Hispanic whites, but this is attributed to language barriers rather than to mistrust. Focus groups of Latino populations show that Latino patients are unfamiliar with the language and documentation of advance care directives, but they are not particularly opposed to the concepts once they are understood (Maller, 2013).

Cultural-Bound Illnesses

Hispanics are diagnosed with many unique illnesses that are not part of the Western medical system. Some common illnesses and their causes are listed in **Table 7.1**.

Susto (literally "fright" in Spanish) is illness that occurs from a frightful experience, and it is similar to anxiety in modern medicine. Symptoms include withdrawal from social interactions, listlessness, not sleeping well, and loss of appetite. Most people who believe in susto deem that anyone can get it; both adults and children can be affected. The soul leaves the body due to a frightening experience, and the body becomes susceptible to illness and disharmony. It can be caused by events such as the sudden, unexpected barking of a dog, tripping over

TABLE 7.1 Culture-Bound Illnesses in the Hispanic Culture and Their Characteristics and Causes

Illness	Characteristics	Cause(s)
Ataque de nervios (nervous attack)	Intense and brief expression of shock, anxiety, or sadness	Believed to be caused by family conflict or anger (e.g., screaming, kicking)
Bilis (bile rage)	Vomiting, diarrhea, headaches, dizziness, migraine, nightmares, loss of appetite, inability to urinate; brought on by livid rage and revenge fantasies	Believed to stem from bile pouring into the bloodstream in response to strong emotion
Caida de la mollera (fallen fontanel)	Childhood condition characterized by irritability and diarrhea	Believed to be caused by abrupt withdrawal from the mother's breast
Empacho	Lack of appetite, stomachache, diarrhea, vomiting, constipation, cramps, or vomiting	Caused by poorly digested or uncooked food or overeating
Fatiga (shortness of breath or fatigue)	Asthma symptoms (especially in Puerto Rican usage) and fatigue	
Frio de la matriz (frozen womb)	Pelvic congestion and decreased libido believed to be caused by insufficient rest after childbirth	
Mal aire (bad air)	Cold air that is believed to cause respiratory infections and earaches	
Mal de ojo (evil eye)	Vomiting, fever, crying, restlessness	A hex placed on children, sometimes unconsciously, that is believed to be caused by the admiring gaze of someone more powerful
Mal puesto (sorcery)	Unnatural illness that is not easily explained	
Pasmo (cold or frozen face; lockjaw)	Temporary paralysis of the face or limbs or spasm of voluntary muscle	Exposure to cold air when body is overheated; caused by a sudden hot–cold imbalance
Susto (fright)	Anorexia, insomnia, hallucinations, depression, weakness, painful sensations	Traumatic experiences or shock

Sources: Adapted from Rhode Island Department of Health (n.d.) and Juckett (2005).

an unnoticed object, having a nighttime encounter with a ghost that keeps your spirit from finding its way back into your body before you wake, or being in a social situation that causes you to have fear or anger.

Mal de ojo, sometimes called "**evil eye**," is illness that is a result of an envious glance from another individual. It mostly affects children. It has been defined as a hex caused by a gaze from a more powerful or stronger person looking at a weaker person (usually an infant or child but sometimes a woman). It may be someone from outside the family looking at the child with envy, or a stare from a powerful person who is admiring the child. It is usually caused inadvertently. Those affected may suffer from headaches, high fever, diarrhea, sleeplessness, increased fussiness, and weeping. It is not fully known what diseases in modern medicine correlate with mal de ojo; however, in severe cases, the symptoms are similar to those of sepsis (the presence of pathogenic organisms or their toxins in the blood or tissues) and should warrant a medical evaluation. Cases of mal de ojo with frequent crying and no other symptoms are thought to be similar to colic.

Empacho (blocked intestines) describes stomach pains and cramps that are believed to be caused by a ball of food clinging to the stomach due to a change in eating habits, eating spoiled food, overeating, or swallowing chewing gum. The disease state of empacho has often been defined as a perceived stomach or intestinal blockage. In most cases, it is not an actual obstruction but rather indigestion or gastroenteritis. Abdominal pain and bloating are symptoms of empacho. Some Hispanic populations also add nausea, vomiting, diarrhea, and lethargy as symptoms that may occur in some cases. Empacho tends to occur more in young children, but people of all ages are susceptible. Empacho is considered a cold illness. Folk medicines used to treat empacho include greta (lead monoxide) and azarcón (lead tetroxide), which are dangerous and can cause lead poisoning. There have been case reports of deaths from these substances.

The ideology of illness and health is rooted in the fabric of the culture, and it is the fundamental element of traditional values. Even though the Mexican American culture utilizes modern medicine, they rely primarily on folk practitioners to treat traditional illnesses.

Healing Traditions, Healers, and Healing Aids

Even though Hispanics generally look to standard primary care doctors and facilities for care, some treatments for illness are provided by family or nonfamily members. On a secondary basis, Hispanics may rely on traditional healing traditions.

In Hispanic cultures, illnesses, treatments, and foods are viewed as having hot or cold properties, although how these are ascribed may vary by country. Some Hispanics consider health to be the product of balance among four body humors (blood and yellow bile are hot, phlegm and black bile are cold). One would balance a hot illness with cold medications and foods and vice versa. This might result in not following a doctor's advice to drink lots of fluids for a common cold, if one believes such drinks add more coldness to the body. Instead, hot liquids (tea, soup, broth) could be recommended (Rhode Island Department of Health, n.d.). **Table 7.2** lists some hot and cold illnesses.

TABLE 7.2   Hot Versus Cold Latino Diagnoses

Cold Conditions	Hot Conditions
• Cancer	• Bilis (bile, rage)
• Colic	• Diabetes mellitus
• Empacho (indigestion)	• Gastroesophageal reflux or peptic ulcer
• Frio de la matriz (frozen womb)	• Hypertension
• Headache	• Mal de ojo (evil eye)
• Menstrual cramps	• Pregnancy
• Pneumonia	• Sore throat or infection
• Upper respiratory infections	• Susto (soul loss)

Source: Juckett (2005).

Healers

Healers names are specific to cultural groups and may include curanderos in Mexico and much of Latin America, Santeria in Brazil and Cuba, and Espiritismo in Puerto Rico. Most of these traditions distinguish natural illnesses from supernatural illnesses. The healing traditions include a variety of methods as shown in **Table 7.3**.

Curanderos

A **curandero** (**curandera** for a female) is a traditional folk healer or shaman who is dedicated to curing physical and/or spiritual illnesses. The curandero is often a respected member of the community and is highly religious and spiritual. In Spanish the word *curandero* means healer. These healers often use herbs and other natural remedies to cure illnesses, but their primary method of healing is the supernatural. They believe that the causes of many illnesses are lost malevolent spirits, a lesson from God, or a curse. There are different types of curanderos/curanderas. Curanderos use herbs and verbal charms or spells to produce a magic effect, sobadores practice manipulation, parteras are midwives, and abuelas (literally "grandmothers," although they are not necessarily related to the patient) provide initial care. Yerberos are primarily herbalists, and hueseros and sabaderos are bone/muscle therapists who specialize in physical ailments.

Curanderos treat ailments such as espanto (Spanish for shock), empacho (Spanish for surfeit, which means to feed in excess), susto, mal aire (literally bad air), and mal de ojo with religious rituals, ceremonial cleansing, and prayers. Often curanderos contact certain spirits to aid them in their healing work. The remedies of the curanderos are often helpful but sometimes have a negative effect on the health of their patients. For example, a common method of healing mollera caída, a condition in which an infant's fontanelle has sunken, is to hold the infant's feet with its head down and perform a ceremonial ritual. Some other traditional treatments, such as azarcón and greta (lead salts) and azogue (mercury), are also

TABLE 7.3   Traditional Latino Diagnoses and Their Related Treatment Methods

Diagnosis	Traditional Treatment
Ataque de nervios (nervous attack)	No immediate treatment other than calming the patient
Bilis (bile, rage)	Herbs, including wormwood
Caida de la mollera (fallen fontanel)	Holding the child upside down or pushing up on the hard palate
Empacho (indigestion or blockage)	Treated by massaging the stomach and drinking purgative tea, or by azarcón or greta, medicines that have been implicated in some cases of lead poisoning
Fatiga (shortness of breath or fatigue)	Herbal treatments, including eucalyptus and mullein (gordolobo), steam inhalation
Frio de la matriz (frozen womb)	Damiana tea, rest
Mal aire (bad air)	Steam baths, hot compresses, stimulating herbal teas
Mal de ojo (evil eye)	The hex can be broken if the person responsible for the hex touches the child or if a healer passes an egg over the child's body
Mal puesto (sorcery)	Magic
Pasmo (cold or frozen face; lockjaw)	Massage
Susto (fright-induced soul loss)	Treatment may include a barrida (spiritualistic cleansing by sweeping the body with eggs, lemons, and bay leaves), herb tea, prayer; repeated until the patient improves

Source: Adapted from Juckett (2005).

harmful because of their lead and mercury content. Other remedies are harmless. For example, a common method of treating mal de ojo is to rub an egg over the body of the sick to draw out the evil spirit that is causing the disease.

These methods of treating health problems often lead to conflict with modern medicine because doctors reject the curandero's healing as superstitious and worthless. As a result, curanderos have often experienced discrimination and been likened to witches by the medical profession and non-Hispanic communities. However, these remedies are important to the Hispanic culture, and disbelief may lead to insult, conflict, or the rejection of modern medicine. Other medical doctors, recognizing the benefits of the spiritual and emotional healing offered by curanderos, have begun to work in conjunction with them, supporting their use of rituals and ceremonies in the healing of the sick while insisting that patients receive modern medical attention as well.

Santeria

Santeria, also known as the "Way of the Saints," is an Afro-Caribbean religion based on beliefs of the Yoruba people in Nigeria, Africa. The traditions have been influenced by Roman Catholic beliefs. Santeria incorporates elements of several faiths and is therefore called a syncretic religion. It has grown beyond its Yoruba and Catholic origins to become a religion in its own right and a powerful symbol of the religious creativity of Afro-Cuban culture. For a long time, Santeria was a secretive underground religion, but it is becoming increasingly visible in the Americas. It was once considered a ghetto religion practiced only by the Caribbean poor and uneducated, but now Santeria has a growing following among middle-class professionals and other ethnic groups, such as whites, blacks, and Asian Americans.

Because of the history of secrecy, it is not known how many people follow Santeria. There is no central organization for this religion, and it is practiced in private, which makes it more difficult to determine the number of followers. There are no scriptures for this religion, and it is taught through word of mouth. The Santeria tradition consists of a hierarchical structure according to priesthood level and authority.

Santeria practices include animal offerings, dance, and appeals for assistance sung to the **orishas**, which resemble the Catholic saints and are spirits that reflect one of the manifestations of Olodumare (God). Animal sacrifice also is a part of Santeria and is very controversial. Followers of Santeria point out that ritual slaughter is conducted in a safe and humane manner by the priests who are charged with the task. Furthermore, the animal is cooked and eaten afterward by the community. Chickens, a staple food of many African-descended and Creole cultures, are the most common sacrifice; the chicken's blood is offered to the orisha, and the meat is consumed by all.

Followers believe that orishas will help them in life if they carry out the appropriate rituals and will enable them to achieve the destiny God planned for them before they were born. This is very much a mutual relationship because the orishas need to be worshipped by human beings if they are to continue to exist. In a 1993 Supreme Court case, Justice Kennedy said in his decision:

> The Santeria faith teaches that every individual has a destiny from God, a destiny fulfilled with the aid and energy of the orishas. The basis of the Santeria religion is the nurture of a personal relation with the orishas, and one of the principal forms of devotion is an animal sacrifice. According to Santeria teaching, the orishas are powerful but not immortal. They depend for survival on the sacrifice. (*Church of Likumi Babalu Aye v. City of Hialeah*, 1993)

Drum music and dancing are forms of prayer and will sometimes induce a trance state in an initiated priest, who becomes possessed and then channels the orisha.

Espiritismo

Espiritismo is the Spanish word for "Spiritism." It is the belief in Latin America and the Caribbean that good and evil spirits can affect human life, such as one's health and luck. An opinion, doctrine, or principle (tenet) of Espiritismo is the belief in a supreme God who is the omnipotent creator of the universe. There also is a belief in a spirit world inhabited by discarnate spiritual beings who gradually evolve intellectually and morally.

Espiritismo has never had a single leader or epicenter of practice, so practice varies greatly among individuals and groups. Espiritismo has absorbed various practices from other religious and spiritual practices endemic to Latin America and the Caribbean, such as Roman Catholicism, curanderismo, Santeria, and voodoo.

A ritual associated with Espiritismo de Corzon, which is a form of Espiritismo practiced primarily in Cuba, is physically, mentally, and emotionally difficult. Those participating in the ritual stand in a circle holding hands while walking in a counterclockwise fashion. At the same time, they chant and beat the floor with their feet and swing their arms forcefully until they fall into a trance. The heavy breathing and stamping, which is heavily associated with chanting in African cults, serves one specific purpose. The noises create a hypnotic sound that leads the medium into a trance. Upon reaching this particular state of mind, the medium can contact the spirits for solutions to problems or ailments (Olmos & Paravisini-Gebert, 2003).

Puerto Rican Espiritismo shares many similarities in its origins with Cuban Espiritismo. Educated Puerto Ricans used Espiritismo as a way to justify their mission of freeing the country from the grasp of Spanish colonialism. However, the religious movement encountered many setbacks in its early years in Puerto Rico. Those who were caught practicing it were punished by the government and ostracized by the Catholic Church (Olmos & Paravisini-Gebert, 2003). Despite all the roadblocks, the movement continued to spread throughout the country, and attempts to achieve spiritual communication through a medium were widely practiced all over the island.

Behavioral Risk Factors and Common Health Problems

The behaviors described here are linked to the common health problems that Hispanics face, but it is important to note that some of their illnesses are not related to behaviors. Their health problems are related to other social factors as well, such as poverty or lack of access to care.

The 10 leading causes of death among Hispanics/Latinos in 2010 were as follows (CDC, 2013):

1. Cancer
2. Heart disease
3. Unintentional injuries
4. Stroke
5. Diabetes mellitus
6. Chronic liver disease and cirrhosis
7. Chronic lower respiratory disease
8. Alzheimer's disease
9. Nephritis, nephrotic syndrome, and nephrosis
10. Influenza and pneumonia

Hispanics have higher rates of obesity than non-Hispanic whites. Approximately 36% of Mexican American men and 45% of women 20 years old and older are obese (body mass index of 30 or greater), compared to 34% for non-Hispanic white men and 33% for women (CDC, 2014). Diabetes and hypertension are closely linked to obesity; 11.8% of Latinos more than 20 years old have type 2 diabetes (13.3% of Mexican Americans), making it the foremost health issue in this population (CDC, 2011a).

Hispanics have lower rates of smoking than most racial and ethnic groups. In 2008, 15.8% of Hispanics smoked. There are significant variations in smoking rates among Hispanic subgroups: 21.5% percent of Cuban Americans, 16.6% of Puerto Ricans, 20.1% of Mexican Americans, 10.7% of Dominicans, and 12.8% of Central and South Americans were smokers in 2008 (American Lung Association, 2010).

Overall, Hispanics are less likely to drink at all than are non-Hispanic whites. In fact, Hispanics have high rates of abstinence from alcohol, but Hispanics who choose to drink are more likely to consume higher volumes of alcohol than non-Hispanic whites (National Institute on Alcohol Abuse and Alcoholism [NIAAA], 2013).

Hispanics, in general, are less likely than non-Hispanic whites and non-Hispanic blacks to report activity limitations caused by chronic conditions. In 2008, the age-adjusted proportion of Hispanics reporting an activity limitation was 10% compared with 15.5% for whites and 17.5% for blacks (National Center for Health Statistics, 2011). Although the Hispanic Paradox shows that Hispanics have health issues similar to non-Hispanic whites or even less in several categories such as cancer, Hispanics do have a particular risk of diabetes. Compared with non-Hispanic whites, Hispanics have higher rates of type 2 diabetes and other manifestations of abnormal glucose metabolism. Diabetes for Hispanics aged 20 years or older from 2010 to 2012 was estimated to be 12.8% compared to 7.6% for non-Hispanic whites (National Center for Chronic Disease Prevention and Health Promotion, 2014).

In 2010, a larger percentage of Hispanic workers were employed in high-risk occupations than non-Hispanic white workers, with exposure to hazardous substances such as silica and fertilizers. They were also at risk from accidental deaths, which was the third leading cause of death (7.3%) following cancer and heart disease. Unintentional injuries were the fifth leading cause of death for non-Hispanic whites (4.8%) and non-Hispanic blacks (4.2%) (Office of Minority Health, 2014a).

What Do You Think?

Life expectancy among Hispanics is 2 years longer than for whites (Office of Minority Health, 2015). Hispanics also have lower mortality rates in 7 out of the 10 leading causes of death, even though they are 2 times more likely to be economically under the poverty line and 3 times more likely to be without health insurance. Hispanics have markedly reduced mortality from cancer (−28%) and heart disease (−25%), two leading causes of death in the United States. Hispanics also have lower smoking rates, better diet, and better general health during the first few years after immigrating. However, CDC statistics show that Hispanics are more prone to die of diabetes, as well as cirrhosis and other chronic liver diseases. What do you think accounts for the paradox related to mortality? Could it be better genetics? Could it be due to lower smoking rates? What about the problems of diabetes and cirrhosis? Could this be due to behaviors developed to try to adapt to the majority culture? Could it be due to lack of access to healthy but more expensive food?

QUICK FACTS

Examples of some important health disparities reported by the CDC (CHDIR, 2012):

- From 2007 to 2010, obesity was more prevalent among female Mexican American adults than among female non-Hispanic white adults.

- In 2010, diabetes was more prevalent among Hispanic and non-Hispanic African American adults than among non-Hispanic white and Asian adults.

- From 2009 to 2010, periodontitis was more prevalent among Mexican American adults aged 30 years and older than for non-Hispanic white adults of the same age group.

- In 2010, Hispanic adults continued to have a substantially higher rate of HIV infection than white adults.

- The teenage birthrate among Hispanic females (Mexicans and Puerto Ricans) in 2010 was higher than that of non-Hispanic white females.

- In 2010, the birthrate for Hispanic females aged 15 to 19 years was approximately 5 times the rate for Asian/Pacific Islanders, 2 times the rate for non-Hispanic whites, and somewhat higher than the rates for non-Hispanic black and American Indian/Alaska Native adolescents.

- Among Hispanic adults 18 to 64 years of age, a larger percentage was without health insurance in 2010 than non-Hispanic white adults of the same age group.

- A smaller percentage of Hispanic adults aged 50 to 75 years reported being up to date with colorectal cancer screening in 2010 than their non-Hispanic adult counterparts.

- Smaller percentages of Hispanics (including Mexican Americans looked at separately) and non-Hispanic African Americans adults with high blood pressure in 2010 had control of their blood pressure compared with non-Hispanic white adults.

- Among Hispanics aged 6 months or older, a smaller percentage was vaccinated against influenza during the 2010–2011 influenza season than non-Hispanic white children.

- If Hispanic adults had the same hospitalization rate as Asian and Pacific Islander adults in 2009, they would have had 240,000 fewer hospitalizations and saved $700 million.

- In 2011, a larger percentage of Hispanic adults did not complete high school and had incomes less than the federal poverty level compared with non-Hispanic white adults. In addition, a larger percentage of Hispanic adults aged 18 to 64 years were unemployed in 2010 compared with their non-Hispanic white counterparts.

- In 2010, a larger percentage of Hispanic workers were employed in high-risk occupations than non-Hispanic white workers.

Source: Office of Minority Health (2013a).

Considerations for Health Promotion and Program Planning

Consider the following concepts when planning and implementing a health promotion program for this target audience:

- Preventive medicine is not a norm for most Hispanics. This behavior may be related to the Hispanic here-and-now orientation, as opposed to a future-planning orientation. It also is related to their fatalistic belief system.

- Some common Hispanic sayings suggest that events in one's life result from luck, fate, or other powers beyond an individual's control. For example:

  Que será, será. (What will be will be.)
  Que sea lo que Dios quiera. (It's in God's hands.)
  Esta enfermedad es una prueba de Dios. (This illness is a test of God.)
  De algo se tiene que morir uno. (You have to die of something.)

- People with acute or chronic illness may regard themselves as innocent victims of malevolent forces. Severe illness may be attributed to God's design, bad behavior, or punishment. Genetic defects in a child may be attributed to the parents' actions.

- Consider sitting closer to Hispanic patients and clients than you would with people from other cultures.

- Be particularly aware of your nonverbal communication messages. Sustained eye contact when speaking to an older person may be considered rude, and avoiding eye contact with a superior is a sign of respect (Purnell, 2013).

- Be aware that Hispanics often have higher exposure rates to environmental hazards due to living in urban environments, and males have high exposure due to their jobs.

- Family and friends may indulge patients, allowing them to be passive, which is an approach that may conflict with the Western view that active participation is required to prevent or heal much disease.

- Some Hispanic sayings support health promotion and illustrate the considerable status given to health and prevention:

  La salud es todo o casi todo. (Health is everything, or almost everything.)
  Es mejor prevenir que curar. (An ounce of prevention is worth a pound of cure.)
  Ayúdate que Dios te ayudará. (Help yourself and God will help you.)

- Vaccination is very important and adhered to for children.

- Western medicine is expected and preferred in case of severe illness, but some Hispanics also may use native healers. The educator and health provider should inquire about the utilization of other healers.

- Use appropriate titles to show respect, such as *Señor* and *Señorita*.

- To show respect, greet the person with a handshake.

- A botanica is a resource store for herbs and other traditional remedies. Some Hispanics may go there before going to a physician or clinic. In many Latin American countries, pharmacists prescribe medications, and a wider range of medications is available over the counter. People may share medicines or write home for relatives to send them medications. Individuals may discontinue medication if it does not immediately alleviate symptoms or after their symptoms abate. Many Hispanics believe that taking too much medicine is harmful.

- When providing nutritional advice or education, use positive examples from Hispanic cultural foods.

- Consider suggesting family-based methods for increasing physical activity, such as dancing or walking with family members.

- If you have the patient's permission, involve the family members in the consultation because it may assist with increasing the listener's adherence to the recommendation(s).

- Consider using peer educators (promotoras) as community outreach workers for community-based efforts; they have been shown to be successful with this community.

- Check for understanding and agreement because Hispanics tend to avoid conflict and are hesitant to ask questions.

- Inquire about complementary and alternative treatments being used as they are frequently utilized by Hispanics.

- Because of historic events, some Hispanics may distrust the health care system (e.g., many Puerto Rican women experienced involuntary sterilization and were adversely affected by birth control pill trials), view the health care system as an extension of a repressive government (Central Americans), or fear deportation, especially if they are in the country illegally.

- Some Hispanics confuse public health programs with welfare and avoid them due to stigma.

- They have a relaxed perspective related to time and may be late for appointments.

Tips for Working With the Hispanic Population

When working with a Hispanic patient or family, it is important to convey respect, some formality combined with a demonstration of personal interest. Traditional family values, diet, reliance on modern medicine, and respect for authority should be encouraged and reinforced. It may be useful to mention the importance of retaining traditional values and practices rather than abandoning them to be more like the U.S. majority, which could be detrimental to their health both physically and mentally.

Caring for Hispanic Patients

Make sure to greet and acknowledge everyone in the room, even the children. Do not act rushed during the appointment. It is better to ask "How can I serve (help) you today?" than "How are you?", which may be taken as a greeting and be answered "Fine and you?"

Avoid instant familiarity, especially when meeting a new person such as during an initial office visit. Formality is a sign of respect when you do not know someone well. The Spanish language differentiates between the formal and the familiar forms of salutations, and should literally be translated and communicated by your conduct. After you have explained something to your patient, use inquiring comprehension checks such as "Tell me what I am proposing to do" because "Do you understand?" may be misunderstood as an insult.

Remember that Latinos embrace alternative therapies and healers. Herbal remedies are second nature to Latinos, and these alternative medicines are typically found in neighborhood stores (botanicas).

Also remember that decisions may need to be made in consultation with family members who may not be present. The Latino family unit has well-defined gender roles. The man is the provider, protector, and the authority figure. The woman is the homemaker, child raiser, and adviser. Even an educated and competent Latino woman may not consent to any significant treatment without the specific permission of her husband (Jimenez, 2014).

Summary

Hispanics total approximately 54 million people in the United States today and are a rapidly growing population, which is predicted to reach 129 million by 2060 (Office of Minority Health, 2014b). Hispanics have strong family ties and have held on to their cultural belief systems and practices. Hispanics incorporate unique features in their health belief systems and healing practices. They have types of healers that are not seen in other cultures. Consider these major differences when providing health care services to this population. One particular challenge is that Hispanic health outcomes deteriorate with loss of traditional lifestyle patterns. Hispanics have equal or better health outcomes even when in lower economic status, but with increasing economic status and acculturation into the majority U.S. culture these advantages are soon lost.

In this chapter, an overview of the history of Hispanics was described, including the fact that part of the United States previously belonged to Mexico. Several culture-bound illnesses have been discussed, such as empacho and susto, along with treatment modalities that include the treatment of hot and cold illnesses. Various types of healing systems have been discussed, such as curanderismo and Espiritismo. Common health behaviors and illnesses among this group have been explained, along with issues for consideration when developing health promotion and education efforts for this target population.

Review

1. Define the terms *Hispanic* and *Latino* and explain why this population is not considered to be a race.

2. Provide an overview of the history of Hispanics in North America and the United States.

3. Explain the socioeconomic conditions of Hispanics in the United States.

4. What are susto, empacho, and mal de ojo?

5. What are curanderismo, Santeria, and Espiritismo?

6. What are some of the common health risk behaviors and diseases among Hispanics in the United States?

Activity

Conduct research on health programs that have been implemented for members of the Hispanic culture. Summarize the literature and identify some best practices.

Develop a fotonovela on a specific health topic. Be sure that the text, images, and other content are appropriate for this target audience.

Case Study

This case focuses on a low-income, non-English-speaking Latino patient and family. As you read this story, pay special attention to issues involved in medical decision making, such as gender roles and values and interest in treatments outside of traditional Western medicine based on culturally constructed folk illness beliefs.

When Alejandro Flores was born, his parents were ecstatic and very proud. Alejandro was their first child born in the continental United States, in a world far away from their traditions and family in Puerto Rico. The Flores family had worked very hard to move to the northeast a year before Alejandro's birth, and they felt that his arrival helped connect them with their new home.

It is 4 years after Alejandro's birth, and the Flores family has grown even larger. There are now five children (three older than Alejandro and one 20-month-old baby) and Alejandro's grandmother living in the same apartment. Alejandro's mother, Señora Flores, takes care of her family as best she can, and she feels lucky to have her mother there to give her advice and a helping hand. Señor Flores works very hard as a custodian at a local school to provide his family with enough income. He has picked up a little English at work, but only Spanish is spoken at home.

Serious asthma problems run in the Flores family, and Alejandro is no exception. Although he looks healthy, Alejandro has had severe asthma for several years. When he was 2 years old, a series of awful wheezing episodes sent him to the hospital multiple times. His parents do their best to care for him, but they are both spread pretty thin and have limited time available. To help with Alejandro's asthma problems, the Flores family recently relocated to a new apartment that has air conditioning, and Sr. Flores has limited his smoking to outside on the patio. The family has two dogs, which could be a problem, but they just couldn't see getting rid of two loved members of their family.

Alejandro also takes a lot of medications for his asthma symptoms. His parents have been taught about asthma and have been given an asthma action plan—all in Spanish. They were told to call the clinic if at any time Alejandro's symptoms worsened. Despite these actions, Alejandro still continues to have heavy wheezing and a tight cough, especially at night.

With Alejandro continuing to have asthma problems, Sra. Flores became skeptical that the medications were not working. Under her mother's guidance, she took Alejandro to an espiritista (in curanderismo, the Mexican American healing system, an espiritista is a healer who serves as a medium for exorcisms and is adept at facilitating the help of benevolent spirits and removing malevolent spirits that surround the client). Sra. Flores took the espiritista's advice and stopped giving Alejandro all of the prescribed medications. She began giving him an herbal tea that she believed, along with prayer, would take Alejandro's asthma symptoms completely away.

Alejandro and his parents attended their regularly scheduled visit to the clinic to see if the new medications were helping to control Alejandro's symptoms. This is the second visit since Alejandro's last hospitalization 6 months ago. Sra. Flores has not contacted anyone at the clinic about Alejandro's asthma getting worse, so the clinic staff assumes the best.

There are several issues to consider about this case:

* Why might Sra. Flores have chosen to consult an espiritista rather than call the clinic when Alejandro was not getting better?

* Do you think traditional Latino gender roles might have some effect on this child and family's experience with the health care system?

* How might it be possible to incorporate alternative folk remedies with mainstream Western medicine in developing a treatment plan for Alejandro?

Source: Cross Cultural Health Care Case Studies (n.d.).

References

Aldrich L., & Variyam, J. N. (2000). Acculturation erodes the diet quality of U.S. Hispanics. *Food Review, 23*, 51–55. Retrieved from http://www.thefreelibrary.com/Acculturation+Erodes+The+Diet+Quality+Of+U.+S.+Hispanics.-a063735911

American Lung Association. (2010). *About smoking, facts and figures, Hispanics.* Retrieved from http://www.lung.org/stop-smoking/about-smoking/facts-figures/hispanics-and-tobacco-use.html

Callister, L. C., & Birkhead, A. (2002, December 16). Acculturation and perinatal outcomes in Mexican immigrant childbearing women: An integrative review. *Journal of Perinatal and Neonatal Nursing, 3*, 22–38. Retrieved from http://www.ncbi.nlm.nih.gov/pubmed/12472187

Centers for Disease Control and Prevention. (2011a). *National diabetes fact sheet: Diagnosed and undiagnosed diabetes in the United States, all ages, 2010.* Retrieved from http://www.cdc.gov/diabetes/pubs/estimates11.htm#1

Centers for Disease Control and Prevention. (2011b). *Obesity, Health Disparities and Inequity Report–United States, 2011(CHDIR).* Supplement, Vol. 60, *Mortality and Morbidity Weekly Report*, January 14, 2011.

Centers for Disease Control and Prevention. (2013). *National Vital Statistics Reports,*

62(6), 55, table 2. Retrieved from http://www
.cdc.gov/minorityhealth/populations
/REMP/hispanic.html

Centers for Disease Control and Prevention. (2014). *Health United States, 2013*. Retrieved from http://www.cdc.gov/nchs/data/hus/hus13.pdf

Church of Likumi Babalu Aye v. City of Hialeah, 508 US 520 (1993).

Cross Cultural Health Care Case Studies. (n.d.). *The case of Alejandro Flores*. Retrieved from http://support.mchtraining.net/national_ccce/case3/case.html

Dixon, S., Gaber, J., & Brooks-Gunn, J. (2008). The roles of respect for parental authority and parenting practices in parent–child conflict among African American, Latino, and European American families. *Journal of Family Psychology, 22*(1), 1–10. Retrieved from http://www.ncbi.nlm.nih.gov/pmc/articles/PMC3125601/

Ford, K., and Norris, AE. (1993). Urban Hispanic adolescents and young adults: relationship of acculturation to sexual behavior, *Journal of Sex Research, 30*(4):316-323.

Interian, A., Martinez, I. E., Guamaccia, P. J., Vega, W. A., & Escobar, J. I. (2007). A qualitative analysis of the perception of stigma among Latinos receiving antidepressants. *Psychiatric Services, 63*(11). Retrieved from http://ps.psychiatryonline.org/article.aspx?articleID=98896&resultClick=3

Jimenez, R. (2014). *American Academy of Orthopaedic Surgeons: Communication skills mentoring program*. Retrieved from http://www3.aaos.org/education/csmp/HispLatCulturallyCompetentTips.cfm

Johnston, L. D., O'Malley, P. M., Miech, R. A., Bachman, J. G., & Schulenberg, J. E. (2014). *Monitoring the Future national results on drug use: 1975–2013: Overview, key findings on adolescent drug use*. Ann Arbor, MI: Institute for Social Research, The University of Michigan. Retrieved from http://www.monitoringthefuture.org/pubs/monographs/mtf-overview2013.pdf

Juckett, G. (2005). Cross-cultural medicine. *American Family Physician*. Retrieved from http://www.aafp.org/afp/20051201/2267.html

Kemp, C. (2005). Mexican & Mexican-Americans: Health beliefs & practices. In *Refugee health-immigrant health*. Cambridge, MA: Cambridge University Press (updated March 2005).

Lobar, S. L., Youngblut, J. M., & Brooten, D. (2006). Cross-cultural beliefs, ceremonies, and rituals surrounding death of a loved one. *Pediatric Nursing, 32*(1), 44–50.

Maller, A. (2013, October 23). Why aren't patients using advance directives? *Clinical Correlations*. Retrieved from http://www.clinicalcorrelations.org/?p=6553

Markides, K. S., & Coreil, J. (1986). The health of Hispanics in the southwestern United States: An epidemiological paradox. *Public Health Reports, 101*, 253–265.

Motel, S., & Patten, E. (2012). *Hispanic trends project; English proficiency and citizenship*. Retrieved from http://www.pewhispanic.org/2012/06/27/iv-english-proficiency-and-citizenship/

National Center for Chronic Disease Prevention and Health Promotion. (2014). *National diabetes statistics report, 2014*. Retrieved from http://www.cdc.gov/diabetes/pubs/statsreport14.htm

National Center for Health Statistics. (2011). Prevalence of complex activity limitations among racial/ethnic groups and Hispanic subgroups of adults: United States, 2003–2009. *Data Brief, Number 73*. Hyattsville, MD: U.S. Department of Health and Human Services, Centers for Disease Control and Prevention. Retrieved from http://www.cdc.gov/nchs/data/databriefs/db73.pdf

National Center for Health Statistics. (2014, October). Mortality in the United States. *Data Brief, Number 168*. Hyattsville, MD: U.S. Department of Health and Human Services, Centers for Disease Control and Prevention. Retrieved from http://www.cdc.gov/nchs/data/databriefs/db168.htm

National Institute on Alcohol Abuse and Alcoholism. (2013). *Factsheet alcohol and the Hispanic community*. Retrieved from http://pubs.niaaa .nih.gov/publications/HispanicFact /HispanicFact.htm

Office of Minority Health. (2013a). *Hispanic and Latino populations, racial and ethnic minorities, populations citing CDC Health Disparities and Inequity Report*. Retrieved from http://www.cdc.gov/minorityhealth /populations/REMP/hispanic.html

Office of Minority Health. (2013b, September 20). *Organ donation and Hispanic Americans*. Retrieved from http://minorityhealth.hhs .gov/omh/browse.aspx?lvl=4&lvlid=72

Office of Minority Health. (2014a). *Hispanic /Latino profile*. Retrieved from http:// minorityhealth.hhs.gov/omh/browse .aspx?lvl=3&lvlid=64

Office of Minority Health. (2014b). *Minority health; populations, racial and ethnic minorities, Hispanic or Latino populations*. Retrieved from http://www.cdc.gov/minorityhealth /populations/REMP/hispanic.html

Office of Minority Health. (2015, May 8). Vital signs: Leading causes of death, prevalence of diseases and risk factors, and use of health services among Hispanics in the United States, 2009–2013. *Morbidity and Mortality Weekly Report*. Retrieved from http://www.cdc.gov /mmwr/preview/mmwrhtml/mm6417a5 .htm?s_cid=mm6417a5_w

Olmos, M. F., & Paravisini-Gebert, L. (2003). *Creole religions of the Caribbean: An introduction from vodou and Santeria to obeah and Espiritismo*. New York, NY: New York University Press.

Paulank, J. B., & Purnell, L. D. (2005). *Guide to culturally competent health care*. Philadelphia, PA: F. A. Davis Company. Retrieved from http://www.hawaii.hawaii.edu/nursing /RNHispanic10.html

Purnell, L. (2013). Transcultural health care. In *Transcultural health care: A culturally competent approach* (4th ed.). Philadelphia, PA: F. A. Davis Company.

Rhode Island Department of Health. (n.d.). *Latino /Hispanic culture & health*. Retrieved from http://www.health.ri.gov/chic/minority/ lat_cul.php

Ruiz, J., Steffen, P., & Smith, T. (2013, March). Hispanic mortality paradox: A systematic review and meta-analysis of the longitudinal literature. *American Journal of Public Health, 103*(3). Retrieved from http://ajph .aphapublications.org/doi/abs/10.2105 /AJPH.2012.301103

Searight, H. R., & Gafford, J. (2005). Cultural diversity at the end of life: Issues and guidelines for family physicians. *American Family Physician, 71*(3), 515–522. Retrieved from http:// www.aafp.org/afp/2005/0201/p515.html

U.S. Census Bureau. (2012). *American community survey: Table B03001*. Retrieved from http:// factfinder2.census.gov/faces/tableservices/jsf /pages/productview.xhtml?pid=ACS_12_1YR _B03001&prodType=table>

U.S. Census Bureau. (2013). *Facts for features: Hispanic heritage month 2014: Sept. 15–Oct. 15*. Retrieved from http://www.census.gov /newsroom/facts-for-features/2014 /cb14-ff22.html

Vega, W. A., Kolody, B., Aguilar-Gaxiola, S., et. al. (1998). Lifetime prevalence of DSM-III-R psychiatric disorders among urban and rural Mexican Americans in California. *Archives of General Psychiatry, 55*(9), 771–778.

Yasmin, S. (2014, January 17). Decoding the Hispanic paradox. *The Dallas Morning News*. Retrieved from http://www.dallasnews.com /opinion/sunday-commentary/20140117- decoding-the-hispanic-paradox.ece

Zayas, L., & Pilat, A. (2008). A suicidal behavior in Latinas: Explanatory cultural factors and implications for intervention. *Suicide and Life-Threatening Behavior, 38*(3), 334–342. Retrieved from http://www.ncbi.nlm.nih .gov/pmc/articles/PMC2662359/

© Jose Gil/Dreamstime.com

CHAPTER 8

American Indian and Alaskan Native Populations

What we see as science, Indians see as magic. What we see as magic, they see as science. I don't find a hopeless contradiction. If we can appreciate each other's views, we can see the whole picture more clearly.
   —Hammerschlag (1988, p. 14)

Everything on the earth has a purpose, every disease an herb to cure it, and every person a mission. This is the Indian theory of existence.
   —Mourning Dove Salish, 1888–1936

Key Concepts

Sand painting
Medicine wheel
Medicine bundle

Sweat lodges
Peyote

Learning Objectives

After reading this chapter, you should be able to:
1. Provide an overview of the social and economic circumstances of American Indian and Alaskan Native populations in the United States.
2. Provide an overview of American Indian and Alaskan Native beliefs about the causes of illness.

© Diana Lundin/Dreamstime.com

3. Describe at least three American Indian and Alaskan Native healing practices.
4. Describe American Indian and Alaskan Native health risk behaviors and common illnesses.
5. List at least six tips for working with American Indian and Alaskan Native populations.

Introduction

The American Indian and Alaskan Native populations include a broad range of people and cultures that existed in North America at the time of its "discovery" by Christopher Columbus. The U.S. Census Bureau identifies this population as a race that includes anyone having origins in any of the original peoples of North and South America (including Central America) who maintains a tribal affiliation or community attachment (U.S. Census Bureau, 2012). A wide range of other terms have been used to describe "American Indian and Alaska Native" such as Native Indians, American Indians, Native American Indians, Indians, Aborigines, Native Alaskans, and Original Americans. Other American Indian and Alaskan Native populations include the Hawaiian and Pacific Islanders, but they are now counted separately by the U.S. Census Bureau. Race is not the same as culture, but Census Bureau information provides a general profile of the combined populations.

Health conditions among the original tribes were directly associated with living off the land and holding a holistic philosophy regarding promoting health. Before Columbus, American Indian and Alaskan Native populations lived a pre-industrial lifestyle much like hunter-gathers and small-scale farmers on other continents. Each tribe or nation had its own practices based on its own culture and geographic region. The Seminoles in Florida, Quinault in Washington, Chumash in California, Inuit in Alaska, and Iroquois in the Northeast were all very different, living on different foods, facing different weather conditions, and developing their own cultural practices and languages. Yet all eventually suffered conquest, and many endured forced dislocation and generally became economically disadvantaged (Management Sciences for Health, n.d.). Today the approximately 2.6 million American Indian and Alaskan Native people are culturally diverse and geographically dispersed (U.S. Census Bureau, 2012).

Current disease patterns among American Indians and Alaska Natives are associated with negative consequences of poverty, limited access to health services, and cultural dislocation. Inadequate education, high rates of unemployment, discrimination, and cultural differences all contribute to unhealthy lifestyles and disparities in access to health care for many American Indian and Alaska Native people (Management Sciences for Health, n.d.).

In a special message on Indian affairs delivered to Congress July 8, 1970, President Richard Nixon declared:

> But the story of the Indian in America is something more than the record of the white man's frequent aggression, broken agreements, intermittent remorse and prolonged failure. It is a record of enormous contributions to this country—to its art and culture, to its strength and spirit, to its sense of history and its sense of purpose.

This chapter provides a brief history of American Indian and Alaskan Native populations and information about their current status in the United States, their beliefs about the causes of illness and healing practices, behavioral risk factors, and the common health problems they face.

Terminology

The various words used to describe American Indian and Alaskan Native populations have varied in popularity and use. None of these terms is accurate because they are derived from mistaken identity of peoples by Columbus and from naming the country after a post-Columbian Italian explorer and map maker, Amerigo Vespucci. Each is based on labels created by Europeans who generally saw the great variety of cultures as one large group of native people. Certainly the Europeans learned to recognize and deal with individual tribes, but a tribe was just seen as a subset of a group of generally less worthy people.

Like most people, American Indian and Alaskan Native people prefer to be referred to by the society with whom they themselves identify. So, for example, Navajo and Blackfeet prefer being identified by their specific tribe or nation. When we refer to American Indian and Alaskan Native people, we are referring to a broad group of cultures similar in scope to the group of cultures included in the label "Europeans." It is intended as a neutral and all-encompassing term for pre-Columbian cultures located in North America. Certainly, Germans still prefer to be called German as much as the English prefer to be called English or British despite being now part of the European Union. Some broad generalizations can be made about such classifications of peoples, but cultural practices and differences can lead to great partnerships as well as great conflicts and to wars. In this chapter, we refer to American Indian and Alaskan Native populations generally, but we also describe some groups more specifically, such as American Indians located within what is now the contiguous 48 United States, Alaska Natives, and specific tribes or nations depending upon the context and available data.

History of American Indians and Alaska Natives in the United States

The American Indian and Alaskan Native populations are descendents of the first humans who migrated from Asia and Europe to North America about 30,000 years ago. Christopher Columbus "discovered" North America in 1492 during his voyage in search for the East Indies.

He used the name "Indians" to describe the native people of the land because he mistakenly thought he was in the Far East.

The European migration initiated what is sometimes called the Columbian Exchange and began in the 15th century. It changed the lives of American Indian and Alaskan Native populations as well as Europeans even before there was physical contact. In the Columbian Exchange, foods, wealth, and customs were transferred back and forth between America, Europe, and Africa. For instance, the modern horse was introduced to North America by the Spanish. When a thousand captured horses were released by American Indians in 1580 after a skirmish with the Spanish, the horses spread into the American Great Plains and changed the way of life for tens of thousands of people who began to use the horse for the first time. This transformed many cultural and economic practices among Plains Indians. It changed their culture into one based on horses that allowed mobility and effective hunting of the vast quantities of bison on the Great Plains. Likewise, corn, potatoes, and tomatoes were transferred to Europe from the Americas.

As transportation and trade increased, new diseases were transmitted by the Europeans, such as smallpox and measles, which spread between American Indian and Alaskan Native tribes even before many even heard of the Europeans. American Indian and Alaskan Native Americans had no immunities to these diseases, and hundreds of thousands of American Indian and Alaskan Native people died. Likewise, it is also believed that syphilis was first transported to Europe from the Americas.

Vast differences in culture caused misunderstanding and conflict. The American Indian and Alaskan Native populations were viewed by the Europeans as a problem. The solution was to eradicate them through wars and to push any survivors to low-valued lands. The Europeans viewed land as something to be held by an owner with various groups managing their own parcels of land. The American Indian and Alaskan Native populations generally viewed land as unbounded except for physical barriers; land was something to be used but not owned. This does not mean life was easy or peaceful. Intertribal wars and preindustrial living off the land presented ongoing dangers and challenges to health and survival. Once it became evident that the Europeans intended to stay and seize land in any way necessary, American Indian and Alaskan Native populations began to initiate their own acts of violence against the Europeans.

In the 19th century, the westward expansion of the United States caused large numbers of American Indians to be moved farther west, often by force, almost always reluctantly. The U.S. Congress, under President Andrew Jackson, passed the Indian Removal Act of 1830, which authorized the president to conduct treaties to exchange American Indian land east of the Mississippi River for lands west of the river. As many as 100,000 Native Americans eventually relocated in the West as a result of the Indian Removal Act. In theory, relocation was supposed to be voluntary, but in practice great pressure was put on American Indian leaders to sign removal treaties.

The United States purchased Alaska from Russia in 1867. In 1906, the Homestead Act granted land to the following individuals:

> Indian or Eskimo of full or mixed blood who resides in and is a native of said district, and who is the head of a family, or is 21 years of age; and the land so allotted shall be deemed the homestead of the allotted and his heirs in perpetuity, and shall be inalienable and nontaxable until otherwise provided by Congress. (Alaska Native Heritage Center, 2000.)

This act was the first to establish land for Alaska Natives, but it left out many tribes. Discrimination and segregation were prevalent in Alaska, especially between Alaska Natives and whites (Russians and Americans). In 1945, Alaska passed a law that ended legal segregation, and this marked the start of a new beginning. According to the Alaska Native Claims Settlement Act of 1971, 40 million acres of land and nearly a billion dollars was awarded to Alaska Natives.

Many steps were taken to "civilize" American Indian and Alaskan Native populations and to change their cultural practices, such as not permitting them to speak their native language and creating Indian boarding schools to keep children away from their tribal setting. The Indian Citizenship Act of 1924 gave U.S. citizenship to American Indians, in part because of an interest by many to see them merged with the American mainstream and also because of the service of many American Indian and Alaskan Native Americans in World War I.

American Indian and Alaskan Native Populations in the United States

There are 566 federally recognized tribes and more than 100 state recognized tribes. As a result of early treaties, the federal government provides health care services to federally recognized tribes through the Indian Health Service (IHS), part of the U.S. Department of Health and Human Services. Comprehensive health services are available to approximately 2 million American Indians and Alaska Natives (Office of Minority Health, 2014a). Some groups of people identify themselves with "tribes" but are not recognized by the states or the federal government.

The majority of those who receive IHS services live on reservations and in rural communities in 36 states, generally in the western United States and Alaska. Thirty-six percent of the IHS service area population resides in non-Indian areas, and 600,000 are served in urban clinics. The urban clientele has less access to hospitals, health clinics, and contract health services provided by the IHS or to health programs in tribal areas. Studies on the urban American Indian and Alaskan Native populations have frequently documented poor health and limited health care options for this group (Office of Minority Health, 2014b).

Since 1972, IHS has embarked on a series of initiatives to fund health-related activities in off-reservation settings to make health care services accessible to urban American Indians and Alaska Natives. Currently, the IHS funds 33 urban Indian health organizations, which operate at sites located in cities throughout the United States. Approximately 600,000 American Indians and Alaska Natives are eligible for this program. The 33 programs administer medical services, dental services, community services, alcohol and drug abuse prevention, education and treatment, AIDS and sexually transmitted disease education and prevention services, mental health services, nutrition education and counseling services, pharmacy services, health education, optometry services, social services, and home health care.

In 2010, almost 28% of American Indians and Alaskan Natives spoke a language other than English at home. American Indian and Alaskan Native populations use many different languages. The Census Bureau recognizes 169 American Indian and Alaskan Native languages, but these languages are spoken by less than half a million people (U.S. Census Bureau, 2011).

For instance, the Alaska Native Language Center currently reports 20 known native languages. However, this organization also reports that many languages will become extinct by the next generation (Palca, 2002).

In 2010 the median family income for American Indian and Alaska Natives was $39,664, compared to $67,892 for non-Hispanic whites. Twenty-six percent of American Indians and Alaskan Natives age 16 and over worked in management and professional occupations, compared to 40% of whites. Also, 28% of this racial group lived at the poverty level, compared to 10.6% of non-Hispanic whites (U.S. Census Bureau, 2012).

Like many other people, American Indian and Alaskan Native populations generally believe in a Supreme Creator; most tribes also have lesser deities and mediators between the spirit world and the earth. They believe that people should try to maintain constant, daily harmony and contact with the Creator, follow all sacred teachings, and treat all life (people, animals, plants, rocks, rivers, rainbows, etc.) with respect.

American Indian and Alaskan Native populations are family based and are taught to respect and obey their elders. The elders are seen as people with much knowledge and they are considered to be the head of the household. After the elders, men are considered to be the leaders of the house. Men also are viewed as the leaders of the tribe, protectors, and fighters. Traditionally, the men would hunt to bring food for the whole community; as a result, they are still seen as the providers for the family.

Women are viewed as being responsible for housework and for teaching the children the ways of the people. The children have to learn the traditions of the tribe and the community and have to respect the elders. The older family members keep an eye on the new generation to make sure that they are following traditions.

In addition to believing in close family relations, American Indian and Alaskan Native populations also believe in living as a community. A person does not need to be from the same tribe or even have blood relations with anyone from the community to be a member of the community. As many as 80 different tribes can live together in one community (West Virginia Division of Culture and History, 2008). The elders are in charge of teaching and guiding the community in the ways of the tribes. They have the responsibility to pass on their history orally and to teach the community the traditional ways of the tribe. They show the new generation how to make traditional arts and crafts and show them the traditional rituals.

One of the rituals is storytelling, or experiencing stories through songs or other performances. Songs play an important part in the lives of American Indian and Alaskan Native populations. These songs are usually ancestral songs that tell the story of the ancestors and of hardships they had to face. Many of the songs are related to nature and hunting. The songs are considered to be the property of the person who created or dreamt them or of the community after that person passes away. If someone wants to reenact the song, they must obtain special permission from the community.

Alaskan Native populations include people from villages or tribes such as Aleut, Inupiat, Yupik, Eskimo, and Athabaskan peoples. Villages consist of mostly related families; however, if residents are not related, they are still treated as one big family. Alaska Natives typically develop close-knit relationships with one another. Village members watch out for one another, and food is always shared when an animal is caught. Alaska Natives believe that if a person shares his or her food, the person will catch more animals in the future. When a young man experiences his first kill, it is tradition for him to give the entire kill to the elders, as a sign of respect and as a way to indicate passing on tradition from generation to generation. The tradition of sharing and giving is a major part of Alaskan Native culture.

American Indian and Alaskan Native General Philosophy About Disease Prevention and Health Maintenance

Traditionally, health was a continual process of staying strong spiritually, mentally, and physically. This strength keeps away or overcomes the forces that cause illness. People must stay in harmony with themselves, other people, their natural environment, and their Creator. Adhering to traditional and tribal beliefs and obeying tribal religious codes is another part of staying healthy; violating tribal tenets or laws may have consequences such as physical or mental illness, disability, ongoing bad luck, or trauma. The violation must be set right before harmony and health can be restored. Some American Indians believe illness is the price to be paid either for something that happened in the past or for something that will happen in the future; therefore, each person is responsible for his or her own health. Illness is not looked upon as abnormal.

This group does not believe in biomedicine or germ theory; they believe illness is caused by personal responsibility, qualities, and spirits (Spector, 2004). Three distinct causes of illness trigger patient suffering: (1) a hostile spirit thrusting a foreign object, such as a sharp stone, insect, or a tangled thread, into the person; (2) the patient's soul leaving the body on its own accord; or (3) the patient's soul being stolen away by enemy spirits (Haas, 2007).

Despite the fact that some Alaska Natives are nonreligious, traditional natives believe that the cause of illness is derived from spirits (Alexandria, 1994). To get rid of an illness, a shaman is needed to remove the ill spirit and restore health. Healing ceremonies can take place in public, and the shaman encourages village members to participate to get rid of the bad spirit that is causing the illness. In addition, some shamans have medical skills that include treating burns with fat, cleaning wounds with urine, amputating frozen gangrenous limbs, and setting broken bones. Traditional natives believe that shamans have the ability to fly and reach the heavens.

Currently, beliefs about the causes of illness are beginning to shift. Alaska Natives noticed that they were less likely to get sick when they traveled in small nomadic bands. However, when Alaska Natives began to settle, they noticed that people were more likely to become ill and die. As a result, they have begun to lean toward the germ theory. Shamans are still used today because it is often difficult to reach health care clinics. In some instances, both a shaman and Western medicine are used in combination to treat illness.

Worldview

Being in harmony is important to the people in these collectivist cultures. Group success is more important than the success of the individual. American Indian and Alaskan Native populations tend to see property as communal. A strong sense of connectedness and an understanding of the world comes from the cycles and natural rhythms of life. Health is achieved through balance. Autonomy is important, but illness is viewed as a family matter. Participation in religious ceremonies and prayer is believed to promote health.

Generally having a fatalistic view, people may not take preventative actions, such as participating in health screenings or treating health issues. American Indian and Alaskan Native peoples also do not recognize silent disease—in other words, if there are no symptoms, then one is not ill. This provides another barrier to participating in health screenings and to treating illnesses that are "invisible" such as cancer.

American Indian and Alaskan Native populations have no precise beliefs regarding what might occur after death. Some believe that humans return as ghosts, or that people go to another world. Others believe that nothing definite can be known about one's fate after this life. Combinations of belief are common. Organ donations and autopsies are generally not desired. Do not resuscitate orders are not acceptable in many tribes because they are believed to bring about negative thoughts and, hence, inevitable loss.

There is high respect for elders, and elders play an important role is passing down cultural traditions to children and grandchildren. In general, respect is a core value and central to all interactions. Respect is viewed as not talking about oneself, bragging, or talking back.

American Indian and Alaskan Native populations select their words carefully and may take long pauses during conversations. Do not interrupt when a person is speaking. Avoiding eye contact and keeping a respectful distance is encouraged. "A primary social premise is that no person has the right to speak for another" (Purnell, 2013, p. 449). Loudness is considered aggressive, and their handshakes are light. They are present focused. Their perspective on time is that it cannot be controlled, and planning for the future may be seen as being foolish (Purnell, 2013).

Amulets, sacred objects, and medicine bags are valued. Do not remove them without asking permission. Remove them carefully and replace them as soon as possible.

American Indian and Alaskan Native populations tend to complain of pain in general terms. For example, the patient may state that he or she is uncomfortable. Pain is often undertreated in this population. This is, in part, because it is viewed as a violation of proscriptive behaviors. When sick, they are often stoic and quiet.

Did You Know?

For some American Indian and Alaskan Native populations, having long hair is not an issue of style; it is related to culture. Cutting one's hair is related to health or mourning the death of a close relative or loved one. If a health procedure requires that hair be cut or shaved, ask if the hair should be returned to the patient or to a family member. This includes needing to shave an area of the body for a surgical procedure. Some members of this culture will wash the hair of the ill person as a custom or ceremony. Touching the hair of a pregnant woman should be avoided.

Pregnancy, Birth, and Child Rearing

Although each American Indian and Alaskan Native culture has its own beliefs and rituals, there are many descriptions of American Indian and Alaskan Native childbirth practices involving the pregnant woman secluding herself, with perhaps a woman helper, and having a private birth experience out of the sight of men. Early accounts of the childbirth practices of the American Indian and Alaskan Native population indicate that pregnant women were to limit their activities and watch their diet and behavior to protect the baby. Certain foods might affect the fetus and cause unwanted physical characteristics. For example, the Cherokee believed that eating raccoon meat would cause illness or death of the baby. They believed that speckled trout could cause birthmarks. Mothers- and fathers-to-be performed rituals to guarantee a safe delivery, such as daily washing of hands and feet.

As the birth grew closer, women and their families observed other rituals to ensure an easy and healthy birth. Some newborns were ceremonially plunged into water on a daily basis for up to 2 years to gain strength. European descriptions of Native American women's quick recovery from childbirth may have been exaggerated. But generally, the excellent physical conditioning of women would have facilitated their recovery from childbirth, allowing most women to return to their regular duties quickly.

Children are considered to be specially linked to the spiritual world and in general are indulged rather than punished. Europeans were surprised at the absence of physical punishment as a means to discipline children. Sometimes the children were chastised by having a little water thrown in their faces, and there were reports of Creek parents occasionally scratching disobedient children and, along with the Chickasaws, allowing young ones to be beaten by someone outside the household. Corporal punishment was clearly the exception rather than the rule, although ridicule or fear of the supernatural might be used to produce obedience.

The transition from childhood to adulthood is well defined. For girls there are sometimes rituals surrounding the onset of menstruation. For boys, whose passage through puberty is less biologically evident, there are more elaborate ceremonies such as the *huskinaw,* a rigorous physical trial, and the vision quest, a spiritual journey. Both involved isolation as well as sensory deprivation and stimulation; their purpose was to begin a new path without forfeiting their upbringing.

Marriage partners might be tentatively chosen by parents, and a young man could be expected to consult the parents of his intended. Yet there was no coercion: both young men and young women had a choice when it came to marrying and deciding whether to remain wed.

Nutrition and Exercise

With regard to their dietary practices, American Indian and Alaskan Native populations believe that certain foods are sacred. For example, some believe the Great Spirit Hashtali gave the people corn as a present, so it is considered to be sacred. Corn is used quite frequently for meals because it can be easily grown and does not require much work. Another sacred food is blood soup, which is made from a mixture of animal blood and corn flour cooked in broth. Blood soup may be used as a sacred meal during the nighttime Holy Smoke ceremony of the Sioux, which is a celebration of Mother Earth that involves the use of the peace pipe (Advameg Inc., 2007). Wolves and coyotes are the only animals that are not hunted for food, because they are regarded as teachers or pathfinders and held sacred by all tribes (Advameg Inc., 2007). At marriage ceremonies, the bride and groom exchange food instead of rings. The groom brings venison or some other meat to indicate his intention to provide for the household, and the bride provides corn or bean bread to symbolize her willingness to care for and provide nourishment for the household (Advameg Inc., 2007).

American Indian and Alaskan Native populations have changed their diet and food practices possibly more than any other group in the United States. Although the current diet of American Indian and Alaskan Native populations may vary by tribe and by personal traits such as age, it closely resembles that of the U.S. white population (Advameg, 2007).

A food guide for American Indians is illustrated in **Figure 8.1**. Although current nutritional practices are similar to those of the general U.S. population, American Indian and Alaskan Native populations originally relied largely on meat, fish, plants, berries, and nuts. The most widely grown foods were maize (corn) and wild rice. Many tribes grew beans and enjoyed them as *succotash,* a dish made of beans, corn, dog meat, and bear fat. Tubers (roots) were also a common food and were cooked slowly in underground pits until the hard tough root became a highly digestible gelatin-like soup.

The American Indian and Alaskan Native populations were shunned and marginalized, but their foods have been integrated into the modern American menu. These include succotash in the South, wild rice dishes in the northern Plains, pumpkin soup in New England, chili in the Southwest, broiled salmon in the Pacific Northwest, and corn on the cob in most areas of the country. Traditionally, American Indian and Alaskan Native peoples lived an active farming and hunting lifestyle that was conducive to better health than the sedentary lifestyle now customary for all population groups in the United States.

Alaska Natives continue to rely substantially on subsistence foods such as fish, terrestrial mammals, marine mammals, and wild plants (Ballew et al., 2004). These foods provide good sources of vitamin A, vitamin B_{12}, omega-3 fatty acids, iron, and protein. Ballew and colleagues' (2004) meta-analysis of recent studies has shown substantial regional and seasonal variation in food intake patterns among Alaska Natives, with an increased use of store foods such as rice, spaghetti, and bread as well as sugared beverages for many months. The analysis reported high total fat and saturated fat intakes and low fiber, vitamin C, folate, and calcium intakes.

When obtaining traditional foods, the men usually do the strenuous hunting, and the women gather berries and plants that will aid in nutrition. Women also prepare and store the food after it is gathered.

Mental Health

American Indian and Alaskan Native populations experience mental disorders at rates similar to those of the overall population. The most significant mental health issues are depression, substance abuse, and anxiety, including posttraumatic stress disorder (PTSD). In some, but not all, American Indian and Alaskan Native groups, alcoholism and illicit drug use disorder rates are much higher than U.S. averages. Although American Indian and Alaska Native groups have high rates of alcohol abuse, most members are not alcoholics (American Psychiatric Association, 2009).

Cultural factors can influence how people feel or describe mental health and their acceptance of mental health issues and treatment. Among Indians/Native people, the concept of mental health has different meanings and interpretations. Often physical concerns and psychological concerns are not separated, and emotional distress may be expressed in different ways. In fact words for "depressed" and "anxious" were not part of the American Indian and Alaskan Native languages,

A Guide to Daily Food Choices

KEY
These symbols show fats, oils, and added sugars in foods.

⬤ Fat
(Naturally occuring and added)

▽ Sugars
(added)

Fat's, Oils & Sweets
use sparingly

Low or Non-fat Dairy Products
Milk, Yogurt & Cheese Group
2-3 Servings

Meat, Poultry, Fish, Dry Beans
Eggs & Nuts Group
2-3 Servings

Vegetable Group
3-5 Servings

Fruit Group
2-4 Servings

Bread, Cereal Group
6-11Servings

Rice, Pasta Group
6-11Servings

FIGURE 8.1

Native American food guide.

Source: CANFIT, Berkeley, CA. For more information, call 510-644-1533 or http://info@canfit.org. Used with permission.

and culturally different expressions of illness, such as ghost sickness and heartbreak syndrome, do not correspond to modern medicine diagnoses (National Alliance on Mental Illness [NAMI], 2014).

Death and Dying

There is a great variety of beliefs about death and dying across the various American Indian and Alaskan Native populations. Some American Indian and Alaskan Native cultures do not speak of death, dying, or of negative outcomes to medical procedures because any mention might cause a negative outcome. Other tribal communities have no difficulty speaking directly about death or dying situations, and wish to have all the information available (e.g., some Pueblo, Lakota, northern Plains, mid-western, and northeastern tribes). These tribes tend to look at death as a natural part of the circle of life, not to be feared, as it may include a reunion with the ancestors who went before.

Cultural-Bound Illnesses

There are no particular illnesses associated with American Indian and Alaskan Native peoples, but many illnesses are associated with a cultural response to acculturation with Europeans. For instance, alcohol, now a major problem for a significant percentage of American Indian and Alaskan Native people, was plied to the tribes for trade and subjugation. The loss of traditional economic and cultural ways to mark life transitions, such as reduction or elimination of right-of-passage into adulthood ceremonies, may contribute to the onset of early smoking. Blatant prejudice has contributed to conditions symptomatic of poor, undereducated, purposely marginalized peoples of any minority group.

A couple of illnesses attributed to American Indian and Alaskan Native peoples may not have a defined cultural base. Ghost sickness is a psychological condition in which a person has an obsessive fear and preoccupation with the death of a person who meant a great deal to him or her. This can be associated with a person's concern that proper burial rites were not followed and that the deceased may not be able to move forward in the afterlife. Some attribute this illness to a severe case of grief and mourning. Concern about burial practices may be just one of many fears that might trigger the condition in any population.

Similarly, a condition called heartbreak syndrome also has been attributed to American Indian and Alaskan Native populations, but it is more probably a general human condition. The American Heart Association has described this condition as involving a sudden onset of heart pain, and even damage, shortly after an intense event such as the death of a loved one or a divorce (American Heart Association, n.d.).

Healing Traditions, Healers, and Healing Aids

Most American Indian and Native American tribes have healing traditions related to their beliefs about the causation of illness and disease, which are not based on Western science. Therefore, many healing traditions and rituals focus on harmony, and the overall purpose is to bring participants into harmony with themselves, their tribe, and all of life. Healing occurs when someone is restored to harmony and connected to universal powers. Traditional healing is holistic. It focuses on the person, not the illness, so the process does not focus on symptoms or diseases but addresses the total individual.

Alaska Native traditional healing practices are rooted in a 10,000-year history and are reemerging today as a holistic healing approach for individuals and communities. These methods are often used in combination with Western-based medical therapies for the purpose of health promotion, disease prevention, pain reduction, and enhancement of psychological wellness (Corral, 2007). Many ancient traditions for healing are still used by Alaskan Natives today.

Despite the emergence of a complementary relationship between Alaskan traditional healing and Western medicine, traditional healing practices are quite distinguishable when compared to the Western medicine mode of treatment. Allopathic medicine focuses on identifying and treating a specific diagnosis, whereas traditional healing strives to restore the patient's sense of natural balance and harmony with self, community, and culture. Traditional healing attempts to nurture the mind–body–spirit connection and to actively involve the patient in finding renewed commitment to lifelong health and wellness (Corral, 2007).

Medicinal plants, such as roots, berries, leaves, and flowers, have historically been used as healing agents throughout Alaska's many regions. These medicinal plants are used in numerous ways to heal everything from the common cold, flesh wounds, and mouth sores to promoting healthy pregnancy and for many other applications (Corral, 2007). The Devil's Club (*Oplopanax horridus* [OH]) is a common medicinal plant widely used in Alaska and British Columbia for treating a variety of ailments, including arthritis, fever, and diabetes. According to Tai and colleagues (2006), ethanolic extract of OH has strong antioxidant activity and has antiproliferative (meaning it prevents the spread and growth of cells) effects on several types of cancer cells. The medicinal plants are aimed more at healing bodily ailments, but other traditional healing modalities focus on the spirit and the mind.

Healing Ceremonies

Ceremonies are used to help groups of people return to harmony; they are not used for individual healing. The ceremonies used by the tribes vary, and there are differences in the way they practice medicine.

For example, the Navajo heal through their **sand painting** (see **Figure 8.2**). Sitting on the floor of a house, the medicine person begins painting at sunrise using ground colored rocks

FIGURE 8.2

Sand painting.

Source: © Bestweb/ShutterStock, Inc.

and minerals. The paintings depict the gods, elements of the heavens, and religious objects. When the painting, which includes complex forms and designs in great detail, is completed, the patient is placed in the center of the painting and the healing ceremony, which includes rituals and chants, is performed. Before sunset, the medicine person destroys the painting. The sands are sent to the desert and scattered on the four winds.

The Iroquois practice medicine through their False Faces, a religious society. Each spring and fall, when most illnesses occur, society members wear strange and distorted masks to drive illness and disease away from the tribe. Wearing these masks and ragged clothes and carrying rattles made from tortoise shells, they perform a dance. After the dance, society members go from house to house to rid the community of evil.

Some tribes use **medicine wheels** (see **Figure 8.3**), and the medicine wheel's large circle measures 213 feet around. The 28 spokes radiating from its center represent the number of days in the lunar cycle. A medicine wheel is a metaphor or symbol that represents the circle of life and the individual journey each person must take to find his or her own path. Within the medicine wheel are the four cardinal directions (north, south, east, and west) and the four sacred colors. The Mother Earth is below the wheel and the Father Sky is above it. The south (white) represents fire and passion, and the associated with it, such as the eagle and lion, represent pride, strength, and courage. The north (blue) represents air and flight and is associated with winged animals that fly, such as the owl and hummingbird. The west (black) is associated with water and emotions and is associated with animals that work in teams and prepare for winter, such as the snake (because it sheds its skin) and the beaver. The east (red) is linked to the earth and wisdom and is related to animals that have layers of fat to sustain them during the winter, such as the buffalo. The wheel helps American Indians to see exactly where they are and in which areas they need to develop to realize and fulfill their potential. They see that people are all connected to one another, and by

FIGURE 8.3

Medicine wheel.

Source: © Dana White/PhotoEdit, Inc.

showing the intricacies of the interwoven threads of life, they can envision their role in life. It helps them understand that without their part in the tapestry, the bigger picture is not as it should be. It is a model to be used to view self, society, or anything that one could ever think of looking into.

Healers

Medicine men, who are prominent healers in the American Indian community, can be male or female. They have knowledge about the interrelationships of human beings, the earth, the universe, plants, animals, the sun, the moon, and the stars (Spector, 2004). These healers are in tune with the way human beings interact with the world around them, and they are able to use their environment to help provide treatment. A healer is held in high regard because it has taken him or her many years of training and apprenticeship to be able to heal the community. Many American Indians first consult a medicine man before seeking other health professionals because of their belief that the treatment they receive from the traditional healer is better than treatment from Western health care establishments (Spector, 2004).

Medicine men have power that other members of the tribe do not have. Their power comes from visions that lead them into studying medicine or by being born into a family with many generations of medicine people. In many tribes, both men and women can serve as medicine people, but in some, like the Yurok in California, only women can be medicine people. Some medicine people are also shamans (holy men and women). A shaman is a healer who goes on a "soul journey" or a "soul flight" to the spirit world, aided by the power of songs, drums, rattles, and other objects, to communicate with spirits and then performs a healing ceremony (Haas, 2007). All medicine people are considered to be learned and are respected members of the tribe.

Medicine people have naturalistic skills. Some medicine people specialize in herbal medicine, bone setting, midwifery, or counseling. Often the medicine man cures people simply because they believe in him or her (placebo effect). Medicine people bring hope, understanding, and confidence to patients, which are often as powerful as modern medicine could have been. They work in the unseen world of good and bad spirits to restore harmony and health.

American Indians believe that they are related to all forms of life. Medicine people make medicine tools out of materials from nature, including fur, skins, bone, crystals, shells, roots, and feathers. They use these tools to evoke the spirit of what the tool has been made of, which helps strengthen their inner powers. For example, a medicine drum is made of wood and animal skins. When medicine people play the drum, they can call up the assistance of the spirits of the tree and the animal from which the drum was made.

Medicine people keep their medicine tools in a **medicine bundle** (see **Figure 8.4**), a large piece of cloth or hide that they tie securely with a thong, piece of yarn, or string. The contents of the medicine bundle are sacred. Each medicine person may own or share different medicine bundles: one's own, the tribe's, and bundles for special purposes, such as seeking visions, hunting, or protection in battle. Some are passed down from one generation to the next. Personal medicine bundles are private, and asking about another person's medical tools

FIGURE 8.4

Medicine bundle.

Source: © Khumina/ShutterStock, Inc.

is forbidden. Some medicine bundles are small enough to be worn around the neck. Medicine bundles that belong to tribes are often called the "grandmothers" because they have the power to nourish and nurture the tribe and promote continued well-being. Tribal medicine bundles grow stronger with each passing year.

Tribes carefully guard the knowledge of their medicine people. Members of the tribe who want to become medicine people must first serve a long apprenticeship with an experienced medicine person. In many tribes, medicine men cannot charge for their services. Gifts, however, are expected. Some tribes do require payment and have set lists of standard gifts. Nearly all tribes recognize tobacco as a gift of respect.

One way medicine men help heal the community is by using various forms of plants and herbal remedies. Medicine men spend many years during their apprenticeship mastering the uses of plants and herbal remedies to be able to cure disease (Bonvillain, 1997). They know which plants or teas cure different illnesses. For example, in the 1500s medicine men used white pine or hemlock to cure scurvy, caused by a vitamin C deficiency (Bonvillain, 1997). Hemlock is an excellent source of vitamin C, according to Frankis (2006). The plant most widely used for healing the American Indian community is tobacco. Tobacco has many useful purposes, such as treating burns, earaches, stomach cramps, and inflammation (Bonvillain, 1997).

Certain people in each tribe are recognized as healers. They receive special teachings. Healing traditions are passed from one generation to the next through visions, stories, and dreams. Healing does not follow written guidelines. Healers work differently with each person they help. They use their herbs, ceremony, and power in the best way for each individual. Healing might involve sweat lodges, talking circles, ceremonial smoking of tobacco, herbalism, animal spirits, or vision quests. Each tribe uses its own techniques. The techniques by themselves are not considered to be "traditional healing." They are only steps toward becoming whole, balanced, and connected.

Sweat Lodges

Sweat lodges are used for healing and balancing. American Indians consider sweat lodges to be a good way to clean one's body and sweat out illness or disease (Bonvillain, 1997). Hot stones covered in water are placed in a small, confined, dark enclosure, creating a steam bath. The stones, considered by American Indians to be their oldest living relatives, are usually lava rocks that do not break when heated. Sweating removes toxins from the body, stimulates the endocrine glands, and makes the heart pump more blood. American Indians believe that sweat lodges also bring balance and health to spirit, mind, and body. They use sweat lodges in many ways, such as before spiritual undertakings, to bring clarity to a problem, to call upon helpful spirits, and to reconnect with the Great Spirit.

Even the building of a sweat lodge is sacred and symbolic. Willow saplings are bent and tied together to form a square with four sides, which represents the four sacred directions. There usually is a single entryway that faces either west or east. The connected poles create a frame that looks like an overturned basket, which symbolically represents items such as the womb or arch of the sky. In some tribes there are 28 poles, which represent either the ribs of a woman, a female bear or turtle, or the lunar cycle. The framework is covered in the skins of buffalo or other animals that represent the animal world (see **Figure 8.5**). The interior of sweat lodges can be created out of many different materials depending on what is available to the community. The interior can be made out of furs, grasses, or various types of bark from trees. A small pit, or altar, is dug in the center of the lodge for the stones. A branch that represents the tree of life is placed in the middle of the altar and is surrounded by small stones. Antlers to move the hot stones and a medicine pipe are placed near the altar.

Before the sweat lodge is used, "The One Who Pours the Water" purifies the surrounding area by smearing it with sacred herbs to ensure that positive spirits will be present. A stone tender stays outside the lodge, heating stones and passing them inside when summoned by The One Who Pours the Water. One heated stone is not used; it is left for the spirits to sweat with and honors the spirits who have come to the ceremony.

FIGURE 8.5

Sweat lodge.

Source: Courtesy of Kirk Shoemaker.

Plants and Herbs

American Indians use herbs to purify the spirit and bring balance to people who are unhealthy in spirit, mind, or body. They learned about the healing powers of herbs by watching sick animals. Only a few of the herbs are discussed here, but a wide variety of plants and herbs are used by American Indians for healing. In fact, there are so many that books have been written about them.

Sage is believed to protect against bad spirits and to draw them out of the body or the soul. American Indians use sage for many purposes, such as to heal problems of the stomach, colon, nasal passages, kidneys, liver, lungs, pores of the skin, bones, and sex organs; to heal burns and scrapes; as an antiseptic for allergies, colds, and fever; as a gargle for sore throat; and as a tea to calm the nerves. Cedar, a tall evergreen tree, is a milder medicine than sage. It is combined with sage and sweetgrass, a plant that grows in damp environments like marshes or near water, to make a powerful mixture used in sacred ceremonies. Cedar fruit and leaves are boiled and then drunk to heal coughs. For head colds, cedar is burned and inhaled. Other herbs often used include acacia, prickly pear, saw palmetto, sunflower, yerba mansa, cliffrose, and cayenne.

Tobacco, often smoked in medicine pipes, is one of the most sacred plants to American Indians, and it is used in some way in nearly every cure. It is smoked pure and is not mixed with chemicals. When American Indians smoke sacred tobacco and other herbs, their breath, which they consider to be the source of life, becomes visible. When smoke is released, it rises up to the Great Spirit carrying prayers. People who share a pipe are acknowledging that they share the same breath. There are many different types of medicine pipes; some are for war, sun, and marriage, and others are tribal, personal, ceremonial, and social pipes. The pipe itself, made of wood with a soft pithy center, is symbolic, and some are shaped like animals. The bowl represents the female aspect of the Great Spirit—Mother Earth. The stem represents the male aspect of the Great Spirit—Father Sky. Together, the bowl and stem represent the union that brings forth life. The bowl in which tobacco is burned also symbolizes all that changes. The stem signifies all that is unchanging. Smoking the pipe is a central component in all ceremonies because it unites the two worlds of spirit and matter.

Peyote, which is a hallucinogenic drug, comes from a spineless, dome-shaped cactus (*Lophophora williamsii*) native to Mexico and the southwest United States. It has buttonlike tubercles that are chewed fresh or dry. Peyote has a history of ritual religious and medicinal use among certain American Indian and Alaskan Native tribes going back thousands of years. Peyote is legal only on Indian reservations. Because of its spiritual and healing properties, it is viewed by American Indians as an agent that allows one to encounter spirits and receive visions or messages from spirits or Gods. American Indians also believe that peyote "can be used to make a person throw up and thus this would expel the illness from the body" (Bonvillain, 1997).

What Do You Think?

Should the use of peyote for religious purposes be allowed in prisons?

> ***Title 42— The Public Health and Welfare, Chapter 21—Civil Rights Subchapter I —Generally, Sec. 1996a***—*Traditional Indian Religious Use of Peyote provides:* **(1)** *Notwithstanding any other provision of law, the use, possession, or transportation of peyote by an Indian for bona fide traditional ceremonial purposes in connection with the practice of a traditional Indian religion is lawful, and shall not be prohibited by the United States or any State. No Indian shall be penalized or discriminated against on the basis of such use, possession or transportation, including, but not limited to, denial of otherwise applicable benefits under public assistance programs.*

However this law also provides for possibly limiting this freedom for prisoners by requiring a balancing of personal rights and compelling governmental interest by indicating:

> **(5)** *This section shall not be construed as requiring prison authorities to permit, nor shall it be construed to prohibit prison authorities from permitting, access to peyote by Indians while incarcerated within Federal or State prison facilities.*

Currently, if a state intends to limit religious rights of a member of an Indian tribe to use peyote, it must confer with tribal religious leaders and narrowly craft a rule that is carefully limited to restrict practice only so much as is required to protect a compelling state interest. With overcrowding and correctional programs designed to end the use of drugs by most inmates, do you think the use of peyote by American Indians is something that should be limited in prisons? Does it create an opportunity for cross-cultural learning? Does it show favoritism for a particular cultural group? If a state allows the smoking of peyote, would it conflict with antismoking laws the state may have adopted to promote health? Does the issue of sincerity come into play when a prisoner claims a right to certain religious practices? What if those practices offend the sensibility of practitioners of another religion?

Dancing

Drumming, dancing, and singing are known to be very powerful sources of healing among Alaskan Natives. The ceremonies incorporate music, movement, and drum rhythms to penetrate within the people involved and aid them in fully expressing emotion, increasing physical energy, making a strong connection with life and one another, and promoting happiness. This also helps promote overall well-being and a sense of love among the community. These ceremonies can be used to prevent drug and alcohol abuse, domestic violence, and suicide, which are some of the most prevalent problems among Alaskan Natives (Corral, 2007).

Behavior Risk Factors and Prevalent Health Problems

Due to the great number and diversity of tribes and locations, it is important for health care professionals to gather data about the specific tribe and geographic region prior to developing any individual or community-based practice. However, some general patterns may be considered.

American Indians and Alaskan Natives have an infant death rate 60% higher than the rate for Caucasians (Office of Minority Health, 2014a). American Indians and Alaskan Natives are twice as likely to have diabetes as Caucasians. An example is the Pima tribe of Arizona, who has one of the highest diabetes rates in the world. American Indians and Alaskan Natives also have disproportionately high death rates from unintentional injuries and suicide. In 2010, their tuberculosis rate was 5.8%, compared to 2% for the white population (Office of Minority Health, 2014a). The 10 leading causes of death among American Indians and Alaskan Natives in 2010 were as follows:

1. Cancer
2. Heart disease
3. Unintentional injuries
4. Diabetes
5. Chronic liver disease, and cirrhosis
6. Chronic lower respiratory diseases
7. Stroke
8. Suicide
9. Nephritis, nephrotic syndrome, and nephrosis
10. Influenza and pneumonia (Office of Minority Health, 2014a)

Native youth aged 12 to 17 years and American Indians and Alaskan Natives adults aged 18 years or older had the highest prevalence of current smoking compared with other racial/ethnic populations (Office of Minority Health, 2014a).

On average, American Indian and Alaskan Native populations are twice as likely as non-Hispanic whites of similar age to have diabetes. As of 2011, 14.2% of the American Indian and Alaskan Natives aged 20 years or older and receiving care by the IHS had been diagnosed with diabetes. At the regional level, diabetes is least common among Alaskan Natives (5.5%) and most common among American Indians in southern Arizona (33.5%) (Office of Minority Health, 2014a).

American Indians have a high risk of motor vehicle deaths and injuries, which is caused by several factors. One factor is that they have the lowest rate of using seat belts in the nation. The other reason is their high rate of drinking and driving. The lands of American Indians do not impose taxes, and they do not have laws that prevent the sale of alcohol and tobacco products to minors. Because of this, the young population easily uses alcohol and tobacco products. Some American Indian and Alaskan Native populations believe that tobacco is sacred, and it is therefore more often used in ceremonies.

The American Indian and Alaskan Native populations also suffer a high suicide rate. American Indian and Alaska Native populations of all ages had a suicide rate of 16.93% compared to 12.08% for the general population. Suicide was the second leading cause of death for American Indians and Alaskan Natives between the ages of 10 and 34 years (Suicide Prevention Resource Center, n.d.).

Alcohol abuse has been linked to many health problems, both directly and indirectly. Generally, American Indian and Alaskan Native peoples abstain more and have fewer regular drinkers than most other populations, but those who do drink are more likely to drink heavily and have serious problems. When results are considered by single race without regard to ethnicity, 22.5% of American Indian or Alaskan Native adults were lifetime abstainers (higher than all other races except Asians at 42%) and had a lower percentage of regular drinkers (40.8%) than any other group except Asians (35.7%). White adults who abstained were 18.5%, and regular drinkers represented 54.7% (National Center for Health Statistics, 2014b).

However, when looking at heavy drinking (more than five drinks a day 12 times in the past year), American Indian and Alaskan Natives topped the list at 11.4%, higher than whites at 10.5%, almost twice as high as blacks at 6%, and 2.5 times greater than Asians at 4.7% (National Center for Health Statistics, 2014b). In 2013, chronic liver disease was the fifth leading cause of death for all American Indians/Alaska Natives, and the third leading cause of death for men, ages 35–64 (Office of Minority Health, 2015).

Alcohol has caused health problems and behavioral issues in many societies, but Alaskan Natives have been struck much harder than most. There are many theories as to why alcohol is such a major issue in Alaska, but one study conducted by the National Center for American Indian and Alaska Native Mental Health Research goes back to the beginning (Seale, Shellenberger, & Spence, 2006). According to this study, alcohol was not a part of Alaska's culture until it was introduced by the Russians, who used it to abuse the natives and take advantage of them. Alcohol quickly became a problem in small villages. The immediate effect was an increase in spousal abuse and neglect of daily chores. This behavior led to shame and guilt, which was often dealt with by more drinking. This behavior is learned by the children in the home, and the cycle continues. The average starting age for drinking is around 9 years old. The traditional culture for many Alaskan Natives is gone, and they are left to live with limited resources for success. Without adequate health education and easy access to medical or mental health care, it has become a difficult task to fight the problem of alcohol abuse.

Another behavioral risk factor that is prevalent among Alaskan Natives is the use of tobacco. Smoking or chewing tobacco is practiced by half of all Alaskan Natives more than the 12 years of age. "Of those patients who were screened for tobacco use during 2006, 46% were smokers. Fifty-nine percent used some form of tobacco" (Alaska Native Epidemiology Center, 2007, p. 30).

Obesity is a problem among Alaskan Natives, with 26% of U.S. whites being obese compared to 41% of Alaskan Natives (Office of Minority Health, 2013). Unintentional injuries and suicides are ranked second and fourth among Alaskan Natives, and both of these health disparities are preventable. The high rate of alcohol abuse among Alaskan Natives contributes to the toll of injuries (Alaska Department of Health & Social Services, 2002). Some of the other contributing factors to the high rate of unintentional injuries are the prevalence of guns in homes, no laws requiring helmets, and inadequate seat belt laws. "Firearm death rates for Alaska Natives are more than four times the national rate" (Alaska Department of Health & Social Services, 2002, p.4). "Guns are readily available in many homes in Alaska due to recreational and subsistence hunting" (Ibid., p.4.).

Mental health problems contribute to the accident and suicide rates as well. "Estimates project about 10 percent of Alaska's children and youths (age 5 to 18) have severe emotional disturbances, and 6.2 percent of Alaska's adult population under age 55 suffer from severe mental illness" (Alaska Department of Health & Social Services, 2002, p. 4). One hundred seventy-five villages in Alaska have no local mental health services other than the occasional itinerant provider.

QUICK FACTS

Health disparities reported in the CDC Health Disparities and Inequalities Report include the following:

- In 2010, the percentage of American Indian/Alaska Native (AI/AN) adults aged 50 to 75 years who reported being up to date with colorectal cancer screening was 11 percentage points lower than the percentage screened among white adults.

- In 2010, the AI/AN birthrate among females 10 to 19 years of age was the third largest (following African Americans and Hispanics).

- In 2011, AI/AN and non-Hispanic white adults were among those with the highest prevalence, frequency, and intensity of binge drinking, compared with other racial/ethnic populations.

- Although smoking prevalence remained highest among AI/AN youth and adults during 2009 and 2010, smoking declined from 17.2% to 13.6% in youth and from 42.2% to 34.4% in adults from 2006–2008 to 2009–2010.

- In 2010, AI/AN and Hispanic adults had the highest age-adjusted mean number of physically unhealthy days in the past 30 days compared with other racial/ethnic populations.

- In 2010, the preterm birthrate for AI/AN infants (13.6%) was higher than for white (10.8%) and Asian/Pacific Islander infants (10.7%).

- During 1999 and 2010, drug-induced death rates in the 30 to 39-year age group were highest among AI/AN compared to other racial/ethnic populations.

- In 2009, the homicide death rate was highest among non-Hispanic blacks (19.9 deaths per 100,000), followed by AI/ANs (9.0 deaths per 100,000).

- In 2008, the infant mortality rate was 53% higher for AI/AN women (8.42 infant deaths per 1,000 live births) compared with non-Hispanic white women (5.52 infant deaths per 1,000 live births).

- In 2009, AI/ANs had the highest motor vehicle–related death rates. Among males, the AI/AN death rate was approximately 2 to 5 times the rates of other races/ethnicities. Among females, the AI/AN motor vehicle–related death rate was approximately 2 to 4 times the rates of other races/ethnicities.

- Although the 2009 overall suicide rates for AI/ANs were similar to those of non-Hispanic whites, the 2005 to 2009 rates among adolescent and young adult AI/ANs aged 15 to 29 years were substantially higher.

- In 2011, the age-standardized prevalence for AI/ANs not completing high school among adults aged 25 years and older was the second largest; second to Hispanics and similar to African Americans.

- In 2011, the age-standardized percentage of AI/AN adults living in poverty was among the highest compared with non-Hispanic whites.

- In 2010, prevalence of unemployment among adults aged 18 to 64 years was highest among non-Hispanic blacks (16.5%) and AI/AN (15.8%).

Source: Office of Minority Health (2013).

Considerations for Health Promotion and Program Planning

Consider the following concepts when planning and implementing a health promotion program for this target audience:

- American Indian and Alaskan Native peoples use their tribal names when referring to themselves, so it is advised that health care professionals ask individuals or groups how they prefer to be addressed.

- Recognize that there are varying degrees of acculturation levels, so health care professionals need to assess where the patient or client is on the continuum of acculturation.

- Recognize that there is great diversity among the tribes, so do not make assumptions.

- Holistic thinking is common and should be used to identify appropriate and acceptable prevention and treatment plans.

- Try to accommodate complementary and alternative forms of healing.

- Do not be surprised or offended by a handshake that is softer or gentler than you are accustomed to.

- Be patient with silence, and give the listener time to reflect on what you said prior to responding.
- Prolonged eye contact should be avoided because it is viewed as being disrespectful.
- Work with the families, and remember that elders are respected.
- Do not encourage or try to reward competitive behavior because cooperation is valued by these cultures.
- Do not appear to be in a hurry; it may give patients a negative impression of you.
- Do not interrupt the person who is speaking as this is considered to be extremely rude.
- Keep nonverbal communication to a minimum.
- With the exception of a handshake, touch is not usually acceptable.
- Remember that listening is more valued than speaking.
- Be aware that suspicion and mistrust may exist.
- When developing community programs, involve the community members.
- Be aware of superstitions such as unlucky and lucky numbers and colors.

Tips for Working With American Indian and Alaskan Native Populations

Some suggestions developed by the Indian Health Services for working with American Indian and Alaskan Native patients include being warm and friendly so the patient feels that you genuinely care about him or her. The first meeting is extremely important because it sets the basis of your relationship. Make the patient feel welcome. Use language the patient can understand (medical terminology may be confusing). If a patient speaks a different language, do your best to explain yourself and to find a staff person who can speak the patient's language.

With the patient's consent, involve the family as they play a crucial role in the patient's outcome and support of family will help speed recovery and raise social well-being. Do not rush the patient. Silence is valued and is not necessarily a negative behavior. Sometimes the patient may require time to think and respond to a comment. Time is viewed more passively, and the people are more task conscious than time conscious. Eye contact is used in varying degrees and should be limited.

Respect traditional healing ways and work to accommodate their beliefs. You can support traditional healing by respecting the people's ways and not degrading their beliefs.

Show great respect to the elderly. Elders are not accustomed to modern health care facilities, the new atmosphere, the noises, the caregivers, or the types treatment used. For many elders, this may be their first trip to a medical facility. It is important to ease their minds and to explain procedures thoroughly (IHS, n.d.).

Summary

American Indian and Alaskan Native populations have a history of being conquered by other nations, having foreign cultures impose upon their way of life, and being the victims of discrimination. Fortunately, they have been able to hold onto their traditional culture in many ways. They continue to express their traditional values within their villages by maintaining close-knit families and using traditional healing modalities to prevent and heal illness. Unfortunately, both groups experience major health disparities, such as a high incidence of suicide, alcoholism, cancer, unintentional injuries, diabetes, and mental illness. Through high-quality, culturally sensitive health promotion programs, perhaps one day better health and access to quality health care can be achieved.

This chapter has described the challenges that these populations encountered historically. These populations do not believe in the germ theory as the cause of disease, although some Alaskan Natives are adopting this belief system now. They have various approaches to healing, such as sweat lodges and ceremonies, and their common behaviors, risk factors, and illnesses are similar. General tips for working with these populations were provided, but we caution that there is a vast amount of diversity within these groups, so it is important not to generalize.

Review

1. Describe the histories of American Indian and Alaskan Native people in the United States.

2. According to American Indian and Alaskan Native beliefs, what are the causes of illnesses?

3. Describe some plants and herbs that are used for healing.

4. Describe what medicine men are and their approach to healing.

Activity

Conduct research on health programs that have been implemented for members of the American Indian and Alaskan Native population. Summarize the literature and identify some best practices.

Review the white bison website (http://whitebison.org/index.php) and reflect on what you learned. Watch the video "The Wellbriety Movement: Journey of Forgiveness" and include comments about it in your paper as well.

Case Study

Don is a 45-year-old, full-blood Indian who is married and has five children. The family lives in a small, rural community on a large reservation in New Mexico. Don was sent to boarding school for high school, and then he served in the war. He recently was treated through Veterans Affairs (VA), which is where he participated in a posttraumatic stress disorder (PTSD) support group. Don suffers from alcoholism. It began soon after his initial patrols in the war, which involved heavy combat and, ultimately, physical injury. He exhibits the hallmark symptoms of PTSD, including flashbacks, nightmares, intrusive thoughts on an almost daily basis, marked hypervigilance, irritability, and avoidant behavior.

Don is fluent in English and his native language, which is spoken in his home. He is the descendant of a family of traditional healers. Consequently, the community expected him to assume a leadership role in its cultural and spiritual life. However, boarding school interrupted his early participation in important aspects of local ceremonial life. His participation was further delayed by military service and then forestalled by his alcoholism. During boarding school, Don was frequently harassed by non-Indian staff members for speaking his native language, for wearing his hair long, and for running away. Afraid of similar ridicule while in the service, he seldom shared his personal background with fellow infantrymen. Don was the target of racism and was called "Chief" and "blanket ass."

Some 10 years after his return from the war, Don began cycling through several periods of treatment for his alcoholism in tribal residential programs. It was not until one month after he began treatment for his alcoholism at a local VA facility that a provisional diagnosis of PTSD was made. Upon completing that treatment, he transferred to an inpatient unit that specialized in combat-related trauma. Don left the unit against medical advice, sober but still experiencing significant symptoms.

Don's tribal members frequently refer to PTSD as the "wounded spirit." His community has long recognized the consequences of being a warrior, and indeed, a ceremony has evolved over many generations to prevent as well as to treat the underlying causes of these symptoms. Within this tribal worldview, combat-related trauma upsets the balance that underpins someone's personal, physical, mental, emotional, and spiritual health. Don did not participate in these and other tribal ceremonies until after he was diagnosed at the VA with PTSD. His sobriety has been aided by involvement in the Native American Church, with its reinforcement of his decision to remain sober and its support for positive life changes.

Though Don has a great deal of work ahead of him, he feels that he is now ready to participate in the tribe's major ceremonial intended to bless and purify its warriors. His family, once alienated but now reunited, is excited about that process.

There are several issues to consider about this case:

- What cultural issues exist in this scenario?

- How did Don's culture help and hinder his situation?

- Are there steps that could have been taken to help prevent Don's alcohol problem?

Source: Adapted from National Alliance on Mental Illness (2003).

References

Advameg Inc. (2007). *Diet of Native Americans.* Retrieved from http://www.faqs.org/ nutrition /Met-Obe/Native-Americans-Diet-of.html

Alaska Department of Health and Social Services. (2002). *Healthy Alaskans 2010, volume 1: Targets for improved health.* Retrieved from http://www.hss.state.ak.us/dph/targets /ha2010/volume_1.htm

Alaska Native Epidemiology Center. (2007). *Regional health profile for Yukon-Kuskokwim Health Corp.* Retrieved from http://www .anthc.org/cs/chs/epi/upload/Regional _Health_Profile_YKHC_0707.pdf

Alaska Native Heritage Center. (2000). *Information about Alaska Native cultures.* Retrieved from http://www.akhistorycourse.org /articles/article.php?artID=195

Alexandria, V. (1994). *People of the ice and snow.* Richmond, VA: Time Life.

American Heart Association. (n.d.). *Is broken heart syndrome real?* Retrieved from http:// www.heart.org/HEARTORG/Conditions /More/Cardiomyopathy/Is-Broken-Heart -Syndrome-Real_UCM_448547_Article.jsp

American Psychiatric Association. (2009). *Let's Talk Facts About Mental Health In American Indians and Alaska Natives.* Retrieved from http://activeminds.org/stor age/documents/2015_conference_docs/ Multicultural-American_Indians__Alas kans.pdf

Ballew, C., Ross, A. Wells, R. S., Hiratsuka, V., Hamrick, K. J., & Nobmann, E. D. (2004). *Final report on the Alaska Traditional Diet Survey.* Alaska Native Epidemiology Center, Alaska Native Health Board. Retrieved from http://www.anthc.org/chs/epicenter/upload /traditional_diet.pdf

Bonvillain, N. (1997). *Native American medicine.* Philadelphia, PA Chelsea House.

Corral, K. (2007). *Alaska Native traditional healing.* Retrieved from http://altmed.creighton .edu/AKNative

Frankis, M. P. (2006). *Picea sitchensis (Bongard).* Retrieved from http://www. conifers.org/pi /pic/sitchensis.htm

Haas, M. J. (2007). *Shaman song.* Retrieved from http://www.shamansong.com/ gpage.html3 .html

Hammerschlag, C. A. (1988). *The dancing heal ers: A doctor's journey of healing with Native Americans.* San Francisco, CA: Harper.

Indian Health Service. (n.d.). *Culturally sensitive care.* Retrieved from https://www.ihs.gov /chr/index.cfm?Module=csc

Management Sciences for Health. (n.d.). *American Indians & Alaska Natives: Health dispar ities overview.* Retrieved from http://erc.msh .org/mainpage.cfm?file=7.3.0.htm&module= provider&language=English#readmoe

National Alliance on Mental Illness. (2003). *American Indian and Alaska Native.* Retrieved from http://www.nami.org /Content/ContentGroups/Multicultural _Support1/ CDResourceManual.pdf

National Alliance for Mental Health. (2014). *American Indian and Alaska Native communities mental health fact sheet.* Retrieved from http://www.nami.org/contentmanagement /contentdisplay.cfm?contentfileid=79888

National Center for Health Statistics. (2012a). *Deaths: Final data for 2009.* Retrieved from http://www.cdc.gov/nchs/data/nvsr/nvsr60 /nvsr60_03.pdf

National Center for Health Statistics, 2012. (2014). *Summary health statistics for U.S. adults: National Health Interview Survey,* table 25. Retrieved from http://www.cdc.gov /nchs/data/series/sr_10/sr10_260.pdf

National Center for Health Statistics. (2012b). *Summary health statistics for U.S. adults: 2012 (2014),* table 26. Retrieved from http://www.cdc.gov/nchs/data/series/sr_10 /sr10_260.pdf

National Center for Health Statistics. (2012c). *Summary health statistics for U.S. adults: 2012,* table 29. Retrieved from http:// www.cdc.gov/nchs/data/series/sr_10 /sr10_260.pdf

Nixon, R. (1970). *Special message on Indian affairs.* Retrieved from http://www.ncai.org /attachments/Consultation_IJaOfGZqlY

SuxpPUqoSSWIaNTkEJEPXxKLzLcaOi kifwWhGOLSA_12%20Nixon%20Self%20 Determination%20Policy.pdf

Office of Minority Health. (2013). *American Indian and Native Alaskan populations, racial and ethnic minorities, populations.* Retrieved from http://www.cdc.gov/minorityhealth /populations/remp/aian.html

Office of Minority Health. (2014a). *American Indian and Alaska Native populations, populations.* Retrieved from http://www .cdc.gov/minorityhealth/populations /REMP/aian.html

Office of Minority Health. (2014b). *American Indian/Alaska Native profile.* Retrieved from http://minorityhealth.hhs.gov/omh/browse .aspx?lvl=3&lvlid=62

Office of Minority Health. (2015). *Liver Disease and American Indians/Alaska Natives.* Retrieved from http://minorityhealth.hhs .gov/omh/browse.aspx?lvl=4&lvlid=32

Palca, J. (2002). *Saving Alaska's native languages.* Retrieved from http://www.npr.org/programs /morning/features/2002/mar/alaska/

Purnell, L. (2013). Transcultural health care. In *Transcultural health care: A culturally competent approach* (4th ed.). Philadelphia, PA: F. A. Davis Company.

Seale, J., Shellenberger, S., & Spence, J. (2006). Alcohol problems in Alaska Natives: Lessons from the Inuit. *American Indian and Alaska Native Mental Health Research: The Journal of the National Center, 13*(1), 1–31.

Spector, R. E. (2004). *Cultural diversity in health and illness.* Upper Saddle River, NJ: Pearson Education.

Suicide Prevention Resource Center. (n.d.). *Suicide among racial/ethnic populations in the US: American Indians/Alaska Natives.* Retrieved from http://www.sprc.org/sites /sprc.org/files/library/AI_AN%20Sheet% 20Aug%2028%202013%20Final.pdf

Tai, J., Cheung, S., Cheah, S., Chan, E., & Hasman, D. (2006, November 24). In vitro anti-proliferative and anti-oxidant studies on Devil's Club *Oplopanax horridus. Journal of Ethnopharmacology, 108*(2), 228–235.

U.S. Census Bureau. (2008). *Population density of the United States, and selected maps of race and Hispanic origin: 2000.* Retrieved from http://www.census.gov/population/www /censusdata/2000maps.html

U.S. Census Bureau. (2011, December). Native North American languages spoken at home in the United States and Puerto Rico: 2006–2010. *American Community Survey Brief* (ACSBR/10-10). Retrieved from http://www .census.gov/prod/2011pubs/acsbr10-10.pdf

U.S. Census Bureau. (2012). The American Indian and Alaska Native population: 2010. *Census Briefs.* Retrieved from http://www.census .gov/prod/cen2010/briefs/c2010br-10.pdf

West Virginia Division of Culture and History. (2008). *Native American communities in West Virginia.* Retrieved from http://www .wvculture.org/arts/ethnic/native.html

© Oscar C. Williams/Shutterstock

CHAPTER 9

African American Populations

I have a dream that my four little children will one day live in a nation where they will not be judged by the color of their skin, but by the content of their character.
  —*Martin Luther King, Jr.*

If I'd known I was going to live this long, I'd have taken better care of myself.
  —*Eubie Blake*

Key Concepts

Tuskegee study   Santeria
Voodoo   Candomblé

Learning Objectives

After reading this chapter, you should be able to:

1. Provide an overview of the social and economic circumstances of African Americans in the United States.
2. Provide an overview of African American beliefs about the causes of illness.
3. Describe at least three African American healing practices.
4. Describe African American health risk behaviors and common illnesses.
5. List at least six tips for working with African American populations.

© Diana Lundin/Dreamstime.com

Introduction

The U.S. Census Bureau racial category "Black or African American" includes people who identify themselves as such and have origins in any of the black racial groups in Africa. Culture is not the same as race, but much data is correlated and available under the racial label. In this chapter we focus on the culture derived from the original Africans brought to America as slaves, which forms the foundation of the somewhat vague term *African American culture*.

Many people who classify themselves as African American do not trace their history back to the early American experience. With many immigrants from African nations, the Caribbean, Central America, and other countries, African American communities across the United States are more culturally diverse now than at any other time in history. For instance, President Obama identifies himself as African American and falls within the Census Bureau definition. However, his father was from Kenya and his paternal family members still reside there. Under Census Bureau guidelines, President Obama could just as well define himself as mixed race because his mother was white and he was raised by her and his white grandparents. Certainly Mr. Obama, and many others like him, lives in a society in which the majority population still imposes assumptions and bias on "black" people of any origin. However, in this chapter we distinguish African Americans from "black" people who can come from any culture. We are looking at the culture that derived from people who were captured and forced to America as individuals torn from their families and communities and compelled to reestablish their lives within a new culture created by white people who wanted the slaves for their labor but not their social company. These Africans had to individually learn a new language, new lifestyle, new eating habits, and live among whites and other slaves from various African locations in essentially a random mix of peoples. They forged a new adapted slave culture, and Michelle Obama, the president's wife, is a descendant of these original African slaves.

This chapter begins with the unique history of African Americans in the United States. This history plays a role throughout the chapter, which includes a discussion about their current socioeconomic position within the United States, beliefs about the causes of illness and how to treat it, health behaviors, and common health problems. Then we discuss how to create a successful community health program that takes these factors into consideration.

Terminology

Historically, African Americans were identified by a number of terms (Negro, colored, black). The correct current term to refer to anyone who has roots in any of the African countries is African American. In the literature, both African American and black are used, but the latter term incorporates a broader population. For example, black Caribbean Islanders fall within the category of "black" but not necessarily "African American." In this chapter, the focus is on African Americans who are descended from slaves, but when referring to research, the terminology found in the original source is used.

History of African Americans in the United States

What is now considered African American culture is a mixture of the oral traditions brought to this country from Africa with modifications developed within a context of slavery, prejudice, discrimination, and poverty. With the massive reduction in potential workers caused by the death of most of the original indigenous population in the Americas due to war and disease, the Europeans in America needed labor and turned to slavery to develop commerce. The African Americans are unique in that they were forced here to be exploited for their labor. To understand the African American culture, it is important to realize this fundamental fact that carries over to the present day.

Slavery has existed throughout the world for thousands of years. Some pre-Columbian indigenous American tribes enslaved their captors, but European settlers did not come to America to be slave owners. However, with the increasing need for labor to raise rice, sugar cane, and cotton, slavery was soon seen to be acceptable and became the status for Africans not only for their lifetimes, but also for generations of their descendants.

The slave trade, which was called the "transatlantic slave trade," was the forced transportation of Africans to the New World, which occurred in or around the Atlantic Ocean (New York Public Library, 2007). It lasted from the 16th century to the 19th century. An estimated 12 million men, women, and children were transported by force to the Americas from their homeland of Africa. Approximately 500,000 were brought to what is today the United States.

The majority of the ancestors of African Americans came from a part of Africa bounded by the Senegal River in the north and by Angola in the south. This area also was called the area of catchment (Perry, 1998). Africans were taken by force, made to be slaves, and shipped to other countries against their will (Perry, 1998). Under these circumstances, it was very unlikely that families stayed intact. Men were separated from women and accounted for about two thirds of the slave population. Most slaves were captured in wars, with some wars conducted specifically to capture people and sell them as slaves. Although the survival and health of the slaves were important to slave traders from an economic point of view, sanitation and health conditions on slave ships were simply filthy and disease ridden, resulting in a death rate of about 20% of the cargo. There was no interest at all in keeping families and groups together, and slaves suffered and struggled to survive individually among strangers of different cultures. One of the first challenges was simply to stay alive and not die of disease.

There was an ongoing difference of opinion among ship captains as to whether to keep the cargo load limited to improve health conditions or to pack as many people on as possible so that after attrition the net load was still very profitable. The trip generally took 30 to 90 days, and up to 290 slaves per ship were keep naked in chains two-by-two on floors and platforms below deck at night with 3 feet or less between the floor and the next level up so that it was impossible to sit up.

If the weather was good, slaves were allowed on deck during the day but remained chained. The ship's crew would require slaves to have some exercise including forcing them to dance. There were usually four buckets, shaped 1 foot wide at the top and 2 feet wide at the bottom, for toilets, which were dumped once a day. Although accessible to the slaves nearest the buckets at night, most captives gave up the struggle at night to crawl past other complaining captives in tight quarters to reach the buckets and just relieved themselves where they lay, mixing their waste with the vomit and waste from the hundreds of others. Each slave was issued a spoon to dip in and eat from a bucket of food shared by 5 to 10 others at once. If the spoon was not available, many simply dipped in and ate with their hands, even after crawling around on the filthy decks. Disease and illness were rampant. There were more than 200 slave rebellions, and some suicides in response to the experience. Many surviving slaves suffered skin lesions from crawling around on bare wet floors and platforms and were cleaned up by the sellers with special cosmetic coloring and grease to make them presentable for sale once delivered (Falconbridge, 1788).

Having been captured, kidnapped, dispossessed, removed from their countries and countrymen, and held in filthy unsanitary conditions, the Africans came to a new culture and a new way of life for themselves and their descendants. At home in Africa, culture was passed between generations through an oral tradition rather than in writing. In America, the slaves relied on their individual memory and continued to transfer and adapt their culture, one person at a time among each other, through oral traditions despite being forced to learn a new language and living a life of confinement and forced labor. Some slaves led stable lives with long-term worksites, but many were sold from place to place. Relationships, both personal and social, were often broken and needed to be redeveloped among strangers.

African enslaved laborers were instrumental in the European colonial expansion in North America, clearing the land, erecting shelters, and constructing forts. They raised commercial and subsistence crops, gathered lumber, raised cattle and hogs, and harvested and produced exports that supported the colonial economies. In some places, such as South Carolina, the population of African American slaves outnumbered the people of European decent. African Americans, free and bound, helped defend the colonies against Indians and against other European colonial powers' attempts at territorial expansion. After the British colonies established territorial dominance along the Atlantic coast, people of African descent—many second and third generation Americans, some free or near-free indentured servants, but most bound in slavery—participated in the American Revolution, on both sides, and in the birth and growth of the United States.

The U.S. Constitution framed the divided view of freedom and slavery, demonstrating that the problem of slavery could not be resolved even among men who were seeking freedom themselves. A House of Representatives was established to provide for representation of all people according to population, including women, each of whom counted as a person. But in areas with substantial slave populations that sometimes outnumbered the possible voters, African American slaves were constitutionally defined each as counting as three fifths of a person (U.S. Constitution, Article I, Section 2). The issues were contentious, and the compromise that allowed movement forward provided that the slave issue could not be addressed further until 20 years after its adoption (Article I, Section 9, Clause 1). In the meantime the states, free or not, were constitutionally required to return escaped slaves (Article IV, Section 2).

Even as African Americans made great contributions to North America, they faced horrific acts of mistreatment, sexual assault, lynching, and other forms of violent acts and discrimination. During the time of slavery, slave overseers were authorized to whip and brutalize noncompliant slaves. Each state had laws (known as slave codes) that defined the status of slaves and the rights of masters; the codes gave slave owners near-absolute power over the rights of their human property and even made it illegal to teach slaves to read.

Did You Know?

Jail and flogging was at one time the official punishment for free African Americans who tried to educate slaves:

passed by the state of North Carolina in 1830—1831,
AN ACT TO PREVENT ALL PERSONS FROM TEACHING SLAVES TO READ OR WRITE, THE USE OF FIGURES EXCEPTED
Whereas the teaching of slaves to read and write, has a tendency to excite dis-satisfaction in their minds, and to produce insurrection and rebellion, to the manifest injury of the citizens of this State:
Therefore,
Be it enacted by the General Assembly of the State of North Carolina, and it is hereby enacted by the authority of the same, That any free person, who shall hereafter teach, or attempt to teach, any slave within the State to read or write, the use of figures excepted, or shall give or sell to such slave or slaves any books or pamphlets, shall be liable to indictment in any court of record in this State having jurisdiction thereof, and upon conviction, shall, at the discretion of the court, if a white man or woman, be fined not less than one hundred dollars, nor more than two hundred dollars, or imprisoned; and if a free person of color, shall be fined, imprisoned, or whipped, at the discretion of the court, not exceeding thirty nine lashes, nor less than twenty lashes.
II. *Be it further enacted*, That if any slave shall hereafter teach, or attempt to teach, any other slave to read or write, the use of figures excepted, he or she may be carried before any justice of the peace, and on conviction thereof, shall be sentenced to receive thirty nine lashes on his or her bare back. *"Act Passed by the General Assembly of the State of North Carolina at the Session of 1830—1831" (Raleigh, 1831)*

These codes indemnified abusers and even required the use of violence. They were condemned by people who opposed slavery as being evil. In addition to physical abuse and murder, slaves were at constant risk of losing members of their families if their owners decided to trade them for profit, punishment, or to pay debts. A few slaves retaliated by murdering owners and overseers, burning barns, killing horses, or staging work slowdowns. After slavery and the Civil War ended, black codes continued to regulate the freedom of former slaves. The black codes outraged some people in the North because it seemed that the South was creating a form of quasi-slavery to evade the results of the war. After winning the 1866 elections, the Republicans put the South under military rule. The new governments repealed most of the black codes, but segregation laws were enforced for the next 100 years. Even with the changes in laws, African Americans still faced informal unequal treatment and discrimination, which continues into the present day despite mixed efforts to end it. Once freed in the South, many African Americans migrated to the urban North to seek greater opportunities. Yet even there they met segregation and discrimination, ironically, many times from new immigrants from Europe competing for opportunities in the newly industrializing United States.

After the Civil War, the United States adopted the 13th Amendment of the Constitution, which gave government the power to root out all attributes of slavery and discrimination, yet the U.S. Supreme Court in *Plessy v. Ferguson* (1896) decided to establish "separate but equal" as a legitimate practice. It took the World War II experience to show that separate "minority" units of African American and Japanese service members performed as well or better than white units. President Truman ended segregation in the military in 1948.

However, separation of the races and cultures was legally authorized until the 1954 U.S. Supreme Court decision in *Brown v. Board of Education* declared "separate but equal" inherently discriminatory. This has had profound effects on education and the provision of health care. Problems continued even after passage of the U.S. Civil Rights Act of 1965, major race riots occurred in the late 1960s, and demonstrations for racial justice continue to this day. In 2014, numerous street demonstrations protested the shooting and killing of unarmed African American suspects by white police officers.

It is difficult to separate the acculturation effect of people living in poverty and aspiring for a better life from actual cultural features of African Americans. The development of what we can consider African American culture did not evolve in one clear locality or uniform manner. Over a period of 150 years, generations of slaves passed oral history and culture along by word of mouth. Music and allegorical stories were shared among people from different African origins and between generations. This resulted in a new African American culture that embodied fundamental characteristics unique to America. Churches and schools, and many other places, were segregated, which inadvertently provided opportunities for African American culture to flourish.

Characteristics of African music made it into church choirs, and allegorical styles became axiomatic for preaching in southern African American churches, but completely new culture forms such as Jazz also emerged. Much of what is considered African American culture evolved from simple poverty. "Soul food" involving greens and all parts of farm animals, which were essentially subsistence and survival food, became associated with African Americans. Yet the African culture added its own parts to the picture with items such as okra and red peas from Africa. Africans adapted "soupikandia," a Senegalese stew, to create gumbo, which is now associated with southern Louisiana.

The concept of family evolved to include people not related by biology as "cousin'" or "brother" or "sister" as a result of affinity of experience and in place of any traceable actual family. The African tradition of respect for elders in an extended family survives in many families to this day.

Despite these hardships, African Americans have demonstrated their capacity to excel in every area of society. Political leaders, Olympic and other sports champions, entertainment figures, scientists, astronauts, Supreme Court justices, military leaders, civic leaders and mayors, religious leaders, award-winning authors and poets, members of the president's Cabinet, newscasters, university presidents, and even a First Lady of the United States have emerged from people sharing the African American culture.

African Americans in the United States

In July 2012, African Americans were the second largest minority population (13%), following the Hispanic/Latino population (17%). In 2011, many blacks or African Americans lived in the South (55%), and in 2012 the largest percentage of African Americans lived in the District of Columbia (51.6%) and Mississippi (38%). New York had the largest total population of African Americans at 3.7 million (Office of Minority Health, 2014); (although slightly earlier, see **Figure 9.1** which presents data from the 2010 national census).

In 2010, the average African American family median income was $39,988, compared to $67,892 for non-Hispanic white families. A total of 27.1% of African Americans, in comparison with 10.6% of non-Hispanic whites, were living at the poverty level (U.S. Census Bureau, 2010). For 2014, the unemployment rate for African Americans was twice that for non-Hispanic whites, 11.1% and 4.9%, respectively (Bureau of Labor Statistics [BLS], 2014). This finding was consistent for both men and women.

African Americans often have strong religious affiliations, especially with Christian denominations, notably Baptist and Church of God in Christ. When the slave trade began, Christianity was only starting to spread in Africa as a result of the European explorers. However, Islam had a much larger influence in Africa at the time, and it is estimated that about 20% of the transported slaves were Muslims. Once in America, there was some debate about whether Christianity should be taught because it might imply some kind of affinity among peoples. Nevertheless, many slaves were taught Christianity, and many continued to follow Islam as well.

African Americans commonly receive disrespect in health care settings, and African Americans experience adverse encounters due to negative assumptions and images, with the most common assumption being related to women's sexual promiscuity (Welch, 2003). Consider the experience of Betty, a 40-year-old African American woman who works in health care. Here she describes her experience with a health care provider during a visit for a Pap smear:

> I went to this doctor. I had an infection. … She said, "How many sex partners do you have?" I said "Gulp" and just looked at her. … She said, "Oh, you don't know how many". … I felt like I was a little piece of garbage. I was just … stereotyped: "There was a little black woman who's out havin' all of these men who comes in here with an infection." (Welch, 2003)

Subtle insults and comments make African Americans feel inferior in health care settings. This mistrust is what leads some African Americans to rely on traditional healing methods or not to seek care until it can no longer be avoided.

African Americans experience discrimination in areas outside of the health care system as well. People who are constantly treated unfairly tend to have more stress, which can lead to emotional, physical, and behavioral problems. When people face discrimination during adolescence,

Black or African American Alone

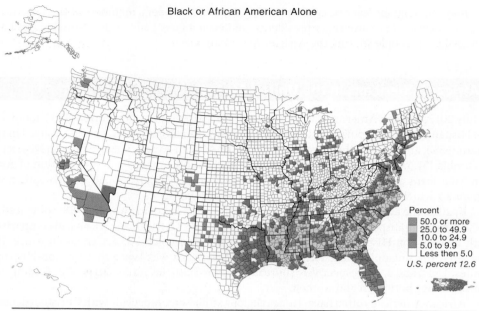

Black or African American Alone or in Combination

FIGURE 9.1

Percentage of population: Black or African American, 2010.

Source: U.S. Census Bureau (2011).

they tend to have behavioral problems that lead to antisocial behavior. Teens can feel out of place among their peers, and because they choose not to talk about it, they may act out their unspoken frustrations. They may engage in aggressive or illegal acts, such as fighting and shoplifting. Young teens may feel that there is nowhere to turn, which may push them to consider suicide.

When adults go through depression because of racial discrimination, they often develop abnormal behaviors, such as being irritable and hostile toward others for no reason, having insomnia, and discriminating against others around them. Growing up around discrimination often causes adolescents to have a hard time concentrating in school and or achieving their goals. Dealing with discrimination and confronting people of other races who think they are better than African Americans can lead to low self-esteem and less satisfaction in their adult lives. When people have had some kind of interaction with racial discrimination, they sometimes believe the world is out to get them. Everywhere they go, they think there is racial discrimination—even when there is no sign of discrimination.

The physical effects of racial discrimination include stress, which can lead to problems such as high blood pressure and a weakened immune system. Another physical effect of racial discrimination is obesity and diabetes. Due to racial discrimination, many unhealthy behaviors arise, such as smoking, drinking, drug use, and binge eating. Another unhealthy behavior is that people who experience racial discrimination may verbally abuse others or be very discriminating toward people outside of their race. People who experience racial discrimination are usually from lower socioeconomic status (SES), which is partially a result of the discrimination that occurs when seeking employment and in the workplace.

The toll on African Americans has been high. The disparities in treatment and the prejudice shown have resulted in African Americans having the worst health profile of any population in the United States.

General Philosophy About Disease Prevention and Health Maintenance

Many African Americans mistrust the U.S. health care system. This distrust is not a paranoid reaction. It has been fueled by incidences such as the **Tuskegee study**, in which the U.S. Public Health Service conducted a study from 1932 to 1972 on hundreds of African American men with syphilis. The men were not treated with antibiotics that would have cured the disease, and indeed most of them died (Clarke-Tasker, 1993). The scientific and medical communities reacted with shock when the study was exposed, but most African Americans saw the study as a blatant act of genocide perpetrated against blacks by whites. As a result, many people in the African American community believe that health care professionals simply do not value their lives.

Many low-income African Americans traditionally separate illnesses into two categories: natural and unnatural illnesses (Welch, 2003). *Natural illness* occurs as a result of God's will or when a person comes into unhealthy contact with the forces of nature, such as exposure to cold or impurities in the air, food, or water. Natural illness also can occur as a punishment for sins. Cures for natural illness include an antidote or other logical protective actions. *Unnatural illness*, on the other hand, is considered to be the result of evil influences that alter God's intended plan. These illnesses are often founded on a belief in witchcraft—that is, that some individuals possess the power to mobilize the forces of good and evil. The use of voodoo healers among Haitians and other West Indian blacks is an example. Treatment or cures for unnatural illness can be found in religion, magic, amulets, and herbs. Many of these beliefs are African in origin, and aspects may be seen among African Americans of all backgrounds (Welch, 2003).

Worldview

Many African Americans believe that health is a gift from God; illness is a result of something that was not pleasing to God or may be determined by fate (Sadler & Huff, 2007). African Americans have historically believed that illness may be due to their failure to live according to God's will. Some African Americans even believe that illness comes directly from the devil. Although most African American communities rely on religion and their relationship with God as a main reason for illness, some community members do not. Sometimes the belief that one's health is in God's hands, a fatalistic perspective, can prevent engagement in preventive measures or treatment.

In general, African Americans are present oriented. Some are rather relaxed about time and may be late for appointments. Time is viewed as circular; showing up for their appointment is more important than being on time (Purnell, 2013). Older persons tend to be more punctual.

Some African Americans use a form of standard English referred to as African American English (AAE), also called Black English or Ebonics. People who hear this dialect may have the impression that the speaker is uneducated; this can be an erroneous assumption because some educated and articulate African Americans use AAE when speaking to one another. African Americans tend to speaker louder than those from other cultures, and it is important not to interpret that as being angry. Many tend to prefer close personal space and are comfortable with touching and hugging. Highly animated nonverbal communication methods are sometimes erroneously misinterpreted as being aggressive. Eye contact is viewed as a sign of respect.

Pain is often expressed openly, but this can vary. With the exception of family members, organ donations usually are not done. As long as the need for an autopsy is explained, the procedure is generally accepted.

What Do You Think?

African Americans, as well as members of other cultures, believe that their health is in God's hands. How can medical providers and public health professionals encourage preventive efforts while respecting this worldview?

Pregnancy, Birth, and Child Rearing

Little has been documented in the literature about African American women's preparation for childbirth (Lu & Halfon, 2003). Like other African American patients, pregnant and new mothers are often made to feel marginalized, stigmatized, and stereotyped because of racism practiced against them.

Like all cultures, traditional beliefs may continue into the present, and many of these beliefs are not supported by medical research. African American beliefs and traditions surrounding pregnancy and birth include the following (Moore, 2007):

- A pregnant woman is not supposed to hold her hands up over her head. It is believed she will strangle the baby.

- A pregnant woman should not cross her legs when sitting. This will cause hemorrhoids.

- A pregnant woman should indulge her food cravings or the baby will have unpleasant physical or personality traits that match the characteristics of the food.

- Babies are not named until it is known if they will survive. It is believed that spirits of the dead cannot see and therefore cannot harm a child who does not have a name.

- The placenta has a spirit of its own and must be secretly buried where it will never be disturbed and negatively affect the child.

- A small portion of the umbilical cord is wrapped in paper and put away to ensure the newborn will not get colic.

- Talismans are used for protection and to connect the child to ancestral powers and the spirits of nature.

- Pregnant women should not have their pictures taken because it will cause a stillbirth.

- New mothers are to rest and be cared for in the initial 4 to 8 weeks after birth, assisted by their family and the community.

- Henna body art is used during the postpartum period. The henna beautification lifts the new mother's spirits, wards off depression, and signifies the mother's new and higher social status.

Nutrition and Exercise

A family tradition of soul food may be problematic for some African Americans. Soul foods traditionally have a high fat, sugar, and sodium content (Andrews, 2007). Many American-born African Americans consume pork products with high salt content, fried foods, and heavy gravy. Common ways that African Americans prepare foods include frying, barbequing, and using gravy and sauces (Purnell, 2013). Their diets are typically high in fat, sodium, and cholesterol with more animal fat, less fiber, and fewer fruits and vegetables than the rest of American society (Purnell, 2013). Studies have shown that African American diets stress the consumption of meat and eggs, which results in a high-cholesterol and saturated-fat diet. African American foods also tend to be lower in complex carbohydrates and dietary fiber. This may contribute to their high incidence of being overweight.

A food guide pyramid was developed to reflect the cultural foods historically eaten by African Americans and to help them improve their nutrition status (see **Figure 9.2**). The African American food pyramid had a foundation of biscuits, corn (corn breads, grits, and hominy), pasta, and rice. In urban communities, store-bought breads have replaced biscuits.

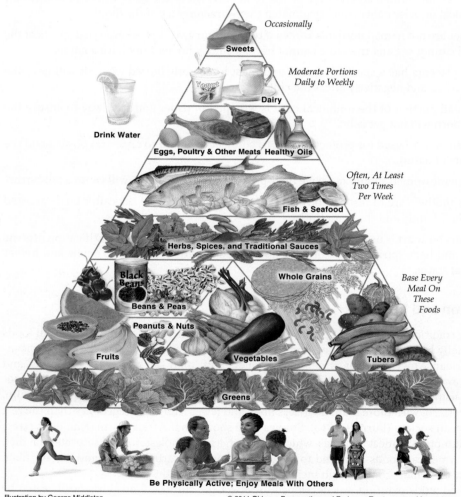

Illustration by George Middleton

© 2011 Oldways Preservation and Exchange Trust   www.oldwayspt.org

FIGURE 9.2

African American food pyramid.

Source: Adapted from sedma.org and Oldways Preservation and Exchange Trust. http://oldwayspt.org/sites/default/files/images/African_pyramid_flyer.jpg

Vegetables (green leafy vegetables—chard, collard, kale, mustard greens—and corn, okra, sweet potatoes, and yams) and fruits (apples, bananas, berries, peaches, and watermelon) make up the middle of the pyramid. Fruit consumption by today's African Americans is considered low compared to other groups. Pork (chitterlings, intestines, ham hocks, and sausages) remains a primary protein source, and frying is still the most popular way of preparing food. Fruit drinks and tea are the drinks of choice over milk, which is consumed primarily in puddings and ice cream (Welch, 2003).

There are many reasons African Americans choose a diet high in fat and sodium. African Americans in general accept larger body sizes, feel less guilt about overeating, and are less likely to practice unhealthy dieting behaviors such as excessive exercising or purging (Andrews, 2007). Although African Americans have a healthy acceptance of a wider range of body sizes, their tolerance may lead to greater obesity and serious obesity-related health problems.

Mental Health

African Americans have about the same degree of mental health issues, or even less, than Non-Hispanic whites. This may be because African Americans often rely on family, church, and community to cope. The level of religious participation among African Americans is high. Although the rate of substance use among African American is lower than for other ethnicities, alcohol and drugs are responsible for more deaths in the African American community than any other chronic disease in the United States (American Psychiatric Association, n.d.). African Americans have a remarkably low suicide rate compared to non-Hispanic whites.

Death and Dying

Generally speaking, in the African American experience, spirituality is a fundamental part of how many people process and reconcile the experience of death. African Americans tend to believe in the sanctity of life and rely on a strong sense of community and family at times of loss. Family-centered consensus is valued in decision making, and there is often a strong need for extended family to gather at times of death. The family should be informed of an impending death so that extended family members who live out of state can be notified.

Many African Americans have a holistic view of death and dying, and birth and death are understood to be part of a cycle or continuum. At the same time, many older African Americans, who believe that death is God's will, may also tend to believe that life support should be continued as long as necessary. Cremation is generally avoided in this community, and organ donation may be viewed by some as a desecration of the body.

In medical settings, so much emphasis is placed on the physical care of the dying that spirituality is often overlooked. Health care providers do not always recognize that this should be an integral part of the continuum of care. In hospital settings, one way to accomplish this is to suggest the support of the hospital chaplain. It would be ideal to involve clergy from the individual's own faith community, but if that is not possible, be sure that the hospital chaplain is available as an integral part of the care team (Carteret, 2011).

Cultural-Bound Illnesses

There are no specific culture-bound illnesses attributed to the African American culture. "Falling Out" or "Blacking Out" have been suggested as culture-bound illnesses, but they are associated with poverty and stress rather than with the African American culture itself (Jackson, 2006). Sickle cell anemia is a genetic condition that has a high incidence in this population, with 1 in 12 African Americans having this trait, but it is not exclusive to African Americans. The disease occurs in about 1 out of every 500 African American births, but it also affects Hispanic Americans, occurring in about 1 out of every 36,000 Hispanic American births (National Heart, Lung and Blood Institute, 2012).

Did You Know?

The CDC has determined that the sickle cell trait may have evolved to provide some protection against malaria. The agency conducted a study in Kenya (Asembo Bay Cohort Project in western Kenya), and the results suggest that people with sickle cell anemia may tend to have shorter lives, but the trait seems to protect young children between 2 and 16 months of age from the effects of malaria (Centers for Disease Control and Prevention [CDC], 2002).

Healing Traditions

African American healing traditions encompass a variety of beliefs and practices. Some of them were brought through slavery and ancestral roots. The ancestral roots from West Africa brought many herbal and spiritual healing techniques. Types of healers that African Americans use include faith or spiritual healers. African American healers may choose to use rituals, charms, and herbs. Today, African Americans can choose whether they want to be seen by a biomedical doctor or a traditional healer. Although they have the freedom to choose their practitioner, certain factors can affect their choice, such as trust, access to care, and insurance, as well as other socioeconomic factors.

Prayer is the most common treatment for illness among people who believe that illness is caused by God's will. Spiritual beliefs form a foundation for the health belief systems of many African Americans. Instead of going to the doctor when they are ill, some African Americans will pray for their actions that caused them to get sick, asking God to make them healthy before seeking the help of Western medicine (University of Washington Medical Center, 2007).

Herbs and remedies are other important aspects of the healing traditions of African Americans. Most home remedies are learned from caregivers, such as mothers or grandmothers (Warner, 2005). Some herbs and remedies that are used include the following (Ansorge, 1999; Spector, 2004; Warner, 2005):

- St. John's wort is used for scrapes, strains, and burns. Today it is known for being a mild treatment for depression.
- Petals from an African plant called okra are used to cure boils.
- Wild yam is used to cure indigestion.
- Rectified turpentine with sugar is used to treat a cough.
- Nine drops of turpentine 9 days after intercourse may act as a contraceptive.
- Sugar and turpentine are used to get rid of worms.
- Dried snake ground up and brewed as tea is used to treat blemishes.
- Cool baths, isopropyl alcohol (applied topically), warming the feet, and cool drinks or popsicles are used to treat fever.
- Catnip, senna extract, chamomile, cigarette smoke, and walking are used to treat colic.
- Whiskey, pennies, eggs, and ice cubes or popsicles alleviate teething pain.

Another type of remedy African Americans commonly use is to wear bad-smelling objects, such as bags containing gum resin or asafetida (rotten flesh), around the neck. Although this traditional method does not have any healing properties, it is said to ward off infectious disease (Ansorge, 1999).

The goal of treatment for unnatural illness is to remove evil spirits from the body. Traditional healers, who are usually women, are consulted. These women possess knowledge about use of herbs and roots as well as mystical voodoo-like powers. Some African Americans who believe that they have been hexed will seek out a voodoo-type healer in addition to or instead of a licensed medical provider (Leininger, as cited in Fields, 2001).

Voodoo (from *vodoun*, meaning spirit) originated in Africa nearly 10,000 years ago. Although its origins remain mysterious and elusive, scholars are fairly certain that its birthplace was somewhere in West Africa. It is recognized as one of the world's oldest religions (Dakwar, 2004). Voodoo was brought to this country in 1724 with the arrival of slaves from the West African coast (Spector, 2004). Historian Sharla Fett identified four themes that link the medical practices of southern slaves to those of the West and Central African cultures: a belief that medicine possesses a spiritual force, that preparing medicine brings the healer closer to spiritual power, that healing maintains relationships between the living and the world of ancestors, and that power can be used for healing and harming (Savitt, 2002). Voodoo is divided into two types: white magic and black magic. White magic is known to be harmless and includes the use of powders and oils that are pleasantly scented. Black magic is quite rare but dangerous and includes the use of oils and powders with a foul and vile odor (Spector, 2004). The practice involves candle-lit rituals and spiritual ceremonies, most commonly held by women. Chest pain, luck, success, attracting money, and evil intentions are just a few reasons people practice voodoo (Spector, 2004).

During the 19th and 20th centuries, voodoo suffered persecution in both the Americas and the Caribbean. The practice of voodoo was illegal, and the spiritual tools of voodoo—fetishes, rods, and sculptures—were confiscated and destroyed (Dakwar, 2004). Simultaneously, a campaign to discredit and disparage voodoo in the public eye began; this led to the popular understanding of voodoo as being malicious, dark, foolish, primitive, dangerous, and violent—ideas that continue to resonate today. Despite this campaign, voodoo is still practiced by millions of people in Africa, the Americas, and the Caribbean (Dakwar, 2004).

Santeria is practiced by some African Americans. It is based on West African religions that were brought to the New World by slaves imported to the Caribbean to work on the sugar plantations. These slaves carried with them their own religious traditions, including a tradition of possession trance for communicating with the ancestors and deities, the use of animal sacrifice, and the practice of sacred drumming and dance. Those slaves who landed in the Caribbean and Central and South America were nominally converted to Catholicism. However, they were able to preserve some of their traditions by fusing various Yoruban beliefs and rituals with elements from the surrounding Catholic culture. In Cuba this religious tradition has evolved into what we know today as Santeria, the Way of the Saints. Today, hundreds of thousands of Americans participate in this ancient religion. Many are of Hispanic and Caribbean descent, but as the religion moves out of the inner cities and into the suburbs, a growing number of followers are of African American and European American heritage.

Another religion tied to the days of slavery is **Candomblé**, which was developed in Brazil by enslaved Africans who attempted to re-create their culture on the other side of the ocean. The rituals involve animal sacrifices, healing, dancing, drumming, and the possession of participants by orishas, which are religious deities said to represent human characteristics such as bravery, love, and honor. Today, Candomblé is widely practiced in Brazil, but because of its secrecy it is unknown how widespread it is in the United States.

Attempts at spiritual healing may be concealed from Western health care providers to avoid the stigma attached to such practices, which may be labeled as devil worshipping or mumbo jumbo by mainstream European American culture (Welch, 2003). When such medical or health-related information is revealed, providers should place it in its proper cultural context.

Behavior Risk Factors and Prevalent Health Problems

Discrimination, poverty, and poor nutrition and exercise habits have resulted in serious health problems for African Americans. The poverty rate is higher among African Americans than any other racial/ethnic groups except American Indian/Alaska Natives (Macartney, Bishaw, & Fontenot, 2013). As a group, African Americans lead all other racial/ethnic groups in low birth weight, infant mortality, obesity, diabetes, asthma, hepatitis B, HIV/AIDS, sexually transmitted diseases, waiting list for organ transplants, and cancer deaths. In 2010, the death rate for African Americans was higher than whites for heart diseases, stroke, cancer, asthma, influenza, pneumonia, diabetes, HIV/AIDS, and homicide (Office of Minority Health, 2014).

Some adverse behaviors that particularly affect the African American community are drug use, smoking, poor nutritional habits, and limited physical activity. The consumption and trafficking of drugs, such as alcohol and cocaine, in the African American community is market driven and stimulated by unemployment, poverty, despair, alienation, depression, hopelessness, and dependency (addiction). Alcoholism is the most significant social and health problem within the African American population. Studies have shown that 60% of homicides in the African American community are alcohol related (Hill, 2007). Despite years of protest from African Americans, their communities are still targeted by billboards with positive messages about alcohol. This means African American youth are exposed to more alcohol advertisements in their neighborhoods than any other youth groups in the United States (Hill, 2007).

The 10 leading causes of death among African American in 2010 were as follows:

1. Heart disease
2. Cancer
3. Stroke
4. Diabetes mellitus
5. Unintentional injuries
6. Nephritis, nephrotic syndrome, and nephrosis
7. Chronic lower respiratory disease
8. Homicide
9. Septicemia
10. Alzheimer's disease (Office of Minority Health, 2014)

In 2011, African Americans were 1.5 times as likely to be obese as non-Hispanic whites. About 80% of African American women are overweight or obese. Diet choices contribute to the fact that African Americans are twice as likely to be diagnosed with diabetes as non-Hispanic whites. In addition, high consumption of fat and sodium increases risk of hypertension (high blood pressure), and African Americans have higher rates of hypertension than any other race (Andrews, 2007; Office of Minority Health, 2014). The diabetes mortality rate is 27% higher among African Americans than among whites (Welch, 2003).

In 2010, African Americans had an infant mortality rate more than twice that of non-Hispanic whites. African American infants were almost 4 times as likely to die from causes related to low birth weight and had twice the rate of sudden infant death syndrome compared to non-Hispanic white infants. Compared to non-Hispanic white mothers, African American mothers were more than twice as likely to begin prenatal care in the third trimester or to not receive prenatal care at all (Office of Minority Health, 2014).

African American men are 34% more likely than white men to develop lung cancer although they represent a lower percentage rate for smoking (21.3%) than white men (22%) who smoke 30 to 40% more cigarettes. African American women tend to smoke less than white women, but the two groups have similar lung cancer rates (American Lung Association, 2010). This is in part because African Americans have a preference for mentholated brands, which are high in tar and nicotine (Ellis, 2005). Almost 84% of African Americans smokers aged 12 years or older reported smoking a mentholated brand of cigarette compared to 24 and

32%, respectively, of their Caucasian and Hispanic counterparts (American Lung Association, 2010). Fortunately, between 1997 and 2007, the smoking rate declined 49% among African American high school students from 22.7% to 11.6%. These students were significantly less likely than non-Hispanic white and Hispanic students to report current smoking in 2007. They also have the highest percentage (58.4%) of smokers trying to quit in the past 12 months (American Lung Association, 2010).

African Americans are the group most affected by HIV, with the rate of new HIV infection in African Americans 8 times that of whites based on population size. They made up about 44% of new HIV infections among adults and adolescents (aged 13 years or older) in 2010 despite representing only 13% of the U.S. population (CDC, 2014a). For African American men, the primary transmission category was sexual contact with other men, followed by injection drug use and high-risk heterosexual contact. For African American women, the primary transmission category was high-risk heterosexual contact followed by injection drug use (CDC, 2014a).

In addition to being at risk from sharing needles, casual and chronic substance users are more likely to engage in high-risk behaviors such as unprotected sex (CDC, 2014a). The Centers for Disease Control and Prevention (2014a) ranks African Americans as having the highest rates of sexually transmitted diseases.

Linked to unprotected sex is the number of teenage pregnancies. Although the number of teenage pregnancies has declined over the years, teen pregnancy rates vary widely by race and ethnicity. In 2012, Hispanic adolescent females ages 15 to 19 had the highest birthrate (46.3 births per 1,000 adolescent females), followed by African American adolescent females (43.9 births per 1,000 adolescent females) and white adolescent females (20.5 births per 1,000 adolescent females; Office of Adolescent Health, 2014). African Americans experience higher rates of other sexually transmitted infections (STIs) compared with other racial/ethnic groups in the United States (CDC, 2014a).

In 2010, African Americans were 1.5 times as likely to die from viral hepatitis compared to non-Hispanic whites, and they were twice as likely to develop hepatitis B in 2011 than the white population (Office of Minority Health, 2014). Among African Americans, chronic liver disease is a leading cause of death. Although the cause is not always known, some cases can be initiated by conditions such as chronic alcoholism, obesity, and exposure to hepatitis B and C viruses. In 2009, chronic liver disease was the twelfth leading cause of death for non-Hispanic blacks (CDC, 2011). African American death rates are higher than those of non-Hispanic whites for all major (of death, and African Americans have a lower life expectancy. African Americans can expect to live 71 years as compared to 76 years for non-Hispanic whites (NCHS, 2013).

Poverty level affects mental health status. Poor African Americans compared to those double the poverty level, are 3 times more likely to report psychological distress. African Americans are 20% more likely to report having serious psychological distress than non-Hispanic whites, but whites are more than twice as likely to receive antidepressant treatments.

Remarkably, African American men have a suicide rate 60% lower than non-Hispanic white men. Even more significantly, African American women have a suicide rate only one quarter that of African American men and less than half that of non-Hispanic white women (CDC, 2014b).

Heart disease is the leading cause of death for African American women in the United States (Office of Minority Health, 2014). As a whole, African American men and women are more likely than people of other races to have heart failure and to suffer from more severe forms of it. They are more likely to have symptoms of heart disease at a younger age, have those symptoms worsen faster, have more hospital visits due to heart failure, and die from heart failure (National Heart Lung and Blood Institute, 2008).

In 2009, African Americans had the highest death rates from homicide among all racial and ethnic groups, with African American males representing the highest rates across all age groups (Office of Minority Health, 2014). African American males constituted 31% of all arrests for violent crime, making up a disproportionate number of arrests for aggravated assault (33.5%) and forcible rape (31%) and about half (48.8%) of all arrests for murder and non-negligent manslaughter in 2009 (Bureau of Justice Statistics [BJS], 2011). Although arrests do not completely represent the extent of violent acts because many acts go unreported and arrests do not always mean guilt, the tremendous disparity in the rates of arrests for violent crimes among African Americans does likely indicate a higher rate of violence (Roberts, n.d.). African American females experienced intimate partner violence at a rate 35% higher than that of white females and about 22 times the rate of women of other races (Rennison & Welchans, 2000). African American males experienced intimate partner violence at a rate about 62% higher than that of white males and about 22 times the rate of men of other races (Rennison & Welchans, 2000).

QUICK FACTS

Health disparities reported in the CDC Health Disparities and Inequalities Report (National Center for Health Statistics, 2012) include:

- African Americans in 2009 had the highest death rates from heart disease and stroke compared with other racial and ethnic populations; these disparities in deaths were also found across age groups younger than 85 years of age.

- From 2007 to 2010, the largest prevalence of hypertension was among adults aged 65 years and older, African American adults, U.S.-born adults, adults with less than a college education, adults who received public health insurance (18 to 64 years old), and those with diabetes, obesity, or a disability, compared with their counterparts. The percentages of African American and Hispanic adults who had control of high blood pressure were lower than among white adults.

- The prevalence of obesity among adults from 2007 to 2010 was highest among African American women compared with white and Mexican American women and men, and the overall obesity prevalence (both sexes combined) of African American adults was also higher when compared with white and Mexican American adults.

- In 2010, the prevalence of diabetes among African American adults was nearly twice that of white adults.

- Although the difference in the number of years of expected life free of activity limitations caused by chronic conditions decreased between white and African American adults from 1999 to 2008, the number of years was still fewer for African Americans than for white adults.

- From 2009 to 2010, the prevalence of periodontitis was highest among African American and Mexican American adults compared with white adults.

- Infants of African American women in 2008 had the highest death rate, which was more than twice the rate among infants of white women.

- African Americans in 2009 had the highest death rates from homicide among all racial and ethnic populations. Rates among African American males were highest across all age groups.

- African American adults in 2010 had the highest HIV-infection rate when compared with adults of other racial and ethnic populations. Prescribed HIV treatment among African American adults living with HIV was less than among white adults.

- In 2010, a larger percentage of Hispanic and African American adults aged 18 to 64 years were without health insurance compared with white and Asian/Pacific Islander counterparts.

- African Americans had the highest incidence and death rates from colorectal cancer in 2008 among all racial and ethnic populations despite having colorectal screening rates similar to those of white adults.

- During the 2010–2011 influenza season, influenza vaccination coverage was similar for African American and white children aged 6 months to 17 years, but African American adults had less coverage than white adults.

- In 2011, similar to other racial and ethnic minority adults aged 25 years or older, African American adults had a higher percentage who did not complete high school compared with white adults. Also, a larger percentage of African American adults (ages 18 to 64 years) lived below the poverty level and were unemployed compared with white adults.

- Although the gap is narrowing, in 2011 the average American could expect to live 78.7 years, whereas the average African American could only expect to live 75.3 years and the average white American 78.8 years.

Factors contributing to poor health outcomes among African Americans include discrimination; cultural, linguistic, and literacy barriers; and lack of access to health care (Office of Minority Health, 2014).

Considerations for Health Promotion and Program Planning

Consider the following concepts when planning and implementing a health promotion program for this target audience:

- Be aware and sensitive to the distrust of the medical community and the government that may exist among African American community members.

- Consider utilizing churches to disseminate information or as a place to conduct health screenings and educational interventions.

- Be aware that peer educators have not been shown to be effective in developing health programs for African American audiences.

- Develop interventions that focus on positive health changes instead of attempting to instill change through fear or negative messages.

- Until invited otherwise, greet African Americans with formal titles.

- Take special care to have congruent verbal and nonverbal communication patterns.

- Be aware of different terminology because there are various regional terms used to describe medical conditions. Among immigrants from Haiti, Jamaica, and the Bahamas, and among many Southern African Americans, for example, blood may be characterized as *low* or *high*, referring to anemia as opposed to hypertension. *Spells*, also called *falling outs*, are perceived to be a result of *low blood*; elderly African Americans especially may refer to *having had a spell*. *Shock* is a common term for a stroke. Other common terms include *having sugar*, *sweet blood*, or *thin blood*, referring to diabetes (Welch, 2003).

- Understand that occasional outbursts of laughter that may appear to be inappropriate for the situation are in fact appropriate because African Americans find solace in laughter and playfulness.

- African Americans are less likely to donate organs or consent to an autopsy. Providers should be aware that talking about organ donation may be an insult to the family (Purnell, 2013).

- African Americans tend to speak louder than those from other cultures; health care providers should not misinterpret this as anger.

- Maintaining good health is often correlated with good religious practice. Many churches maintain a health ministry through which congregations and parish nurses support good health with flu shots, blood pressure checks, and health education (Carteret, 2011). Therefore, health screening programs may best be initiated through community and church activities.

Tips for Working With the African American Population

To improve communication, which enhances the building of a trusting relationship, acknowledge and respect your patients' meaning for their illness. Spend time with your patients and ask about their health beliefs. Listen carefully.

Acknowledging and respecting your patient's understanding of his or her illness will help improve communication, which is a cornerstone of a trusting caregiver-patient relationship. If there is a mismatch, many African American patients will rely on their own explanations before those of medical professionals. Making one medically neutral suggestion that fits your patients' belief system builds rapport quickly.

Assess and acknowledge the significance of spirituality; avoid dominating the content of the discussion, and offer choices for treatment options. Be available to consult with your patient's family, minister, and friends in cases of serious or terminal illness, especially at the time the illness is being explained.

Include your patients in the decision-making process. Answer your patient's questions and concerns about diagnosis and treatment plans. Enlarge the decision-making process to include social decisions.

Show respectful behavior. Your patients may include many people as part of their extended family, some related, and others who may be friends of the family or part of the patient's wider social networks. What is unique about this patient and family that you will not learn from tips or information about their culture?

Before touching patients, always explain what will be done and why. Your patients may prefer that family members of the other gender leave the room (Seminole County Medical Society, n.d.).

Summary

African Americans were originally brought forcibly to the United States through the slave trade. African Americans experience high levels of poverty, discrimination, and violence. Whatever the reason, the overall health of this population is worse than any other group in the United States. The main behavioral risks associated with African Americans are smoking, alcohol consumption, weight management, and lack of physical activity. Some of their beliefs about causes of illness and treatment approaches are related to their religious practices and ancestral roots, so some African Americans will choose to use faith or spiritual healers rather than a biomedical doctor. In some way, African Americans have developed some capacity to cope with stress in a way that results in their having a low incidence of suicide compared to other groups.

In this chapter we discussed the unique aspects of the history of African Americans and how their history has had a negative impact on their trust in the medical system. We learned that religion plays a central role in this community and how that is integrated into their health belief system and practices. General tips for working with these populations were provided, but as usual we caution that there is a vast amount of diversity within this community, so it is important not to generalize.

Review

1. Explain the history of African Americans in the United States.

2. Provide an overview of African Americans' socioeconomic situation.

3. Why is there is general mistrust by African Americans in the medical system?

4. What are some of the behavior risk factors and common diseases that African Americans experience?

Activity

Conduct research on health programs that have been implemented for members of the African American population. Summarize the literature and identify some best practices.

Watch the video *Miss Evers' Boys* on YouTube. Write a reaction paper to the video.

What surprised you? Should the nurse or physician have done anything differently? How does ethics play a role? How do you think this study influences the interactions between African Americans and the health care system?

Case Study

The number of infants who die before their first birthday is much higher in the United States than in other countries, and for African Americans the rate is nearly twice as high as for white Americans. Even well-educated African American women have birth outcomes worse than white women who haven't finished high school. Why?

We meet Andrea Jackson, a successful lawyer, executive, and mother. When Andrea was pregnant with her first child, she, like so many others, did her best to ensure a healthy baby; she ate right, exercised, abstained from alcohol and smoking, and received good prenatal care. Yet 2.5 months before her due date, she went into labor unexpectedly. Her newborn weighed less than 3 pounds. Andrea and her husband were devastated. How could this have happened?

We know that, in general, health follows wealth; on average, the higher on the socioeconomic ladder you are, the lower your risk of cancer, heart disease, diabetes, infant death, and preterm deliveries. For highly educated African American women like Andrea, the advantages of income and status do make a difference in health, but something else is still in play: racism.

There are several issues to consider about this case:

- How may have Andrea's race and culture played a role in her having a low-birth-weight baby?

- Are there any culture-specific protective factors that may have helped Andrea cope with the racism she has faced?

References

American Lung Association. (2010). *Smoking facts and figures, African Americans*. Retrieved from http://www.lung.org/stop-smoking/about-smoking/facts-figures/african-americans-and-tobacco.html

American Psychiatric Association. (n.d.). *African Americans, let's talk facts* [Brochure]. Retrieved from http://www.psychiatry.org/african-americans

Andrews, L. C. (2007). *African Americans and diet*. Retrieved from http://www.netwellness.org/healthtopics/aahealth/healthybody.cfm

Ansorge, R. (1999). Herbs and roots are in African-American folk medicine. *Colorado Springs Gazette*. Retrieved from http://www.texnews.com/1998/1999/ads/ads/health2/roots.html

Brown v. Board of Education of Topeka, 347 U.S. 483 (1954).

Bureau of Justice Statistics. (2011). *Patterns and trends 1980–2009: Arrests in the United States, by sex, age group, and race.* Retrieved from http://www.bjs.gov/content/pub/pdf/aus8009.pdf

Bureau of Labor Statistics. (2014). *Employment status of the civilian population by race, sex, and age,* table A-2 [Economic News Release]. Retrieved from http://www.bls.gov/news.release/empsit.t02.htm

Carteret, M. (2011). *Health care for African American patients/families.* Retrieved from http://www.dimensionsofculture.com/2011/05/health-care-for-african-american-patientsfamilies/

Centers for Disease Control and Prevention. (2002). *Protective effect of sickle cell trait against malaria-associated mortality and morbidity.* Retrieved from http://www.cdc.gov/malaria/about/biology/sickle_cell.html

Centers for Disease Control and Prevention. (2011). Deaths, final data for 2009. *National Vital Statistics Reports,* Vol. 60, No. 3. Retrieved from http://www.cdc.gov/nchs/data/nvsr/nvsr60/nvsr60_03.pdf

Centers for Disease Control and Prevention. (2014a). *HIV among African Americans: Fast facts.* Retrieved from http://www.cdc.gov/hiv/risk/racialethnic/aa/facts/index.html

Centers for Disease Control and Prevention. (2014b). *Suicide rates among persons ages 10 years and older, by race/ethnicity and sex, United States, 2005–2009.* Retrieved from http://www.cdc.gov/violenceprevention/suicide/statistics/rates02.html

Centers for Disease Control and Prevention. (2014c). *Office of Minority Health (2014) Hepatitis and African Americans Minority Population Profiles: Black/African Americans.* Retrieved from http://minority health.hhs.gov/omh/browse.aspx?lvl=4&lvlid=20

Clarke-Tasker, V. (1993). Cancer prevention and detection in African-Americans. In M. Frank-Stromburg & S. J. Olsen (Eds.), *Cancer prevention in minority populations: Cultural implications for health care professionals.* St. Louis, MO: Mosby.

Dakwar, E. (2004). *Voodoo therapy.* Creighton University Medical Center. Complementary and Alternative Medicine. Retrieved from http://altmed.creighton.edu/voodoo/

Ellis, G. (2005). Cigarette companies target African-Americans. *Philadelphia Tribune,* p. 5B.

Falconbridge, A. (1788). *An account of the slave trade on the coast of Africa.* London, England: J. Phillips.

Fields, S. D. (2001). Health belief system of African-Americans: Essential information for today's practicing nurses. *Journal of Multicultural Nursing & Health, 7*(1), 36.

Hill, P. J. (2007). Legacy of addiction, incarceration feeds itself. *Call & Post,* pp. 9–11.

Jackson, Y. (2006). Culture-bound syndromes: Falling out, blacking out. *Multicultural Psychology,* 136–137. Retrieved from http://anthropology.msu.edu/anp204-us12/2012/07/20/falling-outblacking-out-among-afro-carribbeans-and-black-americans/

Leininger, M. (1995). *Transcultural nursing: Concepts, theories, research and practice* (2nd ed.). New York, NY: McGraw-Hill.

Lu, M. C., & Halfon N. (2003). Racial and ethnic disparities in birth outcomes: A life-course perspective. *Maternal and Child Health Journal, 7*(1), 13–30. Retrieved from http://www.ncbi.nlm.nih.gov/pubmed/12710797

Macartney, S., Bishaw, A., & Fontenot, K. (2013). *Poverty rates for selected detailed race and Hispanic groups by state and place: 2007–2011.* Retrieved from http://www.census.gov/prod/2013pubs/acsbr11-17.pdf

Moore, J. (2007). *Traditional health beliefs.* Retrieved from http://www.hawcc.hawaii.edu/nursing/transcultural.html

National Heart, Lung and Blood Institute. (2008). *African American health.* Retrieved from http://www.nhlbi.nih.gov/health/index.htm

National Heart, Lung and Blood Institute. (2012). *Who is at risk for sickle cell anemia.* Retrieved from http://www.nhlbi.nih.gov/health/health-topics/topics/sca/atrisk

New York Public Library. (2007). *In motion: The African-American migration experience.* Retrieved from http://www.inmotionaame.org/home.cfm

Office of Adolescent Health. (2014). *Trends in teen pregnancy and childbearing.* Retrieved from http://www.hhs.gov/ash/oah/adolescent-health-topics/reproductive-health/teen-pregnancy/trends.html

Perry, J. A. (1998). African roots of African-American culture. *Black Collegian Online.* Retrieved from http://www.black-collegian.com/issues/1998-12/africanroots12.shtml

Plessy v. Ferguson, 163 U.S. 537 (1896).

Purnell, L. (2013) *Transcultural healthcare: A culturally competent approach* (4th ed.). Philadelphia, PA: F. A. Davis Company.

Rennison, C. M., & Welchans, S. (2000). *Intimate partner violence* (NCJ 178247). Retrieved from http://www.ojp.usdoj.gov/bjs/pub/ascii/ipv.txt

Roberts, S. (n.d.). *Black youth, health, and society.* Retrieved from http://blackyouthproject.uchicago.edu/primers/reviews/health.pdf

Sadler, C., & Huff, M. (2007). *African-American women: Health beliefs, lifestyle, and osteoporosis.* Retrieved from http://www.nursingcenter.com/prodev/ce_article.asp?tid=710316

Savitt, T. L. (2002). *Medicine and slavery: The diseases and healthcare of blacks.* Champaign, IL: University of Illinois Press.

Seminole County Medical Society. (n.d.). *Communicating with your African-American patient.* Retrieved from http://scmsociety.typepad.com/members_center/files/dscms_culture_africanamerican2.pdf

Spector, R. E. (2004). *Cultural diversity in health and illness* (6th ed.). Upper Saddle River, NJ: Pearson Education.

University of Washington Medical Center. (2007). *African American culture clues: Communicating with your African American patient.* Retrieved from http://www.depts.washington.edu/pfes/pdf/AfricanAmericanCultureClue4_07.pdf

U.S. Census Bureau. (2010). *Population and race; percent black or African American 2010.* Retrieved from http://tigerweb.geo.census.gov/datamapper/map.html

Warner, J. (2005). Folk remedies part of African American tradition. *Fox News.* Retrieved from http://www.foxnews.com/story/0,2933,149791,00.html

Welch, M. (2003). *Care of blacks and African Americans.* Retrieved from http://www.acponline.org/fcgi/search?q=welch+care+of+blacks&site=ACP_Online&num=10

CHAPTER 10

Asian American Populations

Keeping your body healthy is an expression of gratitude to the whole cosmos—the trees, the clouds, everything.
   —Thich Nhat Hanh

Always aim at complete harmony of thought and word and deed. Always aim at purifying your thoughts and everything will be well.
   —Mahatma Gandhi

Sickness is a thing of the spirit.
   —Japanese proverb

Key Concepts

Hmong	Timbang
aAma and aDuonga	Karma
Kior chi force	Shintoism

Learning Objectives

After reading this chapter, you should be able to:

1. Discuss the social and economic circumstances of the various Asian Americans in the United States.
2. Describe the beliefs about the cause of illness for Asian American cultures.
3. Discuss risk factors and illnesses that particularly affect Asian Americans.
4. Describe beliefs about healing practices for Asian Americans.

Introduction

This chapter addresses the cultural health attributes of the approximately 6% of the U.S. population who have immigrated from a large number of countries and locations. These countries are the home of about 60% of the world's population of 7 billion people. The 2010 Census included people who indicated their race(s) as "Asian" or reported entries such as "Asian Indian," "Chinese," "Filipino," "Korean," "Japanese," "Vietnamese," or other detailed Asian responses (Office of Minority Health, 2013).

Race is not the same as culture, and this is particularly true when speaking of Asians in America who come from the most populous and diverse countries in the world, including China with more than 1.4 billion people, India with 1.3 billion people, and Indonesia with 256 million people (U.S. Census Bureau, 2015). The people of China alone speak many different languages and dialects, and it was necessary to establish Mandarin as a language to be learned and used in addition to local languages to enable nationwide communication. All the major religions of the world are practiced by this population including Hinduism, Buddhism, Islam, and Christianity.

This chapter provides a brief history of the Asian population in the United States, along with information about their demographic information, their beliefs about the causes of illness and healing practices, behavioral risk factors, and the common health problems that they face.

Terminology

Asia is the largest land mass on the planet, and referring to a person as an Asian is not particularly descriptive due to the great variety of its peoples and cultures. Some analysts break the continental reference into South Asia, Southeast Asia, and the Far East with the many Asian countries organized into these categories as depicted in **Table 10.1**.

The U.S. Census combines people who describe their heritage as "Asian." Hawaiian and Pacific Islander had been included in this group until separated out in 2000. To complicate the matter, much of the analysis of historical trends and even current literature often refers to "Asian and Pacific Islanders." Including Pacific Islanders adds about one half of the world geography but a very small part of the world population. In this chapter we refer to Asian

TABLE 10.1   Asian American Origins

Far East. China, Japan, Korea, Mongolia, Okinawa, Taiwan
Southeast Asia. Borneo, Brunei, Burma, Cambodia, Philippines, Indonesia, Laos, Malaysia, Singapore, Thailand, Vietnam
South Asia (Indian subcontinent). Afghanistan, Bangladesh, Bhutan, India, Maldives, Nepal, Pakistan, Sri Lanka, Tibet

Source: U.S. Census Bureau (n.d.).

Americans in the same way as the current Census terminology but try to make some distinction among the very different populations and cultures included in the term *Asian*.

History of Asian Americans in the United States

The experience of Asian Americans in the United States differs from that of other major minority groups because it can be generally stated that Asians came to the United States voluntarily seeking to prosper or to avoid persecution in their homeland. Cultural practices within these groups vary greatly depending on country of origin, culture, and when they arrived in this country. The historical background for many of these groups is discussed in this section.

Asian Indian Americans

Asian Indians have generally immigrated to the United States voluntarily. They began immigrating to the United States in greater numbers during the latter part of the 20th century as the population in India increased. Most came to the United States looking for economic opportunity. Asian Indian Americans now are the third largest population group from Asia, after Chinese and Filipino populations (U.S. Census Bureau, 2012a).

Chinese Americans

Although agreement cannot be reached on when the first Chinese people arrived in North America due to lack of records, there is little disagreement about when their immigration exploded. When gold was discovered in California in 1849, word spread to China, and immigrants voluntarily flooded the West Coast. During the gold rush era, Chinese worked, and sometimes succeeded, in the gold fields. Many started businesses to service and support the gold miners who came from around the world to seek riches. When the gold rush diminished, Chinese immigrants began working on the transcontinental railroad. They settled in great numbers in California and established businesses and farms and worked as farm laborers and in factories.

Nevertheless, they were met with strong discrimination. Chinese Americans, as well as other minorities, tended to live in racially segregated areas and established enduring social structures that continue to the present day. Immigration restrictions targeted various Asian populations. The Chinese Exclusion Act of 1882 restricted the admission of unskilled Chinese workers. In 1907 and 1908, an informal arrangement known as the "Gentlemen's Agreement" placed similar limits on Japanese and Koreans, and in 1917 the Immigration Act of 1917 restricted the entry of Asian Indians. In response to a growing population of Filipino immigrants who worked as daily wage laborers in California agriculture, the Tydings-McDuffie Act of 1934 denied entry to Filipinos.

These discriminatory practices continued until the McCarran-Walter Act of 1952 made naturalization available to all races. After the reforms of the Immigration and Naturalization Act of 1965, immigration of Asian people increased dramatically.

Japanese Americans

Many Japanese began immigrating to the United States in the 19th century. At first they moved to Hawaii and the western United States to work on plantations, farms, and in the fishing and canning industries. During World War II, in an act later found unconstitutional by the U.S. Supreme Court, Japanese Americans were interned in concentration camps because of their race and concerns that they would collaborate with the Imperial Japanese government. Even in the face of this discrimination, many Japanese Americans enlisted to assist the country in the war effort. In fact, the U.S. Army's 442nd Regimental Combat Team was composed of Japanese Americans who fought in Europe and was the most decorated unit in U.S. military history. Since the end of World War II, Japanese Americans have grown in their influence on American culture, and currently the U.S. government is engaged in a program of reparation for the suffering endured by Japanese Americans in the camps during World War II.

The people of Asia are not one homogeneous culture and many groups have been in major conflict with one another over the centuries. Vietnam fought wars with China for thousands of years, Japan inflicted major destruction and inhumane treatment on the Chinese during World War II, India and China continue to have border disputes. However, there are many cultural aspects of people from Asia that transcend national boundaries.

Korean Americans

Korean immigration to the United States began in the early 20th century when Koreans immigrated to Hawaii to work on the plantations. Thereafter, a significant wave of immigration was related to the Korean War in the 1950s. That immigration brought many more Koreans to the U.S. mainland, and most settled in the western states (Beller, Pinker, Snapka, & Van Dusan, n.d.).

Vietnamese Americans

The Vietnamese presence in the United States occurred in waves related to U.S. involvement in the Vietnam War. Continuing conflicts in Southeast Asia led to the immigration of Laotians and Cambodians to the United States as well. Vietnamese people who worked with the United States during that conflict fled to the United States when the Thieu government lost power in 1975. It is believed that 130,000 Vietnamese came to the United States in 1975 alone. Most of those immigrants were young, well-educated, English-speaking city dwellers.

Other waves of immigrants were spawned by the invasion of Laos and Cambodia by Vietnamese troops. Between 1979 and 1983, 455,000 Vietnamese, Laotian, and Cambodian refugees came to the United States. These refugees were made up of different ethnic groups and were more rural, less educated, and not as familiar with Western ideas as the first wave of immigrants (LaBorde, 1996).

A third group of refugees from Southeast Asia arrived from 1985 to 1991. This group tended to include both Vietnamese and Chinese who were admitted to the country in family reunification programs (LaBorde, 1996).

Asian Americans in the United States

According to the 2011 Census Bureau population estimate, Asian Americans represent about 4.8% of the U.S. population and number about 14.7 million (U.S. Census Bureau, 2012a). In 2011, there were 4 million Chinese, 3.4 million Filipinos, 3.2 million Asian Indians, 1.9 million Vietnamese, 1.7 million Koreans, and 1.3 million Japanese in the United States (Office of Minority Health, 2013). The states with the top 10 largest Asian populations are shown in **Figure 10.1**.

The percentage of people 5 years or older who do not speak English at home varies among Asian American groups; 52% of Vietnamese, 46% of Chinese, 22% of Filipinos, and 21% of Asian Indians are not fluent in English. About 76.9% of Asian Americans speak a language other than English at home (Office of Minority Health, 2013). Asian Americans are less likely to live in poverty (12.8%), are more likely to be college graduates or hold graduate degrees (50%), and are more likely to be employed in management, business, science, and arts occupations (48.5%) compared with the total U.S. population (15.9%, 28.5%, 36.0%, respectively; Office of Minority Health, 2013). The median family income of Asian American families in 2012 was $70,644, or $14,059 higher than the national median income for non-Hispanic white families; 13% of Asian Americans compared to 11% of non-Hispanic whites live at the poverty, (Office

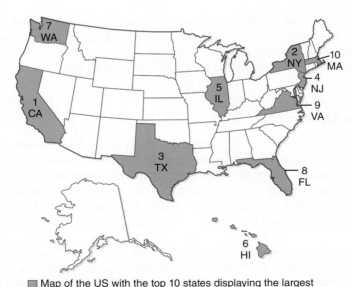

Map of the US with the top 10 states displaying the largest Asian American population according to the Census Bureau

FIGURE 10.1

Top 10 states with largest Asian populations.

Source: Office of Minority Health (2014).

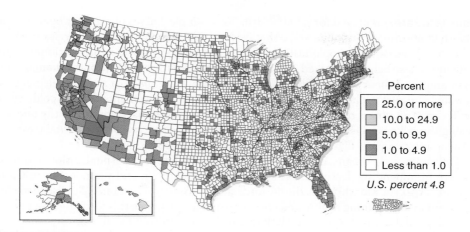

FIGURE 10.2

Asians as a percentage of county population, 2010.

Source: U.S. Census Bureau (2012).

of Minority Health, 2014). **Figure 10.2** depicts the distribution of Asians as a percentage of population as reported in the 2010 Census (U.S. Census Bureau, 2012).

General Philosophy About Disease Prevention and Health Maintenance

Asian beliefs regarding health and illness vary by country of origin and often among districts within the country of origin. However, a common thread through many Asian health practices is the belief that the body must remain balanced to remain healthy. Many Asian cultures are incorporating Western medical systems with traditional practices.

Traditional Chinese beliefs about health and illness stem from the vital energy that flows through the body. Maintaining harmony is essential to health, and restoring the harmony of the energy is necessary to overcome illness. The balance of yin and yang, hot and cold, are often employed in traditional health practices. Yin accounts for "cold" problems such as depression, hypoactivity, hypothermia, abdominal cramps, and indigestion. Health problems influenced by yang include hyperactivity, hyperthermia, stroke, and seizures. The treatment of hot and cold illnesses is accomplished through the use of the opposite force to regain balance (Beller et al., n.d.).

Vietnamese theories of illness and health vary greatly by ethnic groups. The **Hmong**, who originated as mountain-dwelling people, believe in the interrelatedness of medicine and religion. They believe sickness is due to being cursed by the wrath of the gods. A traditional healer is a priest who exorcises bad spirits or intercedes with the gods to remove disease.

Amulets are also employed for good health. For example, babies often wear bua, an amulet of cloth containing a Buddhist verse that is worn on a string around the wrist or neck.

Urban Vietnamese people utilize a health system very similar to traditional Chinese medicine. These beliefs are based on maintaining the balance of **aAma and aDuonga**, similar to yin and yang theory. They believe that living things are made of the four elements: fire, air, water, and earth. The characteristics associated with the elements are hot, cold, wet, and dry. Treating an illness requires employment of the opposite characteristic to the one that is causing the sickness. Like Chinese medicine, herbal remedies, massage, thermal treatments, and acupuncture are utilized to treat illness (LaBorde, 1996).

For traditional Koreans, illness is often seen as one's fate, and hospitalization may be seen as a sign of impending death. Illness is often attributed to yin and yang, just as in Chinese medicine. Also, the **Kior chi force**, the life force similar to chi in traditional Chinese medicine, is important in maintaining health, and efforts are made to balance this force and not to engage in activities that could diminish it. Herbal remedies are utilized for illness.

Filipino health practices incorporate a number of ideas, such as **timbang**, which is described by McBride (n.d.):

> This is a key indigenous health concept that includes a complex set of fundamental principles. A range of "hot" and "cold" beliefs regarding humoral balances in the body, food, and dietary balances includes the following:

- Rapid shifts from "hot" to "cold" lead to illness.
- "Warm" environment is essential to maintain optimal health.
- Cold drinks or cooling foods should be avoided in the morning.
- An overheated body (as in childbirth or fever) is vulnerable; and heated body or muscles can get "shocked" when cooled suddenly.
- A layer of fat ("being stout") is preferred to maintain "warmth" and protect vital energy.
- Heat and cooling relate to quality and balance of air (hangin, "winds") in the body.
- Sudden changes in weather patterns, cool breezes or exposure in evening hours to low temperature, presence of hot sun immediately after a lengthy rain, or vapors rising from the soil, all may upset the body balance by simply blowing on the body surface.

Physical and mental illnesses among Filipino immigrants are considered to be caused by different factors:

1. *Mystical* causes are often associated with experiences or behaviors such as retribution from ancestors for unfulfilled obligations. Some believe in soul loss and that sleep related to the wandering of the soul out of body, known as *bangungot*, or nightmares after a heavy meal may result in death.

2. *Personalistic* causes may be attributed to social punishment or retribution by supernatural beings such as an evil spirit, witch, or *mankukulam* (sorcerer). A stronger spirit such as a healer or priest may counteract this force. For protection, using holy oils, wearing religious objects, or wearing an anting (amulet or talisman) may be recommended.

3. *Naturalistic* causes include a range of factors from nature events (thunder, lightning, drafts, etc.), excessive stress, incompatible food and drugs, infection, or familial susceptibility.

For Filipinos, it is important to prevent illness by avoiding inappropriate behaviors and restoring health through the balance of the life force and the causes of illness (Anderson, 1983).

Asian Indians often practice ayurvedic medicine. This ancient practice is based on the theory that the five great elements—ether, air, fire, water, and earth—are the basis for all living systems. The five elements are in constant interaction and are constantly changing. Asian Indians also employ Western medicine.

Worldview

Islam and Christianity have significant influence for some Asians who view time as linear, comprised of a current life and a hereafter. Most of the world's Muslims live in Asia and believe that guidelines for a successful, even perfect life have been laid down by religious teachings. Personal life can therefore be enhanced by individual decisions to follow the rules. Christians generally hold a similar perspective although they may not believe that individual conduct can help avoid illness and other troubles due to the imperfection of man.

Many other Asians hold a worldview framed by the great religions of Hinduism and Buddhism. The worldview of these religions is that time and history are eternally circular or cyclical, and individuals are involved in a "cycle of rebirths" or "reincarnation." The current life of a person is probably just the most recent of many previous lives and will be followed by many more in the future. Rebirths will continue until the person reaches "liberation" from the cycle of rebirths based on dealing with the universal law that governs rebirths known as **karma**. Unless liberation is achieved by conduct in this life, rebirth will occur, in some form, for another attempt as required by a universal impersonal and indescribable force. This worldview can include the belief that a main goal in life is to rid oneself of all cravings and desires. These beliefs can result in a communication style that may perplex Westerners due to its emphasis on intuition, direct experience, and silence (Kete, Miike, & Yin, 2014).

Japanese **Shintoism** takes a different perspective and is based on a belief that spiritual powers exist in the natural world. It is somewhat external and pantheistic, and individuals can ask for help by turning to divine beings or spirits (Kami) for assistance.

Perspectives on time vary among Asians. Punctuality is highly valued in the Japanese culture. Hmong born in Laos have a different sense of time because there are no clocks or calendars in Laos, so the concept of time may be new to them. Therefore, appointment times for the Hmong are challenging, and they may arrive early in the morning even though their appointment is in the afternoon. This contrasts with Filipino time, which often means arriving one or several hours after the appointment time (Purnell, 2013).

Regardless of differences in worldview of time, most Asians hold a humanistic view that places responsibility on themselves to follow guidelines or work developing personal perfection. This makes them likely to be conducive to learning and following guidance from medical professionals. God and spirits may play some role, but personal accountability also plays a role in many cultural beliefs.

When communicating with Asian Americans, a gentle touch may be appropriate. Respect for those of a higher status is shown by avoiding eye contact. Respect also is shown by bowing the head slightly. Personal space is generally more distant than what is preferred by Euro-Americans. Tone of voice is generally soft. For some, such as those of Japanese descent, self-disclosure is made after trust is established and usually occurs only after it has been elicited.

Modesty and personal hygiene are important. Organ donation is generally not done due to respect given to the body. For this same reason, autopsies are not favored.

Did You Know?

Beliefs in spirituality and afterlife are strong in Asian culture. Ghost money, also known as Joss or spirit money, is one of the gifts that can be given to deceased relatives. The ghost money is burned at funerals of some Asian subcultures, particularly the Chinese, to ensure that the spirit of the deceased has ample good things in his or her afterlife. The Joss paper is typically made from bamboo or rice. The paper is white to represent mourning. The foil typically has a silver or golden shade that represents wealth or money. The sheets are placed carefully and respectfully in the fire.

Pregnancy, Birth, and Child Rearing

Specific practices vary considerably among the various Asian cultures. The Chinese may believe in "lying in" before birth and practicing a "sitting month" after birth when the body is allowed to come back into balance and during which time strict drinking and eating guidelines accompany a prohibition against bathing. Other cultures expect normal activity up to the day of birth, a stoic response to pain, and a rapid return to normal chores shortly after birth. Contact with a child may be limited so as not to make the baby too dependent. In Vietnamese culture, touching may be seen as inviting too much attention to the baby and must be avoided to protect the child from dangerous spirits.

Many Asians look to Buddhist and Confucian beliefs that infants are born as clean slates and only learn improper behavior while growing up. Although some children may be given minor chores and be taught reading and arithmetic earlier, children are expected to begin serious efforts at development and family participation at about 6 or 7 years old. The time is not specific because it is understood that children mature at different paces, but children are expected to exert effort when ready. Generally they are seen as important parts of the continuum of the family and its history and not fully independent. Harmony of the family is highly encouraged, and dishonor or disgrace to one's self or the family is to be avoided. Traditional Asian parents define the rules, and children must comply because respect for elders is critical. Generally, parents expect that they will be judged by the achievements of their children, and they take great interest in their achievements. This does not mean parents are totally cruel and authoritarian, but they do make a strong effort to have close involvement and direct and even demand the effort expected of the child. Rules of conduct encourage self-control, and inner stamina is expected when dealing with a crisis.

Asian patients may not express strong emotion, grief, or pain due to their cultural values (Dewar, 2012).

Nutrition and Exercise

As a group, Asian Americans are not as concerned with nutrition as people from Western cultures. The texture, flavor, color, and aroma of food is much more important in Chinese cooking. The balance of yin and yang, hot and cold, is much more important than food groups.

Because many Asian Americans are lactose intolerant, dairy products are not a large part of their diet. Soy milk and tofu are the staples that provide protein and calcium. The primary food groups for Asian Americans are grains, vegetables, fruit, and meat or fish, and rice and noodles are daily staples (see **Figure 10.3**).

The Asian Indian diet and cooking involves the use of aromatic spices. Asian Indian dietary practices have religious influences from the Hindu and Muslim traditions. Hindus are vegetarians and believe that food was created by a Supreme Being for the benefit of man. Muslims have several dietary restrictions (Bhungalia, Kelly, VanDeKeift, & Young, n.d.).

Mental Health

Asian Americans as a group have similar perspectives on mental health issues. Many traditional Asian cultural and religious beliefs view mental health problems as shameful and disgraceful. Such problems often are not discussed and, consequently, seeking help is often avoided. These views also instruct Asians' view of the world and the differences between Asian cultures and Western societies. **Table 10.2** presents a comparison of the differing approaches to society, family, and behavioral issues between Asian and Western societies.

Many Asians believe that mental illness in a family reflects negatively on family reputation and lineage and on the family member's suitability for marriage. Asians may deny the experience and expression of emotions. These factors make it more acceptable for psychological distress to be expressed through the body rather than the mind (Substance Abuse and Mental Health Services Administration [SAMHSA], 2001).

Death and Dying

Asian culture may affect behavior related to telling the truth to ill persons about their health state, using life prolonging technology, and decision-making styles. Although there is a great variety of beliefs, Asians often do not like to tell a person who is ill of impending death, and many believe even speaking of it may bring bad luck or a poor outcome. Decisions and communication are often considered the responsibility of the oldest male in the family, and can be seen as a moral obligation for that person to act in that capacity. Some of these beliefs can be attributed to Confucian philosophy, which emphasizes perfecting oneself during the current life, including honoring your ancestors, that death is simply another natural challenge to be dealt with in life, and that the afterlife has its own complexity that is not something to focus on or try to fully understand.

FIGURE 10.3

Asian food pyramid.

TABLE 10.2   Comparison of Eastern and Western Values

Values	Eastern/Traditional	Western/Modern
Societal orientation	Family	Individual
Family makeup	Extended	Nuclear
Primary relationship	Parent–child	Marital
Family values	Well defined	Flexible
Relationship emphasis	Interpersonal and harmony	Self-fulfillment and development
Gender roles	Male dominant	Opportunity for females
Control	Authoritative	Democratic
Emotional expression	Suppressive	Expressive
Beliefs	Fatalism/karma	Personal control
	Harmony with nature	Control of nature
	Cooperation	Competition
	Spiritualism	Materialism

Source: Carrasco and Weiss (2005).

What Do You Think?

In the Asian culture, there is a belief that terminally ill patients should not be informed about their prognosis. As a provider, would you respect the cultural practice and not inform the patient about the prognosis? Is there a way for providers to balance the patient's right to know with respect for the cultural practices and beliefs of the family? Is not fully disclosing information to the patient an ethical breach?

Cultural-Bound Illnesses

The Chinese recognize a disorder called neurasthenia. This is a condition characterized by physical and mental exhaustion including headaches, insomnia, and irritability. It may result from other conditions such as depression, stress, or conflict. Although Chinese Americans may experience neurasthenia, health professionals using the standard U.S. diagnostic system may not identify their need for care.

Koreans may have *hwa-byung*, with both somatic and psychological symptoms. *Hwa-byung,* or suppressed anger syndrome, is characterized by sensations of constriction in the chest, palpitations, sensations of heat, flushing, headache, anxiety, irritability, and problems with concentration (Prince, 1989).

Healing Traditions, Healers, and Healing Aids

Many Asian Americans use traditional Chinese medicine and ayurvedic medicine (see Chapter 3). Cambodians use coining, cupping, and pinching to treat many problems associated with "wind illness," which are forms of respiratory illness. Coining is rubbing or scratching the skin of the back, neck, upper chest, and arms with a coin. Cupping and pinching function in the same manner to bring blood to an area of the body. Before or during rubbing, they apply Tiger Balm, herbal liquid medicine, skin lotion, or water on the skin. The technique helps smooth the skin and is believed to improve the coining outcome.

Behavioral Risk Factors and Common Health Problems

Asian American women have the highest life expectancy (85.8 years) of any ethnic group in the United States. Life expectancy varies among Asian subgroups: Filipino (81.5 years), Japanese (84.5 years), and Chinese women (86.1 years) (Office of Minority Health, 2014). However, Asian Americans contend with numerous factors that may threaten their health. Some negative factors are infrequent medical visits due to the fear of deportation, language/cultural barriers, and the lack of health insurance. Asian Americans are most at risk for cancer, heart disease, stroke, unintentional injuries (accidents), and diabetes. Asian Americans also have a high prevalence of chronic obstructive pulmonary disease, hepatitis B, HIV/AIDS, smoking, tuberculosis, and liver disease. In 2012, tuberculosis was 24 times more common among Asians, with a 18.9 cases per 100,000 population as compared to 0.8 for the non-Hispanic white population (Office of Minority Health, 2014).

The 10 leading causes of death among Asian Americans in 2010 were as follows (Office of Minority Health, 2013):

1. Cancer
2. Heart disease
3. Stroke
4. Unintentional injuries
5. Diabetes mellitus
6. Influenza and pneumonia
7. Chronic lower respiratory disease
8. Nephritis, nephrotic syndrome, and nephrosis
9. Alzheimer's disease
10. Suicide

Most Asian Americans can afford health care, but foreign-born Asian Americans have been found to have below average access to both routine care and sick care. They had fewer office visits for talking to a general doctor or specialist but made greater use of emergency rooms (Ye, Mack, Fry-Johnson, & Parker, 2012).

Data from the census and recent research has provided a much better picture of the health behaviors of Asian Americans and the common health problems they encounter. The data indicate that Asian American populations have differing personal practices and susceptibilities to disease.

Most Asian American adults have never smoked; however, for those who do, the highest rate of smoking was among Korean American and Japanese American adults (CDC, 2012). Japanese American adults also were more likely to be current moderate or heavy drinkers. Vietnamese American adults have the highest incidence of alcohol abstinence over a lifetime, and Asian Indian Americans were a close second. Most Asian American adults are in an appropriate weight range, but Filipino American adults were more likely to be obese compared to other Asian American adults. Finally, few Asian Americans reported doing regular physical activity, and Vietnamese Americans were most likely to be inactive during their leisure time (Barnes, Adams, & Powell-Griner, 2008).

Asian American adults are less likely to report being diagnosed with hypertension and high blood pressure than African American, white, or Hispanic adults. Among Asian American populations, Filipino Americans and Japanese Americans are more likely to be diagnosed with hypertension than Chinese Americans, Korean Americans, or Asian Indian Americans. Asian Americans are also less likely to have diabetes than African American or Hispanic Americans. However, within the Asian American population, Asian Indian Americans had a significantly greater incidence of diabetes than Chinese or Japanese Americans. Compared to white, African American, and Hispanic Americans, Asian Americans are less likely to suffer from migraines. Among the Asian American population, Vietnamese Americans and Filipino Americans have the highest incidence of migraines (Barnes et al., 2008).

Immunization rates for Asian American populations are lower than for the other groups overall. Asian Americans are less likely to have received a pneumonia vaccine. They received the hepatitis B vaccine at the same rate as white and African American adults, but they are less likely to obtain HIV testing. Although heart disease occurs less frequently among Asian Americans than any other minority group, it is still a leading cause of death among Asian Americans. Asian Americans are at risk for silent heart attacks, a painless form of the disease that can lead to a fatal outcome as a result of the lack of warning of a problem. Stroke within the Asian American populations is higher than within the white American population (Barnes et al., 2008).

In addition to the various pathologies to which Asian Americans are susceptible, other factors may negatively influence their health.

QUICK FACTS

Asian Americans represent the extremes of both health outcomes and socioeconomic status:

- Asian American women experience the longest life expectancy (85.8 years) of any ethnic group in the United States.
- Leading causes of death for Asian Americans in 2010 were cancer, heart disease, stroke, unintentional injuries (accidents), and diabetes. Death rates for these conditions are less than other racial/ethnic populations.

- Asian Americans also are at risk for chronic obstructive pulmonary disease, hepatitis B, HIV/AIDS, smoking, and tuberculosis. Their liver disease rates are lower than those of other racial and ethnic populations.

- Asian Americans in 2008 had a similar age-adjusted prevalence of diabetes (8.2%) compared with the white population (7.0%).

- In 2010, Asian American women (ages 18+) were least likely to have had a Pap test (68.0%) compared with other women: non-Hispanic white (72.8%), non-Hispanic black (77.4%), Hispanic/Latino (73.6%), and American Indian/Alaska Native (73.4%).

- In 2008, Asian Americans/Pacific Islanders (AAPIs) aged 19 to 24 years had an acute hepatitis B incidence (3.1 per 100,000 population) that was 1.6 times greater than non-Hispanic whites of the same age (1.9 per 100,000).

- Asian Americans and Hispanics in 2006 through 2008 had the greatest percentage of populations residing in counties whose air quality did not meet EPA standards for particulate matter and ozone compared with other racial and ethnic populations.

- Asian Americans are less likely to live in poverty (12.8%), more likely to be college graduates or hold graduate degrees (50%), and more likely to be employed in management, business, science, and arts occupations (48.5%) compared with the total U.S. population (15.9%, 28.5%, 36.0%, respectively).

- Asian Americans contend with numerous factors that may threaten their health, including infrequent medical visits due to the fear of deportation, language and cultural barriers, and the lack of health insurance.

Source: Office of Minority Health (2013).

Considerations for Health Promotion and Program Planning

Health promotion for Asian Americans creates a unique challenge given the varied cultures and traditions involved. Points to consider when developing Asian American programs include:

- Ensure good communication by thorough explanation and language translation where necessary.

- Show respect for family relationships and their needs, and include family in discussions.

- Provide dietary-appropriate meals.

- Inquire about other treatments used for health problems and obtain specific information regarding herbs and other substances that are being used.

Tips for Working With the Asian American Population

Asian Americans, and particularly Chinese Americans, hold strong allegiance to their families, are reluctant to express emotions, show great respect for authority, and prefer direct and immediate solutions to problems. It is important to remember that the oldest male may need to be included in communication and decision making. Younger family members and particularly women may feel they must confer with older family members before making a decision. In addition, the oldest male may believe it is his obligation to make important decisions for the family and particularly for single female members.

In communicating, deference to authority or politeness may result in questions being answered in the affirmative to avoid offending the person asking questions. Asian Muslim women may have a heightened sense of personal privacy and may prefer to be fully clothed during medical exams.

Summary

The term *Asian American* is a generality for many people who trace their heritage to numerous countries, cultures, and traditions across Asia. They continue the traditions of their ancestors and experience health care issues unique to their heritage.

This chapter has provided an introduction to the varied cultures and health practices that comprise Asian Americans through a discussion of their heritage, history in the United States, traditional health practices, and common health risks.

Review

1. Discuss Asian Americans' history in the United States and the influence it has had on their health.

2. What cultural influences affect the health of Asian Americans?

3. Discuss the health behaviors of Asian Americans and how those behaviors affect their health.

4. Discuss some differences among the different populations that are referred to as Asian Americans.

Activities

Conduct research on health programs that have been implemented for members of the Asian American population. Summarize the literature and identify some best practices.

Visit, virtually or in person, a store or website that sells Asian health products. What products did you see that were new to you? What role in health did they have (e.g., to prevent colds, to treat stomachaches)? Write a paper on your findings.

Case Study

An elderly Japanese American woman lived alone in her apartment. Recently it was noted that she was not keeping her apartment and garden up as she did in the past, she has locked herself out of her apartment four times this year, she has forgotten to pay the rent, and last week she left the stove on and burned a pot.

Her friends and family made an appointment for her with a geriatric consultant through her health care provider. She was evaluated by a social worker, and a Caucasian caregiver was hired to assist her with activities of daily living. Since the caregiver has been cooking, the woman has been experiencing diarrhea, cramping, and abdominal pain. She has been using over-the-counter medications for the problem and is being evaluated at the hospital for her symptoms.

Among the things to be considered by the doctors is the possibility that the woman is lactose intolerant, which is prevalent among Japanese people. Because a non-Japanese caregiver now cooks her meals, she may be eating food she is not used to that possibly contains lactose, and she may not be able to discuss this with the caregiver due to communication problems.

Consider the following:

- What can be done to assist this woman in a manner more appropriate to her traditions?

References

Anderson, J. (1983). Health and illness in Filipino immigrants. In Cross-Cultural Medicine [Special issue]. *Western Journal of Medicine*, *139*(6), 811–819.

Barnes, P., Adams, P., & Powell-Griner, E. (2008). Health characteristics of the Asian Adult population: United States, 2004–2006. *Vital and Health Statistics*, No. 394. Hyattsville, MD: National Center for Health Statistics.

Beller, T., Pinker, M., Snapka, S., & Van Dusan, D. (n.d.). *Korean-American health care beliefs and practices*. Retrieved from http://bearspace.baylor.edu/Charles_Kemp/www/korean_ health.htm

Bhungalia, S., Kelly, T., VanDeKeift, S., & Young, M. (n.d.). *Indian health care beliefs and practices*. Retrieved from http://bearspace.baylor.edu/Charles_Kemp/www/korean_health.htm

Carrasco, M., & Weiss, J. (2005). NAMI. *Asian American and Pacific Islander outreach resource manual*. Retrieved from http://www.NAMI.org/Content/ContentGroups/Multicultural_ Support1/AAPIManual.pdf

Centers for Disease Control and Prevention. (2012). *Current cigarette smoking among U.S. adults aged 18 years and older*. Retrieved from http://www.cdc.gov/tobacco

/campaign/tips/resources/data/cigarette-smoking-in-united-states.html#two

Dewar, G. (2012). What research says about Chinese kids and why they succeed. *Parenting Science*. Retrieved from http://www.parentingscience .com/chinese-parenting.html

Kete, M., Miike, Y., & Yin, J. (Eds.). (2014). *The global intercultural communication reader* (2nd ed.). New York, NY: Routledge (Taylor & Francis).

LaBorde, P. (1996, July). *Vietnamese cultural profile*. Retrieved from http://www. ethnomed.org/ethnomed/cultures/vietnamese /vietnamese_cp.html

McBride, M. (n.d.). *Health and health care of Filipino American elders*. Retrieved from http:// www.stanford.edu/group/ethnoger/filipino .html

Office of Minority Health. (2013). *Asian American populations, racial and ethnic minorities*. Retrieved from http://www.cdc .gov/minorityhealth/populations/REMP /asian.html

Office of Minority Health. (2014). *Profile: Asian Americans*. Retrieved from http:// minorityhealth.hhs.gov/omh/browse .aspx?lvl=3&lvlid=63

Prince, R. (1989). Somatic complaint syndromes and depression: The problem of cultural effects on symptomatology *Mental Health Research*, 8, 104–117.

Purnell, L. (2013). *Transcultural healthcare: A culturally competent approach* (4th ed.). Philadelphia, PA: F. A. Davis Company.

Substance Abuse and Mental Health Services Administration. (2001). Mental health care for Asian Americans and Pacific Islanders. In *Mental health: Culture, race, and ethnicity: A supplement to mental health: A report of the surgeon general 1996*, chapter 5. Retrieved from http://www.ncbi.nlm.nih .gov/books/NBK44245/#A1966

U.S. Census Bureau. (n.d.). *Race* .State and County Quick Facts. Retrieved from http:// quickfacts.census.gov/qfd/meta/long_ RHI125212.htm

U.S. Census Bureau. (2012a). The Asian Population: 2010. *Census Briefs*. Retrieved from http://www.census.gov/prod/cen2010 /briefs/c2010br-11.pdf

U.S. Census Bureau. (2012b). The Asian Population: 2010. *Census Briefs*, figure 5. Retrieved from http://www.census.gov/prod/cen2010 /briefs/c2010br-11.pdf

U.S. Census Bureau. (2015). *Country and area ranks, international programs*. Retrieved from http://www.census.gov/population /international/data/countryrank/rank.php

Ye, J., Mack, D., Fry-Johnson, Y., & Parker, K. (2012, October). Health care access and utilization among US-born and foreign-born Asian Americans. *Journal of Immigrant and Minority Health*, *14*(5), 731–737. doi: 10.1007/s10903-011-9543-9

European and Mediterranean American Populations

Sometimes God calms the storm, but sometimes God lets the storm rage and calms his child.
   —Amish proverb

May God give you luck and health.
   —Roma (Gypsy) blessing

Key Concepts

Rumspringa	Gadje
Brauche	Wuzho
Ellis-van Creveld syndrome	Marime
Romany	Drabarni

Learning Objectives

After reading this chapter, you should be able to:
1. Describe the cultural impact on health for the Amish, Roma, and Arab Americans.
2. Discuss the common health risks for European populations in the United States.
3. Describe the behavioral health challenges for these groups.

Introduction

Europeans "discovered" America and made it their own but created a new lifestyle that became the dominant model for the modern United States. This population brought a mix of cultural practices and fundamental beliefs in part based on Christianity, Judaism, and Islam. The current health system in the United States reflects many of the views of this population. Because of its diversity, three subcultures are described in some detail to demonstrate the complexity of this cultural group.

Terminology

This chapter addresses the dominant culture of the United States that can generally be described as European Mediterranean. This cultural group is generally aligned with what the U.S. Census Bureau terms "white" and applies to persons having origins among any of the original peoples of Europe, the Middle East, or North Africa. This is a very broad area that encompasses numerous ethnic and cultural groups. Much has been written about the dominant European groups that inhabit the United States. These cultural groups have fundamentally shaped life throughout the United States and, as a result, have shaped the delivery of health care as well.

History of European and Mediterranean Americans in the United States

Europeans purposefully came to North America to gain wealth and opportunity and to avoid harassment or economic hardship. Early settlers included Spanish, French, and English in what is now the lower 48 states, and Russians in the area that would become Alaska. None came to integrate and adapt to the peoples already on the continent. Compared to the population of Europe, North America seemed empty and wild. In this setting, all came prepared to be self-sufficient and focused on establishing communities of their own kind, eventually free from the control of European countries. In part due to the limited ability to communicate, but primarily due to a culture of self-reliance and initiative, challenges and hardships were addressed locally without particular guidance from leaders in Europe. Settlement was occurring shortly after the onset of the "Age of Enlightenment" in Europe, and rational practical problem solving and the eventual development of the scientific method reinforced a belief that problems could be understood and solutions found by individuals applying their own intelligence, although the help and guidance of a Christian God was often sought and welcomed. A persistent belief in the righteousness of their acts and entitlement as free persons to exploit essentially free natural resources contributed to spread of the population throughout the continent with confidence and self-assurance despite physical and often financial hardship. Indigenous populations were simply displaced to make room for the new European arrivals. In the initial contact, particularly in the interior by the

French fur traders, some measure of coexistence and commercial relations existed, but the westward expansion of the Europeans was ultimately opposed by the indigenous peoples. Of course, other Europeans were also subject to displacement and conquest. The French and English and eventually the Spanish and English Americans engaged in wars to settle territorial claims. Throughout the country's development, but particularly in the late 1700s and after, significant numbers of people immigrated to North America to what is now the United States to escape economic hardship and war. The Scots were driven off their rural lands in their native home by the English, the Irish fled famine due to crop failure, and war drove many Europeans, including Jewish, German, and Armenian populations, to find better opportunities and safety. Like other immigrant populations, the Europeans settled in America generally among peoples of the same or similar cultures. They did not come to change themselves but to have better opportunities to become safer or more economically successful. Concentrations of European subcultures have resulted in regions reflecting these settlement patterns. The Germans in Pennsylvania, the Irish in New York and Boston, the Scots in the Carolinas, and the Scandinavians in the upper Midwest are just a few examples of areas that continue to reflect early settlement concentrations.

During the expansion of the European population in America, a new nation was born that reflected the values of the immigrants. A national government was created to protect against outside intrusion, especially against European rule. Government was not trusted, and states retained much of their autonomy and right to protect local public safety and health. Free enterprise and the autonomy of individuals led to the development of health care systems primarily delivered through private businesses. Government services were—and for many still are—suspect and viewed as inefficient. Self-reliance and autonomy have forged the health care system based on individual insurance coverage and the belief that individuals should take proper steps to take care of themselves and their families without interference from others and also without burdening others.

In addition, the development of the scientific method and the industrial revolution contributed to a belief that humankind could analyze nature and identify or invent solutions to almost any problem, from curing diseases such as yellow fever to developing ways to sustain biologic organisms in outer space. Overlaying this, however, was a predominant and fundamental Christian belief in charity and taking care of the truly needy. Originally charity hospitals served this purpose, and eventually led to universal emergency medical care by local governments. The structure of the Affordable Care Act and implementation of mandatory health insurance is still fundamentally influenced by the free-enterprise, self-reliant view of European Americans with health insurance available through "free marketplace" health exchanges operated by states or, to some people's dismay, the federal government.

Although not participating in the initial territorial conquest and political development of the United States, the peoples of the Middle East and North Africa immigrated seeking opportunities in the new country. These peoples brought a culture based on a third major religion, Islam, which traces its beliefs to Abraham as does Judaism and Christianity. Islam focuses on the teaching of Muhammad, who revealed the lessons of the Quran, establishing rules that must be obeyed according to disciplined daily submission to an all-powerful God. This culture has contributed to both the science and the ethics of health care in the United States.

Did You Know?

Jakob Amman, a Swiss Anabaptist leader, is the namesake of the Amish. Their religion can be traced back through a branch of the Anabaptists to 16th-century Europe during Martin Luther's Protestant Reformation. The Anabaptists would experience subdivision, resulting in groups we know today as the Amish, Mennonites, Church of the Brethren, Hutterites, and many more. The Amish have five religious orders: Old Order, New Order, Andy Weaver, Beachy, and Swartzentruber, with Old Order being the most traditional.

European and Mediterranean Americans in the United States

European Americans represent about 72% (223.6 million) of the current population of the United States, but they are becoming a diminishing percentage of the population as Hispanic and Asian populations grow (U.S. Census Bureau, 2011). The Census Bureau projects that by the year 2060 less than 50% of the total U.S. population will consist of white Americans. European Americans comprise a rich complexity of cultures scattered throughout the country, with the highest concentrations in the Midwest and Northeast, especially in Maine, New Hampshire, Vermont, Iowa, North Dakota, West Virginia, Montana, Idaho, Wyoming, and Colorado (Office of Minority Health, 2010). Despite these concentrations, the fundamental constitutional rights to freedom of religion, speech, and association have fostered a great variety of religious and cultural practices including Catholic, Protestant, Muslim, and a great many other religious groups. One result is a variety of dietary practices and restrictions. Eating fish on Friday, not eating pork ever, avoiding alcohol, and fasting for periods of time are practices in a variety of beliefs. Due to their majority in population, these cultural groups dominate the political process at all levels of government and control the government regulation of health care in the United States.

General Philosophy About Disease Prevention and Health Maintenance

The European and Mediterranean populations generally view disease prevention and health maintenance based on the germ theory view that scientific methods and physical or chemical treatments can be used to prevent and cure illness. Health can be developed and maintained by making advances in understanding biology and science. Science can and must discover cures, and it is just a matter of time before proper preventive practices and medical interventions will be developed to address most health issues.

Worldview

Generally, the European worldview holds that time is linear. Although individuals are autonomous, they are responsible to account for their behavior to a higher being. Self-reliance and free will are important aspects of life, and a great deal of flexibility is allowed within the rules laid down by religious teachings. Informality of expression and dress reflect achievement, and tangible assets are valued over social status alone.

In general, European Americans are a low-touch culture. This has been reinforced by the guidelines and policies related to sexual harassment. Touching should be avoided until people get to know each other as it generally carries a sexual overtone. People of the same sex, especially men, do not generally touch one another unless they are close friends.

Personal space is important, and European Americans generally do not stand or sit close to one another. If health care providers physically distance themselves from a patient who is culturally programmed for close personal space, the provider may be viewed as cold.

Disclosure of personal information is common. European Americans may share very personal information, such as sex or drug use, with people they do not know very well.

Punctuality is important. European Americans do not like to wait as it wastes time. "Time is money" is the common philosophy. People in this culture generally believe that they have control over their future, and hence, do not adhere to the fatalistic belief. People in these cultures are generally future oriented, but they do not like to wait so it has become a fast and "on demand" culture.

Pregnancy, Birth, and Child Rearing

Generally, self-reliance and autonomy lead to a view that children are raised to adulthood and "leave home." Although family relationships continue, association between generations is looser than that of extended families in other cultures. Similarly, parents have independent authority over their own children, and grandparents are not necessarily as influential as in extended families.

Children are generally free to grow up and marry who they wish and earn a livelihood of their own choosing. They are expected to become independent. Even with implementation of the Affordable Care Act, children are expected to be fully independent from family health responsibilities after age 25 when children can no longer be on covered on their parent's health plan.

Culture affects the administration of public health programs. For instance, rules requiring immunizations that have been scientifically proven for common illnesses such as measles must confront parental rights to self-determination in raising their own children with "opt out" procedures established in several states.

What Do You Think?

It is often difficult to see cultural influences when viewed from within a culture. The three great religions of the European population include Judaism, Christianity, and Islam; each recognizes Abraham as a key figure in history. One common cultural practice, circumcision, derives from Abraham's teaching. Research on the health benefits of circumcision are mixed, but it is such a common practice that it is generally accepted as "normal." When the practice is examined from a neutral point of view and is termed "involuntary genital surgery on children," perhaps this culture-bound custom can be viewed for what is—the most common elective surgery in the United States. A majority of infant boys in the United States are circumcised for either religious or hygienic reasons (Owings, Uddin, & Williams, 2013). In 2012, the American Association of Pediatrics (APP, 2012) said that despite potential medical benefits of newborn male circumcision, there was insufficient evidence to recommend routine circumcision of newborns, and the decision should be left to parents based on their religious, ethical, and cultural beliefs. The Jewish culture holds the procedure of circumcision to be of high importance to bind a covenant with God, and a formal ceremony on the 8th day of a boy's life honoring the event is called Brit milah.

Alternatively, many Egyptians and others believe in practicing Pharoenic circumcision on girls during childhood, believing that the girls will be more acceptable for marriage. However, there is a vast difference between that procedure and simply cutting a little skin in the case of boys circumcision. In this procedure, the girl's exterior genitals are cut in a way that damages the sex organs, inhibits pleasure, and causes severe pain and complications for women's sexual and reproductive health. This procedure is usually performed at the request of mothers outside clinical settings or on "medical vacations" to their home country.

A 2015 report showed that over 513,000 women in the United States were subject to, or likely to be subject to, this procedure (Topping, 2015). Something on the order of 90% of adult Egyptian women have had this procedure in Egypt, and mothers do not see it as harmful or abusive. Should this "involuntary genital surgery on children" practice be seen as any different from "harmless" male circumcision? The procedure has been a specific crime in the United States since 1996, and there is a growing international movement to stop "female genital mutilation." What do you think? Is involuntary genital surgery all right for boys but not for girls?

Nutrition and Exercise

The worldview of the majority culture in the United States contributes both to improve health and to harm it. The self-sufficient and autonomous individual is free and is expected to take care of his or her own health. The values supporting individual achievement lead many to be highly active in pursuing health through nutrition regimens, physical fitness routines, and commercial programs. For those without discipline, the "problem solving through science" approach has resulted in commercial health care providing cosmetic surgery to enhance beauty, sex appeal, and weight loss through such cosmetic procedures such as lip enhancement, breast implantation, liposuction, and intestinal bands to reduce weight and improve appearance. On the other hand, cultural emphasis on autonomy allows for self-neglect and abuse such as smoking and drinking to excess. This cultural perspective is always present in public health and medical care provider efforts to encourage good health practices.

Mental Health

Mental health, as in other cultures, carries stigma and misunderstanding. However, the focus on individual rights and self-determination is evident in the care and treatment of mental illness. For instance, only if the state can show that people are likely to be harmful to themselves or others are they compelled to receive treatment. Even if clearly marginally functional in daily living, the culture supporting autonomy and free will allows people to avoid treatment or live without medical care. In addition, the Christian cultural value of charity and assisting others often leads to establishment of charitable programs, such as homeless shelters and meal programs for the poor, which include many mentally ill persons.

Death and Dying

The great variety of subcultures within the European population results in a variety of beliefs and rituals associated with death. Overall, the philosophy of being autonomous transfers to death as well. This is demonstrated by the use of advance directives, hospice programs, and other end-of-life care procedures. Mentally competent patients have the right to refuse medical care and make decisions on life-extending treatments such as artificial life support. The Death with Dignity Act is another example of this end-of-life autonomous decision making.

A great many Christians associate death with old age and something that will be handled later; it is not necessary to think about this today. Muslims, on the other hand, are taught to believe death may occur any day, and this idea is reflected in the importance of five daily prayers. Many deaths that occur in hospitals are possibly due to the "anything can be solved" self-reliant autonomous scientific perspective.

Upon death most will be cremated or buried. Some, such as the Irish, celebrate life with wakes, and others, such as Jewish and Muslims, express various degrees of seriousness and sadness. After death some Christian-based believers may establish elaborate burial events and monuments, whereas Muslims conduct prompt simple and modest burials. The first year after death is often seen as a year of mourning and remembrance. Muslims especially honor the dead for 40 days after death. Muslim women are not allowed to visit cemeteries. Significant variations in burial and death rituals exist within the European American cultural groups.

History, Healing Practices, and Risk Factors for Three Subcultures

The European and Mediterranean American cultural groups are remarkably diverse, and it is probably misleading to suggest that even admitted generalizations are accurate for all. You may already have a general sense of differences between the Italian and English cultures or between Spanish and Scandinavian peoples. Here we describe just three subcultures in this population to provide a sense of the diversity in this group. Included is a brief summary of two small populations, the Amish and the Roma, and a general profile of a large subgroup, the Arabs. Within each group description, culture-bound syndromes and tips for working with the culture are summarized.

Amish Americans

Religious persecution forced the Amish and Mennonites to find a safe haven in the New World. In the 1730s, a group of Amish immigrants joined Mennonite colonists who had already established a community in Lancaster, Pennsylvania. Lancaster houses the oldest Amish community in North America. "More than 90 percent of Lancaster's Amish are affiliated with the Old Order Amish" (Kraybill, 2001, p. 12).

The Amish social environment, including the family structure, child-rearing practices, religion, communication, and pregnancy beliefs, greatly influences the health of this population. The Amish live a simple lifestyle that abstains from material luxuries; it resembles the lifestyle of 16th-century European peasants. For example, they still utilize horses and buggies for transportation, and their lifestyle is agriculturally based. Their unique heritage is ingrained in a belief system that seeks to retain traditional values while avoiding the influences of the dominant culture. The two most valued aspects of their lives include their family and their church district.

The Amish generally have large families because they do not routinely practice birth control and because babies are a welcomed gift from God. Children are believed to be economic blessings; they help maintain the farm and the household. It is not unusual for generations of family members to live in the same house and operate as one unit. Single people and single-parent homes are rare: "Only five percent of Amish households are single-person units, compared to twenty percent for the county" (Kraybill, 2001, p. 100). The average number of people in a household is 12, which may include extended family.

The gender roles within the family are traditional; the males are the dominant figures within the household, directing the farming operations and overseeing their children's work in the fields. Many husbands assist in child care, lawn care, and gardening, but they usually do not assist in other household work. Wives are responsible for washing, cooking, canning, sewing, mending, and cleaning. Church leaders teach that wives must submit to the authority of their husbands according to religious doctrine. Women are not usually employed outside of the home. Their main duties revolve around raising the children, gardening, and assisting with barn chores. The Amish religion is deeply integrated with their family structure. The Amish believe that the Bible is a guide for parents to teach their children the values of their religion while training them to conform to the Amish ways. Cultural beliefs are passed down through the generations in such a way that young Amish children are not exposed to the great variety of cultural practices that modern youth outside of the Amish community accept as normal.

Amish culture is focused on community, and health care expenses are usually covered by the community. The Amish generally do not have commercial health insurance. The ACA exempts the Amish from the health insurance mandate.

A unique part of the Amish culture is **Rumspringa**, which means "running around." This practice was the focus of the documentary *Devil's Playground*. Rumspringa is a time when adolescents are free to explore the world outside the Amish culture. Rumspringa is practiced by young males and females between the ages of 16 and 21 years. During this period, individuals may partake in activities of their choosing, which may include drinking alcohol, using illicit drugs, and experimenting with sexual activities. Rumspringa ends when the young person makes the decision to either live in the outside world or become baptized within the Amish community (Cantor & Walker, 2002).

Beliefs About Causes of Health and Illness Among Amish Americans

The Amish believe that sin is the cause of illness; therefore, their approach to health care is unique compared to other white Americans (Palmer, 1992). The way in which the Amish make decisions about health is affected by their separation from the world and from modern technology.

Health care practitioners should be sensitive to the unique perspective of their Amish patients. For example, considering that the Amish have little contact with medical professionals and technology, health care practitioners should convey descriptions of treatment procedures carefully, avoiding complex medical language (Lee, 2005). Moreover, health care professionals should expect to talk to spouses and family members who are likely to gather in support of the patient. Finally, as much treatment as possible should take place in one visit due to transportation difficulties. These issues should be considered to provide Amish patients with the best possible health care outcomes (Lee, 2005).

Healing Traditions Among Amish Americans

The Amish tend to approach health care as organically as possible with the use of holistic, natural, herbal, and folk medicine, which are readily accessible in Amish communities (Palmer, 1992). Basic natural and herbal remedies may include iron pills, vitamins E and C, herbal tea, and sage tea. Other natural remedies include corn silk tea for an enlarged prostate, aloe vera gel for minor trauma, and poho oil (peppermint oil in a petrolatum base) for respiratory problems (Kriebel, 2000). Additionally, the Amish have been known to utilize reflexology, which is the practice of applying pressure to specific parts of the feet and hands to affect the nervous system (Julia, 1996). The Amish utilize chiropractic procedures and **brauche** practices in which the brauche healer lays his hands over a patient's head or stomach while quietly reciting verses to "pull out" the ailment (Wenger, 1995).

Amish women try to limit their use of technology, even during pregnancy and while giving birth. For example, amniocentesis and other invasive prenatal diagnostic tests are not acceptable. Amish women prefer to use nurse midwives and lay midwives, and to have home deliveries, because it limits the use of technology as well as reduces the number of visits to the doctor, which may be costly (Lemon, 2006).

Women practice certain folk traditions during pregnancy to prepare themselves for giving birth. These practices include not walking under a clothesline because that is believed to cause a stillbirth. Another practice includes not climbing through a window or under a table because both can cause the umbilical cord to wrap around the baby's neck (Lemon, 2006). Women use a medley of herbs, called 5-W, five weeks before their pregnancy ends. These herbs include a mixture of red raspberry leaves, black cohosh root, butcher's broom root, dong quai root, and squaw vine root. The formula is believed to ease the labor by quieting the nerves and relaxing the uterus (Lemon, 2006).

Behavioral Risk Factors and Common Health Problems Among Amish Americans

The Amish have few behavioral risk factors due to various health-promoting behaviors, which, among the adult population, include low rates of tobacco use and alcohol consumption, and high levels of physical activity. However, the Amish are cautious and conservative and may refuse health care services (Armer & Radina, 2006). Furthermore, Amish youth are prone to alcohol abuse, which inspired the Drug Abuse Resistance Education (D.A.R.E.) program to conduct outreach in Amish communities (Ohio Department of Alcohol and Drug Services, 2005).

Amish children and adolescents live in nontechnological farming communities, which results in a population that is physically active and that has a low rate of obesity (Basset, Schneider, & Huntington, 2004). Amish adults also show very high levels of physical activity, which includes consistently walking at moderate to vigorous levels and farming daily. This type of lifestyle, one that promotes physical activity, results in the low prevalence of obesity and positive health outcomes in general for the Amish community (Basset, Tremblay, et al., 2007).

The Amish do not completely prohibit the use of modern medical technology, but they tend to be extremely cautious and may refuse intervention if it is not approved by community leaders. For example, Amish families vary in receptivity to the practice of immunizations for communicable diseases, leading to increased vulnerability to those illnesses. Although the Amish account for less than 0.5% of the national population, they were responsible for nearly all cases of rubella reported in the United States in 1991 (Armer & Radina, 2006). Moreover, the lack of immunizations puts the Amish at risk when they travel outside of their communities because they may not be protected against diseases to which they become exposed.

Certain Amish communities live by laws and precepts that have been passed down for generations. Such customs include marrying within their own community and allowing first cousins to marry. Consequently, a growing number of distinctive recessive genetic disorders have arisen among the Amish (Ember & Ember, 2004). Individuals who have a recessive genetic disorder, such as **Ellis-van Creveld syndrome** (EVC), receive a defective recessive gene from each parent. EVC, a form of dwarfism, is an autosomal recessive disorder in which individuals exhibit an extra digit located next to the fifth digit. In addition, EVC is characterized by individuals having short forearms and legs as well as congenital heart failure (Leach, 2007).

Cartilage-hair hypoplasia, another form of dwarfism, is a genetic disorder that is rarely seen outside of Amish communities (ClinicalTrials.gov, 2007). This rare disorder was not recognized until the mid-1960s when Amish children began to present with features similar to, but more pronounced than, EVC. These signs include fine and underdeveloped hair (hypoplasia of the hair) and underdeveloped cartilage (hypoplasia of the cartilage), resulting in skeletal abnormalities and an inability to fully extend the upper limbs (McKusick, 2000).

The Amish tend to prefer natural home remedies; however, they may seek health care services from medical doctors and complementary health providers, such as reflexologists and chiropractors (Julia, 1996). Due to a relatively stress-free and active lifestyle, positive health outcomes among the population include low rates of obesity, smoking, and cancer (Ferketich et al., 2008). As a result of the lack of vaccinations among the Amish, they are more susceptible to communicable diseases (Armer & Radina, 2006).

Considerations for Health Promotion and Program Planning for Amish Americans

When working with members of the Amish community, the following recommendations should be considered to improve cultural understanding:

- Be cognizant of the cultural differences this group has with society as a whole.
- Recognize the importance of privacy.
- Recognize that Amish people might not understand lifestyle activities and events you consider to be everyday occurrences.
- Be cognizant of the formality of family relationships.
- Explain all procedures and instructions to ensure understanding.
- Be aware that many Amish do not have health insurance.
- Transportation can be challenging as many travel via horse and buggy.
- Telephones are not permitted in the home, which may delay communication (Purnell, 2013).

Roma Americans

Romas, commonly known as Gypsies, a term considered pejorative by these people, are properly termed Roma or the Romani. They are an isolated group who maintains a strong social and cultural bond separate and apart from everyday American society.

The Roma are originally from northern India. They migrated throughout middle and eastern Europe beginning around 1000 CE. They immigrated to the United States in two stages: in the 18th century as a result of being deported from various European countries and at the end of the 19th century primarily from Eastern Europe.

The Roma primarily speak **Romany**, a wholly spoken language derived from Sanskrit, and English as a second language. Most older Roma are not literate, but some younger members have some education. Written forms of the Romany language have been developing with the education of the younger generations.

Roma Americans have a very complicated social structure based on four loyalties: to their nation, clan, family, and vista. They are first divided into nations; the most common nations are the Machwaya, Kalderasham, Churara, and Lowara. The nations are further divided into clans. A clan is a group of families united by ancestry, profession, and historic ties. Each clan has a leader, but there is no such thing as "Gypsy kings" as characterized in popular lore. Some clans are further divided into tribes, but most are composed of families. It is the family that is the most important social group for the Roma. A vista is extended family (Ryczak, Zebreski, May, Traver, & Kemp, n.d.).

Roma Americans purposely isolate themselves from the larger community and tend to be ethnocentric. They maintain separation from people and things that are **gadje**, non-Roma, who are considered to be unclean. The strict code that they live by limits acculturation.

Beliefs About Causes of Health and Illness Among Roma Americans

Roma Americans' beliefs regarding health and illness stem from two concepts: impurity and fortune. The first concept is related to the ideas of **wuzho** (pure) and **marime** (impure). Roma Americans have very strict traditions about what is polluted and how things are to be kept clean. Secretions from the upper half of the body are not polluted, but secretions from the lower half of the body are polluted. Therefore, separate soap and towels are used for the upper and lower halves of the body. Failing to keep the two secretions separate can result in serious illness. Also, because gadje (non-Romas) do not practice body separation, they are considered to be impure and diseased.

Fortune also plays a role in health. Good fortune and good health are thought to be related. Illness can be caused by actions that are considered to be contaminating and, therefore, create bad fortune.

Roma Americans distinguish between illnesses that are of a gadje cause and those that are part of their beliefs. Gadje illnesses can be cured by gadje doctors. Roma Americans avoid hospitals because they are unclean and are separate from Roma society. Illness is a problem to be dealt with by the entire clan. Therefore, if a clan member is hospitalized, family and clan members are expected to stay with them and provide curing rituals and protect them. An exception to the aversion to hospitals is childbirth. Women are considered to be unclean during pregnancy and for a number of weeks after delivery. Childbirth should not happen in the family home because it can cause impurity in the home. Therefore, delivery in hospitals is accepted in the culture.

Finally, older members of a family are very important in health care decision making. They are considered the authorities in the family and carry great weight in all decisions.

Healing Traditions Among Roma Americans

As previously discussed, illnesses can be characterized as those of the Roma or those that are gadje. Roma health treatment is the prerogative of the older women of the clan who are known as **drabarni**, women who have knowledge of medicines. Roma diseases are not connected to gadje diseases; they can only be cured by Roma treatments. Some diseases are caused by spirits or the devil. One spirit, called Mamioro, spreads disease in dirty houses, so keeping a clean home is imperative. The devil has been known to cause nervous diseases. Herbs and rituals are utilized to address these problems.

Behavioral Risk Factors and Common Health Problems Among Roma Americans

In Romani culture, the larger a person is, the luckier he or she is considered to be. A fat person is considered to be healthy and fortunate, and a thin person is considered to be ill and to have poor luck. This belief and other cultural beliefs are sources of health concerns for this group.

As a group, Roma Americans are resistant to immunization because it does not comport with their beliefs regarding purification. Thus, they are at risk for many communicable diseases.

The Roma American diet is high in fat and salt. A great percentage of Roma Americans smoke and are obese. These practices places them at risk for cardiovascular disease, hypertension, and diabetes. The closeness of living conditions leads to an increased risk of infectious diseases such as hepatitis. Romani children are more likely to be born prematurely or with low birth weight, and the increased incidence of consanguineous marriages has led to an increased risk of birth defects (Ryczak et al., n.d.).

Considerations for Health Promotion and Program Planning for Roma Americans

In working with Roma Americans, the following issues should be considered:

- Understand that illness is an issue for the entire society, and the entire clan will be involved in visiting the sick person in the hospital.

- Recognize the primacy of the elders in the family and the clan in making decisions.

- Always remember the importance of what is considered to be clean and unclean and provide separate soap, washcloths, and towels for the upper and lower body parts.

- Understand that this population is mistrustful of non-Roma people and things.

- Understand that Roma Americans are an ethnocentric culture and believe that they must be provided with the best doctors and treatment even if such treatment is not indicated.

Arab and Middle Eastern Americans

Being Arab is not based on race. Arabs are usually associated with the geographic area extending from the Atlantic coast of northern Africa to the Arabian Gulf. The people who descend from this area are classified as Arabs based largely on a common language (Arabic) and a shared sense of geographic, historic, and cultural identity. Arabs include peoples with widely varied physical features, countries of origin, and religions.

Arab and Middle Eastern Americans in the United States

Persons of Arab and Middle Eastern descent are a growing demographic in American society and, not unlike the Amish and Romani, are not well understood by the larger society. This cultural group has also experienced increased discrimination and suspicion since the September 11, 2001, terrorist attacks.

Arabs immigrated to the United States in three waves. The first migration occurred between the late 1800s and World War I; this group was from the area of Palestine and moved for economic reasons. Many of these immigrants were Christians, and their descendants have become firmly acculturated. The second wave began after 1948 with establishment of the state of Israel. This group included many professionals and Muslims. This wave tended to settle in the Midwest and accounts for the large concentration of Arab descendants in the Detroit and

Chicago areas. The third wave began with the 1967 Arab–Israeli War and continues today. This group fled political instability.

Because the vast majority of Arabs are Muslim, the tenets of the Islamic religion are very influential in Arab Americans' lives. Arab American culture is centered around family relationships. The basic relationship is the nuclear family, but each Arab American belongs to a large, extended family and often to an even-more-extended clan that is related by blood kinship (Purnell, 2013).

The Arab American family is the center of Arab American culture. It is a paternalistic structure, but women are respected, especially mothers. Marriage is highly valued and is considered to be the basic structure of society. Divorce is discouraged. Having children is very important in the Arab American culture, and a marriage with many children is considered to be highly blessed. Therefore, the use of reversible birth control is undesirable and irreversible birth control is forbidden (Purnell, 2013). Sickness, birth, and death are events that involve participation by the community.

Cleanliness is a basic tenet of Islam. The Quran, the Islamic holy book, proscribes eating certain foods, including pork or pork products, meat of dead animals, blood, and all intoxicants. Fasting from dawn to dusk every day during the month of Ramadan is required by the religious tenets (Athar, n.d.).

Beliefs About Causes of Health and Illness Among Arab and Middle Eastern Americans

Middle Eastern health beliefs arise from the long-standing traditions of the great Islamic healers of the 7th and 8th centuries. Western theories from Hippocrates and Galen came to Arab medicine through trading routes and were incorporated into the Arabs' knowledge base. They advanced human knowledge of anatomy, physiology, and medical treatments. Thus, the tenets of allopathic medicine form the basis of most Arab beliefs about health and illness. Muslims consider an illness to be atonement for their sins, and they receive illness and death with patience and prayers. Death is part of their journey to meet Allah (God) (Athar, n.d.).

Healing Traditions Among Arab and Middle Eastern Americans

Almost all Middle Eastern people believe in maintaining good health through hygiene and a healthy diet. Women and men are modest and may refuse treatment by practitioners of the opposite gender. This modesty of women contributes to low rates of screening such as Pap smears and mammograms (Purnell, 2013).

Iraqis have a significant history of traditional healing practices. Some common practices include the following (Iraqi Refugees, 2002):

- Cumin, in conjunction with various other ingredients, is used to treat fever, abdominal pain, and tooth pain.

- Respiratory complaints are treated with honey and lemon.

- Infertility can be treated by a placenta being placed over the doorway of the infertile couple's home.

- Henna is believed to have magic healing properties and will be painted on the body to protect against the evil eye and spirits.

- Pregnant women should satisfy their cravings, otherwise they will develop a birthmark in the shape of the food that they crave (Purnell, 2013).

Middle Eastern diets have the following characteristics (Nolan, 1995):

- *Dairy products.* The most common dairy products are yogurt and cheese; feta cheese is preferred. Milk is usually only used in desserts and puddings.

- *Protein.* Pork is eaten only by Christians and is forbidden by religion for Muslims and Jews. Lamb is the most frequently used meat. Many Middle Easterners will not combine dairy products or shellfish with the meal. Legumes, such as black beans, chickpeas (garbanzo beans), lentils, navy beans, and red beans, are commonly used in all dishes.

- *Breads and cereals.* Some form of wheat or rice accompanies each meal.

- *Fruits.* Fruits tend to be eaten as dessert or as snacks. Fresh, raw fruit is preferred. Lemons are used for flavoring. Green and black olives are present in many dishes, and olive oil is most frequently used in food preparation.

- *Vegetables.* Vegetables are preferred raw.

The Mediterranean diet pyramid is shown in **Figure 11.1**.

Behavioral Risk Factors and Common Health Problems Among Arab and Middle Eastern Americans

As a group, Arab and Middle Eastern Americans face the same health concerns as the majority of European Americans. Recent immigrants may be at greater risk for certain inborn genetic disorders as a result of interfamily marriages. Otherwise, their health risks mirror the majority of the population, with heart disease and cancer among the major morbidity factors. Smoking is highly ingrained in the Arab culture, and they have high smoking rates (Purnell, 2013). Due to modesty, screening rates are low.

Considerations for Health Promotion and Program Planning for Arab and Middle Eastern Americans

Considered the following points when dealing with Arab and Middle Eastern Americans in health care:

- Arab and Middle Eastern Americans prefer treatment by a medical provider of the same gender, especially for women.

- Arab and Middle Eastern Americans consider nurses to be helpers, not health care professionals, and their suggestions and advice are not taken seriously.

- Arab and Middle Eastern Americans prefer treatment that involves prescribing pills or giving injections rather than simple medical counseling.

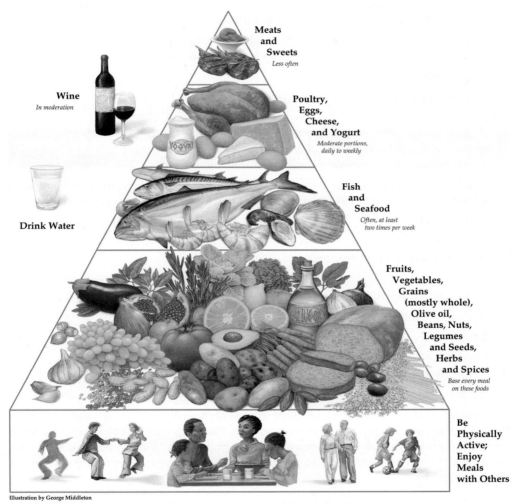

© 2009 Oldways Preservation and Exchange Trust • www.oldwayspt.org

FIGURE 11.1

Mediterranean diet pyramid.

- For orthodox Muslims, follow a halal (Muslim diet), which prohibits some types of meat, like pork, and medications and foods that contain alcohol. Meat needs to be prepared according to Islamic requirements. Also, provide for religious requirements for prayer as often as five times a day, starting before sunrise and ending at night, and provide fasting during the holy month of Ramadan between sunrise and sunset. Although those who are ill are exempted from this practice, devout Muslims may desire to fast anyway.

- Allow for receipt of food into the right hand for Muslim patients. The left hand is considered to be unclean because it is used for cleaning during toileting.

- Respect modesty and privacy.

- Allow for visits and input by the imam, a prayer leader.

Behavior Risk Factors and Prevalent Health Problems for European and Mediterranean Americans

The leading health problems for European and Mediterranean Americans may be directly related to living a comparatively affluent lifestyle. The leading causes of death include:

1. Heart disease
2. Cancer
3. Chronic lower respiratory disease
4. Stroke
5. Unintentional injuries
6. Alzheimer's disease
7. Diabetes
8. Influenza and pneumonia
9. Nephritis, nephrotic syndrome. and nephrosis
10. Suicide (Office of Minority Health, 2010)

Obesity, smoking, and stress contribute to most of these disease, and are associated with living in an advanced, affluent, urban environment. However, these peoples are very diverse economically and also are well represented in the population living in poverty, with poor nutrition and without health care. More than a third of this population is obese (Office of Minority Health, 2010).

QUICK FACTS

- European and Mediterranean Americans (whites) lead other major populations in heart disease (11% of the population), especially when compared to Asian Americans (6.7%).

- European and Mediterranean Americans lead all other major populations with incidence of cancer (8.5%) compared to Asians at 3.5% and Hispanics at 3.8%.

- European and Mediterranean Americans have the lowest percentage of members with diabetes, especially compared to Hispanics (12%) and African Americans (12.5%).

- European and Mediterranean Americans lead all other groups in heart attacks (3.1%) except American Indian and Alaskan Natives (3.8%).

- Fewer European and Mediterranean Americans suffer from stroke (2.4%) than all other groups except Asians (1.8%) (CDC, NHIS, 2014).

- European and Mediterranean populations over age 20 has a high percentage of overweight people (68%), with 34% of men and 32% of women being obese (National Center for Health Statistics, 2014a).

- One third of the adult European and .Mediterranean American population has hypertension (33.1% of men and 33.7% of women; National Center for Health Statistics, 2014b).

- Although teen pregnancy rates have been declining for all ethnic groups, European and Mediterranean teens have a pregnancy rate about half (18.6 per 1,000) that of African Americans (39 per 1,000) and Hispanics (41.7 per 1,000; National Center for Health Statistics, 2015).

- The traditional Mediterranean diet incorporates the basics of healthy eating, plus some flavorful olive oil and even a glass of red wine, and is characteristic of the traditional cooking style of countries bordering the Mediterranean Sea. This diet is associated with a reduced risk of death from heart disease and cancer, as well as a reduced incidence of Parkinson's and Alzheimer's diseases. The Dietary Guidelines for Americans recommends the Mediterranean diet (Mayo Clinic, n.d.).

Tips for Working With European and Mediterranean American Populations

The European and Mediterranean American culture is diverse, so this section includes general tips for caring for peoples of all cultures. Every person is unique, so place yourself in your patients' shoes and consider their unique beliefs, needs, and concerns as you interact with them. Treat your patients as they would like to be treated.

Ask your patients if this is their first visit. If so, take a few moments to orient them. Patients who are new to the system may not know the roles of their health care team, how to report for an appointment, or other health care matters that patients already in the system may know.

If English is the patient's second language, or the patient is deaf or hard of hearing or has vision impairment, make sure to involve an interpreter in all of your care discussions. Do not rely on family members to translate health information. Your patients may include many family members in their care and care decisions. Some may be related, and others may be friends your patients consider to be family and part of their support network.

Use the terms "partner" or "spouse" rather than "husband" or "wife" to avoid making assumptions about sexual orientation. Ask about preferences before acting. Pay attention to patient cues and follow their lead. If they do not establish eye contact or refuse to shake your hand, a cultural custom or spiritual belief may be guiding their behavior. Set the tone for your patient visits by asking questions.

Ask your patients how they would like to be addressed, and remember to continue calling them by their preferred names. Tell your patients why you think they are meeting with you after you ask them why they think they are there. Ask your patients what their goals are for their visit. Remind them they are active partners in their care plans.

Ask what cultural, religious, spiritual, or lifestyle beliefs may affect the kind of health care the patient wants to receive, and document these preferences so other providers can honor them. Continuity of cultural appropriateness within the care team is essential. This is particularly important when you ask who else in their life needs to be involved in making medical decisions about care.

Ask patients to "teach back" the information you give them, and then document their understanding. Offer choices for treatment options. Use open-ended questions (instead of yes/no questions) to make sure you and your patients share a common meaning. Determine whether your explanation of the causes and likely course of the illness match your patients' perceptions and understanding of their illness. If there is a mismatch, some patients may rely on their own beliefs.

Acknowledge and respect your patients' interpretations of their illnesses. Listen carefully. When you talk with your patients, let them know you are listening by nodding your head that you understand, maintain eye contact if that is their norm, or avoid eye contact if that is their norm. Remain on the same physical level as much as possible with your patient.

Explain to your patients what you are writing as you take notes. After you are done taking their medical history, give your patients another opportunity to bring up something they may have omitted or did not feel comfortable talking about at first (especially if this is their first visit with you). They may feel more comfortable discussing something further into the visit. Tell your patients what you are doing and what they will feel if you are doing an exam, procedure, or other care that involves physically touching them (University of Washington Medical Center, 2011).

Summary

People who are characterized as European and Mediterranean Americans, or generally associated with the group defined as white by the U.S. Census Bureau, are not composed of only those of northern European descent. They include people from very divergent backgrounds, such as the Amish, Roma, and those of Arab and Middle Eastern descent. It is important to remember that culture and ethnicity have a significant impact on people's health activities and on their perspectives on health, and merely characterizing a person as European, Mediterranean, or white does not describe those beliefs.

Review

1. Describe the health and illness beliefs of Amish and Roma Americans.
2. Prepare three recommendations to provide culturally competent care for a clinic that deals with Amish or Roma American clients.
3. Describe how Arab American clients might view American health practices differently from other patients.

Activity

Watch the video *Devil's Playground* (Cantor & Walker, 2002), a documentary film about the Amish. Write a three-page reaction paper to the video. What did you learn about the Amish? What surprised you? How would the knowledge about Rumspringa change how health care is provided to the Amish?

Case Studies

Case #1. After his wife gave birth, an Arab man would not allow a male lab technician to enter his wife's room to draw blood. The nurses explained to the man the need for the blood test, and the man eventually agreed to allow the technician into the room. He made sure his wife was completely covered in the bed and exposed only her arm for the lab technician to draw the blood. This protected his wife's modesty and the family honor.

Male providers should be aware of these sensitivities when dealing with Arab American families. In this situation the family's concerns were addressed and respected.

Case #2. A nurse found an Syrian patient on the floor when she entered her room. The nurse was concerned that the patient had fallen, and the patient became upset when the nurse tried to help her out. Because the patient did not speak English, she could not explain to the nurse what she was doing. The nurse later learned that the patient was praying.

Muslims pray to Mecca five times per day. The patient was merely practicing her religious tenets. It is important to be aware of such practices when treating ethnic patients.

Source: Fernandez & Fernandez (2005).

References

American Association of Pediatrics. (2012). *Newborn male circumcision.* Retrieved from http://www.aap.org/en-us/about-the-aap/aap-press-room/Pages/Newborn-cMale-Circumcision.aspx#sthash.Rca4BHGr.dpuf

Armer, J. M., & Radina, M. E. (2006). Definition of health and health promotion behaviors among Midwestern old order Amish families. *Journal of Multicultural Nursing & Health, 12*(3), 44–53.

Athar, S. (n.d.). *Information for health care providers when dealing with a Muslim patient.* Retrieved from http://www.islam-usa.com

Basset, D., Jr., Schneider, P. L., & Huntington, G. E. (2004, January). Physical activity in an old order Amish community. *Medicine & Science in Sports & Exercise, 36*(1), 79–85.

Basset, D. R., Jr., Tremblay, M. S., Esliger, D. W., Copeland, J. L., Barnes, D., & Huntington, G. E. (2007, March). Physical activity and body mass index of children in an older Amish community. *Medicine & Science in Sports & Exercise, 39*(3), 410–415.

Cantor, S. (Producer), & Walker, L. (Director). (2002). *Devil's playground* [Documentary]. United States: Stick Figure Productions.

Centers for Disease Control and Prevention. (2014). *Summary Health Statistics for U.S. Adults: National Health Interview Survey, 2012, Table 2* Vital and Health Statistics, Vol 10, Number 260 retrieved from http://www.cdc .gov/nchs/data/series/sr_10/sr10_260.pdf

ClinicalTrials.gov. (2007, September). *Genetic studies in the Amish and Mennonites.* Retrieved from http://clinicaltrials.gov

Ember, C. R., & Ember, M. (2004). *Encyclopedia of medical anthropology: Health and illness in the world's culture* (Vol. 2). New York, NY: Kluwer/Plenum.

Ferketich, A. K., Katz, M. L., Paskett, E. D., Lemeshow, S., Westman, J. A., Clinton, S. K., et al. (2008, Winter). Tobacco use among the Amish in Holmes County, Ohio. *Journal of Rural Health, 24*(1), 84–90.

Fernandez, V. M., & Fernandez, K. M. (2005). *Transcultural nursing: The Middle Eastern community.* Retrieved from http://www .culturediversity.org/mide.htm

Iraqi Refugees. (2002). Retrieved from http:// www3.baylor.edu:80~Charles_Kemp/ Iraqi _refugees.htm

Julia, M. C. (1996). *Multicultural awareness in the health care professions.* Needham Heights, MA: Simon & Schuster.

Kraybill, D. B. (2001). *The riddle of Amish culture.* Baltimore, MD: Johns Hopkins University Press.

Kriebel, D. W. (2000). *Belief, power, and identity in Pennsylvania Dutch brauche, or powwowing.* Ann Arbor, MI: UMI.

Leach, B. (2007, February 1). Scienceline. *The road to genetic cures.* Retrieved from http:// www.scienceline.org/2007/02/01/biology -hapmaps-leach/

Lee, D. (2005). *Our Amish neighbors: Providing culturally competent care* (Multicultural Health Series) [Videotape and handout]. Ann Arbor, MI: UMHS, PMCH, Cultural Competency Division.

Lemon, B. C. (2006, Fall). Amish health and belief systems in obstetrical settings. *Journal of Multicultural Nursing & Health,* 1–7.

Mayo Clinic. (n.d.). *Mediterranean diet: A heart-healthy eating plan.* Retrieved from http:// www.mayoclinic.org/healthy-lifestyle /nutrition-and-healthy-eating/in-depth /mediterranean-diet/art-20047801

McKusick, V. A. (2000). Ellis-van Creveld syndrome and the Amish. *Nature Genetics.* Retrieved from http://www.nature.com/ng /journal/v24/n3/full/ng0300_203.html

National Center for Health Statistics. (2014a). *Healthy weight, overweight, and obesity among adults aged 20 and over, by selected characteristics: United States, selected years 1988–1994 through 2009–2012,* table 64. Retrieved from http://www.cdc.gov/nchs /data/hus/2014/064.pdf

National Center for Health Statistics. (2014b). *Hypertension among adults aged 20 and over, by selected characteristics: United States, selected years 1988–1994 through 2009–2012,* table 60. Retrieved from http:// www.cdc.gov/nchs/fastats/white-health.htm

National Center for Health Statistics. (2015). *Final data for 2013. Birth rates per 1,000 females ages 15–19, by race/ethnicity, 1990–2013,* table 1. Retrieved from http://www .hhs.gov/ash/oah/adolescent-health-topics /reproductive-health/teen-pregnancy /trends.html

Nolan, J. (1995). *Cultural diversity: Eating in America. Middle Eastern.* Retrieved from http://ohioline.osu.edu/hyg-Fact/5000/5256 .html

Office of Minority Health. (2010). *White populations*. Retrieved from http://www.cdc.gov/omhd/Populations/White.htm

Ohio Department of Alcohol and Drug Services. (2005, Spring/Summer). Amish D.A.R.E. program shining example of SDFSC funds, innovation at work. *Perspectives, 3*(1), 5–6.

Owings, M., Uddin, S., & Williams, S. (2013). *Trends in circumcision for male newborns in U.S. hospitals: 1979–2010*. Retrieved from http://www.cdc.gov/nchs/data/hestat/circumcision_2013/circumcision_2013.htm

Palmer, C. V. (1992). The health beliefs and practices of an old order Amish family. *Journal of the American Academy of Nurse Practitioners, 4*, 117–122.

Purnell, L. (2013). *Transcultural healthcare: A culturally competent approach* (4th ed.). Philadelphia, PA: F. A. Davis Company.

Ryczak, K., Zebreski, L., May, M., Traver, S., & Kemp, C. (n.d.). *Gypsy (Roma) culture health refugees immigrants*. Retrieved from http://bearspace.baylor.edu/Charles_Kemp/www/gypsy_health.htm

Topping, A. (2015, February 5). FGM affects three times more people than originally thought. *The Guardian*. Retrieved from http://www.theguardian.com/society/2015/feb/05/fgm-numbers-affected-us-women

University of Washington Medical Center. (2011). *Culture Clue™: Communication guide: All patients*. Retrieved from https://depts.washington.edu/pfes/PDFs/CommunicationGuideAllCultures.pdf

U.S. Census Bureau. (2011). The white population, 2010. *Census Briefs*. Retrieved from http://www.census.gov/prod/cen2010/briefs/c2010br-05.pdf

Wenger, A. F. Z. (1995). Cultural context, health and health care decision making. *Journal of Transcultural Nursing, 7*(1), 3–14.

© Fleyeing/Dreamstime.com

CHAPTER 12

NONETHNIC CULTURES

We draw our strength from the very despair in which we have been forced to live. We shall endure.
    —*Cesar Chavez*

If God had wanted me otherwise, He would have created me otherwise.
    —*Johann Wolfgang von Goethe*

Key Concepts

Sexual identity   Refugee
Gender identity   Asylee
Transgender   Immigrant
Bisexual   Alien
Gay   Illegal alien
Lesbian

Learning Objectives

After reading this chapter, you should be able to:

1. Describe the differentiating characteristics of lesbian, gay, bisexual, and transgender (LGBT) people.
2. Discuss the health risks encountered by the LGBT population.
3. Describe the problems often encountered by LGBT people when accessing health care services.
4. Discuss steps that can be taken to improve cultural competence within the medical community in caring for LGBT patients and their families.

© Diana Lundin/Dreamstime.com

5. Discuss health disparities of people with disabilities and ways to address their health needs.
6. Describe how the culture of commerce and health are related and the health effects of the culture.
7. Describe the challenges farmworkers encounter in obtaining health care.
8. Discuss ways to decrease farmworkers' health risks.
9. Discuss the unique situations of new immigrants and refugees and ways to address their health needs.

Introduction

Although culture can be easier to identify in ethnic and racial groups, it also exists in other human relationships. Culture is not restricted to race, ethnicity, or heritage; it includes customs, beliefs, values, and knowledge that influence our behavior and affect our health. Therefore, understanding the health of cultural groups not defined by race or ethnicity is just as important. A culture can develop within any group or community of people who share customs or beliefs. Athletes share a "sports culture," and illegal drug users may share a "drug culture."

This concept of culture becomes clear when we examine how the cultural relationships of gay people, people with disabilities, farmworkers, and new immigrants and refugees affect their health. Cultures can also be based on common beliefs or lifestyles such as a culture of people suffering discrimination, a culture of consumers, and a culture of people living in poverty. Finally, cultures are affected by and affect other cultures.

Introduction to the "Culture of People Suffering Discrimination"

People from most cultures have a tendency to develop discriminatory attitudes toward other cultures. In some sense, this is a way to maintain the integrity of the original culture. However, historically discrimination has gone well beyond personal preference to imposing hardship on the people of other cultures. Two examples of a common cross-culture "culture of discrimination" are the treatment of gay people and of persons with disabilities.

History of Gay Americans in the United States

There are references to gay people throughout the ages, but gay people did not begin to emerge as a culture in the United States until the 20th century. For the greatest part of American history, what is now pejoratively termed "homosexual" activity was outlawed through state sodomy laws. Members of the lesbian, gay, bisexual, and transgender (LGBT) community lived underground to avoid legal entanglements and a prevailing culture of discrimination.

In the 1950s, small groups of gay men and lesbian women formed to establish rights for gays and lesbians. Most notably were the Daughters of Bilitis, which is credited as the first lesbian rights group, and the Mattachine Society, the first group to advocate on behalf of gay men.

Societal changes in the 1960s also included changes for gay people. As black Americans strongly advocated civil right, gay Americans were beginning to object to the legal restraints placed on their lives as well. Years of resentment came to a head in the Stonewall riots in 1969. Prior to this event, it was common for police to raid gay and lesbian bars and arrest the patrons. In a New York bar named the Stonewall Inn, the patrons protested and a riot broke out. Over the next few days, gay people continued to riot, demanding their right to assemble. This event sparked gay and lesbian activism across the country, resulting in the birth of the gay rights movement, which overturned many laws.

Significant strides have been made in obtaining equal status in the United States. In 1973, the American Psychiatric Association declassified "homosexuality" as a mental disorder. The diagnosis of "ego-dystonic homosexuality" was removed from the *Diagnostic and Statistical Manual of Mental Disorders (DSM)*, and for the first time gay Americans were no longer considered to be mentally ill. Legal advances have been made as well. In 2003 the U.S. Supreme Court found laws against consensual sex among adults to be unconstitutional. However, about a dozen states continue to have antisodomy laws on their books. In June 2015, the U.S. Supreme Court found laws prohibiting marriage of persons of the same sex to be unconstitutional.

Gay Americans in the United States

There are more than 8 million adults in the United States who are lesbian, gay, or bisexual, comprising 3.5% of the adult population, and approximately 9 million Americans identify as LGBT when transgender persons are included (Gates, 2011). Population-based data sources that estimate the percentage of adults who are transgender are very rare. The Massachusetts Behavioral Risk Factor Surveillance Survey represents one of the few population-based surveys that includes a question designed to identify the transgender population. Analyses of the 2007 and 2009 surveys suggest that 0.5 percent of adults aged 18 to 64 identified as transgender (Conron, Scott, Stowell, & Landers, 2012).

Terminology

Gay people, referred to as lesbian, gay, bisexual, and transgender (LGBT) individuals, exist in all cultures, communities, and subgroups of American society. Therefore, biologically and ethnically LGBT persons tend to be as different as the varied cultures from which they arise. However, LGBT culture has its own values, beliefs, traditions, and behaviors.

It is often difficult to identify members of this culture without their self-identification. Historically, the secrecy of the culture has been an effort at self-preservation. Today, the LGBT culture is emerging and being given a place in society.

Key to understanding this population is to understand some terms. **Sexual identity** is usually defined as a person's physical, romantic, emotional, and spiritual attraction to another person. **Gender identity** references a person's internal, personal sense of being male or female, boy or girl, man or woman. Gender identity and sexual identity are not the same. For **transgender** people, their physical, birth-assigned gender does not match their internal sense of their gender. Transgender is usually defined as individuals who live full- or part-time in the gender role opposite to the one in which they were physically born. **Bisexual** refers to those whose sexual identity is to both men and women. **Gay** individuals' gender identity is consistent with their physical sexual characteristics, but their sexual identity is to persons of the same sex, and it usually refers to gay males specifically. **Lesbian** refers to gay women specifically.

Behavioral Risk Factors and Common Health Problems Among LGBT Americans

Research suggests that LGBT individuals face health disparities linked to societal stigma and discrimination. Much of the negative response by other people results from reaction to the group members' own risky health behaviors that have become highly associated with the HIV/AIDS epidemic and the fear, dread, and expense associated with the disabling health condition it represents. Nevertheless, discrimination against LGBT persons has been associated with high rates of psychiatric disorders, substance abuse, and suicide. Experiences of violence and victimization are frequent for LGBT individuals and have long-lasting effects on the individual and the community. Personal, family, and social acceptance of sexual orientation and gender identity affects the mental health and personal safety of LGBT individuals (CDC, n.d.).

LGBT health requires specific attention from health care and public health professionals to address a number of disparities, including:

- LGBT youth are 2 to 3 times more likely to attempt suicide.
- LGBT youth are more likely to be homeless.
- Lesbians are less likely to get preventive services for cancer.
- Gay men are at higher risk of HIV and other sexually transmitted diseases (STDs), especially among communities of color.
- Lesbians and bisexual females are more likely to be overweight or obese.
- Elderly LGBT individuals face additional barriers to health because of isolation and a lack of social services and culturally competent providers. (CDC, n.d.)

Transgender individuals have a high prevalence of HIV/STDs, victimization, mental health issues, and suicide and are less likely to have health insurance than heterosexual or LGB individuals.

LGBT populations have the highest rates of tobacco, alcohol, and other drug use. Young people who identify as lesbian, gay, bisexual, and transgender also frequently become victims of commercial sexual exploitation (CSE) (Walker, 2013). Youth who are LGBT "are at an increased risk for becoming sexually exploited due to their over-representation in the homeless youth population (20 to 40 percent of homeless youth in California identify as LGBT)" (Walker, 2013). LGBT youths' vulnerability can be attributed to a variety of factors such as history of running away from home, physical and sexual abuse, rejection by parents, and child welfare placements. Many youth who are LGBT have been turned out of their homes, often for reasons related to their sexual orientation or gender identity (Walker, 2013). Because LGBT youth are disproportionately homeless, it is especially challenging to identify and engage them in intervention services. Very few LGBT youth shelters exist, and it is common for these children to exchange sex for money or basic necessities such as food, shelter, and clothing, a practice known as "survival sex." One study estimates that more than 1 in 4 homeless LGBT children, and nearly half of gay or bisexual boys, have been victims of CSE (Walker, 2013). The onset of acquired immunodeficiency syndrome (AIDS) in the 1980s brought devastation to the lives of gay men. Although discrimination and a belief that these men deserved their fate was the initial response to the epidemic, with time a better understanding of the disease and its risk factors have enlightened the discussion. The importance of distinguishing between sexual identity and sexual behavior has been emphasized in dealing with this disease.

Research has found that men who have sex with men are most at risk (see **Table 12.1**). Those men characterize themselves as gay, bisexual, and heterosexual. Therefore, focus must be placed on behaviors and not labels. Also, bisexual men were often unlikely to disclose their bisexuality to their female partners (Dean et al., 2000).

Changing behavior remains the primary way of reducing the spread of the human immunodeficiency virus (HIV). Education about safer sex practices has been strongly supported

TABLE 12.1 Cumulative Estimated Number of AIDS Diagnoses, Through 2010[a]			
Transmission Category	**Cumulative Estimated Number of AIDS Diagnoses, Through 2010[a]**		
	Adult and Adolescent Males	**Adult and Adolescent Females**	**Total**
Male-to-male sexual contact	555,032	NA	555,032
Injection drug use	187,938	89,800	277,738
Male-to-male sexual contact and injection drug use	80,902	NA	80,902
Heterosexual contact[b]	77,521	136,675	214,196
Other[c]	11,975	6,427	18,402

[a]From the beginning of the epidemic through 2011.
[b]Heterosexual contact with a person known to have, or to be at high risk for, HIV infection.
[c]Includes hemophilia, blood transfusion, perinatal exposure, and risk not reported or not identified.
Source: CDC (2013b).

within the gay community, and research has shown that most gay men report having protected sex most of the time.

Little research has been done on AIDS in the lesbian community. The few studies that have been done indicate a small incidence and no evidence of female-to-female transmission. It is presumed that lesbians who contract the disease have either used intravenous drugs or had intercourse with a man. However, research to determine the true risk factors within this population is needed.

Cancer

Although definitive studies are lacking, the information to date indicates that gay men and lesbians are at higher risk for certain cancers: Kaposi's sarcoma (KS), non-Hodgkin's lymphoma (NHL), cervical cancer, Hodgkin's lymphoma, anal cancer, lung cancer, and liver cancer. Gay men are at higher risk for Kaposi's sarcoma, which is associated with HIV infection, and AIDS-related non-Hodgkin's lymphoma (Yanik et al., 2015). It has also been noted that survival time for gay men with cancer is less than for the population at large. It is speculated that this is due to HIV/AIDS comorbidity and delay in detection and treatment (Dean et al., 2000).

Lesbians have been found to be at higher risk for breast cancer than heterosexual women due to increased risk factors, including alcohol consumption, obesity, and not having children. Lesbians receive less frequent gynecologic care and breast cancer screening.

Substance Use

When compared with the general population, LGBT individuals:

- Are more likely to use alcohol and drugs
- Have higher rates of substance abuse
- Are less likely to abstain from alcohol and drug use
- Are more likely to continue heavy drinking into later life (CDC, 2013a)

Alcohol and drug use among some men who have sex with men (MSM) can be a reaction to homophobia, discrimination, or violence they experienced due to their sexual orientation and can contribute to other mental health problems. Substance abuse is associated with a wide range of mental health and physical problems. It can disrupt relationships and employment and threaten financial stability.

Alcohol and illegal drug use in some gay and bisexual men also contributes to increased risk for HIV infection and other STDs, especially the use of methamphetamines, amyl nitrates (poppers), and drugs used to treat erectile dysfunction. Individuals under the influence of drugs or alcohol may increase their risk for HIV transmission by engaging in risky sexual behaviors or through sharing needles or other injection equipment (CDC, 2013a).

Mental Health

As previously noted, declassification of "homosexuality" as a mental illness occurred in 1973. However, the LGBT population is at increased risk for certain mental health issues as a result of stressors related to antigay societal attitudes and internalization of negative social attitudes.

Significant among the problems encountered by this group are mental disorders and distress, substance use, and suicide. As with other health issues faced by this population, few scientifically significant studies are available in this area.

The transgender population is at risk for mental health problems comparable to others who undergo major life changes, minority status, discrimination, and chronic medical conditions. Studies indicate increased rates of depression, substance use, and anxiety disorders. Unfortunately, suicide attempts and completed suicides are more common in the transgender population, and genital mutilation is also reported at significant rates (Dean et al., 2000).

Aging

Surveys have shown that LGBT elders are more likely to live alone than elders in the population at large (Hoctel, 2002). Furthermore, few agencies exist to meet the social service needs of this group, and the availability of long-term care facilities is virtually nonexistent. Finally, due to their age, LGBT elders are less able to deal with discrimination in the health care system than younger members of the LGBT community.

Considerations for Health Promotion and Program Planning for LGBT Americans

To investigate United States hospitals' policies and procedures related to LGBT concerns, the Human Rights Campaign Foundation and the Gay and Lesbian Medical Association (HRC, 2007) devised the Healthcare Equality Index to evaluate how the health care community responds to the needs of the LGBT community. The focus of the inquiry was on five criteria: patient nondiscrimination, hospital visitation, decision making, cultural competence training, and employment policies.

The project began in 2007, and all participants were given anonymity for their responses. Requests for participation were sent to 1,000 hospitals. Responses from 78 hospitals in 20 states were obtained. The results showed that 50 hospitals had policies providing the same access to same-sex partners as is provided to married spouses, 56 allowed the designation of a domestic partner or someone else as medical surrogate, only 45 had a policy allowing same-sex parents the same access to medical decision making for their minor children as married spouses, and 57 provided staff training on specific issues affecting LGBT patients and their families (HRC, 2007).

Efforts to improve LGBT health include:

- Implementing antibullying policies in schools.

- Providing supportive social services to reduce suicide and homelessness risk among youth.

- Appropriately inquiring about and being supportive of a patient's sexual orientation to enhance the patient–provider interaction and regular use of care.

- Providing medical students with access to LGBT patients to increase provision of culturally competent care.

- Expansion of domestic partner health insurance coverage.

- Establishment of LGBT health centers.
- Dissemination of effective HIV and STD interventions (CDC, n.d.).

The LGBT community experiences barriers to accessing care. The lack of health insurance for individuals and their partners, cultural barriers, and a poor understanding of their health care needs all affect the health of this group. For health promotion to occur, efforts need to be made to address these problems. Cultural competence must be addressed within the provider community as well. **Table 12.2** and **Table 12.3** provide objectives for creating LGBT cultural competence.

TABLE 12.2   LGBT Cultural Competence Strategies

Use gender-neutral language in forms and practice.
Do not make assumptions about sexuality.
Utilize nonbiased behavior and communication.
Do not use labels; focus on behavior.
Conduct a thorough sexual-risk evaluation.
Be aware of LGBT health risks.
Be knowledgeable about the health needs of the LGBT community.

Source: Gay & Lesbian Medical Association (2001).

TABLE 12.3   Recommended Community Standards for Gay, Lesbian, and Transgender Persons

1. Create and promote open communication and a safe and nondiscriminatory workplace.
2. Create comprehensive policies to ensure that services are provided to LGBT clients and their families in a nondiscriminatory manner.
3. Have procedures available for clients to resolve complaints concerning violation of policies.
4. Prepare and implement assessment tools to meet the needs of LGBT clients and their families.
5. Maintain a basic understanding of LGBT issues within the organization.
6. All personnel who provide direct care to LGBT clients shall be competent to identify and address the health issues encountered by LGBT clients and their families and be able to provide appropriate treatment or referrals.
7. The organization shall ensure the confidentiality of client information.
8. Community outreach shall include the LGBT community.
9. The board of directors of the organization should have an LGBT representative.
10. The organization shall provide appropriate and safe care and treatment to all LGBT clients and their families.

Source: Gay & Lesbian Medical Association (2001).

Introduction to People With Disabilities

Another example of a culture not defined by race or ethnicity is the culture of people living with disabilities. Steven Brown, the cofounder of the Institute on Disability Culture, states that those with disabilities have created a group identity. He describes the culture of disability as follows:

> We generate art, music, literature, and other expressions of our lives and our culture, infused from our experience of disability. Most importantly, we are proud of ourselves as people with disabilities. We claim our disabilities with pride as part of our identity. (Brown, 2002, p. 48)

Since the Americans with Disabilities Act was enacted in 1990, many social barriers have been removed or reduced for people with disabilities and progress is continuing. Good health is important to be able to work, learn, and be engaged within a community.

Did You Know?

Deaf people typically do not view themselves as having lost their hearing or being handicapped, impaired, or disabled. The Deaf celebrate and appreciate their culture as it provides them with the unique privilege of sharing a common history and language.

The dominant cultural patterns in Deaf culture is collectivism, and they view all Deaf people as part of that culture. The group of Deaf people is generally close-knit and connected. Deaf people find pleasure in being in the company of other Deaf people and actively seek ways to accomplish this. When Deaf people first meet, they typically begin the communication with identifying where the other person is from and whether they have Deaf friends in common. A person's physical appearance is acknowledged and remembered because it is the landscape for all signed communication. Sometimes a person's name may not be revealed until the end of the conversation. Open communication is valued, and having secrets or withholding information is usually not done as it does not support the interconnectedness that occurs in this collectivist culture (Siple, Greer, & Holcolm, 2003).

Like all cultures, this one has deep roots as well. An example is the way that Deaf people say good-bye to one another. The departure process is lengthy, which is different from the typically process for the hearing culture. In Deaf culture one approaches each group to say good-bye, which often results in further conversation. The entire process may take more than an hour to accomplish. This behavior is because of the interconnected culture of the Deaf and the communication challenges that can occur when they are apart (new technologies are breaking down these barriers, but prior to email and other technology sign language was the main communication method) (Siple et al., 2003).

TABLE 12.4   Disability Among U.S. Adults 18 and Older by Race and Ethnicity, 2004–2006

Race/Ethnicity	Disability
Non-Hispanic white	20.3%
Non-Hispanic black or African American	21.2%
Hispanic	16.9%
Asian	11.6%
Native Hawaiian or Other Pacific Islander	16.6%
Native American or Alaska Native	29.9%

Source: Centers for Disease Control and Prevention (2014b).

Terminology

In section 504 of the Rehabilitation Act of 1973, a "person with a disability" includes any person who (1) has a physical or mental impairment, which substantially limits one or more of such a person's major life activities; (2) has a record of such impairment; or (3) is regarded as having such an impairment (Black Hawk College, 2014). Disabilities can affect people in different ways, even when one person has the same type of disability as another person. Some disabilities may be hidden and difficult to see. There are numerous types of disabilities, including these categories:

Physical disability means a visual, hearing, mobility, or orthopedic impairment.

Communication disability is an impairment in the processes of speech, language, or hearing.

Learning disability is a persistent condition of presumed neurological dysfunction that may exist with other disability conditions. This dysfunction continues despite instruction in standard classroom situations.

Psychological disability is a persistent psychological or psychiatric disorder, or emotional or mental illness.

One in 5 adults in the United States is living with a disability (CDC, 2014b). A higher percentage of American Indians have disabilities than other racial and ethnic groups (**Table 12.4**).

Behavioral Risk Factors and Common Health Problems Among People With Disabilities

Disability is often equated with poor health, but people with disabilities can and should have the same opportunity for good health as people without disabilities. However, they report being in poorer health than those without disabilities (**Table 12.5**).

Reports of fair or poor health among adults with a disability by race and ethnicity were:

- Hispanic, 55.2%

- American Indian or Alaska Native, 50.5%

TABLE 12.5   Self-Reported Health Status Among U.S. Adults With and Without Disabilities, 2004–2006

Self-Report Health Status	With Disability	Without Disability
Excellent/very good	27.2%	60.2%
Good	32.5%	29.9%
Fair/poor	40.3%	9.9%

Source: Centers for Disease Control and Prevention (2014b).

- Non-Hispanic black or African American, 46.6%
- Non-Hispanic white, 36.9%
- Native Hawaiian or Other Pacific Islander, 36.5%
- Asian, 24.9% (CDC, 2014b).

Smoking, lack of physical activity, lack of access to medical care due to cost, poor oral health, infrequent mammograms, and obesity all disproportionally affect people with disabilities (CDC, 2014b). For example, in 2011 adults (ages 18 years and older) with disabilities were more likely to smoke (25.5%) than adults without disabilities (18.2%). This finding was observed in all states. In that same year, adults (ages 18 years and older) with disabilities were more likely to be obese (38.1%) than adults without disabilities (23.9%). This finding also was observed in all states (Institute on Disability, 2012).

Considerations for Health Promotion and Program Planning for People With Disabilities

When working with people with disabilities, focus on their abilities, not on disabilities. Remember a person is a person first, with a disability second. For example, whenever possible, try to use "people first" language, such as "people who are blind" rather than "blind people" or "the blind." When communicating with an individual with a disability, speak directly to the person with the disability rather than to his or her companion or interpreter. If you would like to offer assistance to a person with a disability, always ask first, wait until the offer is accepted, then listen patiently and follow instructions. If the person declines your help, respect his or her decision and do not proceed to assist. If the person uses a service animal, do not pet or distract the animal. Consider these tips for working with people who are deaf or hearing impaired, for people who are blind or have a visual impairment, and for people who have a mobile impairment.

Deaf or Hearing Impaired
Making eye contact

- Essential for effective communication
- Important because people who are deaf read the nuances of facial expressions and body language for additional information

Attention getting

- Hand waving is most common
- Tapping the shoulder or arm is acceptable
- Flickering lights on and off is also common
- Using a third person to relay attention in a crowded room

Meeting others within the Deaf community

- Greetings often include hugs instead of handshakes
- Conversations tend to include elaboration about lives and daily occurrences
- Conversations tend to be open and direct
- There is an interest in other people and connection with the Deaf community (Minnesota Department of Human Services, 2013).

Blind or Visually Impaired

- On an organization level, many changes can be made to assist a blind or visually impaired person such as using Braille labels or using software to enlarge the print on computer screens.
- Do not feel overly conscious or obsess about being politically correct when talking to someone who is blind.
- People who are blind are generally not offended by words like "see," "look," and "watch" in everyday conversation.
- There is no need to avoid using the words "blind" or "visually impaired." Don't tip-toe around it.
- It is acceptable to use descriptive language, such as making reference to colors, patterns, designs, and shapes.
- Do not speak in a loud voice or talk down to a person who is blind.
- Avoid pointing to objects or people; instead, verbalize by saying, "It's on your left."
- Identify yourself when someone who is blind or visually impaired enters a room or when you are approaching the person. For example, say, "Hi, Sam. It's Ann."
- If you are in a group, try to address a person who is visually impaired by name so that he or she knows who you are talking to.
- Introduce a blind person to other people in the room, such as in a meeting or at a lunch table. When leaving a room, it is courteous to let a blind person know that you are leaving (Shuval, Gabriel, & Leonard, 2015).

Mobility Impairments

- Consider a person's wheelchair or walker as an extension of his or her body. Leaning on the wheelchair or walker, or placing your foot on a wheel, is not acceptable.

- Speak to a person who uses a wheelchair, walker, cane, or crutches in a normal voice strength and tone.

- Talk to a person who uses a wheelchair at eye level whenever possible. Perhaps you can sit rather than stand.

- Feel free to use phrases such as "walk this way" with a person who cannot walk. Expressions such as this are commonly used by wheelchair users (University of Washington, 2015).

Introduction to the Culture of Commerce

One aspect of all people of all cultures in the United States is adapting to the fundamental cultural contribution of Europeans. They brought the modern, free enterprise, marketplace economic model to America, and everyone interacts with this fundamental feature of the country. In fact the U.S. Constitution was drawn up after 10 years of experience with the Articles of Confederation, in part to facilitate the free flow of goods and services across state lines. This has been met with any number of responses by various cultures as part of the acculturation process when "fitting in" to American society in general.

Some free enterprise activities that emerged from commerce have improved the health of all peoples. For instance, drug manufacturing, physical fitness gymnasiums, vitamin companies, hospitals, and health insurance companies have all flourished under the free enterprise system. In addition, the development and sale of cell phones and computers that enable improved communication with health providers instantly though email, texting, and telemedicine have greatly improved the delivery of health care for everyone. On the other hand, commerce has led to tremendous negative health consequences as well. In this section, we look at its impact on three nonethnic groups affected by the culture of commerce: consumers, hired farmworkers, and recent immigrants.

Consumers

Commerce is based on engaging people who buy goods and services—consumers—with opportunities and enticements to purchase necessities and a great number of optional or even unnecessary products and services. Marketing and peer pressure in a consumer-oriented society can compel people to remain engaged in an unceasing stressful struggle to make money. This can have negative effects on the mental and physical health of consumers. Examples of the impact of commerce on consumer health are a sedentary lifestyle, high stress levels, eating an unbalanced diet, not getting enough rest, overconsumption of stimulants such as caffeine, fewer relationships with individuals and less of a community connection, and depression. Yet there is little correlation between increased income and increased happiness across society. Since World War II, per capita income in the United States has tripled, but levels of life satisfaction remain about the same. Studies also indicate that many members of capitalist societies feel unsatisfied, if not outright deprived, however much they earn and consume because others make and spend even more (Etzioni, 2012).

Some negative consequences from consumers responding positively to commercial enticements generate additional encouragement of unhealthy activities and products. For instance, negative impacts come in the form of tobacco use and lung cancer, coal mining and black lung disease, automobile smog and emphysema, and supersized fast food and obesity. The fast food industry has capitalized on the fast-paced environment, and rates of obesity, diabetes, and other health problems are on the rise. The fast food industry spends a large amount of money on advertising, leading to an annual exposure to consumers of thousands of commercials for junk food and fast food. In addition, TV time means lost play time. Medical research confirms that the more television children watch, the more likely they are to be overweight (Shuval et al., 2013). Childhood obesity is worse in some minority communities. Part of the reason is that African American children watch more television on average than do other children (Shuval et al., 2013).

Although cigarette ads have been taken off television, ads directed at potential consumers (direct-to-consumers) for prescription drugs have increased dramatically. The United States and New Zealand are the only two developed countries that allow direct-to-consumer advertisements on television and radio, on billboards, and in magazines and newspapers. The average American television viewer can expect to spend as much as 16 hours per year watching such ads (Frosch, Krueger, Hornik, Cronholm, & Barg, 2007). Expansion into broadcast direct-to-consumer advertisements climbed due to a change in federal regulations in the late 1990s. The new regulations require broadcast ads to include only "major statements" of the risks and benefits of the drug along with directions to alternate information sources for full disclosure. Direct-to-consumer advertisements spending subsequently increased from $150 million in 1993 to $4.24 billion in 2005 (Dave, 2010). In addition to potential misuse, the costs of direct-to-consumer advertisements increased drug prices and the use of more expensive drugs in place of equally effective lower-priced drugs. Higher drug and health care expenditures in general tend to raise insurance premiums (Dave, 2010).

The impact of the pursuit of profit has not been uniform across U.S. cultural groups, but it has affected everyone from all cultures. In the next section, we describe how the culture of farmworkers has been affected by the culture of commerce, and its impact on farmworkers' health.

What Do You Think?

In some geographic regions, a higher sales tax is imposed on certain unhealthy products, such as tobacco, soda, and alcohol. Do you think that is ethical? What products, if any, should have a higher sales tax and why? Does a higher sales tax infringe on people's personal choices? Should some items, such as alcohol, be made illegal? What role does the culture of commerce have on these laws and policies?

Farmworkers

Farmworkers in the United States are the backbone of the farming community and agribusiness. These workers and their families live a life driven by personal economic need, and a major commercial sector benefits from their lifestyle. Many farmworkers travel from one location to another, following changing locations of agricultural work opportunities.

Farmworkers in the United States

It is difficult to track trends in this population because accurate statistics are difficult to find due to the fact that "52 out of every 100 of all farmworkers do not have authorization or any legal status in the U.S." (Gonzalez, 2008). Because many workers and their families are unauthorized, they are reluctant to provide any demographic information about themselves or their community due to the risk of deportation.

In 2006, an average 1.01 million hired farmworkers made up a third of the estimated 3 million people employed in agriculture. The remainder included self-employed farmers and their unpaid family members (Kandal, 2008). Half of the paid farmworkers were in California, Florida, Texas, Washington, Oregon, and North Carolina. These farmworkers are disadvantaged in the labor market, and on average hired farmworkers are younger, less educated, likely to be foreign-born, less likely to speak English, and less likely to be U.S. citizens or to have a legally authorized work permit (Kandal, 2008).

History of Hired Farmworkers in America

Mexican workers are the largest population of hired farmworkers in U.S. agriculture. Farmworkers are also from other countries, including Guatemala, Honduras, Puerto Rico, Dominican Republic, Southeast Asia, Philippines, Jamaica, Haiti, and other Caribbean islands. Farmworkers are predominantly Hispanic, and 7 out of 10 farmworkers are foreign born. Of the foreign-born workers, 94% are from Mexico (U.S. Department of Labor, Employment and Training Administration, 2009). Prior to the Mexican workers' emergence, Chinese workers filled the labor pool. Nearly 200,000 Chinese were legally contracted to cultivate California fields until the Chinese Exclusion Act. Thereafter, Japanese workers replaced the Chinese field hands (PBS, 1999).

Mexican immigration began during the 1850s to geographic regions like California that were still considered to be part of Mexico. In the 1920s, the Mexican government addressed complaints of abuse with the United States by securing contracts with the United States to try to trace immigration and provide some type of labor protection to their citizens who traveled to the United States for work. The first was the de facto Bracero Program, which allowed workers to bring their families. During World War II, the United States signed another Bracero treaty to legalize immigration for Mexican workers to fill the labor gaps left by soldiers who were participating in the war. Under this program, approximately 4 million Mexican farmworkers came to support the agriculture industry between 1942 and 1964 (PBS, 1999).

More recently, the United States has entered into trade agreements that directly affect farmworkers, including the General Agreement on Tariffs and Trade (GATT) and the North American Free Trade Agreement (NAFTA). The Immigration Reform and Control Act also has played a role in the legalization and fluctuation of farmworkers and their services.

In 2008 almost 75% of farmworkers earned less than $10,000 per year, and 3 out of 5 farmworker families lived in poverty. Few farmworkers had assets of any import, and about one third owned, or were buying, a house or trailer in the United States (U.S. Department of Labor, Employment and Training Administration, 2009). Given their low incomes, many households qualify for social services and housing assistance. However, many migrant workers do not apply for those services for fear of deportation.

According to the National Agricultural Workers Survey (NAWS), migrant farmworkers are poorly educated. More than one third are school dropouts, and of those who attend school, 17% are at a grade level lower than their same-age peers (U.S. Department of Labor, Employment and Training Administration, 2009). The most recent data show that the approximate median level of education for the population is sixth grade, and there is only a 50.7% high school graduation rate among migrant teenagers (U.S. Department of Labor, Employment and Training Administration, 2009).

Behavioral Risk Factors and Common Health Problems Among Farmworkers

Many factors affect farmworkers' health. They tend to be geographically isolated and constantly move from place to place, which makes access to care difficult. In addition, a lack of health education contributes to poor knowledge of good health practices.

Health standards for farmworkers are similar to that of third-world countries, even though they work in the United States. Unsanitary working and housing conditions place farmworkers at risk for many health problems. Most farmworkers cannot afford to take time off from work and also risk losing their jobs to attend doctor appointments (National Center for Farmworker Health, Inc. [NCFH], 2002).

Farmworkers are exposed to many different types of diseases and injuries related to the sun, chemicals and machinery they use, including musculoskeletal injuries, respiratory illness, tuberculosis, HIV, and others. Musculoskeletal injuries are very common in farmworkers. The labor done by farmworkers consists of heavy lifting and constant, quick movements of certain body parts, such as the wrists. Workers are also encouraged to work at a quicker pace to finish early (NCFH, 2002).

Respiratory illnesses, including asthma, occur due to exposure to pesticides, dust, pollen, and molds. Exposure to these pollutants for long periods of time can have long-term effects on the workers (NCFH, 2002).

Tuberculosis is common among migrant farmworkers due to the prevalence of tuberculosis in their home countries. The disease is transmitted to workers in the United States and spreads amongst the population (NCFH, 2002).

AIDS is prevalent in migrant populations and is associated with increased rates of sexually transmitted diseases and prostitution in labor camps. Wives of the men who travel to the United States for work are at risk for infection transmitted by their husbands (NCFH, 2002).

Considerations for Health Promotion and Program Planning for Migrant Farmworkers

Guidelines for working with farmworkers include the following:

- Recognize the concern farmworkers have regarding immigration issues and the possibility of deportation.
- Ensure that appropriate translations services are available.
- Remember to include family members in decision making.
- Determine a person's living situation before planning.
- Understand that fear and mistrust exist.

The motivation for economic improvement and participation in the United States economy continues today among other groups of immigrants as well. The attraction has been so compelling that the government has established limits on how many people can immigrate every year. The overall annual limit in 2015 was 675, 000 for regular immigrants, 70,000 for refugees, and no limit for asylees (American Immigration Council, 2015). We look at the lives of these new immigrants and refugees next.

Introduction to People Who Are Recent Immigrants or Refugees

Most Americans have descended from immigrants or refugees. Many noncitizen immigrants residing in the United States have lived here for decades and have adapted to life, either through acculturation or by maintaining their own cultures. However, recent immigrants and refugees confront the reality of living in another culture as new arrivals to the United States.

Terminology

A **refugee** is a person who has fled his or her country because of fear of persecution. Under U.S. immigration law, a refugee is a person who has been or has a well-founded fear of being persecuted for reasons of race, religion, nationality, membership in a particular social group, or political opinion, and who is unable to avail him- or herself of the protection of that country. This definition focuses on persecution as the defining characteristic and excludes people who have been displaced because of civil war, ethnic strife, natural disaster, or economic reasons.

An **asylee** is a person who has shown that he or she meets the definition for refugee—meaning he or she has a well-founded fear of persecution based on one of the five enumerated grounds—and has been provided asylum. Asylum status and refugee status are closely related. Their major difference lies in where a person applies for asylum or refugee status. Applicants requesting refugee status do so outside the United States, whereas those seeking asylum status request it from within the United States. However, all people who are granted asylum must meet the definition of a refugee. Both refugees and asylees have the right to live and work indefinitely in the United States and to apply for lawful permanent residence after one year. In addition, both refugees and asylees are eligible for certain assistance from the Department of Health and Human Services Office of Refugee Resettlement. This assistance includes benefits such as cash and medical assistance, employment preparation and job placement, skills training, English language training, legal services, social adjustment, and aid for victims of torture.

The top 10 countries of refugee origin entering the US in 2014 were Iraq, Burma, Somalia, Democratic Republic of the Congo, Cuba, Iran, Eritrea, Sudan, Afghanistan (Zong, 2015). The overall number of refugees allowed into the United States in 2014 was 70,000 (American Immigration Council, 2015).

An **immigrant** is a person who migrates to another country, usually for permanent residence. Under this definition, an immigrant is an alien admitted to the United States as a lawful permanent resident. The emphasis in this definition is on the presumptions that (1) the immigrant followed U.S. laws and procedures in establishing residence in our country; (2) he or she wishes to reside here permanently; and (3) he or she swears allegiance to our country or at least solemnly affirms that he or she will observe and respect our laws and our constitution.

By contrast, an **alien** is generally understood to be a foreigner—a person who comes from a foreign country—who does not owe allegiance to our country. An **illegal alien** is a foreigner who (1) does not owe allegiance to our country and (2) who has violated our laws and customs in establishing residence in our country. He or she is therefore a criminal under applicable U.S. laws. The term "undocumented immigrant" is an oxymoron (the parts conflict). An immigrant is synonymous with a "permanent legal resident." Proper terms for the undocumented are "illegal alien" or "undocumented alien, unauthorized worker."

Behavioral Risk Factors and Common Health Problems Among People Who Are Immigrants or Refugees

Many health conditions may affect the health of refugees; therefore, CDC provides guidelines for health care providers who may see refugees at any point during the resettlement process. These guidelines aim to:

- Promote and improve the health of the refugee
- Prevent disease
- Familiarize refugees with the U.S. health care system

Because of the vast diversity of immigrants and refugees and the varied ways in which they enter the United States, a national snapshot of their health status is not available.

Did You Know?

The United Nations Health Refugee Agency collects health information in refugee camps and reports this information in their health information system. Services include pediatrics and integrated management of childhood illness, reproductive health, psychiatric consultation, emergency medical services and referrals, basic laboratory services, tuberculosis management, voluntary testing and counseling for human immunodeficiency virus/acquired immune deficiency syndrome (HIV/AIDS) with referral services for antiretroviral treatment, and nutrition promotion.

The Bhutanese refugee population, originally ethnic minorities expelled from southern Nepal, have several health issues including anemia, vitamin B_{12} deficiency, and mental health issues. Most Bhutanese refugee women have never had a mammogram or a Pap smear. They may not feel comfortable discussing sexuality and gynecological issues with nonfamily members, especially male clinicians. Sexual assault, rape, trafficking, polygamy, domestic violence, and child marriage have all been reported in the camps. Domestic violence is probably the most pervasive form of gender-based violence suffered by Bhutanese refugees (CDC, 2014a).

Considerations for Health Promotion and Program Planning for People Who Are Immigrants or Refugees

Considerations for health promotion for newly arrived immigrants and refugees follows the same pattern as for people from different cultures. A foundation of cultural awareness must be developed to understand the means of communication, values, attitudes, and cultural practices. Cultural awareness and competence are not only useful for delivering health care services but will likely also be appreciated and facilitate the delivery of care or acceptance of prevention measures.

The diversity of nationalities, ethnic groups, religions, and other dimensions is apparent in many refugee settings. Urban refugee populations often consist of people from numerous national, ethnic, and religious backgrounds. In these situations, target audience segmentation is challenging. One approach is to develop simple messages in languages that are most common in that setting. Visual communication materials, such as pamphlets and brochures, featuring neutral images that are not specific to any particular groups are preferred. In some settings, neutral cartoon characters have been well received. It is important to ensure representation of all groups in formative assessment, pretesting of materials, and in interpersonal communication channels. During pretesting, the target group's responses to draft communication materials should be sought and materials revised to ensure comprehension and acceptability, and to promote effectiveness.

Differences between displaced and host communities also significantly affect access to effective communication. Similarly, refugees and internally displaced people often come from areas of long-standing conflict with interruptions in schooling resulting in low levels of basic education and literacy (Burton & John-Leader, 2009).

Summary

In this chapter we have discussed the barriers to care and challenges encountered by cultures not defined by race or ethnicity in achieving good health and their interactions with health care services. Some cultures, such as LGBT, are less likely to seek care because of fear of discrimination, and they tend to have higher incidences of diseases as a result. Farmworkers account for approximately 3 to 5 million people in the United States. They are mostly Hispanic people who work in almost every state. Poverty, unsettlement, legal issues, low education level, and harsh working conditions are their main challenges. They are at major risk for skin diseases and exposure to the sun and pesticides. AIDS is common among farmworkers due to lack of education, an increase in sexually transmitted diseases, and prostitution.

People face a wide variety of disabilities. People with disabilities have health challenges related to access to medical care and preventive services, oral health, high rates of smoking, and obesity.

Immigrants and refugees may have low literacy skills and have an array of physical and mental health issues. Refugees, in particular, are displaced peoples, and they may be unfamiliar with U.S. culture and face fear, depression, and other mental health issues, as well as physical problems such poor nutritional status.

All people from every culture in the United States confront, in various degrees, the influence of commerce and are consumers who are enticed to make purchases, often without reference to their ethnic culture. Consumers are all subjected to enticements to buy unhealthy products (cigarettes), consume larger portions of food (supersizing), and live and travel in response to economic opportunities whether health resources are available or not. It is the culture of commerce that drew most people of other cultures to the United States, and it is one of the most common cultures to affect all other cultures in the country.

Review

1. Describe three roadblocks to accessing health care that are encountered by the LGBT community and farmworkers.

2. Prepare three cultural competence recommendations for a clinic that provides services to farmworkers.

3. Outline what areas should be covered in a staff training session to address the needs of LGBT clients.

4. Describe how discrimination toward farmworkers and LGBT people affects their health and health care.

5. Describe some types of disabilities and cultural considerations to be considered when providing health services.

6. Define immigrant, asylee, alien, and refugee.

7. Explain how commerce affects health.

Activities

1. Select a nonethic subculture such as athletes, veterans, rural residents, or prison inmates, and write a paper about the group. Discuss topics such as their demographics, culture, health issues, practices, and beliefs.

2. Watch the video titled *Super Size Me* (http://www.snagfilms.com/films/title /super_size_me) and write a brief summary of your thoughts on how commerce affects diet.

3. Watch the video titled *Affluenza* (http://www.filmsforaction.org/watch /affluenza_1997/) and write a brief summary of how commerce affects people's sense of well-being and stress.

Case Study

A specific example of the culture of commerce is television advertising for prescription drugs targeted at the general population. Television viewers represent members of all cultures (except perhaps the Amish). Viewers cannot buy any of these products without a prescription from their doctor. These drug ads are regulated by the Federal Trade Commission and not the Food and Drug Administration (FDA, 2012). The FDA Division of Drug Marketing, Advertising and Communication(DMAC) is responsible for regulating direct-to-consumer ads. Drug companies are required to submit copies of their ads at the same time that they are disseminated, but no preclearance is yet required. If a direct-to-consumer ad is found to be in violation of FDA regulations, the FDA can issue warning letters for serious violations, which may lead to regulatory action by the FDA. However, if a company refuses to comply, the FDA cannot impose

fines, except through administrative hearings. The United States is only one of two countries that allows direct-to-consumer ads (U.S. House of Representatives, 2008).

In a physician survey, the FDA found that 8% of physicians felt very pressured and 20% felt somewhat pressured to prescribe the specific brand name drug when the patient asked the physician to do so. Most physicians suggested alternative courses of action (Woodcock, 2003).

Direct-to-consumer television advertising fell 11.5% to $3.47 billion in 2012. Even so, Nielsen, the television monitoring organization, estimates that an average of 80 drug ads air every hour of every day on American television (Palmer, 2013).

Most ads (82%) made some factual claims and made rational arguments (86%) for product use, but few described condition causes (26%), risk factors (26%), or prevalence (25%). Emotional appeals were almost universal (95%). No ads mentioned lifestyle change as an alternative to products, though some (19%) portrayed it as an adjunct to medication. Some ads (18%) portrayed lifestyle changes as insufficient for controlling a condition. The ads often framed medication use in terms of losing (58%) and regaining control (85%) over some aspect of life and as engendering social approval (78%). Products were frequently (58%) portrayed as a medical breakthrough. Despite claims that ads have educational value, the study found ads provide little information about the causes of a disease or who may be at risk. Ads illustrate characters who have lost control over their social, emotional, or physical lives without the medication; and they minimize the value of health promotion through lifestyle changes (Frosch et al., 2007).

References

American Immigration Council. (2015). *Refugees: A fact sheet*. Retrieved from http://immigrationpolicy.org/just-facts/refugees-fact-sheet

Black Hawk College. (2014, October 2). *Types of disabilities*. Retrieved from http://www.bhc.edu/student-resources/disability/types-of-disabilities/

Brown, S. E. (2002). What is disability culture? *Disability Studies Quarterly. 22*(2), 34–50.

Burton, A., & John-Leader, F. (2009). Are we reaching refugees and internally displaced persons? *Perspectives, United Nations High Council on Refugee Status, Bull World Health Organ, 87*, 638–639. Retrieved from http://www.unhcr.org/4b4dc15f9.html

Centers for Disease Control and Prevention. (n.d.). *Healthy people 2020*. Retrieved from http://www.healthypeople.gov/2020/topicsobjectives2020/overview.aspx?topicid=25

Centers for Disease Control and Prevention. (2012, March 27). *Immigrant and refugee health*. Retrieved from http://www.cdc.gov/immigrantrefugeehealth/about-refugees.html

Centers for Disease Control and Prevention. (2013a, March 22). *Gay and bisexual men's health*. Retrieved from http://www.cdc.gov/msmhealth/substance-abuse.htm

Centers for Disease Control and Prevention. (2013b). *HIV surveillance report: Diagnoses of HIV infection and AIDS in the United States and dependent areas* (Vol. 25). Retrieved from http://www.cdc.gov/hiv/statistics/basics/

Centers for Disease Control and Prevention. (2014a). *Bhutanese, refugee health profiles*. Retrieved from http://www.cdc.gov/immigrantrefugeehealth/profiles/bhutanese/index.html

Centers for Disease Control and Prevention. (2014b, April 2). *Disability & health*. Retrieved from http://www.cdc.gov/ncbddd/disabilityandhealth/data.html

Conron, K. J., Scott, G., Stowell, G. S., & Landers, S. (2012). Transgender health in Massachusetts: Results from a household probability sample of adults. *American Journal of Public Health, 102*(1), 118–122. Retrieved from http://www.ncbi.nlm.nih.gov/pmc/articles/PMC3490554/

Dave, D. (2010, June 3). *Direct-to-consumer advertising in pharmaceutical markets: Effects on demand and prices*. Retrieved from http://www.voxeu.org/article/consumer-adverts-pharmaceuticals-impact-prices-and-sales

Dean, L., Meyer, I. H., Robinson, K., Sell, R. L., Sember, R., Silenzio, V. M. B., et al. (2000). Lesbian, gay, bisexual and transgender health: Findings and concerns. *Journal of the Gay and Lesbian Medical Association, 4*(3).

Retrieved from http://glma.org/document/docWindow.cfm?fuseaction=document.viewDocument&documentid=17&documentFormatID=26

Etzioni, A. (2012, September 4). *The crisis of American consumerism.* Retrieved from http://www.huffingtonpost.com/amitai-etzioni/the-crisis-of-american-co_b_1855390.html

Food and Drug Administration. (2012). *Prescription drug advertising: Questions and answers. Information for consumers (drugs).* Retrieved from http://www.FDA.gov/Drugs/ResourcesForYou/Consumers/PrescriptionDrugAdvertising/UCM076768.htm#control_advertisements

Frosch, D. L., Krueger, P.M., Hornik, R.C., Cronholm, P. F., & Barg, F. K. (2007). Creating demand for prescription drugs: A content analysis of television direct-to-consumer advertising. *Annals of Family Medicine,* 5(1), 6–13. Retrieved from http://www.annfammed.org/content/5/1/6.full

Gates, G. (2011). *How many people are lesbian, gay, bisexual and transgender?* Retrieved from http://williamsinstitute.law.ucla.edu/research/census-lgbt-demographics-studies/how-many-people-are-lesbian-gay-bisexual-and-transgender/#sthash.tP57Wgyv.dpuf

Gonzalez, E., Jr. (2008, May 27). *Migrant farmworkers: Our nation's invisible population.* Retrieved from http://www.extension.org/pages/Migrant_Farm_Workers:_Our_Nation's_Invisible_Population

Hoctel P. D. (2002, January-February). Community Assessments Show Service Gaps for LGBT Elders, Aging Today, 5–6. Cited by https://www.lgbtfunders.org/files/AgingInEquity.pdf

HRC, GLMA release inaugural healthcare equality index. (2007, October 7). *The Advocate.* Retrieved from http://www.advocate.com/health/health-news/2007/10/02/hrc-glma-release-inaugural-healthcare-equality-index

Institute on Disability. (2012). *Annual disability statistics compendium.* Retrieved from http://www.disabilitycompendium.org/archives/2012-compendium-statistics/2012-health

Kandal, W. (2008). *A profile of hired farmworkers: A 2008 update.* (Economic Research Report No. 60). Retrieved from http://www.ers.usda.gov/media/205619/err60_1_.pdf

Minnesota Department of Human Services. (2013, February 11). *Deaf culture.* Retrieved from http://www.dhs.state.mn.us/main/idcplg?IdcService=GET_DYNAMIC_CONVERSION&RevisionSelectionMethod=LatestReleased&dDocName=id_004566

National Center for Farmworker Health Inc. (2002). *Factsheets about farmworkers.* Retrieved from http://www.ncfh.org/?pid=5

Palmer, E. (2013). *Top 10 DTC pharma advertisers.* Retrieved from http://www.fiercepharma.com/special-reports/top-10-dtc-pharma-advertisers-h1-2013

PBS. (1999). *Mexican immigrant labor history.* Retrieved from http://www.pbs.org/kpbs/theborder/history/timeline/17.html

Shuval, K., Gabriel, K.P., & Leonard, T. (2013, May 15). *How to communicate with someone who is blind.* Retrieved from http://chicagolighthouse.org/programs-and-services/working-someone-who-blind-or-visually-impaired/how-communicate-someone-who-bli

Siple, L., Greer, L., & Holcolm, B. R. (2003). Deaf culture. *PEPNet Tipsheet.* Retrieved from http://www.pepnet.org/sites/default/files/71PEPNet%20Tipsheet%20Deaf%20Culture.pdf

University of Washington. (2015). *Strategies for working with people who have disabilities.* Retrieved from http://www.washington.edu/doit/strategies-working-people-who-have-disabilities

U.S. Department of Labor, Employment and Training Administration. (2009). *The national agricultural workers survey*. Retrieved from www.doleta.gov/agworker/report/ch1.cfm

U.S. House of Representatives. (2008). *Direct-to-consumer advertising: Marketing, education, or deception?* Subcommittee on Oversight and Investigations of the Committee on Energy and Commerce, House of Representatives, One Hundred Tenth Congress, Second Session. Retrieved from https://House.Resource.Org/110/Org.C-Span.205243-1.Raw.Txt

Walker, K. (2013). *Ending the commercial sexual exploitation of children: A call for multi-system collaboration in California*. California Child Welfare Council. Retrieved from http://www.youthlaw.org/fileadmin/ncyl/youthlaw/publications/Ending-CSEC-A-Call-for-Multi-System_Collaboration-in-CA.pdf

Woodcock, J. (2003, July 22). *Regulating prescription drug promotion*. Retrieved from http://www.fda.gov/NewsEvents/Testimony/ucm115080.htm

Yanik, E. L. et al. (1215). *High cancer risk among the HIV-infected elderly in the United States*. Conference on Retroviruses and Opportunistic Infections (CROI), Seattle, abstract 725. Retrieved from http://www.aidsmap.com/Study-finds-high-rates-of-cancer-among-older-people-living-with-HIV/page/2950216/

Zong, J. Batalova, J, Refugees and Asylees in the United States. (2015). Migration Information Source, Migration Policy Institute, October 28, 2015. Retrieved from http://www.migrationpolicy.org/article/refugees-and-asylees-united-states#Refugee Countries of Origin

UNIT III

Looking Ahead

CHAPTER 13

Closing the Gap: Strategies for Eliminating Health Disparities

It is time to refocus, reinforce, and repeat the message that health disparities exist and that health equity benefits everyone.
 —Kathleen G. Sebelius, Secretary, Health & Human Services
 (HHS Action Plan to Reduce Racial and Ethnic Health Disparities, n.d.)

The future health of the nation will be determined to a large extent by how effectively we work with communities to reduce and eliminate health disparities between non-minority and minority populations experiencing disproportionate burdens of disease, disability, and premature death.
 —Guiding Principle for Improving Minority Health
 (Office of Minority Health & Health Disparities, 2007)

Key Concepts

Best practices	Cultural competence
Telehealth	

Learning Objectives

After reading this chapter, you should be able to:

1. Describe at least six strategies for reducing or eliminating health disparities.
2. Explain the role of the Affordable Care Act is reducing inequalities.

Health disparities in the United States are extensive, as has been demonstrated by the differences in the incidence and consequences of diseases and mortality rates for various populations. The causes of health disparities are complex, systemic, personal, integrated, and multifactorial, and there are no easy and immediate solutions to reduce or eliminate them. The complexity of the problem should not deter our efforts to work on reducing, and eventually eliminating, these differences in health because these disparities have a negative impact on the people of our nation. The changing demographics anticipated over the next decade will amplify these problems; hence, the importance of addressing disparities in health today. Groups currently experiencing poorer health status are expected to grow as a proportion of the U.S. population, and the future health of the United States as a whole will be influenced substantially by our success in improving the health of these groups. A national focus on disparities in health status is particularly important as major changes unfold in the way health care is delivered and financed (Office of Minority Health & Health Disparities, 2007).

The government has highlighted the need to reduce health disparities, and this focus is reflected in the *Healthy People 2020* objectives (U.S. Department of Health and Human Services, 2015). *Healthy People 2020* is designed to achieve four overarching goals:

1. Attain high-quality, longer lives free of preventable disease, disability, injury, and premature death.
2. Achieve health equity, eliminate disparities, and improve the health of all groups.
3. Create social and physical environments that promote good health for all.
4. Promote quality of life, healthy development, and healthy behaviors across all life stages.

In April 2011, the U.S. Department of Health and Human Services (DHHS) announced a nationwide plan to reduce health disparities. The plan is described in the *National Stakeholder Strategy for Achieving Health Equity,* which is a common set of goals and objectives for public and private sector initiatives and partnerships to help racial and ethnic minorities and other underserved groups reach their full health potential. The strategy incorporates ideas, suggestions, and comments from thousands of individuals and organizations across the country. The five goals outlined in the document are:

Goal 1: Awareness: Increasing awareness of the significance of health disparities, their impact on the nation, and the actions necessary to improve health outcomes for racial, ethnic, and underserved populations.

Goal 2: Leadership: Strengthen and broaden leadership for addressing health disparities at all levels.

Goal 3: Health system and life experience: Improve health and healthcare outcomes for racial, ethnic, and underserved populations.

Goal 4: Cultural and linguistic competency: Improve cultural and linguistic competency and the diversity of the health-related workforce.

Goal 5: Data, research, and evaluation: Improve data availability, coordination, utilization, and diffusion of research and evaluation outcomes (National Partnership for Action to End Health Disparities, 2011, p. 108).

The 42 topic areas are listed in **Box 13.1**.

BOX 13.1   Healthy People 2020 Topic Areas

1. Access to Health Services
2. Adolescent Health
3. Arthritis, Osteoporosis, and Chronic Back
4. Blood Disorders and Blood Safety
5. Cancer
6. Chronic Kidney Disease
7. Dementias, Including Alzheimer's Disease
8. Diabetes
9. Disability and Health
10. Early and Middle Childhood
11. Educational and Community-Based Programs
12. Environmental Health
13. Family Planning
14. Food Safety
15. Genomics
16. Global Health
17. Healthcare-Associated Infections
18. Health Communication and Health Information Technology
19. Health-Related Quality of Life and Well-Being
20. Hearing and Other Sensory or Communication Disorders
21. Heart Disease and Stroke
22. HIV
23. Immunization and Infectious Disease
24. Injury and Violence Prevention
25. Lesbian, Gay, Bisexual, and Transgender Health
26. Maternal, Infant, and Child Health
27. Medical Product Safety
28. Mental Health and Mental Disorders
29. Nutrition and Weight Status
30. Occupational Health
31. Older Adults
32. Oral Health
33. Physical Activity
34. Preparedness
35. Public Health Infrastructure
36. Respiratory Diseases
37. Sexually Transmitted Diseases
38. Sleep Health
39. Social Determinants of Health
40. Substance Abuse
41. Tobacco Use
42. Vision

Source: CDC. (2011, May 11). *Healthy People 2020*. Retrieved from http://www.cdc.gov/nchs/healthy_people/hp2020/hp2020 _topic_areas.htm

---

In November 2010 the DHHS was charged with developing a department-wide action plan for reducing racial and ethnic health disparities. The outcome was the document titled *HHS Action Plan to Reduce Racial and Ethnic Health Disparities* (n.d.). The action plan includes transforming health care and expanding access, building on the provisions of the Affordable Care Act related to expanded insurance coverage and increased access to care. The plan also calls for more opportunities to increase the number of students from populations underrepresented in the health professions, train more people in medical interpretation to help serve patients with a limited command of English, and train community workers to help people navigate the system.

Within the framework of the *HHS Action Plan*, the five overall goals for reducing disparities and associated action steps include:

1. Transform Health Care: Action steps include expanding insurance coverage, increasing access to care through development of new service delivery sites, and introducing quality initiatives such as increased utilization of medical homes.

2. Strengthen the Nation's Health and Human Services Workforce: Action steps include a new pipeline program for recruiting undergraduates from underserved communities for public health and biomedical sciences careers, expanding and improving health care interpreting and translation, and supporting more training of community health workers, such as promotoras.

3. Advance the Health, Safety, and Well-Being of the American People: Action steps include implementing the CDC's new Community Transformation Grants, and additional targeted efforts to achieve improvements in cardiovascular disease, childhood obesity, tobacco-related diseases, maternal and child health, flu, and asthma.

4. Advance Scientific Knowledge and Innovation: Action steps include implementing a new health data collection and analysis strategy authorized by the Affordable Care Act, and increasing patient-centered outcomes research.

5. Increase the Efficiency, Transparency, and Accountability of HHS Programs: Actions steps include ensuring that assessments of policies and programs on health disparities will become part of all HHS decision making. Evaluations will measure progress toward reducing health disparities (U.S. Department of Health and Human Services, n.d.).

Both plans call for federal agencies and their partners to work together on social, economic, and environmental factors that contribute to health disparities. Many other federal agencies and states have developed strategic plans to eliminate health disparities. These plans can be useful to organizations when they are developing their own objectives and interventions.

Eliminating health disparities will require enhanced efforts and changes in research, improving the environments of people who are affected by health disparities, increasing access to health care, improving the quality of care, and making policy and legal changes. These five areas are the spokes of the overarching goal of this chapter, which is to provide information about strategies for reducing health disparities.

What Do You Think?

What is your opinion of these national priorities to reduce health disparities? Are there any you would add or remove? Do you think any of the goals are a higher priority than the others? What steps would you take to achieve these national goals?

Strategies for Reducing or Eliminating Health Disparities

A variety of approaches are needed to reduce health disparities. This task requires a systematic, coordinated, and collaborative effort to effectively implement the strategies. The methods necessitate implementation at different ecological levels with community, local, state, and national organizations and politicians at the helm.

Cultural Competence

Implementing change does not mean imposing a uniform solution. Cultural variation and a variety of approaches to achieving good health should be fostered and encouraged to ensure optimal results. Fundamental to this approach is proceeding on a course involving cultural competent understanding. There is no universally accepted definition of cultural competence in health care. In general, **cultural competence** is a set of congruent behaviors, attitudes, structures, and policies that come together to work effectively in intercultural situations (National CASA Association, 1995–1996). That set of behaviors can be adopted and practiced by a solitary professional or an entire organization. Cultural competence requires a set of skills by individuals and systems that allows an increased understanding and appreciation of cultural differences as well as the demonstrated skills necessary to work with and serve diverse individuals and groups.

According to the National CASA Association (1995–1996), the culturally competent organization:

- values diversity,
- conducts cultural self-assessments,
- is conscious of and manages the dynamics of difference,
- institutionalizes cultural knowledge, and
- adapts services to fit the cultural diversity of the community served.

Did You Know?

The National Center for Cultural Competence at Georgetown University (http://nccc .georgetown.edu/) has a wealth of resources on the topic. Its site includes information about projects and initiatives and data vignettes. There are a large variety of self-assessment tools as well as resources. In addition, there is information about distance learning opportunities and promising practices.

Cultural competence entails the willingness and ability of individuals and a system to value the importance of culture in the delivery of services to all segments of the population at all levels of an organization. It includes activities such as policy development and implementation, governance, education, promoting workforce diversity, and the reduction of language barriers.

Becoming culturally competent is an ongoing process. It requires a dedication to growing with a changing society that is becoming more diverse and to serving the individuals and communities with the most culturally appropriate, and hence highest quality, care possible.

Improving cultural competence levels should begin with an assessment to determine where an individual or organization can improve. It can assist with directing training and education for the workforce, policy development, and other systematic changes. We included an individual and an organizational cultural competence assessment tool in Chapter 2.

Research

Eliminating health disparities requires new knowledge about the determinants of disease, causes of health disparities, effective interventions for prevention and treatment, and innovative ways of working in partnership with health care systems. From a culturally informed perspective, the advances in knowledge about topics such as genetics and best practices need to be put into action and applied to the health care industry and not just lie in the pages of professional journals.

Best practices of disparity reduction initiatives and programs are being identified and shared. This needs to continue and be magnified. Government organizations and researchers need to continue to work to document and publicize those programs and policy changes that have been proven to be effective, but it is just as important to identify programs that do not work! Most of what is published in journals and on websites illustrates the successes, but the unsuccessful programs and policies add to the knowledge as well. Knowing what does not work helps prevent health care professionals from channeling valuable resources to interventions that have already been shown not to produce positive effects.

Data on specific populations also is needed. A majority of the data report on broad categories of race and ethnicities, such as Asians and American Indians. In addition, much of the research combines groups, such as Asians with Pacific Islanders and American Indians with Alaska Natives. There is great diversity within these groups, so more specific data is needed to help identify the health problems within the subpopulations and successful strategies for reducing them. This problem also can obscure successful health strategies among subpopulations. Researchers and government agencies are encouraged to collect and report data for racial and ethnic subgroups instead of the current commonly used broad categories.

In the United States, socioeconomic status has traditionally been measured by education and income. Surveys also should capture information about a range of contextual variables that have been found to be explanatory in health differences, such as social support, social networks, family supports, levels of acculturation, social cohesion, community involvement, perceived financial burdens, discrimination, and differences in the health status of foreign-born versus U.S.-born individuals, which at times also are linked to socioeconomic status.

Improving the Environments of People Affected by Health Disparities

Health disparities have complex origins. Not all are due to traditional concepts of social culture. For instance, the cultures of poverty, discrimination, and commerce have significant cross-cultural importance. There is little doubt that neighborhood characteristics are important elements associated with health. Residents of socially and economically deprived communities experience worse health outcomes on average than those living in more prosperous neighborhoods. Neighborhoods may influence health through relatively short-term influences on behaviors, attitudes, and health care utilization, thereby affecting health conditions that are more immediate. Neighborhoods also can influence health on a long-term basis through "weathering," whereby the accumulated stress, lower environmental quality, and limited resources of poorer communities experienced over many years negatively affects the health of residents.

Members of minority cultures are more likely to live in poor neighborhoods. These neighborhoods often have poor performing schools, high crime rates, substandard housing, few health care providers and pharmacies, more alcohol and tobacco advertising, and limited access to grocery stores with healthy food choices. These social determinants of health can accumulate over the course of a life and can be detrimental to physical and emotional health.

Increasing Access to Health Care

Not all cultures endorse "modern medicine," but no culture intentionally rejects any kind of health care. Lack of access to the modern health care system is generally based on economic barriers. In March 2010, President Obama signed comprehensive health reform into law, the Patient Protection and Affordable Care Act (ACA). The law is intended to make preventive care—including family planning and related services—more accessible and affordable for many Americans. Tax credits, mandates, and covering those with preexisting conditions are some ways the law is intended to improve access to care and make it more affordable.

Access to care also is related to having health care providers within every geographic region. There are imbalances in how the health care workforce is distributed, and this leads to lower access to care in some geographic regions of the United States. Poor neighborhoods tend to have a lower person to health care provider ratio than more affluent regions. **Telehealth** is the use of technology to remotely deliver health care, health information, or health education at a distance. Examples include telepsychiatry, in which mental health services are provided using video conferencing, and teleradiology, in which films are electronically forwarded to providers in remote locations. Telehealth can be used to provide medical services to medically underserved geographic regions.

Government incentives programs also help improve access to care. These programs offer incentives and competitive salaries to providers who work in low-income regions.

Improving Quality of Care

Improving quality of care is related to training of health care providers, providing equal care, reducing language barriers, and increasing diversity in the workforce. Each of these four areas is discussed in the following paragraphs.

With regard to training health care providers, fostering a culturally competent health care system that reflects and serves the diversity of America must be a priority for health care reform. States and academic centers that train health care professionals can develop, and some already have, requirements for training in this area. This can assist with providing equal treatment.

The groundbreaking report *Unequal Treatment: Confronting Racial and Ethnic Disparities in Healthcare* (Smedley, Stith, & Nelson, 2003) showed that racial and ethnic minorities receive lower-quality health care than Caucasians, even when insurance status, income, age, and severity of conditions are comparable. The report's first recommendation for reducing these disparities is to increase awareness of the issue among the public, health care providers, insurance companies, and policy makers. It also recommended the standardized collection of data on health care access and utilization by patients' race, ethnicity, socioeconomic status, and, where possible, primary language.

Language barriers can lead to numerous problems, such as damage to the patient and provider relationship, miscommunication with regard to the health problem and treatment approach, medication and correct-dosage mistakes, and legal problems. Health care has a language of its own and can make communication with people with limited English proficiency skills even more difficult. Barriers can be reduced by multilingual signage, providing interpretive services, noting a patient's native language and communication needs, and having documents (such as consent forms and educational materials) available in languages that reflect the demographics of the region served.

Diversity in the workforce is another goal. The health care workforce is underrepresented by people who are nonwhite, yet people of color are more likely to practice in federally designated underserved areas, to see patients of color, and to accept Medicaid patients. As stated in a Commonwealth Fund report (McDonough et al., 2004), racial concordance of patient and provider leads to greater participation in care and greater adherence to treatment.

Policy Changes and Laws

The ACA, as stated previously, intends to provide more affordable coverage, put an end to preexisting condition limitations as well as an end to limits on care and coverage cancellations (Health Care That Works for Americans, n.d.). In addition to the ACA, policies and laws that mandate cultural competence training for medical professionals have been shown to be effective. A few of these laws are discussed here.

In 2005, New Jersey became the first state to address the issue of equity in health care and cultural competence training of physicians (Senate Bill [SB] 144). The law requires medical professionals to receive cultural competence training to receive a diploma from medical schools located in the state or to be licensed or relicensed to practice in the state. Each medical school in New Jersey is required to provide this training.

California has taken several steps to ensure cultural competence across the state's health care infrastructure. In 2005, Assembly Bill 1195 required mandatory continuing medical education courses to include cultural and linguistic courses. In the previous session, SB 853 was enacted, which requires commercial health plans to ensure members' access to linguistic services and to report to state regulators steps being taken to improve the cultural competence of their services. Similarly, the state's Medicaid program, Medi-Cal, requires all health plans providing services for Medicaid patients to ensure their linguistic needs are met, including 24-hour access to interpretive services and documents in native languages.

The state of Washington enacted SB 6194 in 2006, which requires all medical education curricula in the state to include multicultural health training and awareness courses. All of these laws strive to establish cultural competence among health care professionals.

Summary

To achieve quality and affordable health care for all, health care reform must include concrete steps to reduce health disparities. Ensuring access to coverage is only part of the answer. Other strategies include reducing barriers to quality health care for people of color by requiring cultural competence training of medical professionals, recruiting a diverse workforce, eliminating language barriers, coordinating public and private programs that target disparities, providing more funding to community health centers, and improving chronic disease management programs by making them more responsive to minorities. Health disparities reflect and perpetuate the inequity and injustice that permeates American society. Eliminating health disparities will help create equal opportunity for all Americans in all sectors of our society.

In this chapter, a variety of methods for reducing health disparities are presented. These include strategies such as diversifying the health care workforce, changing policies, training health care professionals in the area of cultural competence, and conducting additional research. These changes can help reduce the gap in health among Americans, and this needs to continue to be a priority for our nation, particularly in light of the changing demographics of the United States.

Cultural competence is a process, and there is still a lot to learn. No one can learn all there is to know about the numerous cultural groups in the United States, but it is important that you are aware of the major differences, challenge your assumptions, respect and embrace values and beliefs that are different from your own, and provide the same high standards of care to all people, regardless of race, ethnicity, gender, sexual preference, or other attribute. Our hope is that you will go beyond this by advocating for equality and striving to improve health care systems to help close the gaps in the levels of health that exist among certain groups. We leave you with this final thought:

Cultural differences should not separate us from each other, but rather cultural diversity brings a collective strength that can benefit all of humanity.

—Robert Alan

Review

1. Describe what cultural competence is and why it is important.
2. List at least four national goals for eliminating health disparities.
3. Describe strategies to reduce or eliminate health disparities.

Activity

Write a letter to the president of the United States. Provide suggestions about how to reduce the health disparities in the United States. What changes need to be made in terms of policy, training, or other areas.

Case Study

Cambridge Health Alliance set out to increase mammography rates among women 50 to 69 years of age. Screening rates for all women were below 60% when the initiative began. The initiative focused on three areas: developing patient tracking systems and other information systems (such as improving communication within and between facilities), improving access by enhancing the capacity of the radiology department to reduce appointment wait times, and conducting outreach to difficult to reach and unscreened patients.

The outreach process included staff and patient education. Outreach staff work individually with the 15 clinics, reviewing their breast health screening rates and lists of patients due for mammograms and identifying factors that contribute to unscreened patients. This review assisted the clinic staff with understanding the clinic population. The clinic and outreach staff worked together and sent unscreened patients a personalized letter from their primary care provider. The content of the letter encouraged the patient to go to the clinic for a screening.

After the letter was sent, a follow-up personal phone call was made to the patient. The patient was called up to three times. During the call, the staff offered to schedule, and occasionally transport, women to the clinic for their screening. Letters and phone calls were provided to patients in their own languages.

Special Saturday events took place to assist working women with having the screening. The patients were often able to attend a session with friends. The Saturday sessions provided group education and individual screenings.

At the end of the initiative, screening rates were at 86% and rates for all language groups were above 80%; the screening rate for Spanish speakers was 92% and the screening rate for Portuguese speakers was 94% (Eliminating Disparities in Care, n.d.).

There are several issues to consider about this case:

Why do you think these initiatives were successful?

Do you think these program changes would be helpful with other groups? Why or why not?

What health outreach program changes have you seen other programs make (e.g., on billboards, on television) to improve the health among specific groups?

References

Centers for Disease Control and Prevention. (2011, May 11). *Healthy People 2020.* Retrieved from http://www.cdc.gov/nchs/healthy_people/hp2020/hp2020_topic_areas.htm

Eliminating disparities in care. (n.d.). Retrieved from http://www.aha.org/content/00-10/08disp-xbrscancer.pdf

Health care that works for Americans. (n.d.). Retrieved from http://www.whitehouse.gov/healthreform/healthcare-overview

HHS action plan to reduce racial and ethnic health disparities. (n.d.). Retrieved from http://minorityhealth.hhs.gov/assets/pdf/hhs/HHS_Plan_complete.pdf

McDonough, J. E., Gibbs, B. K., Scott-Harris, J. L., Kronebusch, K., Navarro, A. M., & Taylor, K. (2004). *A state policy agenda to eliminate racial and ethnic health disparities.* New York, NY: The Commonwealth Fund.

National Partnership for Action to End Health Disparities. (2011, April). *National stakeholder strategy for achieving health equity.* Rockville, MD: U.S. Department of Health and Human Services, Office of Minority Health.

Retrieved from http://minorityhealth.hhs.gov/npa/files/Plans/NSS/NSS_07_Section3.pdf

National CASA Association. (1995-1996, Fall/Winter). *What is cultural competence?* Retrieved from http://www.casanet.org/library/culture/competence.htm

Office of Minority Health & Health Disparities. (2007). *Eliminating racial & ethnic health disparities.* Retrieved from http://www.cdc.gov/omhd/About/disparities.htm

Smedley, B. D., Stith, A. Y., & Nelson, A. R. (Eds.). (2003). *Unequal treatment: Confronting racial and ethnic disparities in health care.* Washington, DC: National Academies Press.

U.S. Department of Health and Human Services. (n.d.). *HHS action plan to reduce racial and ethnic health disparities.* Retrieved from http://www.minorityhealth.hhs.gov/npa/files/Plans/HHS/HHS_Plan_complete.pdf

U.S. Department of Health and Human Services. (2015, February 16). *About healthy people.* Retrieved from http://www.healthypeople.gov/2020/about/default.aspx

Glossary

aAma and aDuonga: Vietnamese belief of balance in all things, similar to yin and yang in traditional Chinese medicine.

acculturation: The process of adapting to another culture by acquiring elements of the majority group's culture.

acupuncture: Traditional Chinese medicine treatment that involves stimulating specific points along the meridians to achieve a therapeutic purpose. The usual practice involves inserting a needle into one of the acupoints along a meridian that is associated with an organ or function.

advance directive: Pertains to treatment preferences and the designation of a surrogate decision maker in the event that a person should become unable to make medical decisions on his or her own behalf.

ahimsa: A Buddhist and Hindu doctrine that expresses belief in the sacredness of all living creatures and urges the avoidance of harm and violence.

alien: A person who is generally understood to be a foreigner, i.e., comes from a foreign country and does not owe allegiance to the United States.

alternative medicine: A variety of therapeutic or preventive health care practices, such as homeopathy, naturopathy, chiropractic, and herbal medicine, that do not follow generally accepted medical methods and may not have a scientific explanation for their effectiveness; used instead of Western medicine.

animal sacrifice: The ritual killing of an animal as part of a religion.

assimilation: The process of becoming absorbed into another culture, adopting its characteristics, and developing a new cultural identity.

asylee: A person granted legal status in the United States based on applying, upon arrival in the US, for refugee status due to a well-founded fear of persecution (must meet the criteria for a refugee).

autonomy: The ethical principle that embodies the right of self-determination.

Ayurvedic system: India's ancient and traditional natural system of medicine that provides an integrated approach to preventing and treating illness through lifestyle interventions and natural therapies.

beneficence: The state or quality of being kind and charitable; a principle that requires doing good or removing harm.

best practices: The assertion that there is a strategy that is more effective at delivering a particular outcome than any other technique, method, or process.

biomedical (allopathic) medicine: The system of medicine that uses pharmacologically active agents or physical interventions to treat or suppress symptoms or pathophysiologic processes of diseases or disorders.

biomedical worldview: The perspective that disease is caused by primarily biological factors.

bisexual: Individuals whose sexual preference is to both men and women.

brauche: Amish practice whereby a healer lays his hands over a patient's head or stomach while quietly reciting verses to "pull out" the ailment.

Candomblé: A religion developed in Brazil by enslaved Africans that involves rituals such as animal sacrifice, drumming, and dancing.

collectivism: The view that the group should be the priority rather than the individual.

complementary medicine: Treatments that are utilized in conjunction with conventional Western medical therapies prescribed by a physician.

cultural adaptation: The degree to which a person or community has adapted to the dominant culture or retained its traditional practices.

cultural competence: The ability to interact effectively with people of different cultures; a set of congruent behaviors, attitudes, structures, and policies that come together to work effectively in intercultural situations.

cultural relativism: The principle that one's beliefs and activities should be interpreted in terms of one's own culture and that no culture is superior to another.

culture: The set of learned behaviors, beliefs, attitudes, values, and ideals that are characteristic of a particular society or population.

curandero (male) or curandera (female): A traditional folk healer or shaman who is dedicated to curing physical and spiritual illnesses.

digital divide: The disparity in access to electronic information resources.

discrimination: The practice of treating people differently on a basis other than merit.

dominant culture: The total, generally organized way of life, including values, norms, institutions, and symbols that reflect the largest culture.

doshas: In Ayurvedic medicine, the three vital energies that regulate everything in nature.

drabarni: Roma women who have knowledge of medicines.

durable power of attorney: A legal document that gives someone that you select the ability to make decisions for you when you are not able to do so for yourself.

Ellis-van Creveld syndrome: Genetic disorder found among the Amish in which there is a defective recessive gene from each parent.

empacho: In the Hispanic culture, a description of stomach pains and cramps.

Espiritismo: A Latin American and Caribbean belief that good and evil spirits can affect human life, such as one's health and luck.

ethics: Externally defined principles that govern the standards of behavior for individuals within a group regarding what is good or bad.

ethnicity: Large groups of people who are classified according to common racial, national, tribal, religious, linguistic, or cultural origin or background.

ethnocentricity: When a person believes that his or her culture is superior to that of another.

euthanasia: Act or practice of ending the life of an individual who is suffering from a terminal illness or an incurable condition.

evil eye: Also referred to as mal de ojo. In the Hispanic culture, an illness thought to be caused by jealousy; the Spanish translation is "bad eye." This belief is held by many migrant farmworkers.

familismo: A strong loyalty and identification with one's nuclear and extended family.

fate versus free will: The belief that events are predetermined and cannot be changed (fate or destiny) versus humans being able to determine the direction of their life (free will).

fidelity: Ethical principle that entails keeping one's promises or commitments.

five elements: The traditional Chinese medicine theory based on the perception of the relationships among all things. These patterns are grouped and named for the five elements: wood, fire, earth, metal, and water.

fotonovela: An illustrated novel.

gadje: All things non-Roma; considered to be not clean.

gay: Term that refers to homosexuals in general and is usually used to refer to male homosexuals specifically.

gender identity: A person's internal, personal sense of being male or female, boy or girl, man or woman.

germ theory: The theory that microorganisms in the body causes specific diseases.

health disparity: Also referred to as health inequalities. Gaps in the quality of health and health care across racial, ethnic, sexual orientation, and socioeconomic groups.

Healthy People 2020: A program that provides a prevention framework for the United States. It is a statement of national health objectives designed to identify the most significant preventable threats to health and to establish national goals to reduce these threats.

heritage consistency: The degree to which people identify with their culture of origin.

Hill-Burton Act: Also referred to as the Hospital Survey and Construction Act of 1946. It provided federal assistance to state governments for the construction and modernization of hospitals and other health care facilities. The original statute required recipient hospitals to make services available "to all persons residing in the territorial area of the application, without discrimination on account of race, creed, or color."

Hispanic paradox: The apparent contradiction reflected in the fact that Hispanics generally have better health and live longer than more affluent non-Hispanic whites and other cultural groups within the United States.

Hmong: Mountain-dwelling people from Cambodia and Vietnam.

holistic medicine: An approach to well-being that integrates the whole person (body, mind, and spirit).

humoral system: The system of liquid components of the blood and other tissues in the body (e.g., blood plasma) that do not contain cells.

hydrotherapy: A treatment used by naturopathic practitioners based on the therapeutic effects of water. Thought to assist in ridding the body of waste and toxins, it utilizes hot and cold baths, compresses, wraps, and showers as treatment modalities.

illegal alien: A foreigner who (1) does not owe allegiance to the United States and (2) who has violated U.S. laws and customs in establishing residence in this country.

immigrant: A person who migrates to another country legally and who usually seeks permanent residency.

individualism: The outlook that places high importance on the individual and individual self-reliance.

justice: The ethical principle stating that people should be treated equally and fairly.

karma: The total effect of a person's conduct during the successive phases of existence, which is expected to determine the person's destiny.

Kior chi force: Korean belief in a life force similar to chi in traditional Chinese medicine; it is important in maintaining health, and efforts are made to balance this force and not to engage in activities that could diminish it.

lesbian: Term that refers to homosexual women specifically.

living will: A set of instructions that documents a person's wishes about medical care.

mal de ojo: Also referred to as evil eye. In the Hispanic culture, an illness thought to be caused by jealousy; the Spanish translation is "bad eye."

marime: Roma concept of impurity, which is foundational to their health beliefs.

medicine bundle: A wrapped package containing objects such as tobacco, a flute, eagle feather, or other items thought to contain spiritual significance, used by American Indians for religious and healing purposes.

medicine wheel: A symbol that represents harmony and peaceful interaction.

meditation: A group of mental techniques intended to provide relaxation and mental harmony as well as to quiet one's mind and increase awareness.

meridians: The traditional Chinese medicine concept of channels through which qi, blood, and information flow to all parts of the body.

mind–body integration: Seeing the mind and body as a consolidated unit.

mindfulness meditation: The concept of increasing awareness and acceptance of the present.

minority: A group that is smaller in number than another group; a part of a population that differs in characteristics, often resulting in differential treatment.

morality: A subset of philosophy that addresses concepts of right and wrong, proper conduct, good and evil that are usually implemented by individual interpretations of these concepts and are often based in philosophical and religious teachings.

multicultural evaluation: Integrates cultural considerations into an evaluation's theory, measures, analysis, and practice.

multicultural health: The provision of health services in a sensitive, knowledgeable, and nonjudgmental manner with respect for people's health beliefs and practices when they are different from your own.

naturalistic theories of disease: The belief that illness is caused by a person's imbalance with the natural environment.

naturopathy: Healing practice based on ancient beliefs in the healing power of nature and that natural organisms have the ability to heal themselves and maintain health. The body strives to maintain a state of equilibrium, known as homeostasis, and unhealthy environments, diets, physical or emotional stress, and lack of sleep or fresh air can disrupt that balance. Natural remedies, such as herbs and foods, are used instead of surgery or drugs.

nonmaleficence: The principle that one should practice competently.

orishas: A spirit that reflects one of the manifestations of God in Yoruba religion and is expressed in practices such as Santaria.

personalistic belief system: The belief that illness is caused by the intervention of a supernatural being or a human being with special powers and is related to one's behavior.

peyote: A spineless, dome-shaped cactus (*Lophophora williamsii*) native to Mexico and the southwest United States. The plant has buttonlike tubercles that are chewed fresh or dry as a narcotic, hallucinogenic drug by certain Native American peoples.

prakriti: The combination of the doshas at the time of conception that are unique to each individual.

promotores (male) or promotoras (female): Community members who promote health in their own communities.

proxemics: The scientific study of the amount of space that people feel is necessary to have between themselves and others.

qi: In traditional Chinese medicine, the vital life force that animates all things.

qigong: Translates to "energy work." A part of traditional Chinese medicine that involves movement, breathing, and meditation that is intended to improve the flow of qi through the body.

race: The concept of dividing people into populations or groups on the basis of visible traits and beliefs about common ancestry.

racism: The belief that some races are superior to others by nature.

reciprocity: The exchange of like or similar things of value for mutual benefit.

refugee: A person who has fled another country due to fear of persecution because of his or her race, religion, nationality, social group, or political opinion and requests legal status before entering the United States.

Reiki: A form of alternative medicine in which the healer uses his or her hands to channel healing energy.

religion: An organized collection of beliefs, cultural systems, and worldviews that explain the meaning of life and the universe.

respect: A sense of admiration, honor, value that invokes a belief that a person or object should be treated seriously and with courtesy.

respeto: A Spanish word meaning respect.

rituals: A set of actions that usually are very structured and have a symbolic value or meaning.

Romany: A language derived from Sanskrit that is spoken by the Roma people.

Rumspringa: An Amish practice that allows adolescents to be free to explore the world outside of the Amish culture.

sand painting: The art of creating paintings using sand for the purpose of healing.

Santeria: An African-based religion that combines the worship of traditional Yoruban deities with the worship of Roman Catholic saints.

sexual identity: A person's physical, romantic, emotional, and spiritual attraction to another person.

Shintoism: The formal state religion of Japan, which is based on a belief in the importance of developing harmony and balance in life and with other people with the help of the spiritual beings, including some that are within nature and objects such as trees and stones.

shrine: A place of religious devotion or commemoration.

spirituality: The belief in a higher power, something beyond the human experience, and its intercession in healing.

susto: In the Hispanic culture, an illness thought to be caused by soul loss or fright.

sweat lodge: A kind of sauna, usually a domed or oblong hut, that is used in a spiritual ritual by some American Indians.

tai chi: A traditional Chinese medicine exercise designed to improve the flow of qi through the body and encourage balance and harmony.

talking circles: A method used by many American Indians to discuss a topic or what is present for them in their lives. The group members sit in a circle and make comments on the topic of discussion, following specified rules.

telehealth: The use of technology to remotely deliver health care, health information, or health education at a distance.

temporal relationship: A relationship involving time.

timbang: Filipino belief in a range of "hot" and "cold" humoral balances in the body and food and dietary balances.

transcendental meditation: A technique that allows a practitioner to experience ever-finer levels of thought until the source of thought is experienced.

transgender: Individuals who live full- or part-time in the gender role opposite to the one in which they were physically born. They may be heterosexual or homosexual.

Tuskegee study: An unethical study that the U.S. Public Health Service conducted from 1932 to 1972 on hundreds of black men who had syphilis.

veracity: An ethical principle that involves being truthful.

vitalistic system: The theory or doctrine that life cannot be explained entirely as a physical and chemical phenomenon and that life is partially self-determining through one's energy or soul.

voodoo: A religion that originated in Africa and was influenced by Roman Catholics in which a supreme God rules deities, deified ancestors, and saints who communicate with believers in dreams, trances, and ritual possessions.

worldview: The overall perspective from which one sees and interprets the world.

wuzho: A Roma belief of what is pure, which is a foundation of their health traditions.

yin and yang: The traditional Chinese medicine theory that everything is made up of two polar energies.

yoga: An ancient system of exercises and breathing techniques designed to encourage physical and spiritual well-being.

Index

philosophy about disease prevention and
      health maintenance held by, 152–160
pregnancy, birth and child rearing, 154–155
religion and, 153–154
terminology, 150–151
tips for working with, 167–168
in U.S., 151–152
worldview of, 153–154
HIV. *See* human immunodeficiency virus
Hmong, 27–28, 231–233
holistic approach, 37–38, 38*t*
holistic medicine, 39
homeostasis, 82
Homestead Act, 176–177
homicide, African Americans and, 217, 219
homosexuality, declassification of, as mental
      illness, 271
hope, religion and, 108
hot *vs.* cold Latino diagnoses, 159, 160*t*
human biology, as health field, 14
human immunodeficiency virus (HIV)
      in African Americans, 218
      in LGBT Americans, 270–271
      prevention of, 122
      substance use and, 271
humoral system, 34, 34*t*
huskinaw, 181
hwa-byung, 237
hydrotherapy, 81
hygienic practices, 37
hypertension, religion and, 101–102, 102*t*

I

IHS. *See* Indian Health Services
illegal alien, 283
illness. *See also* disease prevention and health
      maintenance philosophies; health and
      illness theories
      mystical and naturalistic causes of, 233
      natural and unnatural, 209–210
      response to, 63–64
      terminal, disclosure of, 237
      theories of, 32–37
immigrants, 26
      Arab, 256–257
      Asian American, 228
      behavioral risk factors and common health
            problems among, 283–284

defined, 283
health promotion and program planning for,
      284–285
Mexican, 280
terminology, 282–283
immunizations, 49, 248
      Amish Americans and, 253
      Asian Americans and, 239
impure. *See* marime
Indian Citizenship Act, 177
Indian Health Services (IHS), 177
Indian Removal Act, 176
individualism, collectivism *vs.*, 54–55, 54*t*
individualistic cultures, 55
infant mortality rates, African Americans and,
      217, 223
influenza and pneumonia
      in American Indian and Alaskan Native
            populations, 192
      in Asian Americans, 238
      in European and Mediterranean
            Americans, 260
      in Hispanic and Latino American
            populations, 163
integration, 10–11
      mind-body, 64
interactive media, 123
Internet, 120–124, 127
intimate partner violence, African Americans
      and, 219
Iroquois, 186
Islam, 98*t*, 233, 246, 263

J

Jackson, Andrew, 176
Japanese Americans, 229. *See also* Asian Americans
Joint Commission for the Accreditation of
      Hospital Organizations (JCAHO), 110
Jones-Shafroth Act, 151
Judaism, 98*t*, 248–249
      Hasidic, 115–116
justice, 26

K

karma, 62, 233
Kior chi force, 232
Korean Americans, 229. *See also* Asian Americans